FUTBOLERA

FUTB

A HISTORY *of* WOMEN *and* **SPORTS** *in* LATIN AMERICA

OLERA

BRENDA ELSEY

JOSHUA NADEL

UNIVERSITY OF TEXAS PRESS ✧ AUSTIN

Joe R. and Teresa Lozano Long Series in
Latin American and Latino Art and Culture

Title page photo: Members of Deportivo Femenino de Costa Rica
FC walking out for the first kick. Courtesy of the Bonilla Family.

Cover and interior design by Amanda Weiss

Requests for permission to reproduce material
from this work should be sent to:
 Permissions
 University of Texas Press
 P.O. Box 7819
 Austin, TX 78713-7819
 utpress.utexas.edu/rp-form

♾ The paper used in this book meets the minimum
requirements of ANSI/NISO Z39.48-1992 (R1997)
(Permanence of Paper).

Names: Elsey, Brenda, author. | Nadel, Joshua H., author.
Title: Futbolera : a history of women and sports in Latin
    America / Brenda Elsey, Joshua Nadel.
Other titles: Joe R. and Teresa Lozano Long series in Latin
    American and Latino art and culture.
Description: First edition. | Austin : University of Texas
    Press, 2019. | Series: Joe R. and Teresa Lozano Long series
    in Latin American and Latino art and culture | Includes
    bibliographical references and index.
Identifiers: LCCN 2018037054 | ISBN 978-1-4773-2234-5
    (paperback : alk. paper) | ISBN 978-1-4773-1858-4 (library e-book)
    | ISBN 978-1-4773-1859-1 (non-library e-book)
Subjects: LCSH: Sports for women—Latin America—History. |
    Sports for women—Social aspects—Latin America. | Women
    athletes—Latin America—History. | Soccer for women—Latin
    America—History. | Soccer—Social aspects—Latin America. |
    Soccer—Latin America—History.
Classification: LCC GV709.18.L37 E57 2019 | DDC 796.082098—dc23
    LC record available at https://lccn.loc.gov/2018037054

doi:10.7560/310427

JOSHUA:

For Sofia, Rafael, and Evanthia, σας αγαπω πολύ.

BRENDA:

For Maya, with all my love.

CONTENTS

FIGURES

FUTBOLERA

FIGURE 0.1. Ángel Zárraga, *Las futbolistas*, 1922 (Paris). Women's football captured the imagination of Latin Americans well before the sport was officially acknowledged.

INTRODUCTION

"WHY WOULD YOU KEEP PLAYING? ALL THE HOMOPHOBIA and humiliation, no financial gain—why? Why not do something easier?" I asked Marina, a former player for the Argentine national women's football, or soccer, team. We were in a café in Queens, New York, on a frigid winter day. She had immigrated to the United States in 2010 to pursue opportunities to play professionally. While her dreams of a salaried career had not come to fruition, Marina continued to play and referee when she wasn't at her job cleaning offices. She answered, "The more difficulties there were, the more I wanted it. I didn't have education, money, or other weapons. I was only armed with talent for soccer. It's all I wanted to do."[1] Marina's reactions echoed those of thousands of women who have played organized sports in Latin America since the late nineteenth century. Their exclusion is key to understanding how gender and sexuality developed in the region. Women's communities and activities within sports are also vital to understanding social history. This book focuses on the relationships of women to civic associations, including sports clubs, physical education teams, or union leagues, and the significance that sports have in women's lives.

There are many powerful female icons in Latin American history: Mexico's Adelita, Argentina's Eva Perón, Brazil's Escrava Anastácia. Whether real, imagined, or a composite, they serve as flash points for understanding women's lives in the region. Yet these iconic women were exceptional in one way or another, and the focus tends to be on their activities that made them so, rather than on the more mundane common experience. *Futbolera* is a deceptively straightforward way to refer to a girl or a woman who plays football, or soccer. Futboleras have disappeared and reappeared throughout the twentieth and twenty-first centuries. They have been, for the most part, ignored in popular stories of sports and in Latin American history more generally. They thus serve as metaphors for women's appearance in the historical narrative. When raised in public debate, the futbolera was shorthand for a woman who went "too far," a red herring, or a strange monstrosity. Today, from international to national federations, organizations justify their neglect of women athletes based on the purported lack of tradition and the portrayal of women as newcomers to sports. This book discusses the history of women's role in sports other than football, but given the importance of the sport, football occupies a special role in understanding sportswomen and the ideologies of gender, class, race, and sexuality in Latin America.

History telling can confer legitimacy on its subjects, just as it can deny it in the same instance. The neglect of women's historical participation in Latin American sports has served to naturalize gender differences in society more broadly and to justify the denial of resources to women athletes. Focusing on women's activities within sports illuminates a site of women's creativity and community. The media's disinterest in women's sports has given historians a difficult track to follow. Frequently, the athletes themselves preserve the history of women's sports, offering up their memories, photographs, jerseys, and press clippings to journalists and historians. Much like the history of samba or of drag shows, these enthusiasts retain the details of their performances as raw material that historians then weave into narrative. This is not an attempt to give voice to the voiceless, nor to put together an exhaustive account of women's sporting history, but rather to record and situate the traces available, and hopefully to open up new paths for research.

To understand futboleras, there is a longer history to comprehend, one that involves the construction of the state in Latin America. Physical education programs were part of expanding state agencies that formed new schools and institutes to train students throughout the region in the late nineteenth and early twentieth centuries. Physical education regimes differed across countries and also based on national goals and local adaptations. This book uses Latin America cautiously and aspires to use comparative cases to highlight the heterogeneity of the region. Walter Mignolo's critique of the idea of Latin America, which demonstrated the subjugation of indigenous and African peoples embedded within the term, is central to keep in mind.[2] Indeed, experts throughout the Americas designed programs to replace any indigenous or African "habits" with European ones. In the first decades of the twentieth century, they mostly operated on the assumption that only Europeans had traditions of physical culture worth adopting as state policy.

It is hard to imagine a more direct exertion on children than school programs instructing them in how to move their bodies. Even though physical education was conceived of as voluntary, and even enjoyable, for students, the state sought still to control the ways students stretched, jumped, ran, and even stood. Physical education reinforced gender differences as immutable, and creating proper heterosexual behaviors was paramount. Although sportswomen stepped outside the margins of what was socially acceptable, they nevertheless operated on a spectrum of participation in sports and physical education. However, girls' and women's ideas about physical education often deviated from the states' nationalist projects. The communities that women formed and the intensity of exchanges across national borders merits attention in any study of sports. In addition to studying transnational relationships, this book puts forward comparative cases that reflect how distinct histories of gender created different landscapes for women's athleticism.

The embrace of gender, which underscored the process and contingency of categorizations of male and female in the United States and in European academies, reaches at least as far back as the publication of Joan Wallach Scott's foundational essay, "Gender: A Useful Category of Historical Analysis," in 1986. Gender opened up a wide range of methodologies and sources to scholars interested in the history of how societies constructed, naturalized, and reproduced difference along the lines of masculinity and femininity. Over time, these terms have become pluralized—genders, masculinities, femininities, sexualities—to recognize competing ideas surrounding them. Gender has enabled historians to account for the importance of women to labor, property, and politics even when they aren't represented "in the flesh." One can understand how laws that fail to mention women, often written without women's participation, have been designed both linguistically and in practice to award capital to men. It is crucial to remember that gender identities do not exist in a vacuum. They relate to class, race, nation, and sexuality as well. To the extent possible, we have tried to account for these intersectionalities, as they are known. As research in evolutionary biology and medical ethics has advanced, the boundaries between sex and gender have become more nebulous in recognition that the two sexes lie within a spectrum of characteristics.

The growth in gender history and women's history resulted in a number of important studies that have forced us to rethink traditional historical narratives. Histories of women workers, for example, demonstrated not only their workplace experiences but also their importance to Latin American economies.[3] Ideas that men and women deserved different pay and benefits shaped the politics of labor unions, especially in terms of restrictions on women's work and labor organizing. New understandings of women's participation in political movements—across the ideological spectrum—have demonstrated both their importance to politics and marginalization from it. As social workers, teachers, and civil servants, women had responsibility to implement state projects on an everyday basis.[4] Social histories of women also gave depth and nuance to the way in which one can understand the significance of state projects like land reform.[5] Given the overlapping inequalities throughout the region, feminist scholarship has explored the way in which racism, classism, and homophobia have intersected with sexism to shape people's everyday lives.[6]

Gender history and women's history rely on each other for insight, but they are not the same. Despite all of the progress made in the 1990s and early 2000s, women's social history in Latin America remains a neglected area of research. In part this is because of greater focus on the study of gender, which inevitably sheds more light on men because they appear with greater frequency in source materials. In other words, while gender history and women's history are certainly not at odds, they cannot be conflated either.[7] Gender histories, many of which are more suggestive than definitive, have produced insights of major importance that also contribute to women's history, and their contributions to the history of sexuality have forced us to reevaluate normative legal prescriptions, private lives, and alternative communities.[8] Histories of the family—the social, religious, and productive foundation for most of Latin American history—have been revolutionized by new research in the history of sexuality. Social histories of women are sorely needed to continue to understand better how people contest, adapt, and uphold ideological constructs like masculinity and femininity.

The study of women in underground communities and their activities in a subject like sports, which is seldom considered politically important, cannot rely on the same type of documentary base as a history of formal feminist organizations or women's charities, for example. Methodologically, this study occasionally reads as media history, because we frequently rely upon traces of women's participation noted in the press. Argentina and Chile have had stable sports publications, whereas other countries, like Mexico, present a greater challenge. The uneven attention that women's sports has received in the press makes the search for women's sporting history—and the creation of cohesive narratives about it—akin to searching for needles in haystacks. In addition to newspapers and magazines, we have utilized government documents—particularly from physical education departments—oral histories, informal memoirs, fan websites, photographs, and club documents. The chapters on Brazil must be prefaced with a huge acknowledgment to the Museu do Futebol in São Paulo and its director, Daniela Alfonsi, and enthusiastic collector, Aira Bonfim. The scarcity of source material is, of course, exaggerated by the social constraints placed on women's sports and its dismissal by most collectors. These social histories of football, and sports more broadly, although rarely focused on women, have provided important analyses of the role of sports in national identity and political, ethnic, and social class formation.[9]

While this book attempts to cover considerable territory, geographically and thematically, much remains to be investigated. The most glaring geographical ommissions are the Andes and the Caribbean. This reflects our prior research experiences, as well as

FIGURE 0.2. Women's football team, Pradera, Colombia, 1952. Photo property of Archivo del Patrimonio Fotografico y Filmico del Valle del Cauca (AFFVC).

our interest in understanding the handful of well-known histories of women's sports. The decision to focus on Mexico, for example, emerged from our previous investigations of the women's world football championship of 1971. In the course of our research, we have found ample sources to suggest that vibrant women's sports, including football, developed in places not covered in this volume—such as Colombia and Peru. We look forward to future research on these areas. Thematically, this project is consciously focused on women's history. Much remains to be researched on the multiple ways in which class, race, ethnicity, and sexuality shaped the meaning and experience of women. The history of sexuality within sports also deserves much greater attention, both regionally and globally. In oral histories, queer sportswomen explained that they found a supportive community among their fellow athletes. Questions remain about how vigilance of women's sexuality and violence against lesbians affected women athletes. Authorities and media spent less time studying lesbians than gay men. New work in this area will undoubtedly deepen our understanding of gender in Latin America.[10] A more local frame could also account for how indigenous communities adapted, rejected, or embraced European sports.

Historians traffic in time. However, the basic chronologies and events of Latin American women's sports have not been sketched out. Cognizant of the pitfalls and problems involved in such an endeavor, we have constructed a rough chronology of the field, and this book is loosely structured around this time line. Throughout the region, girls' education began in earnest in the 1880s. This was particularly the case in the Southern Cone, but in Mexico, Costa Rica, and elsewhere the importance of schooling for girls was also recognized. Soon thereafter, educators began creating physical education programs, as they saw a link between a healthy body and a healthy mind. These programs opened previously unavailable opportunities for sports and exercise, particularly for working-class girls. Liberal reformers, military officers, and, to a lesser extent, conservative Catholics negotiated the outlines of physical education curricula. Across the political spectrum, the idea that sports could improve the eugenic health of the nation was incredibly powerful and inherently involved both girls and boys. As with many other ideological currents at the time, Latin American statesmen looked to Europe to guide the creation of agencies, policies, and curricula that would bring "modern" and scientific ideas to their programs. Racial hierarchies shaped the way bureaucrats, teachers, and reformers understood the goals of physical education. The assumption that people of African, indigenous, Asian, or mixed descent needed to model their movements and habits on Europeans in order to improve their racial makeup was presented as "common sense." Influenced by European practices, women dominated teaching positions for girls' physical education in this era. They frequently expanded their teaching beyond the classroom and organized clubs and tournaments.

By the end of the 1920s, Latin American feminism emerged as a diverse set of movements and ideologies. This coincided with the increasing participation of women in the workforce and in suffrage campaigns around the region. At the same time, leisure activities expanded rapidly, delivered by new technologies to urban crowds. The international image of the flapper, with short hair and athletic clothing, was closely tied to women's sports. Women's commentary, fandom, and participation in sports increased markedly. Celebrity culture, especially around film stars, strengthened the conflation of beauty and health. Entrepreneurs capitalized on these trends, creating products to help women stay attractive and youthful. Radio programs and magazines encouraged women to follow exercise routines in the home rather than in sports clubs, sending the message that women's sweat, exertion, and competition were a shameful public spectacle. Furthermore, they underscored that women needed to prioritize their domestic obligations rather than their personal fulfillment.

Sports associated with upper-class European women, such as tennis and swimming, gained widespread acceptance. Although some celebrated the new trends, others ridiculed the flapper as vain and sexually promiscuous. Elite writers worried that these new trends blurred the lines between genders and social classes and threatened the purity of "respectable" women who could be mistaken for any streetwalker if they appeared at a stadium or with a bob. These arguments moved beyond the pages of elite magazines and spilled into the streets. In Mexico in the 1920s, for example, men attacked women (and one another) over women's embrace of flapper style.[11] As much as Latin American educators might have wanted to adopt European norms, they reacted with suspicion to the global flapper trend, as well as to the new feminine model: the athletic body. As sports, particularly football, became strongly associated with proper masculinity and nationalism, journalists and experts found women's presence increasingly abhorrent. Club leaders, journalists, and educators questioned the sexuality of women who chose to practice sports, particularly team sports.

In the 1940s and 1950s, greater state investment in culture and leisure meant an expansion in subsidized facility construction, physical education, and elite amateurism, such as Olympic teams. It also meant increased state intervention in the sporting life of citizens.

This intrusion by the state is most starkly visible, in the case of women's sports, with the legal prohibition of women's football, rugby, and wrestling (among other sports) in Brazil in 1941. There and elsewhere in the region, the professionalization of sports medicine, physical education, and sports clubs further restricted women's athleticism. And, as women's sports organizations strengthened, they faced greater resistance from those opposed to female athletic activities—from both men and women. Many states in Latin America expanded significantly in the midcentury and in the process came with a renewed patriarchy. A minority could capitalize on this expansion, such as women's basketball teams in the Southern Cone. The growth of basketball and volleyball in the 1940s and 1950s had created international opportunities for players. Women traveled together, organized fund-raisers, and spent quite a bit of time "hanging out." Although male coaches acted as chaperones, there were freedoms not normally afforded to women involved in these clubs. However, attacks from experts and restrictions by state agencies drove many communities of women's sports underground, as well as into conflict with local police. Nevertheless, they persisted. Without access to media, state subsidies, or cultural capital, some women athletes continued to play the sports they loved with one another. If the women viewed their persistence as feminist, we have almost no way to know, because of the scarcity of sources. However, their fight for leisure time, appeal for access to public space, and defiance of restrictions on sports challenged central pillars of modern patriarchy.

In the 1960s and 1970s, young women who rejected the model of domesticity found themselves in a difficult position. The historian Valeria Manzano has demonstrated that young women "practically contested prevalent ideas of 'home' by remaining longer in the education system, fully participating in the labor market, helping shape youthful leisure activities, daring to experiment with new courtship conventions and to acknowledge publicly that they engaged in premarital sex, and marrying later in life."[12] In this way they challenged the equation of women with wifehood and motherhood. Perpetual moral panics generated discussion, recriminations, and in extreme cases (though not as extreme as it may seem) violence against women. As women entered universities and labor unions in greater numbers in the 1960s, they took a keen interest in participating in sports. However, as national women's teams solidified and gained prestige, male coaches displaced their women counterparts. Male coaches frequently viewed their players with hostility and saw their positions as merely a stepping-stone to working with male athletes. The military dictatorships of the 1970s and 1980s in Argentina, Brazil, Chile, and Uruguay, which curtailed civic associations and promised a return to traditional gender roles, hurt the progress made in women's sports in the late 1960s. In that era, international bodies, notably the International Olympic Committee and the Fédération Internationale de Football Association (International Federation of Association Football, FIFA), received increasing pressure to create more opportunities for women athletes. While the former found ways to include more women, although never as equals, the latter created stronger structural barriers to women's participation. As athletes regrouped in the 1990s and early 2000s, they continued to face discrimination with a new justification: the market.

This loose chronology of women's sports and gender history over the course of the twentieth century identifies changes in the broadest of terms. At once promoted as healthful and necessary and feared as transgressive by state actors and elites, women's athletic endeavors occupied an in-between—and dangerous—space. Although the state at times supported girls' physical activity, parents and conservative activists took a much more negative view. For them, the increase in girls' activities outside the home and the church would lead to perdition. The effects of girls' physical fitness on their fertility and future motherhood was *the* focus of public and expert debates. Fatherhood, on the other hand, was not the primary concern when it came to boys' physical education. Even when there was debate about the benefits of one type of exercise over another for girls, a consensus existed in the physical education community in regard to girls' primary role as mothers.

Our study begins with outlining the emergence of physical education and sports in the Southern Cone, where we find the earliest attempts to create programs for girls and women. While the state had a vested interest in the development of girls' physical education, it was wary of female sporting practices as well. At the same time that girls' physical education was promoted, female athletes were kept under the watchful eyes of teachers and so-called public health experts. These experts, as we show, had little knowledge of women's physiology and tended to worry more about appearance as a measure of sports' value. Appearance mattered not only for the purported experts in the health field but also in the sporting magazines of the day. There was little consensus on how to treat the sportswoman, but we suggest that two tropes appeared: the woman athlete as athlete and the woman athlete as object of male ridicule. The treatment of sportswomen varied due not only to differences of opinion on the health benefits of women's athletics but also to different prescriptions across class. This reflected the intersection of class prejudice and eugenics. If the countries of Latin America were to create healthier populations, then the femininity and health of its "better" citizens were paramount. As a result, discussions of women's sports often dovetailed with discussions of social class and race. Certain sports, such as tennis and swimming, were deemed healthful and appropriate, based on their supposed harmony with women's capacities, level of exertion, and lack of physical contact. Others, such as football and basketball, became the focus of intense debate, occasional support, and near constant suspicion. The potential of women's empowerment through team sports frightened sporting and state institutions.

The development of women's sports, and women's participation in the sporting environment, takes center stage as we move to early twentieth-century Brazil in the second chapter. As men's football embedded itself so deeply in Brazilian society, women's football came to be seen as anathema to the ideals of the country. A healthy Brazil, and healthy Brazilian women, needed to focus more on mothering skills than on sporting prowess. The values, skills, and relationships fostered in football clubs were seen as the exclusive dominion of men. This chapter traces the development of women's football around the country. As a part of the trajectory of women's football, state efforts at developing girls' physical education played an important role. In Brazil, as in Argentina and Chile, concern over women's sexuality and physical appearance informed debates over women's public health. Experts promoted gymnastics, dance, and light exercises that supported women's supposed feminine fragility by encouraging rhythm and harmony. Others, "rough games," like football, did not. They threatened the female "aesthetic." So too social class worried the Brazilian authorities. For many Brazilians, the development of women's football became concerning only after white elite women began to play the game and men of color integrated into top clubs. At that point, critics pointed to it as a threat to the nation. They had ample "evidence" to support them. The *Lancet*, the world's premier public health journal, had published studies on the problems of girls' and women's sporting activities in the 1920s. England cited this evidence in its ban of women's football, and, twenty years later, Brazil would follow suit. By the time of the ban, Brazilian women had been playing football for at least twenty years in places as varied as circus tents, factory grounds, and schoolyards. They had formed a strong league of teams in Rio de Janeiro that traveled around the country. Women's sports, particularly football, went from a marginalized spectacle toward the mainstream in a very short time. As the sport gained popularity, its critics became increasingly vocal, leading the newly centralized Brazilian state to ban the women's sport as a threat to the survival of the nation.

Despite the ban on women's football, play continued, particularly outside of the capital city. The continuation of the sport, combined with women's involvement in Brazil's sporting landscape as members of the media and in ancillary club roles, meant that the apparent sudden appearance of futboleras in the early 1980s was no more than a reemergence into the public sphere. In other words, had anyone bothered to look for women's football in Brazil from 1941 to 1981, they would have found it. Still, the sport needed an "appropriate" cover for its technically illegal activity. By calling women's football matches charity matches, organizers and players alike were able to avoid the legal and social stigma of playing. Even raising money for charitable causes, however, did not fully neutralize the opposition to the game. Editorials in newspapers lobbied against the sport. By the 1960s, the sport had grown enough that the Conselho Nacional de Desportos (National Sports Council) was forced to reiterate its stance against the game and investigate men's clubs, such as Santos, that had decided to support women's teams. Official opposition notwithstanding, we show that networks of personal relationships allowed women's football to continue. Such was the case with Clube Atlético Indiano, organized by the sister of José María Marin, who would go on to head the Confederação Brasileira de Futebol (Brazilian Football Confederation) and be charged in the 2015 FIFA scandal. Finally, by the end of the 1970s, Brazilian authorities relented and permitted women's football once more, though the end of the ban only came fully in 1981. We end the chapter by exploring the debates about women's football that continued until the 1990s. Feminist magazines began covering the sport and lauding its potential transformative power, but Brazilian women continued to face challenges throughout the 1980s and 1990s, particularly with perceptions about the game's purported effects on their health and sexuality. Nevertheless, the chapter shows that the political opening in Brazil contributed to a broader social and cultural space for women's sports.

From Brazil, we move to Mexico and Central America, where the role of the state takes center stage as we examine the development of girls' physical education and sports. Here, as elsewhere, eugenic interest in "improving" the nation led to increased interest in motherhood as a patriotic function. The Mexican Revolution (1910–1920) created a state apparatus geared toward engineering new forms of citizenship from the top down. Accordingly, successive revolutionary governments sought to extend secular education into rural Mexico. Both the rural schools, developed by the Secretaría de Educación Pública (Secretariat of Public Education) in the 1920s, and the cultural missions, begun in the late 1920s, had an explicit sporting component to them. Sports in rural areas was seen as a way to create camaraderie and a sense of local, regional, and national pride. Girls were encouraged to compete in basketball, volleyball, and other sports, though only occasionally football. Still, the idea of physical education and sports for girls rankled many in more conservative regions of the country, causing tensions between the state and the population. In Mexico, the use of physical activity to create mass spectacle was raised to new heights by the state. Workers' sporting parades were common in the 1930s, with tens of thousands of government workers descending on Mexico City to show off their physical prowess. Young women played as important a role in these scenes as men, presenting gymnastic exhibitions, marching, and dancing. So too in the 1930s the government organized national championships for amateur sports under the auspices of the Confederación Deportiva Mexicana (Mexican Confederation of Sports), including women's basketball and volleyball championships. The focus on girl's physical education, and the training of women physical education teachers, meant that it was a matter of time before women began playing football, which slowly emerged as the national sport. Mexico was joined by Central American republics, including Costa Rica and El Salvador, where the state promoted physical activity in the name of improving the population. In Costa Rica, early twentieth-century physical education programs and a vibrant women's movement led to the development of the first women's football teams in Central America, in the late 1940s. From San José, the sport spread throughout Costa Rica and into much of Central America and the Caribbean. El Salvador offers a contrasting case. There, rhetorical interest in women's physical education did not translate to increased funding for programs, and thus sporting opportunities opened more slowly.

Concerns over sexuality were present, though not dominant, during the brief boom of women's football in Mexico, which occurred from about 1968 to 1975, and which forms the basis of the fifth chapter. With the erosion of the power of the Mexican state, more cultural spaces opened for women in the 1960s, including sporting spaces. Building on earlier attempts at women's football leagues, and the growth of women's sports fandom as well, a number of women's football leagues developed in and around Mexico City. These were bolstered by Mexico's entry and success in the first women's world championship, hosted by the Federazione Internazionale

Europea Football Femminile (Federation of International and European Women's Football) in 1970 in Turin.[13] Mexico hosted the second tournament a year later. However, the futboleras faced many struggles to play. Chief among these, as elsewhere, were resistance by the male-dominated football institutions (both national and international) and resistance from family. The former made it difficult to find fields on which to practice; the latter made it difficult for women to get to such fields as were available. Still, allies existed in the Mexico City government and in the press, which offered the sport the space it needed to take root. When the official Federación Mexicana de Fútbol (Mexican Football Federation) took over the sport in efforts to "protect" women from unscrupulous businessmen and proceeded to ignore it, the players themselves had developed a strong enough network to keep the sport alive.

This, ultimately, is one story of women's sports in Latin America. Women's sports were always there, but always existed just below the surface and remained on the margins of acceptable behavior. In the case of football, although it began almost simultaneously with the men's game, from the outset women who played were seen as violating the norms of respectable behavior. As football became increasingly a part of national identities in the region, women faced greater exclusion. It was not women's sporting practices per se that sporting institutions objected to. Indeed, for the length of the twentieth century certain sports and physical activities were promoted by the state to create healthier mothers as a means to create healthier citizens—when under the tutelage of state-sponsored girls' physical education programs or undertaken as part of a beauty regimen. But once women began organizing on their own and demanding leisure time, public space, and community resources, all considered men's domain, they encountered resistance in and outside of the home. Both in the media and through official apparatus, avenues for the practice of women's football slowly closed. No longer considered spectacle, the threat it caused to notions of appropriate womanhood, to masculine hegemony, and to perceptions of women's public health, were too much to be ignored. Yet, as we show, the sport continued, ultimately laying the groundwork for today's futboleras. Beyond the realm of sports, women athletes in Latin America have created new models of ideal body types, challenged men's monopoly on resources, and forged important communities.

1

PHYSICAL EDUCATION AND WOMEN'S SPORTS IN ARGENTINA AND CHILE

IN 1902, JUANA GREMLER PETITIONED THE CHILEAN MINISTRY of Public Education requesting funds for the girls' school she directed. Among her requests, she asked for outdoor space and resources for physical education.[1] Specifically, Gremler wanted to promote team sports and ball games among her pupils. She had arrived in Chile from Germany with a passionate dedication to girls' education. In 1895, she took the helm of the prestigious public school Liceo de Niñas no. 1.[2] Gremler's curriculum prioritized physical education because she believed that in addition to physical health, it built moral fortitude. Her curriculum served as a model for girls' education in other Chilean schools, as well as in neighboring Argentina and Peru. In her school, girls spent an average of two hours per week in physical education—more than in history or natural sciences.[3] Physical education became an important site of intervention into the bodily habits and minds of girls and young women.[4] In its earliest years, physical education offered a radical departure from societal conventions that emphasized the importance of women's softness, calm, and spiritual focus. As state agencies, physical education experts, and physicians took an interest in it, physical education became dominated by men who, based on little scientific evidence, argued for the fundamental differences between males and females and instructed girls in their inferiority.

Juana Gremler was part of a small but influential circle of teachers who pioneered girls' education in late nineteenth- and early twentieth-century Latin America. The Brazilian teacher Clara Korte, for example, created a postsecondary program, the Instituto Femenino de Educación Física (Women's Institute of Physical Education), in Rio de Janeiro in 1916.[5] Her curriculum went far beyond physical

17

instruction and included courses on hygiene, infant health, and home economics. Like similar programs in Argentina and Chile, its primary purpose was to produce scientific teachers who would shape the physical activities of thousands of girls. Typically single, these women were praised for sacrificing motherhood and marriage to the teaching profession.[6] However, the traces of their lives indicate they were not cloistered ascetics, but travelers, community organizers, and capable professionals. They formed civic associations with colleagues, students, and alumni beyond the classroom. And, importantly, they pioneered women's sports around the continent.[7]

Throughout the Southern Cone at the turn of the twentieth century, physical education teachers promoted their students' exercise within schools and sought to establish girls' sports clubs in the wider community. This chapter examines the growth of girls' physical education and sports, with a particular emphasis on Argentina and Chile. These two countries, followed closely by Brazil, integrated girls into physical education the earliest, and we hypothesize that this encouraged women's sports development. State bureaucrats, medical experts, and educators pinned their hopes on physical education programs to produce fit soldiers, disciplined citizens, and eugenically improved populations, primarily with boys in mind. However, this last goal opened spaces for girls' and women's participation in sports and physical education activities. Their future as childbearing vessels alternately justified or doomed girls' participation in the eyes of physical education experts. Yet, for all of their claims of expertise, the understanding of women's bodies was shockingly inaccurate among the wider medical community until the mid-twentieth century and beyond. Very little scientific research focused on the effects of exercise on girls' and women's health. Therefore, when girls and women were included in the long treatises on physical education, experts put forward wildly contradictory recommendations.

The histories of physical education and women's sports reflect the importance of transnational relationships among teachers and athletes. Yet the uneven number and types of sources available on women's history in the early twentieth century presents a challenge to anyone attempting a seamless chronology. In Bolivia, Ecuador,

Mexico, Paraguay, and Peru, for example, much of the source base comes from physical education manuals and government publications, whereas in Chile and Argentina, magazines such as *Estadio* and *El Gráfico* provided stable coverage of sports throughout the early twentieth century. No sooner, in other words, do we make the argument for looking at the region transnationally than uneven documentation complicates such a project. Nevertheless, this chapter begins to put forward arguments and categorize themes around girls' and women's physical education, while acknowledging that our sources often come from sporadic publications and traces of evidence.

Generally speaking, three ideological camps shaped the politics of sports in the early twentieth century. The most prominent in the early 1900s were liberal reformers, working within the state, who hoped that under European tutelage exercise could help to reform poor people's habits. Civic associations, frequently religious or charitable in nature, formed another locus of activity. They sought to promote "moral" behavior, particularly in regard to sexuality and alcohol. Sports clubs emerged as the largest of these secular voluntary organizations. Gender disparity in leisure time, family resources, and access to public space meant women found themselves excluded from clubs until the mid-twentieth century. The relationship between physical education and organized sports, despite involving many of the same people, was thorny. In light of the fanaticism and sociability of sports clubs, some educators saw them as antithetical to proper, scientific, physical education. A third group of leaders worked in the military. The military created sports clubs, physical education curricula, and Olympic associations. For example, in Brazil, the military created its own football league in the 1910s. Military sports directors tended to favor martial sports, such as shooting and equestrian events, and to a lesser extent fencing and swimming. Not surprisingly, military clubs and personnel in charge of state institutions encouraged vertical structures with clear chains of command. Military sports directors viewed physical education as a vehicle for the glorification of the nation-state and the development of healthy soldiers. As far as women were concerned, whereas liberal reformers and conservative associations conceived of a place for women within physical education curricula—mainly as a way to shape behavior—military directors ignored women entirely.

Precious little research focused on women's health, so early twentieth-century reformers spun fantasies and worked from convoluted ideas of women's anatomy. Women fit within liberals' education projects as future mothers of a racially engineered and modern society. In Latin America, the emerging "science" based on "racial improvement" was intricately tied to immigrant and labor-movement threats to elite power, as well as to processes of urbanization and industrialization. The series of crises that these changes produced have been termed the "social question." Policy makers looked to Europe for solutions to the region's supposed racial and social problems but ultimately created local policies that addressed their specific concerns and unique perceptions of their nations' ethnic makeup. Educational pioneers like Juana Gremler struggled to convince their colleagues that girls should be educated for their own development, not only for their roles as future mothers and wives.[8]

An exemplary case of liberal eugenics driving physical education took place in Bolivia. Liberal statesmen there considered indigenous habits and customs to be primary obstacles to modernization. Bolivian lawmakers faced two distinct challenges: minimal state resources and political resistance from an indigenous majority not easily convinced of the superiority of European programs for their children's education. In 1904, the country adopted the Argentine curricular model, which they viewed as having successfully dealt with Argentina's "Indian problem."[9] Educators designed the curriculum in hopes that students would acquire the discipline necessary for a future industrialized society. Inspired by the Swedish educator Henrik Ling, Bolivian teachers advocated that students practice gymnastics above all else. As the Bolivian state devised national curricula, it contracted advisors from Ling's Stockholm institute to create mixed-sex physical education. Bolivian bureaucrats hoped that Ling's methods for women's fitness would improve the racial health of their future offspring.[10] In the early twentieth century, the Bolivian government hired Henry Genst, from Belgium, to implement the Ling method in La Paz, Sucre, Oruro, and Potosí. Genst maintained his advisory position until returning to Brussels in 1929.[11] Genst and his colleagues integrated folkloric dances and indigenous games into the curriculum, albeit in a tangential way. Along with Genst's work in developing curricula, the Bolivian government created a department of physical education in the 1930s. While Genst advocated different levels of strenuousness for male and female students, girls were always part of his broader program. After Genst's departure, however, the Bolivian military played a larger role and demonstrated less interest in girls' physical education.[12] The Prussian system of marching and work on the parallel and horizontal bars appealed to the developers of these military programs. In Prussian and Swedish curricula, however, teachers pushed for inclusion of outdoor games, including football.[13] The prevailing opinions among educators that girls could not handle such competitive stress, as well as aesthetic arguments that women's play looked unfeminine and unseemly, shut off another avenue for their participation in physical education.

Coupled with liberal physical education programs, the Young Men's Christian Association (YMCA) encouraged the integration of girls and women into team sports, particularly basketball, across Latin America. The YMCA established a branch in Brazil in 1893 and was present in Argentina as early as 1902, where it provided welcome technical support for physical education teachers.[14] By the 1910s the YMCA established centers throughout the Americas, frequently running into controversies because of its Protestant missionary purpose. In 1919 the archbishop of Lima forbade any Catholic from entering YMCA facilities.[15] YMCA personnel, including the "fathers" of Argentine basketball, Paul Phillips and Frederick Dickens, came from a context in which women had already played basketball, football, tennis, and many other sports for decades.[16] At a 1914 YMCA conference of representatives from Argentina, Brazil, Chile, and Uruguay, delegates discussed how to include women in basketball. The Uruguayan delegate commented, "the Latin Girl needs athletics very badly."[17] While it is unclear what needing athletics badly might have meant, the differences between participation of girls and women in the United States versus the Southern Cone were notable.

YMCA agents went on to shape physical education and sports in South America in important ways. For example, Frederick Dickens served as director of physical education at the Buenos Aires YMCA before being promoted to the South American YMCA as continental director of physical education. Dickens then led the Argentine Olympic delegation to Paris (1924) and Amsterdam (1928). He also served as a professor at Argentina's National Institute of Physical Education until 1938. Perhaps because the YMCA stayed clear of football, which was already institutionalized (and demonized by some), basketball, swimming, and track and field dominated women's sports in Argentina and Chile. In contrast, in the United States and Europe women's football thrived in the 1920s. Given the regular exchanges among physical education experts, one can assume that in Latin America they were well aware of developments in the women's game elsewhere. During their 1922 tour, Dick Kerr's Ladies, a football club from England, played throughout the United States. Interestingly, in New York the club played the women's club Centro-Hispano FC, comprised mainly of Latin American immigrants.[18]

PHYSICAL EDUCATION, MEDIA, AND SPORTSWOMEN IN ARGENTINA

Argentina has long been characterized, and satirized, as a country that idealized European culture. Perhaps not surprisingly, Argentine ideas about the benefits of exercise and sports hewed closely to European models, particularly Swedish and Prussian gymnastics methods. At the same time, communication with its neighbors and the particularities of Argentine institutions fundamentally changed imported programs. Argentine state crafters promoted physical education for girls quite early. In 1839, when Domingo Sarmiento took directorship of the Colegio de Niñas Pensionadas de Santa Rosa, he included dance and gymnastics in the girls' curriculum.[19] In the 1870s, Dr. Francisco Berra wrote a physical education text that became a standard in both Argentina and Uruguay. In it, Berra asserted that physical education was just as important for girls as it was for boys. Meetings such as the 1882 Buenos Aires Pedagogical Congress brought Berra and his counterparts in Brazil, Chile, and Uruguay into direct dialogue.[20] Berra viewed girls' physical education as a way to prevent women's nervous conditions, as well as to avoid deadly diseases such as tuberculosis.[21] Enrique Romero Brest, Berra's successor, stood out as the most influential physical education expert of the early twentieth century. Romero Brest not only saw a need for physical education for girls in schools, but also wanted to extend physical culture for girls and women outside of school. To that end, he founded the girls' and women's sports club Atalanta in 1902.[22] Romero Brest pointedly declared that the purpose of women's physical education was to better the "race" by adopting Germanic and Anglo-Saxon habits.

The integration of girls into physical education meant that the Argentine Ministry of Education created a vehicle for the daily and corporal enactment of gender differences. Medical doctors and teachers placed social qualities onto biology when they claimed that girls needed harmony and balance of movement while boys needed vigor and action. Above all, Argentine physical educators repeated ad nauseam that girls' exercise was needed to enhance beauty. Enhancing beauty meant that girls stayed at a healthy weight but did not build muscles. As Pablo Scharagrodsky has noted, while improved maternal health was the end goal for girls' physical education, the same standard—parenthood—was not a concern for boys.[23] The emergent fields of physical education and sports medicine emphasized girls' eventual maternal fitness, but not boys' capacity for fatherhood. Romero Brest, for one, opposed the military exercises that had been popular for boys in the nineteenth century. Instead, he advocated outdoor games that would form boys into moral citizens.

The case of women athletes in Argentina stands out for several reasons, despite Argentina's commonalities with and influence over its neighbors. First, Argentine physical educators and sports commentators prioritized the role of exercise in beauty, perhaps even more than in motherhood. Second, the national sports magazine *El*

Gráfico, which had regional coverage and influence, covered female athletes with regularity and relative nuance. This is especially true when compared to Brazil or Chile, which had similar physical education programs and women's sports participation. Finally, the resources channeled to sports organizations by the Peronist government opened unprecedented sporting opportunities for women. While the opportunities were hardly equal to those of men, women's sports nevertheless received a temporary boost in state support. Perón's interest in opening space for the working class within traditionally elite sports also provided opportunities for women practicing less popular sports, such as polo.

Beyond monitored physical education classes for girls, experts disagreed as to whether women should exercise at all. Physical education teachers, doctors, and journalists concurred that women's character was simultaneously lazy and high strung.[24] These experts thought that exercise regimens should be designed to help women relax their nerves and balance their supposedly drastic mood swings. Women's magazines and physical education specialists encouraged women to exercise in the home rather than in the more public sporting clubs. Entertainment magazines focused on fitness routines of popular cinema actresses who advocated for home workouts.[25] These magazines, such as *El Hogar* and *Caras y Caretas*, cautioned women against exercising in public. Writers assumed that women had too much domestic work to spend time at the local athletic club.[26] Moreover, these writers assumed women would be ridiculed and thus cautioned them to keep their activities private. Radio programs in the 1930s instructed women on exercises they could perform at home, especially stretches and small resistance movements. Gymnastics was universally promoted because it invigorated the body without the "disfigurement" of more rigorous exercise. Experts also recommended rhythmic dance, which would help the nervous system while beautifying the body. These recommendations sent the message that women should keep their exertion, sweating, and straining in private.

Images of sportswomen exploded in the media between the early 1900s and the 1920s, creating new representations of girls and women. At the outset of the twentieth century, magazines and newspapers pictured women exercising with their legs rigidly kept together and dressed from ankle to neck. Aided in part by changes in the textile industry, which had developed and popularized lighter fabrics, heavy uniforms gave way to shorter suits and uncovered legs by the 1920s. Argentina's sports magazine of record, *El Gráfico*, began publication in 1919 and played a highly important role in the creation of these new images of women and sports. Surprisingly, the third edition of the magazine, published on July 12, 1919, featured women tennis players on the cover.[27] Throughout the 1920s the magazine, known as the "bible of sports," published many photographs of women athletes. *El Gráfico* pictured women with sports equipment, on the field or in action. Although traditional women's publications suggested cloistering women's exercise, sports media of the period encouraged women to practice in public. Because they presented women as active subjects instead of passive objects and highlighted their physical prowess instead of *only* their beauty, these images disrupted the visual culture of Argentina in the 1920s and 1930s. Throughout the 1930s, about 15 percent of *El Gráfico*'s front cover pages featured women. Although still a minority, the frequency with which sportswomen appeared far exceeded that of any similar publication on the continent, and likely played a role in normalizing the idea of sportswomen. Not only did *El Gráfico* feature women regularly on the covers, it also featured their accomplishments throughout the pages of the magazine. Women's magazines such as *El Hogar*, on the other hand, featured society ladies and starlets. One of its few covers that featured women in active poses showed a woman on a diving board in ballet shoes.[28] In other words, instead of showing active subjects, most magazines pictured women as passive objects to be admired for their beauty, grace, or wealth.

Another way that *El Gráfico*'s coverage highlighted women's participation in sports was its frequent identification of women's club memberships. By noting which athletic clubs they belonged to, *El Gráfico* helped to normalize women's sporting activity and included women as part of the larger sporting community. From those descriptions, we gather that many elite sportswomen belonged to exclusive clubs of the British, German, Scandinavian, and French expatriate communities. Scholarship has generally assumed that the diffusion of sports began with urban elite women and trickled down to the working class.[29] Certainly, wealthy women had greater access to leisure time and frequently attended European schools, which more commonly promoted girls' physical education. At the same time, the nature and number of articles that expressed anxiety over the popularity of sports among women indicate that—as with men's sports—women's physical activity quickly went beyond elite circles.

The growth of women's sports in Argentina coincided with the consolidation of sports medicine in universities, clubs, and national sporting associations. Not surprisingly, leaders in sports medicine could not reach a consensus in regard to girls' and women's participation in sports. The historian Patricia Anderson has shown the contradictory and uninformed nature of the debates about the effect of exercise on girls and women in the early twentieth century.[30] By the mid-twentieth century, there emerged distinctions in recommendations for physical activity based on women's age. Academic articles and other scholarly texts recommended sports for girls more consistently, but only until puberty. However, opinions diverged widely on physical activity after the onset of menstruation. Once women were potential child bearers, protecting and policing their bodies became much more important for state and society. For example, faculty at the University of Buenos Aires thought women should cease all sports activities with the onset of menstruation.[31] Even the strongest advocates of physical activity emphasized the need for restraint and supervision. Notably, Ruth Schwarz de Morgenroth thought exercise was advisable for pubescent women, but only when under the supervision of a female expert. If opinion was divided on menstruation and sports, experts universally rebuked women for exercising during pregnancy. Part of the intense anxiety surrounding pregnancy might have stemmed from the decrease in the birth rate in Argentina, which decreased from 1910 to 1930 by 54 percent.[32] Sportswomen became targets of medical scorn, as experts—without any evidence, scientific or otherwise—blamed athletics and other modern leisure activities for distracting women from motherhood and harming fertility.[33]

Medical experts recommended exercise in the postpartum period, mostly for beauty enhancement and weight loss rather than any other benefits. Beginning in the 1920s, doctors in Argentina delineated a very fine line between obesity and *lipofobia*, or a fear of fatness. These experts postulated that women had a natural tendency toward the former, and that those who suffered from the latter had an overly angular and thin figure. In other words, beauty—the goal of physical education—was difficult to attain and maintain. Without enough activity, women would be "obese." Too much activity, and they would be too thin. In the magazine *Eva's* medical columns from the 1940s, doctors advised postpartum women to apply more makeup, wear stronger girdles, and brush their hair with even greater enthusiasm than normal.[34] Once women became menopausal, they became nonsubjects for sports medicine. This further underscored the view of sports science that exercise was for an aesthetic ideal or maternal fitness, rather than for the health of women.

With the professionalization of medicine, education, and sports management, and an increase in their prestige, women found themselves edged out of employment in those fields. Beginning in the late 1930s, certain physical education leaders sought to reduce the number of women instructors. Raúl Blanco, a director of institutions in both Argentina and Uruguay and the author of a major work on the history of physical education, declared the Argentine physical education program a failure, in part because there were too many female teachers.[35] Blanco accused women of pursuing a teaching career in physical education for the comfortable schedule it offered rather than a true passion. He also opined women spent far too much time in gymnasia and did not inculcate students with morals and discipline. In response to similar criticisms, in 1939 the Argentine president Roberto Ortíz divided the Instituto Nacional de Educación Física (National Institute of Physical Education) into separate schools to train female and male physical education teachers. Women remained at the national institute, while men moved to the newly opened Instituto de Aplicación General Belgrano (General

Belgrano Institute of Practice) in San Fernando.[36] This growing number of specialists organized the first Pan-American Congress on Physical Education in Buenos Aires in 1941. Although women attended, which we know from their writings, they do not appear in the official records of the congress.[37]

The increase in resources for Argentine male sports in the Peronist period dwarfed that of women's sports. Despite the professionalization of men's football in 1931, the Argentine Football Association continued to rely on state support in a variety of ways, which only increased during the 1940s and 1950s. As football emerged as the unrivaled national sport, futboleras found it more difficult to claim a space there. However, increased state support to both amateur and professional clubs, ostensibly for football, trickled down to other women's sports. Women participated enthusiastically in the Pan-American Games, hosted by Argentina in 1951. In fact, Argentine women achieved important victories in 1951, earning the top three spots in fencing, as well as medals in track and field and swimming. Throughout the 1950s Argentine women excelled at the Pan-American Games. Club Atlético San Lorenzo de Almagro became an important club for sportswomen training in these events. One of those women was Ingeborg Mello, whose Jewish family fled Germany in the late 1930s.[38] Mello won gold in the shot put and discus events of the Pan-American Games. While competing for Argentina in neighboring countries during the 1940s, Mello and her Jewish teammates confronted Nazi sympathizers within the track-and-field community.[39] Mello's sporting achievements helped her obtain naturalization in Argentina. She continued to train at San Lorenzo and participated on the national team in Olympic competition. Mello experienced sports as a vehicle for integration into social life in Buenos Aires.

The role of women in sports clubs remains more elusive than their participation in Olympic events. A feature in the magazine *Fray Mocho* published photographs of three women's football teams in Buenos Aires in 1923.[40] The photographs' subjects are identified as members of the first women's football club, named Río de la Plata, which consisted of at least three women's football teams. Two of the

FIGURE 1.1. Early women's football in Argentina, 1923. *Fray Mocho*, October 2, 1923.

teams appear to pit criollas against their British and German counterparts, defined as "Team Argentina" versus "Team Cosmopolita." The futboleras appeared experienced, with proper uniforms, and the images of their play in action indicate that they were well versed in the game. Moreover, the magazine identified officers of the club, so it appears that the women adopted a similar structure to men's clubs. Futboleras popped up on factory teams in increasing numbers with industrialization in the 1930s. Yet many of these workplaces, such as meatpacking plants, cigarette factories, and sugar refineries, were segregated along gendered lines. Factories were charged with tension around women's mobility in the workforce. Even with separate work sections, men found themselves working alongside women with greater frequency.[41]

The dissemination of basketball, spurred by groups like the YMCA, helped women carve space in neighborhood and union clubs. Vélez Sarsfield, a sports club founded in 1910 as a men's football club in the Liniers neighborhood of Buenos Aires, started a women's basketball team in 1954 and became a national powerhouse in the sport.

FIGURE 1.2. Juan Perón at a women's basketball game, Argentina, 1952. Courtesy of Biblioteca Nacional de Argentina.

The important textile workers' union, the Asociación Obrera Textil, also had a very active women's basketball program.[42] Considering how basketball is played today, there would seem to be little rhyme or reason as to why it was more acceptable than football for women. In the early and mid-twentieth century, however, the game was much slower, requiring players to shoot from a stationary position. Physical contact between players was more regulated, and basketball was played indoors, away from the elements. These factors notwithstanding, we argue that the greater acceptance of women's basketball across the continent stemmed from football's unparalleled popularity and power as a symbol of national identity.

As women's sporting activity increased, so too did concern over its impact. The public health debates over appropriate physical activities for women intertwined sexism with rampant homophobia. While male footballers were seen as models of virility and heterosexual prowess, journalists, officials, and fans cast doubt on women athletes' femininity and heterosexuality. Among psychologists, lesbianism was usually subordinated to the discussion of male homosexuality in Argentina. Medical experts characterized lesbianism as an incomprehensible perversion, supposedly caused by inadequate sexual experiences with men, or as a psychological maladjustment whereby women acquired male personality traits.[43] Thus, experts warned that women's adaptation to men's clothing and behavior could influence their sexual orientation and psychology. As sports had been defined as essential to building and exhibiting proper masculinity, it constituted a dangerous terrain in terms of its potential to masculinize women. Medical experts, state officials, and journalists, among others, policed spaces where women socialized or otherwise collaborated. They suspected that places such as women's prisons, hospitals, and schools served as underground communities where lesbianism was rampant.

CHILEAN SPORTSWOMEN, TEACHERS, AND THE RISE OF "EXPERTISE"

The history of women's physical education and sports in neighboring Chile demonstrates interesting overlaps with, and departures from, Argentina. The dominant ideologies of amateur sports clubs rested on a shared idea of proper masculinity that excluded women from the spaces of the clubhouse and the pitch. Amateur sportsmen drew upon British ideals of sports as a way to cultivate restrained masculinity, emotional control, and "fair play." Football dominated the sports scene in Chile, and football clubs were essential to the integration of working-class men into local politics. They served as spaces of democratization, and by the 1950s and 1960s, political radicalization.[44] The extreme marginalization of women from football created further obstacles to women's participation in connected social spheres, such as unions and political parties. Although shut out from organized football, women created spaces for athletic competition in basketball in particular, but also in volleyball, track and field, tennis, and swimming. The media occasionally paid attention to women's sports teams because of their international success. They sporadically received support from their male-dominated parent clubs. Government resources were absent, however, even by comparison with Argentina or Brazil. Moreover, despite the strong contingent of women in the field of education and the success of these sportswomen, sports clubs and the media created higher informal barriers to women's football.

At the turn of the twentieth century, Juana Gremler, the teacher who opened this chapter, traveled across Europe in search of the proper curriculum for Chilean girls. At this time, the training of physical education teachers was quite balanced in terms of gender. Boys and girls were both encouraged to be physically active, and both men and women received training in normal schools to become physical education teachers. In Chile, Joaquín Cabezas played the most important role in shaping the institutions and the direction of physical education. In 1888 the Chilean government sent Cabezas to Sweden to study the physical education program based on the Ling method.[45] On his return, he established the Instituto Superior de Educación Física y Manual (Superior Institute of Physical Education and Manual Labor) in 1906, which explicitly adopted physical education as a way to prepare children for labor and proper citizenship rather than the military. Perhaps because of the influence of the Swedish system, the Instituto Superior accepted women immediately. The institute provided professional training for physical education teachers, as well as vocational training. The first graduating class of physical education teachers from the institute included seventeen female and nineteen male students. Cabezas was also close to liberal teachers' associations, supported by politicians including Manuel Salas and Arturo Alessandri. He would later champion the expansion of public education to girls and poor communities, helping to create the Pro Popular Sports Committee, endorsed by the Popular Front in the late 1930s. The female physical education teachers trained at the institute shaped women's sports far beyond their classrooms. For example, teachers formed independent sports centers, not only for students but also for themselves and their former students. In the 1920s, Liceo Paula Jaraquemada, in Santiago's popular neighborhood Recoleta, began as a sports club where diverse generations played team sports outside of the school.[46]

The Chilean sporting press began in fits and starts in the early twentieth century. In the 1920s, *Los Sports* dominated the field, to be replaced by *Estadio* from the 1940s until the 1980s. However, hundreds of small newspapers, community bulletins, labor newsletters, and provincial outlets provided sporting coverage at any given moment. Moreover, radio comprised a major component of sports media.[47] The sports media developed two opposing caricatures of femininity that dominated popular visual culture for much of the century. Photographs, advertisements, and comics tended to portray women either as ethereal beings, such as angels and nymphs, or as castrating wives. The angelic archetype cast women as virginal and dispassionate, much like the younger and less maternal images of Catholicism's Mary. This image frequently borrowed from a popular idea of classical Greek beauty, insofar as the positions and dress echoed Greek figurative poses and outfits. In addition to supposedly classic aesthetics, Victorian optics of whiteness and fragility also influenced Chilean visual culture. In contrast, the castrating wife was depicted as overweight, shouting, and almost always in the private sphere of the home or a very local place. These women were frequently depicted with rolling pins and brooms to reinforce their supposed place in the home. Cartoonists and humorists frequently portrayed the angry wife with curlers in her hair or as dowdy. Sportswomen were occasionally featured in visual media, but fit uncomfortably with the dichotomous models.

In popular culture, sportswomen ruptured common images and appeared as exceptional, at best, and monstrous, at worst. Not fitting precisely into either the "angelic" or "castrating" molds, media and sports club materials exoticized women athletes as Amazons who existed outside of normal development. For example, the most popular sports magazine in the 1920s, *Los Sports*, began to publish a topless woman "athlete" of the month in 1928, sometimes with a spear, other times on horseback. The photographs reinforced sportswomen as exotic, rather than picturing women with standard equipment, such as a tennis racket or javelin. By having the women pose topless, they also objectified and sexualized them. Rather than thinking of sportswomen as athletic, these images suggested that they be considered objects of desire or ridicule. International sporting associations also conjured Amazons when discussing sportswomen; for example, the International Equestrian Association's official rules forbade women, whom it called "Amazons," from competing in men's events.[48] The term *amazona* for a female horseback rider was widely accepted in international sports associations and press. Perhaps the fictional, exotic, and anachronistic Amazon provided a nonthreatening template for horsewomen.

The flapper, a reflection of urbanization and changes for women in the 1920s, also challenged polarized images of Chilean women in the sports press. Sportswriters and club directors expressed frightening hostility toward the flapper who ventured into the stadium. Misogynist cartoons created fantasies of violence against young, single female spectators. For example, one cartoon showed a woman with short hair and makeup entering the stadium. When she sat down to watch the game, the ball hit her in the face. The joke is that her makeup has made a replica of her face on the ball, which is now thrown and kicked around.[49] Frequently, the jokes of cartoons or anecdotes in the sports press and club magazines revolved around violence against women for trespassing into stadiums and clubs. This included women being bound and gagged to prevent them from speaking, suffering black eyes from all sorts of mishaps, and receiving plenty of head wounds from their husbands. In looking through media, correspondence, and memoirs of the time, it is apparent that men viewed sports clubs as an escape from domestic life. Women's presence, unless as spectacle, ruined that escape from familial obligations in the eyes of many men.

The more accepted football became as a way to develop proper masculinity among young men, the further physical education teachers and club directors pushed girls and women away from it. There is evidence that women played football in Chile by 1900, and likely before. The earliest evidence comes from photographs at the Museo Histórico Nacional de Chile (Chilean National Historical Museum). One such photograph features Team Talca from that town's normal school, dated c. 1900. The caption reads: "It would never have

Development of sport leads to the uglcess of women

FIGURE 1.3. Women's football in Talca, Chile, 1900. Courtesy of Museo Histórico Nacional Chile.

occurred to us that there could exist in Chile a football club formed by young members of the weak and beautiful sex."[50] It continues, criticizing the women for "robbing" men of all their spheres. The typeset text indicates the caption was intended to be published in a magazine. Another photograph from the museum, eighteen years later, also pictures futboleras from Team Santiago of Talca.[51] The photograph's caption reads exactly the same as the photograph from 1900, but the players are entirely different. Both photographs picture women in ankle-length dress with frills and feminine hairstyles. The women are seated around a table in the second photograph. The Team Talca photographs deviated from the standard men's team photographs in that although the women have a football front and center in the image, they are in formal school uniforms and are not wearing athletic clothing or insignias. Team Talca is not the only instance of women's football in turn-of-the-century Chile. In 1905, Badminton Football Club organized a match with a team of young women playing against one of men to raise money for a children's hospital.[52] Though an impromptu event, it suggests women's familiarity with the sport.

By 1919, women's familiarity with the sport was made clear. In May and June of that year, *El Mercurio* published a number of short notices about women's football, which was apparently experiencing something of a boom. On May 11, the newspaper announced a match between Flor del Sport and Delicias del Sport, two women's teams, as the first event in a day of football matches. On its own this article might suggest that women's football remained something of a spectacle, with matches organized haphazardly. However, that same day representatives of nine women's teams gathered in *El Mercurio*'s offices to form a women's football association.[53] The article's author had some knowledge of the women's teams, describing Flor de Chile as "the founder of women's football," Progreso Femenino as "disciplined and enthusiastic," and Bélgica Star as having some "very good" players. That the article described seven of the nine teams suggests that women had been playing football for some time, a suspicion reinforced by *El Mercurio*'s description of the team Compañía Chilena de Tabacos (Chilean Tobacco Company, likely a team sponsored by the company). The team, the newspaper wrote, "had always been at the head of the clubs of its sex."[54] Two weeks later, the paper noted upcoming matches between four of the teams. It also informed the public about an exhibition match between Flor de Chile and Delicias del Sport as part of a sports festival sponsored by Club Motociclista Nacional (National Motorcycle Club), which included an aviation show and a motorcycle race. *El Mercurio* again implied that women's football was common, noting that the match represented "the first time" that the teams would play in front of "not the usual crowds that attend football games."[55] By late June, the newspaper was publishing the results of executive board elections of women's teams and announcing registration periods for the clubs. This practice was common with men's clubs; doing the same for women suggests a normalizing of the women's game.[56]

If playing football was somewhat rare, women's participation in sports clubs was not. Sports clubs typically provided auxiliary membership for women, often grouped in categories with children, lacking the rights to voice or vote. In many of the larger sports clubs, especially immigrant ones, such as Unión Española and Audax Italiano, women formed auxiliary departments by the 1910s. However, the increasing role of the military in sports during World War I and during the dictatorship of Carlos Ibáñez shut down women's teams, as the Ibáñez government joined with larger clubs to funnel support toward professionalization. It also buoyed clubs associated with military and police regiments. Not surprisingly, under Ibáñez, sporting institutions tied to the military, such as the Student Shooting Association, received more government support.[57] Despite the lack of state support and the media's derision, sportswomen persisted in creating organizations for athletic competition. In 1927, sportswomen inaugurated the Asociación Deportiva Femenina (Women's Sports Association, ADF), in Valparaíso.[58] Members of the ADF competed in basketball, swimming, table tennis, track and field, and volleyball. In an interview with *Los Sports*, ADF's secretary, Azucena Villanueva, declared that "men have the idea that we cannot manage without them but we are going to prove otherwise. We must show evidence that a woman and a man can enjoy sports together."[59] When asked about other sports, such as football, Villanueva stated, "Everything has its limits. Just as there are appropriate sports for women, there are also reasons that assist women to combat stale ideas." In the same interview, Villanueva informed the readers that ADF was created to celebrate the fiftieth anniversary of the 1877 law that opened access to university education for women. In the last paragraphs of the interview, the author wrote that the conversation with Villanueva "was far from being a lecture about feminism."[60] Although the ADF decided football was beyond the scope of their organization, there is evidence that the sport diffused quickly among women.

In 1928 a journalist from the Chilean magazine *Match* commented that it was common to have seen women play football and take "pleasure from the manly sport."[61] The same article mentioned an unexpected buzz about women's football in cafés and restaurants of Buenos Aires. The sport had grown enough to alarm a Catholic priest in Argentina who began a campaign against women's football. Despite stern warnings from the pulpit, women continued to play. Articles and editorials critical of women's football appeared, indicating the growth of the sport.

Women athletes and their allies sought space within the thriving Chilean labor movement, which had some of the most stable sports organizations in the country.[62] Their efforts to build alliances often used the same language as the Church and conservative politicians, ultimately falling back on women's roles as mothers in the "future prosperity of the nation."[63] Women's football emerged in the Chilean workplace, and frequently beyond the main cities. In 1928, a team named Aurora Porteña, formed in Coquimbo, posed for a team photograph. The picture showed eleven women who worked in the laundry service of the Fontz family in the northern port city.[64] The photograph was donated to a Chilean library sometime in the 1930s, and the typed description, presumably by the local library, is telling. It reads that the photograph features the first women's football team and that "the players are today respectable wives, many of them, among others, Sra. Anselma de Arriagada, Sra. Araya, Sra. Rojas, etc." The librarian clearly wanted to establish the respectability of the young women, who perhaps would have been judged harshly for their participation in football, by demonstrating they had successfully married. However, the women in the photograph appear entirely unconcerned with typical feminine aesthetic. All eleven have bobbed haircuts and wear caps. None smile or pose coquettishly. Instead, most look straight at the camera, holding their hands either on their knees, on their hips, or to their sides. Their cleats, socks, and uniforms matched, and perhaps the only gestures toward their gender were the ribbons on the front of the uniforms.

The growth of women's sports prompted fairly predictable and extreme reactions. Authors rarely signed the more extreme editorials that appeared on women in sports. The antagonism toward feminism in Chilean mainstream media outlets persistently tried to isolate sportswomen from larger projects of gender equality by either

FIGURE 1.4. Aurora Porteña, Chile, 1928.

categorizing them as reasonable compared to feminists or ignoring the larger implications of women's participation in sports. In 1929, *Match* published an article conceding that women's sports might be positive for the improvement of Chilean "race," but that they were negative for marriages.[65] According to the article, in the "pre-athletic era, during which women were docile, soft and obedient," men could expect their wives to accept their subordination.[66] The muscular and confident women created by athletics caused serious anxiety among their male family members. The effect of women's sports activities on husbands was a central consideration of the mainstream press. A woman who practiced gentle and soft calisthenics would only be more pleasing to her husband, according to *Los Sports*.[67] In this sense, Chilean media mirrored that of much of Argentina, though Chilean journalism lacked the dynamic coverage of female athletes that *El Gráfico* provided and placed greater emphasis on family harmony. Beauty was a vehicle to bond a woman's boyfriend or husband to her, but not necessarily to be pursued for sexual gratification or for its own sake.

Proponents of girls' physical education sought allies in the labor and feminist movements, which made sense given the frequency with which girls left school for the labor market at young ages.[68] These efforts to build alliances often used the same language as the Church and conservative politicians, ultimately falling back on women's roles as mothers in the "future prosperity of the nation."[69] Feminists did, in fact, advocate for women's sports. Unión Feminina de Chile, the country's strongest suffrage group, had a sports section in its newsletter, trying to build connections between women participating in basketball, swimming, and tennis.[70] Sports club directors appear to have felt threatened by feminist interest in sports, and advocated women's sports as a corrective to feminism. For them, women athletes recognized their own inferiority, unlike the feminists fighting for equality, whom they referred to as "vulgar."[71] Alarm bells in the provinces indicate that football had gained popularity among women in the north of Chile as well. An editorial in Antofagasta urged women's organizations to carefully select sports that could enhance elegance, such as tennis, rather than football—which only detracted from women's femininity.[72]

The early and near complete acceptance of women's tennis illustrates the importance of class and race in determining which sports became socially permissible for women. The elite circles of Valparaíso and Santiago embraced tennis as appropriately paced for women. It also involved very little, if any, physical contact. Its association with British Victorian culture, which represented the pinnacle of white civilization for many Chilean elites, meant tennis escaped nearly all criticism normally directed at women's sports. Magazines commented that while tennis was associated with foreigners, Chileans had picked it up too quickly for clubs to accommodate all of those hoping to play, proving that Chileans were already disposed to British habits.[73] Women and men began playing tennis at roughly the same time. The Santiago Lawn Tennis Club, a luxurious club in Parque Cousiño replete with a chalet and gardens, was a center of elite men's and women's tennis. Members of the club referred to its women's tennis section as "a happy triumph of feminism."[74] In this context, women's tennis provided little challenge to the prevailing gender hierarchies. For women who excelled at it, however, tennis provided a rare opportunity to practice sports seriously without social castigation. Despite the near total neglect of women's sports in the Chilean press of the 1920s, *Los Sports* and other publications accepted mixed doubles tennis without reservation.[75] Mixed doubles was the least popular tennis event, but it was a regular part of tournaments. It represented a unique instance in which men and women competed in the same space and on the same team. The success of Anita Lizana, who became one of the world's best tennis players during the late 1930s, further normalized the sport in Chile; however, it did not spur increased investment by the Olympic committee or the ministries responsible for sports.

While tennis was the most acceptable sport, the most popular organized sport among Chilean women across class—like their Argentine counterparts—was basketball. The first women's matches in Chile were played in Santiago and Valparaíso in the early 1920s.[76] Chilean physical education teachers promoted basketball enthusiastically within schools, but also within labor unions and neighborhood clubs.[77] Still, from the outset, some girls faced resistance to their participation from their families, who worried they would become "marimachos."[78] The worry that their daughters might become too masculine connected with fears that they would develop attraction to other women. Despite some level of discouragement, women persisted in forming teams within clubs. One of the first clubs to promote the sport was Club Gath y Chaves. Gath y Chaves was a high-end department store in Santiago and Buenos Aires in the early 1900s. Once the store began selling women's clothing, it hired young women as salesclerks. These women took advantage of the impressive sports facilities the department store offered its employees, including football fields and basketball courts. The second wave of clubs included Badminton, Escuela de Artes, Universitario Tabú, and General Baquedano. As intriguing as some of these clubs are, we know little about the way that women's basketball teams developed

within them. We do know, however, that women's clubs joined the
Santiago Basketball Association at least as early as 1933. Sara López
Ramírez, a physical education teacher, served as the first president
of the Asociación Santiago de Basket-Ball Femenino. The associa-
tion integrated nine clubs: Estrella Polar, Enrique Correa, Comercio
Atlético, Flecha, Manuel Montt, Cabrera Gana, Universitario Tabú,
Badminton, Escuela de Artes, and General Baquedano. Once the
Federación Chilena de Basket-Ball Femenino (Chilean Women's
Basketball Federation) was established, provincial associations joined,
including Valparaíso, Concepción, Temuco, Osorno, Rancagua,
María Elena, Talcahuano, Tomé, Chuquicamata, Sewell, and San
Fernando. Women enthusiastically took up basketball and soon
began to traverse their cities, provinces, and even the country looking
for competition. Northern clubs dominated Santiago and Valparaíso
in the early years.[79] Despite covering the season closely, *Estadio* was
surprised when the women from the small northern town of María
Elena defeated Santiago at the fifth national tournament, held in
1944 in Concepción. The victory of this regional team indicates that
basketball had likely been established for decades in the provinces,
even if it was not officially integrated into national associations.

The 1940s and 1950s were a "golden age" in Chilean women's
basketball, in terms of international success and fan attendance. The
sportswear store Casa Olímpico began to advertise its line of basketball clothing for women in popular magazines and newspapers. By
the 1940s, women shed the bulky athletic suits of the past in favor of
satin shorts and short sleeves. Moreover, basketball became a vehicle
for girls to travel. For example, the Liga Escolar de Deportes (School
Sports League) supported girls' basketball extensively, and provincial students participated in tournaments in Santiago, Concepción,
and Osorno. Consider the case of Cabrera Gana, a small club in
the center of Santiago.[80] It began as an excursion club, one of the
many formed to organize trips to the countryside, especially for
mountain climbing. One of its members, Haydée Piñeiro, became a
top basketball player and helped to build the top women's basketball
team in Chile, among the best in South America. The women took a

minibus and toured the provinces of Argentina, something *Estadio* described as dangerous, uncomfortable, and "a crazy thing."[81] Ten women traveled for forty days; one of them brought her husband along and he drove. They played in seven cities, losing to River Plate and Boca Juniors in Buenos Aires. A trip of this extent in the 1940s of unaccompanied women was unusual, but the sports engagements they had arranged provided a unique incentive and structure to their travels.

The boom in women's basketball occurred within and beyond schools. Indeed, it coincided with a boom in amateur sports in Chile more broadly. This effervescence was a result of increased state resources under the center-left government of the Popular Front for sports projects targeting the working class. Large clubs like Colo Colo incorporated women's basketball in the late 1930s, as did immigrant clubs, small neighborhood clubs, and factory clubs.[82] In fact, the growth of basketball in Argentina, Brazil, and Uruguay helped the sport in Chile as well, because international rivalries built interest among audiences and the press. Chile hosted the first South American women's tournament in 1946, when it defeated Argentina in the finals to claim the title.[83] The finals were held in the Teatro Caupolicán, and six thousand people attended. According to one commentator, "Never had basketball, in any country of South America, succeeded in bringing so many people to women's games. Never."[84] During the tournament, women held the first South American Congress of Women's Basketball, which forged a network of continental leaders in the sport.

The international success of women basketball players thrilled journalists. *Estadio* raved about the performance of the Santiago champions of 1949, Famae (Fábrica y Maestranza del Ejército), a team of the state-owned arms factory. Famae traveled to Peru that year for the third South American championships, and the Peruvian fans marveled at their skill, according to the Chilean press.[85] Their fans felt certain that the women's basketball team was "without a doubt" the top talent on the continent, having proven so in Argentina, Bolivia, and Peru.[86]

The popularity of women's basketball drew athletes from all so-cial classes, but working-class players dominated the top rosters. The biography of the star player Natacha Méndez provides a lens on the women who led Chile's early national teams. Méndez grew up in Población Pedro Montt, where she started playing in Club Deportivo Pedro Montt. Her parents were directors of the club, which had produced several national players. Once her talent was recognized, Famae scouted Méndez, who transferred there. Popular histories of the Pedro Montt neighborhood emphasized her beauty and skill, noting that she was elected a Spring Queen and also Queen of the Pacific in the South American championships of 1951.[87] The local press appeared adamant in establishing Méndez's femininity. According to the newspaper *La Cuarta*, Méndez was so attractive that audiences in Lima went crazy for her. This type of adulation for a sportswoman was objectifying, but also disruptive of conservative ideals of appropriate activities for women. Méndez remained active within the sports community well after her playing career ended, and she went on to manage a well-known sports facility.

As women's basketball grew—and as Chilean women excelled in it at the continental level—it gained acceptance. Increased press coverage of the sport led to greater knowledge of the players. The rise of the sport culminated in 1953, when the directors of sports associations and sports journalists named the women's basketball star Hilda Ramos as Chilean athlete of the year, representing the first time that a woman received the prize.[88] Ramos captained the 1953 team that finished second in the world championships, losing in the finals to the United States. However, this progress proved short-lived. The following season the women's basketball team received fewer resources, and men replaced the female directors of the Chilean Women's Basketball Federation. According to Georgina Oyarzún, a basketball coach from the era, the 1953 world championship marked the beginning of the decline of Chilean women's basketball.[89]

The idea that Chilean women's basketball declined, in part, be-cause men took over its administration once it achieved a certain level of success makes sense, given the attitudes of the men involved.

For example, the coach of the women's national team in the 1950s, Osvaldo Retamal, declared that "basketball was not a sport for women."[90] Retamal was not only a coach, but also a professor at the Institute of Physical Education. Retamal believed that basketball was too fast and rough a game for women to play. When asked how he could sustain these beliefs and still train the women's team, he replied that he had firsthand knowledge of their incapacities.

In international basketball governance, Latin American women participated in the International Basketball Federation (FIBA) to the extent possible. Of the seven members of FIBA's women's commission, four were men. Among the remaining three seats, the Chilean Amelia Reyes Pinto held one.[91] By 1960 even fewer women served on the commission; Reyes Pinto was the only remaining woman of eleven members after 1960. The only other Latin American woman listed in the international governing bodies was the representative to the International Federation of Volleyball, "Miss de la Fuente," who was secretary-treasurer of the Mexican federation.[92]

Similar to the case of basketball, the international success of women track-and-field athletes helped them to garner domestic support. Track and field was structured in such a way that Chilean media could use timing, height, and distance to gauge how their athletes fared compared to others even without traveling to a tournament.[93] This was important for a country that struggled to arrange travel for athletes, both for sending its own athletes abroad and for organizing international meets at home. So, for example, the magazine *Estadio* could compare the running times of US women with those of Chilean and Argentine women and determine that the South Americans stood a chance against the top North American athletes, especially those from the United States and Cuba. The Pan-American Games, first held in 1951, provided the most important opportunity for women's track-and-field competition.[94] For female athletes, like Chile's Eliana Gaete, the Pan-American Games motivated them to continue training even after starting a family. Gaete won gold in 1951 and 1955, in between which she married and had her first child.[95] The success of Gaete, along with that of Marlene Ahrens and Betty Kretschmer, among others, encouraged the organization of athletics tournaments for girls, as well as the expansion of women's track-and-field teams within larger sports clubs.

Despite their success, female athletes were often treated harshly by Chilean federations, which refused to address—among other things—the problem of sexual harassment. Marlene Ahrens was suspended for one year at the height of her career as a result of remarks she made to a Chilean magazine. In 1959, she had refused the advances of the head of the rowing federation, Alberto Labra, who went on to preside over the Chilean Olympic Committee from 1963 to 1965. Despite an appeal and subsequent investigation that supported Ahrens, the sports directors refused to relent, upholding her suspension, which prevented her from competing at the Tokyo Olympics of 1964.[96] She promptly retired. Female athletes were not immune to holding sexist views themselves, even if they frequently found themselves championing women's equality. The press eagerly highlighted women's criticism of fellow women athletes. For example, the Chilean sprinter Adriana Millard dismissed the performance of Fanny Blankers-Koen, a star of the London Olympics in 1948, because "she ran and jumped like a man."[97] Moreover, Millard complained that Blankers-Koen's muscles were too much for a woman. Blankers-Koen had shocked the sporting world by returning to the sport after having two children and then claiming four gold medals in the 1948 Olympics. Still, Millard advised that young women instead emulate Maureen Gardner, who was thinner and more traditionally feminine in appearance.

As journalists began to publish popular histories of Chilean sports, especially football, in the 1950s and 1960s, they portrayed women as obstacles to progress. Pepe Nava's chronicles portrayed the first sportsmen as being rebels, and he described them as "crazy for sports."[98] Nava claimed that young women prevented the growth of football because of their anachronistic thinking. According to Nava, sports clubs threatened women's hopes for marriage proposals. For that reason, he claimed, young women formed organizations that opposed sports.[99] In response, a group of upper-class young men held a match at Club Hípico to convince their girlfriends of football's value. The women were so impressed that they threatened to become "foot-ball girls."[100] The article is accompanied by a stunning photograph of a young women's football team, neither named nor dated. The caption reads, "After being disgusted by football at the outset, the Chilean young ladies took to it with so much enthusiasm they formed a team."[101] The uniforms appear to be official, perhaps from a girls' school in the 1920s. The players are all wearing cleats and the goalkeeper is identified. "Fortunately, the idea did not spread," said Nava.[102] Pepe Nava never elaborated on why women's football did not catch on. Indeed, the Chilean media's rejection of women's football, like that of the Argentine press, is difficult to analyze, in part because it was left unexplained and in part because the sport itself was barely visible.

Oral histories point toward the constant underground presence of women's football. For example, the track-and-field trio Eliana Gaete, Marlene Ahrens, and Betty Kretschmer all began their athletic endeavors with football. Ahrens recalled that women played quite a lot of football in the 1940s.[103] In a 2013 interview she corrected a reporter who claimed that women played football "now" by noting that in her youth she "played so much football."[104] Ahrens explained that on her father's ranch she played with the sons of the *inquilinos* (tenant farmers) every afternoon, sometimes with shoes and other times without. For her part, Betty Kretschmer complained that she wasn't allowed to compete in football, which was her favorite sport. She later became a journalist, primarily writing about football.[105]

The Chilean physical education community asserted its expertise with increased intensity during the 1950s and 1960s. Yet the intellectual materials of the field had changed little in regard to gender. In physical education journals, authors asserted immutable differences between men and women, based on anatomical differences (such as curvature of the spine) and attributes of the "nervous system."[106] Specifically, physical education experts pointed out women's excitability, lack of concentration, and inability to control their emotions, which began in adolescence.[107] Because of the "inalterable" natural differences between men and women, particularly men's stronger muscles and larger bones, the experts recommended segregated education along gender lines. So too pedagogical instructions differed for teaching boys and girls. The rules for teaching girls included avoiding all strong and brusque actions, focusing on movement and harmony, without falling into the category of dance. Teachers were reminded to be aware of girls' limited attention span and strength. Manuals also suggested avoiding competition because girls' fragile psychology could not handle the pressure of winning or losing. In arguing for the differential treatment, experts frequently drew analogies to differences between animal species. While one article conceded that there was little research on human subjects, it noted that one could see from the animal kingdom that the female was weaker in all species.[108]

While most of the growth in women's sports participation occurred in basketball and volleyball, working-class clubs in Chile began to integrate women's football by the 1950s.[109] The first women's football teams to garner attention were Las Atómicas and Las Dinamítas from San Miguel. As with other pioneering women's teams in the region, the two teams toured Chile, playing preliminary matches before men's games. Attendees at a women's match that took place in Limache raved about the performance.[110] As a result, the sports magazine *Gol y Gol*, which was more focused on amateurism than *Estadio*, received dozens of letters in response from women who hoped to organize matches.[111] Despite its popularity among women, however, women's football sparked controversy within the sports pages. Conservative journalists expressed hostility toward women players and fans. In 1952, *Estadio* mentioned women's football and boxing as an "invasion."[112] Still, the debate provides a window into a broader subterranean practice: journalists indicated that women played football throughout the country, not only in the major cities.[113] In defense of women's football as a tradition, some readers sent in photographs of teams from the 1920s.[114] Readers of *Gol y Gol* sent in details of women's provincial football teams, such as Colo Colo of Iquique.[115] The club wrote to the magazine again on the occasion of their first anniversary, with photographs of the club's directory, which comprised three men and two women.[116] Other teams sprang up rapidly in the provinces throughout the 1960s, including Las Malulas and Latino from Vallenar. Women's matches often served as benefits for traditional feminized charities, such as maternity wards of hospitals.[117]

Despite the growth of women's football, physical education experts continued to reject its benefits. At the National Institute of Physical Education at the University of Chile, students could specialize in gymnastics, track and field, basketball, swimming, or men's football. Only men were allowed to enter classes on football. The curriculum also required women take two courses on childcare and dance. Interestingly, between 1945 and 1955 more women than men attended the institute, probably reflecting broader trends in women as teachers. This trend began to change in the mid-1950s. While being pushed out of coaching and governance, female physical education teachers continued to organize communities and contribute to academic publications.[118] Marta Briceño Vásquez, a teacher at the Liceo de Niñas no. 3, wrote a short editorial piece in 1951 about the stagnation in Chilean women's physical education. Briceño Vásquez considered the Pan-American congresses on physical education preliminary steps to connect women in the field. She wrote a summary of the Congreso Internacional de Mujeres Interesadas en la Educación Física Femenina (International Congress of Women Interested in Women's Physical Education). This congress met for the second time in Copenhagen in 1949, but Argentina seems to have been the only South American delegation that participated. Briceño Vásquez commented that there were no formal declarations of the congress, simply a vibrant exchange of ideas about everything from the role of sports and dance in physical education to teacher training and international exchanges.

Women's increasing entrance into higher education helped expand their opportunities for team sports. Universities had facilities, social spaces, and physical education programs already established. In the early 1960s, parents would likely have been more willing to allow daughters to spend their leisure time at university events than barrio clubs.[119] In addition to basketball, University of Chile students organized a women's volleyball league, with teams representing the different majors. The coverage of female athletics in the university sounded similar to coverage of women's sports in 1910. One *Gol y Gol*'s reporter commented, "The traditional beauty of our women puts a beautiful mark on the beginning of this tournament."[120] There was little to no attempt to analyze the tactics or composition of teams.

The popularity of women's basketball began to decrease in the late 1960s and early 1970s. Players attributed the decline to sexism, particularly the displacement of female coaches and the disproportionate support for men's teams.[121] In 1966 Chile came fifth out of six participants in the South American championship, which was the worst showing of Chilean women's basketball to that point. The erosion of paternalist factory policies, which included support for sports clubs, hurt women's amateur sports. For example, in 1970 Club Antonio Labán, the most decorated team in history, according to *Estadio*, removed its budget for sports altogether. Many hoped that the return of the Colo Colo club to women's basketball competition in 1970 would help make up for this loss.[122] It did not. Still, contrary to the trends in sports clubs, girls' athletics steadily grew within elite high schools. By the late 1960s, there was an interschool competition for girls that included seventeen high schools and nearly five hundred young sportswomen.[123] Many of these schools emerged from immigrant communities. Women's swimming also became popular among elite European high schools, including Stade Français, Cambridge School, and Dunalastair.[124] Moreover, dominant swimmers emerged from German and Scandinavian immigrant communities, including Inge von der Forst and Gisela Nissen.[125]

FANS, GODMOTHERS, AND AUXILIARY MEMBERS

Athletes are central figures in the history of women and sports in Latin America. However, the female club member, fan, and *madrina* (or godmother) also contributed to sports culture. The figure of the club *madrina* was one of an older, matronly woman who cooked meals, sewed uniforms, and provided advice for the players. For example, Ida de Cariola, the wife of Carlos Cariola, the well-known journalist and dramatist, accompanied Colo Colo's tour of Latin

America and Europe in 1927. One of the players described Ida de Cariola as "the fairy godmother of the delegation." The player further recalled "her kindness, her cordial and pleasant spirit, filled with affection, so that everyone loved her. She was a good friend to all, caring and friendly, she knew how to lift everyone up, her exquisite femininity was always a security blanket for the delegation."[126] It is important to note that Colo Colo, which quickly became Chile's most popular club after its foundation in 1925 and spearheaded the move to professionalism in 1933, permitted women members as early as 1930. In the club's statutes, the first article stated: "The corporation will be formed by members belonging to both sexes, that apply to the practice of sports, that will create all the branches of sports that the board of Colo-Colo F.C. considers appropriate to its goals, giving preference to those that cultivate a popular fan base."[127] Women could still face discrimination, however, because new member applications required recommendations from current members. Green Cross was another club with the structure that had a separate category of membership for women.[128] Women were able to qualify for a voice and a vote in the club so long as they paid the appropriate dues.

Throughout the twentieth century, football fans organized into the largest, and sometimes most violent, sports communities in Latin America. In the early 1900s, clubs offered free admission to women in the hopes that their presence would discourage men from violence in the stands. Despite the threatening environment as fandom became more brusque in the middle of the century, die-hard female fans elbowed their way into organized groups. Photographic evidence shows that women attended games in large numbers and with notable frequency in Argentina, Brazil, Chile, and Uruguay. Only in the 1960s did female fandom became a topic of interest for journalists and club directors. Most dismissed women's fandom because they assumed women lacked experiential knowledge essential to understanding the game.[129] They also accused women of pretending to enjoy football in order to attract men. Still, in Argentina's most prominent rivalry, two women succeeded in leading the *barras* (fans). María Esther Duffau, known as "La Raulito," of Boca Juniors, and Haydée Luján, or "La Gorda Matosas," of River Plate, took the mantle in the 1960s. They accumulated power within their clubs, controlling ticket allotments, club "gifts," and organizing international travel. La Raulito and La Gorda opted for masculine clothing, hairstyles, and language. In media portrayals, they abandoned their female identities to become "real fans."[130] Both Duffau and Luján came from difficult circumstances. Duffau, as popularized in the 1975 film about her entitled *La Raulito*, had grown up on the streets and often passed for a boy. Luján, too, was an orphan. Both women understood the football club as their extended family. Luján portrayed the club in a way not unlike the way that Eva Perón portrayed the Argentine nation—as her fictive kin. Luján claimed that her fiancé could not understand her love for the club. She described River Plate as her boyfriend, her children, and her husband.[131] It is striking to imagine the environment in which these women led fans in chants that ridiculed rivals by linking them to femininity and sexual submissiveness. Fan chants of many clubs ridiculed the opposing teams for their supposed homosexuality. In this way, clubs created a hostile environment for women, as well as for gay spectators.[132]

The 1980s were marked by an increase in fan violence in the stadiums, making it even more difficult for women to participate. Despite the early examples of women fan leaders, researchers in the 1990s found that women fans achieved limited acceptance.[133] Male fans denied that women possessed real knowledge or passion for the clubs, in part because they expected real passion to be conveyed through violence, which women were generally excluded from. In fact, women discussed that male protection was readily available whenever a fight broke out. While women reported that they did not feel discrimination, they also said that there were specific lines they knew better than to cross. For example, female Boca fans knew precisely which areas of the fan sections they could enter.[134] Several women fans described the violent ways in which they were excluded from the inner circles of fan groups. In ethnographies with female fans, social scientists have found that women were acutely aware of the connection between discounting the knowledge of women fans and the lack of female representation in sports media. Many female fans outwardly criticized women's football, complaining that it was a poor imitation of the men's game. The researchers Mariana Conde and María Graciela Rodríguez found that men claimed to tolerate women fans, but when asked to elaborate, the male informants also doubted the femininity and sincerity of female fans.[135] Interestingly, the World Cups of the 1990s ruptured previous tournaments in that women's fandom was highlighted, but women were presented as sexualized objects, and fans of the nation, in a carnivalesque moment. The ongoing integration of groups based on their potential as consumers has also driven the inclusion of women as a sector within football fandom.[136]

The activities of women fans, godmothers, and club members have been largely erased in the histories produced by clubs. For example, Unión Española commissioned a club history on the occasion of its fiftieth anniversary. Unión Española was an important professional club in Chile that emerged in the early twentieth century from a consolidation of civic associations of Spanish immigrants. In a short book that recorded the club's history, the directors constructed an allegory of the club as a family, more specifically a fraternity.[137] "Birth doesn't happen without pain. The mother and child's pain," wrote the directors on the club's creation.[138] Before professionalism, the women's section was very popular, but it remained unimportant for the directors who wrote the history of the club. While Unión Española offered some dances for young people in the community, many photographs depicting grand banquets from the 1920s and 1930s showed hundreds of members, all men.[139] According to their records, in 1936 the football club counted 2,289 *socios* (members), including 405 women and children.[140] In club records from 1941, women's numbers were separated from men, and they made up 201 of the 2,500 *socios*.[141] The Chilean Football Federation's official history, written in 1945, contained no mention of women.[142]

As women joined unions in greater numbers, they also took part in the sports clubs within their workplaces. Reflecting women's greater participation in sports, Club Deportivo del Sindicato Industrial de Cristalerías de Chile (Chilean Industrial Glassworkers Sports Club) elected a sports queen for the spring festivities instead of a beauty queen.[143] Women formed sections of barrio clubs at an increasing pace in the mid-twentieth century. For example, women members of Club Pedro Aguirre Cerda, of Conchalí in Santiago, organized dances, sports tournaments, and other social events.[144] The Club Cultural Población Miguel Dávila, which worked closely with the Socialist politician Mario Palestro, created a women's basketball section in 1949, directed by Rosa Gomes. Women also joined clubs as board members in this period.[145] For example, in Lanco, a relatively small town in southern Chile, Club Diablitos was organized in the municipal offices. Originally founded exclusively by men in 1960, by 1963 enough women joined to form a women's basketball section. The coach of women's basketball joined the board of directors, "inaugurating a new era in the life of the club."[146]

The international social movements of the 1960s, including anticolonialism, feminism, and revolutionary movements in the global South, did little to change the mainstream discourse of women and sports. New youth publications reiterated the same antagonism that women supposedly harbored toward sports. In 1965 one young woman wrote to an advice column fretting that her boyfriend loved her but clearly loved football more.[147] Despite the growth of women's sports and the influence of feminism on sectors of the Latin American left, women athletes were ignored among those trying to recast sports as tools of popular rebellion. Antonino Vera's history *El fútbol en Chile* contained only two references to women.[148] One came in the very first paragraph of the book in efforts to establish the popularity of the sport. He wrote, "Children, youths and older men—and now even women have made 'the English game' their favorite pastime."[149] Changing history meant including the male working class. The next appearance of women came in Vera's description of the entrance of the teams of the University of Chile and the Catholic University, in 1938 and 1939, respectively, to the professional league. Vera claimed that the university matches drew women to stadiums for the first time.[150] Yet we know his version is inaccurate. In the early 1900s there were plenty of women present at football games, as their photographs were splashed across the society pages. In fact, in 1912 sportswriters were complaining that the coarse behavior of players was diminishing women's attendance at football matches.[151]

A RETURN TO FOOTBALL

For all of the suppression of women's football in South America, it is remarkable that Argentina sent a team to the second women's world championship, held in Mexico in 1971, and that other South American nations considered attending. Informal communication networks were crucial, as there was little or no press reporting in South America prior to the event.[152] Chile's *Estadio* made one mention of it in February 1971, stating briefly that Mexico was preparing to host a women's football tournament.[153] But when the championship took place, *Estadio* did not cover it at all. It did, however, report on the 1971 women's football championships in the United States, featuring a photograph of empty stands as evidence that nobody wanted to see women play football.[154] Still, among South American sports journalists, there seemed to be a general awareness of Costa Rican, and Central American, women's success in football. When discussing a Fédération Internationale de Football Association (International Federation of Association Football, FIFA) decision against affiliating women's organizations, Chilean writers mentioned that Central Americans, in particular, would be disappointed.[155]

While both Chilean and Brazilian women were rumored to be organizing teams for the tournament, Argentina was the only South American delegation to compete in the 1971 world championship in Mexico.[156] But where did the players come from? With scant coverage in the Argentine press, the mere existence of women's football might have come as a surprise. But from media reports as far afield as Spain and Mexico, it would appear that Argentina's largest clubs were the engines of a growth in women's football in the late

1960s and early 1970s. And there was some diffusion: a tournament between Universitario, Real Torino, Sporting, and Rosario was aired on television to very high ratings.

Soon after Mexico announced it would host the 1971 women's championship, Argentina's newly formed Association of Women's Football committed to attend. The association listed six affiliated clubs and planned, according to vice president Raúl Rodríguez, to organize the first national tournament after participating in the world championship.[157] The Mexican newspaper *El Heraldo de México* named Daniel Fabri as the coach for the women's team, though Fabri did not travel to Mexico.[158] The futboleras who composed this pioneering squad remember neither Fabri nor Rodríguez, meaning either that the press was mistaken or, more likely, that it named men who were marginal to the sport in order to present the reading public with male authority figures. The Mexican press indicated that Brazil would also send a delegation, perhaps on the assumption that Brazil would participate in anything football related.

The Argentine squad was concentrated around one club, Club Universitario, which sent thirteen members of its team to represent the country in Mexico. Two other clubs sent two players each: Real Italiano and Sporting. As none of the clubs was flush with money, the Argentine Association of Women's Football struggled financially to travel to the Mexican tournament.[159] The players, too, had few resources to spend on travel. Most of the players were factory workers who played football in their free time, though four were university students. It is unclear if they all lived in Buenos Aires, as newspaper reports suggest that women played in La Plata and Rosario. The age of many of the players—some as old as thirty-three—suggested that they had been playing organized football for a decade.[160]

The lead-up to the tournament gives a glimpse of the existence of women's football in the region. The Mexican national team planned a trip to Argentina to play a series of friendly matches, scheduled to be played in Estadio Gimnasia y Esgrima in Buenos Aires.[161] But the trip was extended as a result of requests to play elsewhere in South America. The Mexican women's federation received requests

FIGURE 1.5. Club Universitario, Buenos Aires, 1971. Photograph of the Argentine team that participated in the second women's world football championship in Mexico. *El Heraldo de México*, July 3, 1971.

from both Peru and Venezuela—which had hosted a four-team tournament in 1960—to play matches there.[162] While it did not travel to Caracas, the Mexican women's team played representatives of Peru in the Estadio Municipal de Lima as part of the municipality's sesquicentennial independence celebration, led by Mayor Eduardo Dibós Chappuis.[163] The Limeñas, playing in sneakers, lost 2–3.[164] The match in Buenos Aires, initially slated for July 16, 1971, was rained out. In the meantime the organizers sold so many tickets that they moved the venue to the stadium of Club Atlético Nuevo Chicago because it had a capacity for fifty thousand spectators.[165] The match was a violent affair. The Mexican national team lost 3–2 and was so upset by the officiating, specifically a penalty they received for roughing the goalkeeper, that they temporarily withdrew from the match. Some minutes later they returned to the field, where they promptly received another penalty. The Mexican player Irma Mancilla and the Argentine Betty Garcia were expelled for fighting.[166]

The Argentine futboleras who traveled to the second world championship of women's football, in Mexico, sacrificed quite a bit to be there. As workers and students, they missed work and classes in order to attend. They had wanted to participate in the first world championship, in Turin, but could not raise sufficient funds for travel. Even for the Mexico trip, the team's financial situation was so dire that the delegation arrived in waves in order to save money on accommodations.[167] The Argentine captain, Maria Angélica Cardoso, explained that the team "suffered quite a bit to get here and still we have to struggle; we cannot return to our country defeated."[168] They were coached by a Mexican stand-in, as their own trainer could not make the trip. With all the difficulties, Argentina finished the tournament in fourth place, losing the match for third place in a rough affair against Italy in front of a crowd of fifty thousand in Guadalajara.[169] Today, the veterans of the 1971 Argentine team call themselves Las Pioneras—the Pioneers. Through social media, they have reconnected with one another and created their own history of the experience. In the process, they have begun documenting the wider history of women's football in Argentina.[170]

When Juana Gremler lobbied for more resources for physical education programs for her school in 1902, perhaps she envisioned the impact that girls' sports and physical education would have. After all, she placed more importance on sports than on other "traditional" subjects. The first wave of women's sports advocates believed in the role that physical education could play in improving women's health and the fitness of the nation. At the same time, they encountered strong resistance to women's sports. Still, few would have predicted that generations of women would struggle for their place in the sporting world. Women like Gremler, throughout the Southern Cone and beyond, who worked inside the state structure, were at once arbiters of change and guardians of official policy. Indeed, physical education and sports for girls and young women remained topics of intense debate within state institutions, the sporting community, and the public sphere more broadly. Government officials, private associations, and public health "experts" and educators believed that they had the answers to how much and what type of physical activity was helpful for future mothers. As the fields of medicine and education professionalized, women found themselves displaced by their male counterparts. However, in reality, most experts relied on little to no evidence to support their theories of female sports and physical activity. Rather, these experts based their knowledge on personal prejudices and political positions. Yet the decisions they made—from Bolivia to Argentina, Chile to Brazil— directly shaped the physical education curricula and girls' ability to participate in sports, both within school and beyond. Sexist attitudes notwithstanding, girls and women forced their way onto the court and the field. Whether in basketball or football, tennis or track and field, women and girls transgressed the boundaries meant to keep them in the home.

As the numbers of women participating in sports grew, so too did their representation in the press. But just as there was no unified vision as to whether or how women should participate, the sports media in Latin America had distinct views on the matter. In Argentina, *El Gráfico* opted for a relatively inclusive image of the sportswoman. As noted, the magazine often opted to show women in action, and in so doing normalized, intentionally or not, the idea of women playing sports. Though it was the most influential sports magazine in the region, its message did not necessarily extend to other countries. In Chile and elsewhere, sportswomen were treated in the press as anomalies: transgressors of gender norms as athletes, and interlopers on male-only spaces as fans.

The development of international competitions in women's sports further legitimized the presence of women. From Chilean basketball to Brazilian swimming, success brought more positive media coverage, which helped to place more emphasis on the importance of physical education and sports for girls. Yet there were limits to the impact of regional and international events. The support that they garnered tended to be shallow. Men still dominated the sports media and sporting institutions, as well as ministries of education and public health. As a result, schoolgirls and women athletes remained dependent on male allies. Women who spoke out found themselves sidelined. Moreover, hand in hand with that focus came greater access to physical education and sports, if only as ways to "beautify" the nation and to create healthy citizens. In both Argentina and

Chile, female teachers and students of physical education promoted sports among girls and women beyond the classroom, sparking the creation of independent teams and vibrant, if somewhat ephemeral, communities.

2
POLICING WOMEN'S SPORTS IN BRAZIL

WHEN THE BRAZILIAN MUSEUM OF FOOTBALL, HOUSED IN THE Estádio Pacaembu, launched the first exhibition dedicated to women's football in 2015, curators aptly titled it *Visibility of Women's Football*. Given the international attention to Brazilian football and its fabled role in everyday life, the silence surrounding the history of women in the sport is striking. Brazilian women's football is framed by perhaps the most prohibitive landscape anywhere in the Americas. From the 1940s until the 1980s, women's football was prohibited by law. In the 1970s, as the ban was called into question, journalists and popular commentators dismissed its impact as insignificant, claiming that women had never played much football. Yet historical evidence demonstrates that women's football established a successful fan base and a pool of players early in the twentieth century. At the time that the Getúlio Vargas government banned women from playing the national game, in 1941, the sport was expanding rapidly. In fact, we argue, the growth in popularity of women's football and concern over its impact on young women by public health experts prompted its prohibition. This chapter seeks to understand why futboleras posed a danger to Brazilian society, how they persisted in playing, and what the significance of their struggle reveals about gender in midcentury Brazil.

That women's football became a cause of concern for patriarchal sports organizations across class lines is not surprising considering the broader historical context. Getúlio Vargas rose to power in the 1930s on promises of reform that had been percolating since the late 1800s. Along with the broader expansion of the state, the Vargas regime also sought to more directly regulate women's lives and behavior. Lawmakers, from the 1890 penal code to the early twentieth-century civil code, defined women's and men's rights differently.[1] Efforts by reformers such as Clóvis Beviláqua to grant women more equal status in civil cases were rebuffed on the basis that women were "incapable" under civil law, a category they shared with children and the "insane."[2] Women's participation in public health debates, including those that surrounded the development of physical education, was limited from the outset. The barriers to women's education prevented them from being doctors or being considered experts. Even though medical programs allowed women to study in 1879, very few upper-middle-class or elite white women managed to do so. The paucity of female voices ensured that men drove the public discussion of women's sports and physical education.[3] In turn, the dominance of men in such debates made physical education one more domain of patriarchal control.[4]

At the vanguard of women's football in Brazil were the players, although we hear from them less frequently in the historical record than we do pundits, journalists, and state officials. Women footballers faced restrictive gender prescriptions, hostility from sporting institutions, and a lack of resources. There were challenges to participation in other sports as well, but none as restrictive as football. As football diffused from elite social clubs to the popular classes, the sport's growing association with violence and working-class leisure made it more difficult for young women to play. Still, beginning in the 1910s, women entered football as fans and club matrons, as well as players. More commonly, women participated in rowing and horseback riding, which were associated with the upper class.[5] The Olympic movement offered another avenue for athletes, and Brazilian women flocked to swimming, tennis, and later basketball, track and field, and volleyball. In the early part of the twentieth century, newly minted "experts" recommended women avoid team sports. In their view, dance and gymnastics were optimal, but at least tennis and swimming avoided overt physical contact, brusque movements, and excessive muscle development. Women's sports were almost exclusively promoted by middle- and upper-class sports clubs, as well as by educational institutions to which relatively well-off, mostly white Brazilians had access. However, even though experts deemed football detrimental to women's health, women ignored the official proscriptions of the medical and educational establishment.

Men's football might have dominated Brazil's sports landscape in the 1920s, but many viewed its health benefits and social significance with skepticism. Those who embraced the nineteenth-century ideal of amateurism viewed the growth of passionate football fandom as antithetical to that ideal's disinterested pursuit of "sports for sports' sake." The diffusion of football among the popular classes, particularly the masses of fans without the guidance of elite athletic organizations, worried politicians and police. Furthermore, as football became a mass spectator sport, the mission of the sport to civilize the population and strengthen bodies for citizenship and military duty became more and more difficult to promote. As a result, the Brazilian legislature launched an investigation into organized fans as threats to public order in the early 1920s.[6] Race and class played a factor in these hearings; the degree to which working-class and black Brazilians participated in a sport bore direct relation to its perception as violent. And while boxing was understood by its nature to be violent—and received criticism for it—the focus on aggression in football was largely absent from reports of games played by early participants ensconced in the upper class. Despite the claims that including players of color revolutionized Brazilian football, elite white men continued to direct the clubs and sporting institutions. The increasing importance of football in social life and as an economic enterprise coincided with extensive stadium construction in cities and greater government resources in the 1930s. By then, however, the print media commonly referred to football as the "violent sport."[7] The exclusion of women took place at the very moment when the narrative of the sport as a democratizing and unifying force of national identity, particularly in terms of race, took hold.[8]

SHAPING GIRLS INTO MOTHERS

Physical education frequently provided the only opportunities for girls to play sports and to exercise on a routine basis. The growth of physical education, despite its deeply sexist foundations, introduced sports to a broader cross section of girls. Programs of girls' gymnastics emerged in the late nineteenth century, driven by

European immigrants who integrated these programs into their athletic clubs.[9] The Brazilian teacher Clara Korte, for example, created a postsecondary program called the Instituto de Educação Physica das Mulheres (Women's Institute of Physical Education) in Rio de Janeiro in 1916.[10] Her curriculum went far beyond exercise instruction and included courses on hygiene, infant health, and home economics. There is evidence to suggest that these physical education teachers played an important role in carving spaces within the major football clubs for women. Korte, for instance, organized events in Rio's storied Club Fluminense, where she taught the women's section rhythmic gymnastics and hosted women's tennis tournaments.[11] Physical education for girls often included dancing, which was not considered rigorous enough for boys. Following World War I, the military lobbied for an expanded physical education curriculum to improve the fitness of incoming soldiers.[12] The medical community joined the army's plea for more physical education and reinforced the need for genetic improvement through physical regimens. The military preferred marching, marksmanship, and strength training. In general, physical education leaders suggested that following the models of the "Anglo-Saxon" race, Brazilian racial health could also be improved by prioritizing modern sports, like cricket.[13] Early leaders viewed African, Asian, or indigenous heritage as detrimental to national racial health. Physical education leaders from the medical and sports communities mounted a significant resistance to the Ministry of War's attempts to create obligatory physical education programs at the end of the 1920s precisely because they lacked the scientific understanding of eugenics.[14]

The expansion of sports clubs and physical education coincided with a broader proliferation of urban leisure activities in the early twentieth century. As cities across the world experienced the Roaring Twenties, new technologies motored the rapid dissemination of popular culture in urban Brazil.[15] These technologies enabled physical and sensory mobility and included mass train travel, aerial views in film reels, radio programs, and easily accessible photographs. New respect for youth developed as part of the political and economic elite's warm embrace of technology and modernity. The interest in youth also sprang from their role in a growing consumer culture. In this context, football clubs, fields, and stadiums emerged as a central part of social life, not only in Rio de Janeiro and São Paulo, but also in northern cities like Salvador and Recife. Along with samba schools, football clubs integrated significant migrant populations and acted as forces in local politics.

Because sports and athleticism were tied to ideas about the nation, women's participation was bound up with the "social question," eugenics, and a fractured Brazilian nationalism in the 1920s. As in neighboring Argentina and Uruguay, Brazilian physical educators looked to the Swedish gymnastics movement as a model for physical education. Fernando de Azevedo, a leading figure in Brazil's physical education curricula, advised that women should pursue Swedish gymnastics, including using apparatus like the bars, dancing, and walking, with occasional marching or limited jogging.[16] Azevedo promoted physical education that not only reflected, but also encouraged, different bodily development in men and women. Whereas men needed strength and vigor, developed in rough sports, women needed grace and harmony to enhance their feminine nature. Women thus received instruction, both in educational institutions and through the media, in dance, rhythmic gymnastics, and "gentle" sports. The recommended dances did not draw upon African and indigenous traditions in Brazil, but instead looked to European classical ballet for inspiration. As a writer, academic, and public official, Azevedo shaped policy. In a career that spanned from the 1920s to the 1960s, he wrote for the newspaper O Estado de São Paulo and served as secretary of education and health and director general of public education for the state of São Paulo. In these roles he helped to write the education code in the 1930s that obligated physical education in high schools. His views disseminated widely beyond educational circles, to social and sporting clubs and to popular audiences, through his features in magazines such as Jornal dos Sports and his numerous books. New disciplines, such as physical education and sports medicine, coalesced and gained traction as science itself became more prestigious. This was a transnational movement that resulted in the creation of new international regulatory bodies, which demanded a standardization of rules and regulations at the national level. This process limited women's participation in club sports because the governing bodies set out different rules for men and women and frequently barred women altogether. Essentially, standardization formalized women's exclusion or second-class status within clubs.

Early physical education leaders sought to distinguish scientific sports practice from what they considered "bawdy" entertainment and spectacle. Physical education experts worried above all that women's sports would harm the female aesthetic. They feared that changes to women's physique, such as building muscle, would blur gender difference.[17] In their advocacy, these experts employed fascinating pseudomedical concepts, particularly around nebulous measurements of hormonal balance. Classical dance, inspired by Isadora Duncan and others, was promoted to stop the development of women's muscles. Once again, physical education experts showed the depth of their ignorance in regard to women's anatomy and musculature. Frequently, in cautioning women against developing large muscles, writers used hyperbolic comparisons, such as women exercising to the point of having muscles like Hercules.[18] In the 1920s, invigorated efforts began to exclude women from football within physical education programs. In part this was due to the perceived physicality of the game, in part due to its supposed masculinizing nature. Moreover, the increasing identification of football as the national sport heightened its representative power. The process of professionalization of men's football in the early 1930s and its perception as violent, as mentioned earlier, created new market approaches to the sport that increased its penetration into social life. The state interest in the national team's success increased steadily following the Brazilian victories in the South American championships and the international recognition of neighboring Argentina and Uruguay. Women's exclusion from the national sport, particularly as it became a cornerstone of Brazilian identity writ large, was part and parcel of marginalizing them as active agents of the nation.

In the early twentieth century, a notable difference existed between the way in which Brazilian educators and their counterparts in neighboring countries conceived of physical education. In the case of Brazil, education leaders and sports directors focused more on the relationship between physical exercise and beauty, and included a focus on whiteness. Attitudes that highlighted light skin as beautiful dovetailed with eugenics in a way that preoccupied Brazilian leaders in a profound way. While whiteness was a part of the rhetoric in Chile, for example, the discussion there centered more around the moral and spiritual values of women. How sports shaped women's temperament was a more important question for Chilean educators, insofar as women carried the responsibility of creating the proper home environments for their husbands and children. In both cases, however, physical education professionals advised women they needed the guidance of scientific experts, assumed to be male. Only under male tutelage, women were told, could they avoid potential hazards of overexertion and body modification. The more football club directors emphasized the sport's role in developing proper masculinity, the more dangerous women playing it became.

The sports media popularized these ideas about physical education and women's sports. In the 1920s, sports media grew exponentially in Brazil. Not only did sports publications proliferate—going from fewer than ten in 1912 to over sixty in 1930—but mainstream newspapers and magazines further elevated the status of physical activity and education.[19] As the mass diffusion of sports occurred, there were important ways in which it was coded as universally male. One such way was that many larger features on sports included very small pieces on women and women's sports, if at all. This reinforced for readers that save for exceptional cases, reading the sports pages meant reading about men. The naming of sports also naturalized their masculine nature. Reporters covered basketball or women's basketball, or wrote about tennis and women's tennis. Even women active in sports were called female "sportsmen," with publications using the English term to imply they were elite, amateur, and, therefore, acceptable. Moreover, sports language and metaphor drew upon activities already coded as exclusively masculine. This is true of metaphors in regard to war, but also "human nature" and articles that stressed the changes of modernity, such as the rise of office work.

Proposals to mandate physical education curricula sparked debates in government agencies, among educators, and also in the popular press. The army played an important supporting role in the diffusion of the subject by creating early public institutes directed at boys who would be future soldiers. Changes to physical educational curricula sparked debates and resistance, often about coeducation. The historian Jeffrey Dávila has shown the circulation and prominence of eugenicists in implementing physical education programs.[20] Leaders such as Antônio Carneiro Leão believed in scientifically measuring intelligence and physical fitness in order to promote proper matches for reproduction. Modern sports, they argued, were eugenicist; the country would improve its gene pool through physical education for both men and women. Vargas made physical education compulsory in high schools in 1932. However, teachers struggled to find the adequate space and time to implement the curriculum. The Vargas government's belief in physical education for girls as central to fit citizenship forced a rare confrontation with the Catholic Church.[21] In a letter to the administration, the bishops of São Paulo criticized the indecent clothing and physical examinations performed on girls. The government rebutted with assertions that the clothing was "modest" and that women nurses handled the examinations. In the eyes of the bishops, girls in motion and in loose clothing incited desire among the boys in their classes. The Vargas regime's refusal to capitulate in 1940 might have had more to do with its support of eugenics then with the promotion of new roles for girls and women. The support of the military, schoolteachers, the popular press, and the medical community might have meant more than the support of the Church to the government, which sought allies and legitimacy, particularly in the absence of elections.

Women playing football rarely appeared in the press during the 1910s and 1920s, and when they did, they were frequently pictured as carnivalesque, or sometimes literally as part of the carnival itself. Serious efforts of women athletes to organize competition coexisted with theatrical representations of them. For example, the elite literary magazine *A Cigarra*'s review of the carnival season in 1926 included a suggestive photograph of "women footballers," who may have actually been men dressed in drag.[22] Alongside the more traditional fare of the magazine—social news, engagements, and birth announcements, as well as reports on elite leisure activities, such as rowing and automobile and horse racing—appeared many photographs of men dressed as women in carnival processions. Photographs of men dressed as women football players fit with other transgressive celebrations featured in the issue, including men dressed as Cleopatra or wearing the costume of indigenous women. When elite urban men adopted the costume of native Brazilians, they reinforced their status as white. The photo in this chapter of women football players of the Queirolo circus was apparently taken during a game with Club Palestra Italia. Given that there are eight players in the picture, four in each color jersey, one could assume it was a four-on-four match, which would not have been routine in 1920s Brazil. While it is difficult to say with absolute certainty what the photograph is supposed to portray, it was not an isolated image. Photographic evidence indicates that women participated in significant numbers in sports clubs of the period. In the very same issue, *A Cigarra* published a photograph, of a serious nature, of Rio's elite mingling in the club Saldanha da Gama. Women comprised about half of the pictured members of Club Saldanha, which had teams for rowing and football. This was not out of the ordinary; a 1920 photograph of Club Mangueiras, which fielded a major Carioca football team, showed half of its members to be women.[23]

The first match of women's football was once thought to have been played in 1913 as a Red Cross benefit, until the historian Eriberto José Lessa de Moura debunked the story. That match, he argued convincingly, was actually played by men in drag.[24] What can we make of the repeated appearance of men dressed as women playing football? The desire to adopt women's dress and movement, as these men understood them, must have held a certain allure, either to break from the strict social mores or to capture some of what they perceived to be a pleasurable identity or one with freedoms of expression, perhaps allowing physical affection toward male friends. While there was likely a degree of derision involved, we cannot assume that as the only motivation. Just as studies of the history of carnival, gender, and sexuality caution against assuming that cross-dressing indicated any widespread tolerance of homosexuality in urban Brazil, mimicking women's supposed mannerisms and dress perhaps only underscored the derision of feminine qualities.[25]

While early reports of women's soccer tended to emphasize the carnivalesque, models existed for elite Brazilian women to think about the game as a viable possibility. Pioneering sportswomen from abroad appeared more frequently in the early twentieth-century Brazilian press. For example, the elite magazine *Sport Ilustrado* published a report, including a photograph, of a women's football match between France and England, noting that an unnamed French team defeated the English club Dick Kerr in a brilliant match.[26] It is apparent from glancing at the women pictured in the magazines that European and North American women's sports began to influence fashion trends. While Brazilian women might not have been as quick to adopt loose clothing and short haircuts, they weren't far behind either. Of course, doing so challenged not only gender norms, but also those of sexuality and class. However, European trends were not embraced wholesale, nor were they always held up as bastions of feminism. In another article that appeared in *Sport Ilustrado*, the writer discussed a controversy that erupted in London because of the supposed growth in women's hands as a result of their sporting activities, which alarmed British men.[27] The columnist, identified as Doutora Lanteri, claimed that this should not discourage women from sports, because "no reasoned person could prefer the fragile hand of an unfit doll, unable to hold a cup of tea, to a strong, healthy, and lively woman who knows how to lead a horse and wield an oar with dexterity."[28] In the end, Doutora Lanteri asked, what were a few millimeters of hand growth? These pieces on foreign sportswomen opened avenues for Brazilian journalists to safely discuss their views on controversial issues close to home. The author, Doutora Lanteri, was most likely the Italian Argentine Julieta Lanteri, one of the first women physicians in Latin America and a prominent advocate of women's rights.

While women athletes caused some consternation in elite circles, the female sports fan did not arouse such hostility. She was an accepted figure in elite Paulista and Carioca society in the 1920s. The sports press, still in the process of gaining a foothold in the publishing world, merged sports with the society pages. One way they tried to broaden their audience was to feature notable people—often young, single women—related to sports. For example, *Sport Ilustrado* featured a photograph of the "well-known" sportswoman Herminia Carneiro.[29] Despite the description, Carneiro was pictured with her daughter, holding a parasol, and there was no further comment on her relationship to sports. In these pieces, women appear as decorative. The coverage differs markedly from the respectable coverage of Argentina's *El Gráfico* or the nudes in the Chilean *Los Sports*. The magazine also held beauty contests for the best-looking sports fan in Rio.[30] Contests such as these sent strong messages to young women about the terms that made their presence at sporting events acceptable. Essentially, women fans held value for beautifying the audience and increased the stakes for male players. They also ensured that there was a heteronormative element to the homoeroticism of men's team sports. Women viewed their role as far more than ornamental. In the 1920s, women choreographed halftime dances and chants to inspire their teams. Women of Fluminense not only danced on the "rinks" or velodrome surrounding the field but also competed with dancers of Rio's other big football clubs, Flamengo, Botafogo, and América.[31]

The beauty contests organized by sports clubs and newspapers provide a window on widely disseminated views about what made women beautiful. The description of contestants revealed that fragility and vulnerability were considered important qualities of beauty, though these features were presented in abstract terms. Take for instance the feature on Dina Coelho Netto, one of Fluminense's female fans. Although Coelho Netto's photograph headlined the article, the writer, identified as Rezende, spent an entire page expounding upon his views of beauty without referencing Coelho Netto, putatively the subject of the article.[32] When focus finally turned to Coelho Netto, the author waxed poetic on her small feet and ivory arms (thereby assuring readers of her whiteness), and described her beauty as soft and fearful. The reader was never told why Coelho Netto liked football or why she supported the club. Early sports sections demonstrated the extent to which organized fan clubs connected members across the cities, often through the press, and included women. When the "beautiful" Nila Castex, a die-hard fan of América FC stopped attending games, an article in *Sport Ilustrado* publicly beckoned her back. The author lamented that Castex stayed cloistered at home to the great sadness of her fellow fans.[33] The magazine seemed unable to feature a woman without describing her beauty. Apparently, Nila Castex was "brunette like the daughters of Amazonia," with "black eyes, black hair, [and] an angelic face."[34]

The increasing visibility of women in public roles and spaces, like stadiums, met with broad resistance. The historian Barbara Weinstein's work has demonstrated that limitations to women's work outside the home increased in the 1920s and 1930s, through reforms that included restricting women's vocational education to the domestic arts.[35] Industrialists, state agencies, and reformers created obstacles to women's employment in textiles or other industries. Because of their supposed weakness and lower intelligence, women were deemed unsuitable for additional activities outside the home.[36] While Getúlio Vargas, as president, supported the extension of suffrage to women in 1932, much of his populist dictatorship, from 1937 to 1945, promised a return to social conservativism, particularly in terms of gender. Even followers of the Marxist movements of the time were unprepared to step outside of the patriarchal bounds, criticizing the author Patricia Galvão for the "feminist perspective" in her novel *Parque Industrial*.[37] Nevertheless, in the face of this resistance women began carving out larger spaces for themselves in Brazilian society. In the early 1920s public high schools finally accepted women, allowing a path for greater numbers of women to study at the university.[38] Still, in 1930, only eighty-three women graduated from university.[39] Nevertheless, the desire to embrace

FIGURE 2.1. Queirolo circus, 1930. Courtesy of Museu do Futebol, São Paulo.

modernity, which elite Brazilians still assumed to be European, meant that the restructuring of patriarchy was in order. Women's integration into work and education was not only circumscribed but also heavily supervised. While most working-class women worked outside of the home, and economic conditions forced even reticent women into the workforce, increasingly women's ideal place was in the private sphere.

CIRCUSES AND WOMEN'S FOOTBALL

In the early twentieth century, the line between respectable and disreputable leisure activities was not so sharply drawn as one might think. Circuses were one of the main places where "high" and "low" pastimes converged. A circus might feature a Shakespeare performance one night and "exotic" human talents the next. As a space that often allowed for social transgression, it is perhaps unsurprising that it became one of the few places where women regularly played football. The circus featured novelty acts, to be sure, but women's football was not the only sport to use the relatively safe space as an incubator. Jujitsu and other emergent sports diffused through the circus, which could be as much a local festival as a spectacle of the bizarre. More established sports, such as men's football and particularly gymnastics, campaigned throughout Latin America to distinguish themselves from the circus. Members of physical education societies and authors of the somber guides to scientific exercise went to great lengths to demonstrate the difference between their techniques and those of circus performers. Women's football, on the other hand, because of its rareness in the early twentieth century, found a home of sorts within circuses.

The earliest appearances of women's football in the circus occurred in the 1920s. One of the most popular circuses, the Circo Irmãos Queirolo (Queirolo Brothers Circus), featured the sport on a regular basis. The Queirolo circus showcased animals, clown shows, and oddities, but also had serious theatre on its playbill. Begun by an Argentine-Uruguayan couple, the circus traveled across the Americas, including to New York City. In this particular iteration of the circus, the show was divided into three parts; the first was clowns, the second a comedy act, and the third a women's football "tournament." In the earliest years, the games appear to have been five-on-five affairs, described as contested between "pretty and graceful ladies."[40] In Rio de Janeiro in 1930, the women's football tournament played as the rival Brazilian and Argentine national teams.[41] By mimicking rivalries of men's teams, the women added a theatrical element to their play. In Curitiba, the capital of the southern state of Paraná, the women in the circus played as two rival clubs of the region, Curitiba and Paranaense.[42] In other performances in that same tour, women players represented the Britannia and Palestra Italia football clubs, another local rivalry.[43] It is possible that the circus teams comprised the same women, and adapted the local names as a way to increase the novelty of the spectacle, but it is likely that they sought women outside of the circus to join them. The Queirolo circus was not the only one to feature women's football in this period. Their competitor, Circo Nerino, also featured women footballers.[44] After one show, a local paper estimated a crowd of 2,500 spectators gathered to watch the troupe, a number that would have been a respectable audience for an amateur men's football match. Reporters gave the circus rave reviews and complimented its organization and quality. The inclusion of women's football in circus performance continued through the 1940s, even after legal prohibition of the sport.

It is difficult to assess how spectators or players perceived these tournaments. In a positive review of the Circo Irmãos Garcia (Garcia Brothers Circus) that traveled through the Southern province of Santa Catarina in 1940, the newspaper O Dia featured women's football. In this report, at least, it is clear that the women's match was not perceived primarily as a joke.[45] As with other circuses and prior stops for the Garcia circus, the women adopted the team names and uniforms of the local rivalry. In this case women represented Recreativo Brasil and Blumenauense. The teams were tied at the half in a match that the reporter described as "sensacional." *Sensacional* is one of the most common words used in match reports and could be interpreted to mean "spectacle," which may indicate the audience considered women's football an oddity. However, it is also a word that means "amazing" or "fantastic" when used to describe intense matches between men. Other details in the article make it clear that the reporters found the match interesting for the competition itself and that the fans took it seriously. According to observers, the circus offered a trophy, and the fans for each squad came out in "colossal" numbers. Circuses continued to organize women's football games after the prohibition in 1941. In 1943, for example, the Queirolo circus held a women's tournament, once again in Santa Catarina.[46] In fact, one of the places where women's football had the opportunity to survive the initial years of the ban might have been the circus. As sites of regular, staged transgressions of social norms, circuses provided women the cover that they needed to continue to play. Unintentionally, the farce of the circus might also have helped local officials who preferred not to enforce the ban to avoid having to pursue futboleras.

WOMEN FANS AND THE MARIA-CHUTEIRAS

Brazilian women were ardent fans of football. Although there might have been significant overlap between players and fans, they were not interchangeable groups. One of the earliest celebrity female football fans, who occupied both the field and stands, was the poet Anna Amélia de Queiróz. According to popular legend, Queiróz translated the football rule book from English to Portuguese. She played football in the 1910s in Usina Esperança, a steel mill run by her father in Itabirito, Minas Gerais.[47] There, she introduced the game to workers and used her influence to claim space on the pitch. While attending a match of América FC, she met her future husband, Marcos Carneiro de Mendonça, the first-choice goalkeeper of the Brazilian national team and the eventual president of the powerful club Fluminense. Supposedly inspired by Mendonça, in 1922 Queiróz wrote the poem "O salto" (The jump), which some call the first poem dedicated to Brazilian football. In recent media coverage of Queiróz's life, her love of football has been subsumed as part of her love for Marcos Carneiro de Mendonça. Her granddaughter referred to her as Brazil's first *maria-chuteira*, or a woman who pursues romantic relationships with famous football players.[48] In fact, Queiróz's football poetry has never been taken seriously. Rather than being perceived as the work of a serious poet who sought to capture movement, "O salto" and other poems about football have been interpreted as part of her effort to capture Mendonça's affections. They are, in other words, seen as part of her singular desire to "land" her husband. Yet Queiróz was an important feminist, scholar, and football player. "O salto" appeared in her popular and prizewinning book *Alma* (Soul), published in 1924.[49] Queiróz dedicated different parts of her book to different people, corresponding to the stages of the soul and the history that she writes about. The sections were dedicated, in order, to her mother and her father. Queiróz opened the book with a poem called "Dúvida" (Doubt), in which she lamented that impossible hope and ambition caused great suffering. Queiróz explored a number of transgressive themes in the book, including experiencing religious doubt and envying the faith of women who had seen their children die.

"O salto" is one of the best-known poems in Queiróz's book, but it is not the only one that explores athleticism. The poem beforehand, "Poean," discussed the beauty of the male athletic body. Steeped in Greek mythology, the poem was explicitly sexual and positioned Queiróz, the narrator, as the initiator of the relationship. In the poem she compared the athlete to the warriors of ancient Greece who inspired lust. "O salto" continued the same theme, comparing the male athlete to an Olympic hero, "glorious, passionate, intrepid, beautiful, Greek perfection."[50] Queiróz's discussion of her trembling body at the sight of athletes, not explicitly football players, must have shocked conservative Brazilians. It is not surprising, then, that journalists would try to tame the sexuality of these poems by analyzing them as mating calls to her future husband. In the final section of the book Queiróz continued her exploration of ancient characters, placing women in central, active, and heroic roles. The women include Sophonisba, Andromeda, and Cleopatra, among others. As she began the book, Queiróz ended by lamenting failed ambitions and restricted aspirations that deadened the soul. Curiously, women do not appear as athletes themselves, despite Queiróz's own activities in football and other sports. Queiróz did not stop her sporting activities after marriage and motherhood, even serving as president of the Women's Automobile Club through the 1940s.[51] Though her reliance on themes and forms of classical antiquity might have bound her to a masculinist tradition, she also placed women's gaze, emotions, and reflections at the center of her work.[52]

Throughout the region, magazines portrayed upper-class young women in the 1920s as interested in sports as a fashionable trend. Just as they depicted Anna Amélia de Queiróz, the mainstream media focused on sports as a device to discuss women's devotion to men. A short story published in 1920 in O Paiz, called "Amor e futebol" (Love and football), is an example of how popular writers understood women as decorative accents to discussions of sports.[53] The protagonist, Murilo, is an aspiring footballer who becomes smitten with Alba, a wealthy fourteen-year-old girl. When Murilo first approaches Alba, she is reading the sports section of a local magazine. He asks if Alba is a "sportsman," but she explains that she is reading about a very handsome athlete, João Jório. Jório would have been a topic of interest in 1920 as he represented Brazil in the Olympics in water polo and rowing. Her choice of leisure activity, leafing through magazines and working on her musings, sent a clear message about her class status. Yet Alba's role in the story is solely as a plot device. The joke is built into Alba's admiration of Jório's charms rather than a serious engagement with his athletic achievement. The display of the male body in sports competitions could transgress conservative codes of sexuality when gazed upon by men or by women. This dangerous quality was aggravated when black players integrated into sports clubs, particularly football clubs. Alba is not the only character placed as an auxiliary to the protagonist. The elderly gardener, a black man who is close to Alba, insults Murilo by insinuating that the young man approves of professional football. Ultimately, the story serves as a platform for an editorial on amateurism. Women and black people appear as decorative characters for the monologues of the young, presumably white Murilo. Popular fiction that included women as sports fans emphasized their feminine and heterosexual qualities. Any association with sports called into question women's normal sexual development, but the medical community and journalists typically reserved their fears of lesbianism for women athletes.

Photographs from the 1910s onward show that women attended football matches regularly, often unaccompanied by men. In a retrospective piece on women football fans written at the end of the 1930s, journalists recalled fervent female fan groups made up of elite women.[54] However, these fan groups expanded beyond elite circles. The piece features a photograph from the 1920s of a group of women beaming into the camera as they arrive at the Campeonato Sudamericana de Fútbol (South American Football Championship), likely the iteration held in Rio in 1922. Sports journalists connected sports spectatorship with the birth of the modern woman. The football stadium acted as a runway to display the newest fashions and a space to socialize with friends. In a feature from 1939, one journalist lamented that female fans of his time lacked the enthusiasm of those in the 1920s. This editorial, and similar ones, fit uncomfortably alongside evidence that by the 1930s women were at the forefront of organized fan clubs, or *torcidas*.[55] Women led chants and hymns, and choreographed dances for their teams. Although most evident in urban centers, women's fandom caught on outside of cities as well. Take, for example, a grainy photograph from a game played in Campo do Bomsucesso in August 1935.[56] Just outside of Rio, the Bomsucesso club was a pillar of the Carioca league since its founding around 1913. The photograph is an image of a dirt field and a wooden stadium with about twelve rows and 1,500 spectators. A feeble gate separates the crowd and the players, to the extent that the players could touch, talk to, and otherwise communicate easily with fans. The fans were dressed formally and engrossed in the match. Women's heels stick out in the front row as they leisurely cross their legs at the ankles. And while the majority of the crowd comprises men, women are interspersed, and appear in the back with small children as well. The stands are surprisingly integrated, demonstrating plenty of fans of color, including a black woman in a white dress in the back row, who nervously watches the game.

There is evidence from elsewhere in Latin America that women football fans not only attended matches but also frequently played matches as fan groups. In December 1933, for example, female supporters of the two most powerful Uruguayan men's football clubs, Nacional and Peñarol, played a match at Estadio Centenario, a stadium whose continental importance would be hard to overstate. The stadium was built for the finals of the first men's World Cup in 1930 and represented the global prominence of South American football. The women's game on December 20, played over the opposition of public health experts, was well attended. Thousands of people, both men and women, witnessed the match.[57] For months prior to the match, the two women's teams practiced in preparation, highlighting two important points: women played the sport, and sufficient numbers of women were fans as well. That there is no other available information on the match highlights a third: the almost complete lack of press coverage of women's team sports in Uruguay.[58]

EFFERVESCENCE IN WOMEN'S FOOTBALL

At the same time that women's football gained popularity in circuses, it began to appear in less spectacular locales. In 1921, the first "official" women's match, in the sense that it was recorded in a mainstream newspaper, was played between squads from Cantareira and Tremembé, which were sequential train stops on the northeastern peripheries of São Paulo. The match, played on the grounds of Tremembé FC, reportedly occurred at 3:00 p.m.[59] While information about the match appeared prior to the game in newspapers, we have been unable to find a report of the match itself. It is difficult to ascertain with any certainty how many spectators attended and what their reactions might have been. One can speculate, based on the way that *A Gazeta* predicted it would be a "very interesting" match, that there was an element of novelty and spectacle involved. So too in September 1923, *Revista da Semana* featured a page of photographs and commentary on SC Feminino Vasco da Gama, the women's team of Club de Regatas Vasco da Gama, one of Rio's oldest teams. That year, the Vasco da Gama men's team won the Carioca league, fielding the first mixed-race team in a major Brazilian league. That a club of this level would include women's football suggests that the sport was more widespread. According to the magazine piece— which included the names of the sportswomen—the women's team practiced on the same field as the men.[60]

Women's football thrived in social and club life in 1930s Brazil. Developments in neighboring countries, such as the match in Uruguay mentioned before, encouraged its acceptance. During a trip abroad, one writer came across a women's sports club in Montevideo, and he felt inspired to urge Brazilian women to foray into sports, particularly football.[61] In typical fashion, however, the writer seemed entirely ignorant of women's efforts to start such clubs in his own city, or in the rival city of Rio de Janeiro, more than ten years earlier. The case of the club in Montevideo, which evidently caught the journalist's attention, is a fascinating one. Not only did the female athletes organize a football tournament, but they also founded a women's section of the club Dublin oriented toward competing in basketball, volleyball, track and field, and tennis. The football tournament they organized in 1935 was held in Estadio Parque Central.[62] The response of journalists to these high-profile women's football matches exposed the power of a male normative sports culture even as they claimed to support women's football. The writer assumed that his readers would find women's efforts to play football comical. He urged them instead to consider these women as brave pioneers. So, on the one hand the author expressed admiration for women's football, while on the other he conveyed the message that people would laugh at it. At the same time, he showed his complete ignorance that women's football was already a regular activity in Brazil. Still, that Brazilians should look to Uruguay for football guidance in the 1930s should not be surprising given Uruguay's gold medals in the 1924 and 1928 Olympics and its victory in the 1930 men's World Cup. Dublin Sports Club was undoubtedly at the vanguard of women's sports on the continent, in procuring Parque Central, fielding a women's football team, and creating a sports club for women.

As Brazilian women's football became more visible, newspaper coverage grew. *Jornal dos Sports* began to have semiregular articles about women's football in 1931, though the articles were hardly flattering. In one of the first pieces about the women's sport, the anonymous author noted that the days when "our female compatriots had no interest in sports" were gone. With slight alarm the author commented that most sporting clubs were developing women's sections in "volleyball, tennis, [and] fencing," but that once "football grabbed the attention of the women of Rio," they began playing with relish.[63] According to the article, the teams Lina Alves and Manoel Pereira, the latter affiliated with Brasil Suburbano FC, were to play a match later in the week. Both teams had already given impressive displays of their skill. Still, the author focused on something other than football as the draw for the match: men, "barbados," flocked to the field "to see what the lovely players could do for them." The interpretation of women's football as a sexualized spectacle laid the groundwork for later persecution of the sport.[64] Women playing football was seen as inherently immoral, as it—among other things—required that they show off their bodies without the proper modesty. Policing women's femininity was connected to ensuring their proper sexual development. Studies of sexuality had become medicalized in the 1920s and 1930s, although women's homosexuality was either ignored or almost always subsumed by literature on sodomy and male homosexuality. The medical community, physical education experts, and journalists overlapped in their beliefs that proper femininity rested on the opposite side of the spectrum from masculinity. Therefore, if men needed to hone their aggression, ideal women exhibited subservience, sacrifice, and humility. The self-control so often touted as a characteristic of good athletes meant controlling the excess of these behaviors or the expression of the other gender's supposed innate traits. These were prescriptive rather than descriptive recipes, but influential in making policy nonetheless.

The trend away from conservative attire and toward women's greater visibility in the public sphere began in the early twentieth century, culminating in the 1920s with the arrival of the "modern girl." Attacks on the fashionable flapper raged throughout the Americas, including Brazil, where criticism of modern mores extended into the 1930s and 1940s—the precise moment that women's football grew in popularity. Conservative forces pushed back on efforts for reproductive rights and sought to limit suffrage; however, changes in fashion toward looser and more comfortable clothing for women seemed impossible to stop. Media and politicians refused to recognize that these trends had been around for quite some time. A *Sport Ilustrado* article in 1938 explained that the "club woman" was a fashionable type. A woman of privilege, she passed her days in leisure at the sports club, brightening club fields and grounds with her elegance and beauty. For activity, she played tennis, swam, or practiced gymnastics.[65] The language in the article is nearly identical to that published in the same magazine seventeen years earlier: the ideal sportswoman remained a *new* icon. The magazine reinforced the elite and white nature of the sportswoman, with photographs of women captaining yachts and playing tennis in luxurious clubs. Despite the anxieties expressed about the proper clothing for women, manufacturers and sports goods stores saw an opportunity to sell women sateen basketball outfits and other versions of short pants made of lighter fabric and allowing for freer movement of their legs.[66]

By the latter 1930s, prominent magazines, such as *Sport Ilustrado*, developed editorial lines that advocated for the mass adoption of women's sports.[67] The magazine hoped to convince the skeptical public of the need for women's physical education and of Brazil's potential as a continental leader in this area. Yet even the most passionate advocates typically premised their arguments by "conceding" that women had neither the strength nor the energy of men. These declarations appeared consistently as facts that needed no evidence to support them. Based on these spurious facts, the editors suggested women's prohibition from violent or stressful sports, such as football. Ranking sports appropriate to women, the magazine gave top billing to swimming and tennis. Journalists pointed to the swimmers Piedade Coutinho and Maria Lenk as evidence that swimming was the premier sport of Brazilian women. Water, according to the public health experts, provided a female environment, one that cushioned blows, protected fertility, and connected women to the natural world. An issue of *Correio Sportivo* credited the popularity of tennis with its opportunities for women, and mentioned that it was invented for women, specifically the bored wives of colonial officials in India.[68] The colonial and elite history of tennis aside, women's competitions increased in intensity. In 1930 Rio hosted an international tennis tournament for women that included the Spanish champion and feminist Lili Álvarez. Álvarez shocked audiences in Europe and the Americas by wearing a "divided" tennis skirt, akin to short pants. Throughout the 1930s, leagues in Rio and São Paulo thrived and sent women players around the country. The next group of acceptable, but not ideal, sports included track and field, basketball, and volleyball. Not content merely to advocate for women's sports, the sportswriters from *Sport Ilustrado* credited themselves with the development of women's sports. Despite the hyperbole of the editors at *Sport Ilustrado*, there were instances where women's inclusion in the sports pages disrupted popular images of women's roles. For example, the illustrations that accompanied the article, by Alberto Lima, were at odds with the patronizing tone of the journalists.[69] Lima depicted three different women, a javelin thrower, a high jumper, and a tennis player. None of the athletes were objectified, sexualized, or parodied.[70] Instead, they were treated as serious athletes, deep in the concentration of competition.

In the late 1930s, volleyball and basketball were growing in international popularity among women. These sports were created in Massachusetts at the turn of the twentieth century and championed by the Young Men's Christian Association (YMCA) and Young Women's Christian Association (YWCA). From the beginning, both organizations conceived of volleyball and basketball as appropriate for women. Brazilian women seemed particularly taken with volleyball. Physical education instructors promoted the sport among female students in schools like Escola Wenceslau Braz and Colégio Sylvio Leite in Rio, and soon sports clubs began to organize events for women.[71] The club Icarahy de Regatas organized important tournaments among clubs, including Praia das Flexas, Canto do Rio, and Celeste, among others.[72] All teams came from Nitheroy (now Niterói), an affluent suburb of Rio. Photographs of the Icarahy club team underscore the nexus of class, race, and women's sports: all participants were very young white women. Even if volleyball was less threatening than sports like football, sportswomen represented a sharp departure from the dominant image of women splashed on movie posters and newspapers of the static debutante. Articles contrasted the "calm" required to play volleyball with the physical nature of football. Assuming its readers were men, *Sport Ilustrado* explained that men's psychology responded better to games with physical confrontation.[73] It seems nonsensical to posit that volleyball required calm and gentle coordination, and was therefore appropriate to women, yet this logic ruled the day.[74] In the coverage of women's sports, the absence of football is conspicuous, especially given its growth in popularity.

Women's football flourished in Brazil in the decade before its legal prohibition in 1941, as had been the case in England prior to the ban on women's football by its national association in 1921. Because of the intense activity of a new generation of sportswomen in the 1930s, a Rio newspaper called women's football "the order of the day" in 1940. Women's teams in the nation's capital organized a greater number of tournaments, as well as played preliminaries to men's matches and at cultural festivals. It appears that many women's clubs in Rio had some affiliation with larger and more established sports clubs. The first women's football match reported on by *Jornal dos Sports* took place on May 18, 1931, in Piedade on the fields of Brasil FC. The match saw the team Madame Lessa Alves defeat Madame Macedo 1–0. Given the intentional emphasis on "Madame" these teams were perhaps named after well-known Carioca women. Reporters were skeptical of the women's game. The women played enthusiastically and occasionally excited the crowd. However, the game quickly "deteriorated toward brutality," as the players Odette and Clelia began fighting after a hard foul.[75] Later that year the team Manoel Pereira, affiliated with the men's club Brasil Suburbano, traveled to Ypiranga FC to play in a night festival.[76] The link between the women's team and the men's club highlights the support that women's football received from some established quarters during the 1930s. Another early match occurred at the Oriente Atlético Clube of Santa Cruz, which was on the west side of Rio. During a sporting festival on club grounds in September of 1931, one of the three football matches featured women of Madame Lessa Alves and Manoel Pereira.[77] The Oriente men's team competed in the same league as Brasil Suburbano, Liga Metropolitana de Desportos Terrestres (Metropolitan League of Field Sports). These types of relationships indicate that women's teams emerged from connections between women who were already members of clubs, who gained access to fields, and who likely met one another at routine club functions.

Women's football expanded throughout the 1930s, and appeared to be on solid ground by 1940. Women's teams most actively thrived in Minas Gerais, especially Belo Horizonte, and in Rio de Janeiro.

Sports festivals in both cities included women's football with greater frequency.[78] Further supporting that women's clubs emerged from the fabric of larger sports clubs, the 1940 festival in Rio featured a woman's team from Cruzeiro FC.[79] The newspaper coverage of the match also noted the first names of the Cruzeiro team members, which remained a common practice for *Jornal dos Sports* in 1940. Thus, coverage of women's matches in the paper provided a rare moment of notoriety for players. *Jornal dos Sports* quickly became a major source of encouragement and information on women's football. Its reporters followed the clubs around Rio fairly closely— for example, the Brasileiro sports club and Frei Miguel FC. The teams frequently played on the fields of the Casino de Realengo, in Realengo—an established working-class neighborhood on the periphery of the city.[80] For its ninth anniversary celebration, *Jornal dos Sports* held a series of celebratory events on March 13, 1940, in conjunction with the cigarette manufacturer Fábrica Sudan. A central part of the celebration was a women's football match, where teams competed for the Mario Rodriques Filho Cup at the fields of SC Tavares, using lights for the first time.[81] A group of students founded SC Tavares in 1931 in northern Rio and for a time had a stable field. The newspaper either truly supported women's football or saw it as a way to draw a large crowd to watch a spectacle, or both. The former seems possible, as two other articles in the same issue note the skill with which women played. One item reported on the "sensational match" between the "disciplined teams" of Casino de Realengo and SC Brasileiro.[82] The other, accompanying a picture of Brasileiro, suggested that the teams could show "the strong sex how to play football with technique and discipline."[83] The directors of SC Tavares also organized a match under the lights between Eva FC and Brasileiro.[84] The teams played once again the following month in a preliminary to the match between SC Anchieta and SC Royal.[85] Unfortunately, the press only listed the first names of players, and information about these women has proven elusive.

By the end of 1940, *Jornal dos Sports* was not only reporting on women's matches, but also actively promoting the sport. It published notices that invited futboleras to its offices for meetings to discuss important matters with local teams.[86] In much the same way that a symbiotic relationship, with overlapping interests, developed between the media and men's football, *Jornal dos Sports* actively sought to help women's football, not only by reporting on it with increasing frequency but also by sponsoring tournaments and arranging meetings of the women's football community. The sport was not limited to preliminaries, and by all indications women players capitalized on the momentum gathered from their festival appearances and newspaper support. According to a magazine report, "four of the big [women's football] clubs in the city," Brasileiro, Eva, Casino de Realengo, and Valqueiro, gathered to play on the fields of Bomsucesso to celebrate the May 1 holiday. The fields of Bomsucesso were located in the northern industrial neighborhood of the same name in Rio. The sport, according to the article, "always raised great interest, and was becoming more interesting than men's games" because of the dedication of the players.[87] The notion of women's teams competing for the attention of fans would have rattled the metropolitan league. At that point, many of the women's matches lasted only thirty minutes, with fifteen-minute halves. The final was typically a sixty-minute affair.[88]

Throughout 1940 the presence of women's football increased exponentially. On May 19, 1940, Del Castillo FC hosted its first women's football match, which pitted Valqueiro FC against AC Independente for the unofficial title of champions of the suburban zone. Both teams were considered to be strong, with Independente having beaten the powerful SC Brasileiro in a memorable match and Valqueiro "imposing itself" on other teams.[89] Such a synopsis demonstrates a familiarity with the teams' records. That August, SC Brasileiro played another night match against the women's team of SC Unidos, on the grounds of SC Abolição.[90] Brasileiro dominated that crucial season, at least in Rio de Janeiro. In September, the team defeated Mavillis FC by a score of 5–0, even after lending Mavillis three of its best players. As with many matches, this served as a preliminary to a match between professional teams—Nitchroyense and SC Bemfica.[91] Women's clubs did emerge from major clubs, but like men's football, most players represented small or ephemeral organizations. Mavillis FC and SC Bemfica are the only two that belonged to the men's league, and both were amateur. After a full day of football, with a schedule of five men's matches starting at 10:30 a.m., a women's match between Verissimo Machado FC and Independente was to kick off at 5:00 p.m.[92] Coverage in Rio was not entirely positive, however. One Carioca sportswriter lamented that women athletes invited criticism because of how badly they played. His concern pretended to protect women from a scornful public while actually attacking their performance.[93] The author called for the authorities to stop women's football for their own good. This echoed the language of reformers seeking to curtail women's partici- pation in politics and the workforce, while claiming to have women's interests at heart.

While Rio was an epicenter of women's football, it was not the only site of activity. The women in Rio may have acted as mission- aries for the women's sport in other states. A brief but provocative announcement appeared in a local paper in 1940 that announced the formation of a women's football club in Belo Horizonte, called Mineiras FC.[94] Club football offered women the opportunity to travel and gain public accolades for their athleticism. Neither of these should be underestimated. For example, in April 1940 Flamengo— one of Rio's most important clubs—traveled to São Paulo FC to play at the inaugural festivities at the municipal stadium Estádio Pacaembu. The stadium could hold over thirty-seven thousand spec- tators, and Getúlio Vargas and other high-ranking officials frequently made appearances there. One wonders if Vargas watched one of the women's matches, given his draconian actions against the sport less than a year later. Two women's teams, Casino de Realengo and SC Brasileiro, took the 420 kilometer trip to São Paulo with Flamengo.[95] According to *Jornal dos Sports*, this would be the first opportunity for residents of São Paulo to see a women's football match, which they were waiting for with "much curiosity."[96] Although women played football matches throughout São Paulo and the suburbs, ap- parently women's football there had not organized to the degree of that it had been in Rio. The trip also highlights the importance of media's role in the active promotion and proselytizing for women's football. Travel was arranged ("a difficult task when it comes to women's teams") by Carlos Gonçalves, a representative of the São Paulo league, and sponsored by *Jornal dos Sports*, which called a meeting of the clubs' directors to finalize plans.[97] The women footballers joined women tennis players, swimmers, and track-and-field stars at the inaugural festivities of the stadium. The most celebrated athletes were Brazil's two Olympic swimmers, Maria Lenk and Cecilia Heilborn.[98] The prominence of futboleras, demonstrated by their inclusion in these festivals, has been erased in popular memory.

According to journalists, the match between women's football teams at the stadium's inauguration was unprecedented for São Paulo. Carioca women's teams had gained enough popularity to negotiate their stipends. Newspapers in Rio criticized futboleras for demanding too much spending money.[99] The writer Salathiel Campos defended the women, noting that most amateurs required some subsidies to play the sport.[100] Campos explained as well that as a novelty act, the women drew a large crowd and so deserved a portion of the gate receipts. This reveals the extent to which football organizers and writers conformed to market logic since the advent of professionalism in men's football in the early 1930s. Campos's characterization of the women, however, differs drastically from the way in which the women's teams and their trainers presented the delegation. Upon their arrival, the Rio delegation of women's football, represented by SC Brasileiro and Casino de Realengo, gave an informal press conference at the train station.[101] Oscar Leal, the trainer of SC Brasileiro, spoke at length regarding technical differences between the two teams. He emphasized that the Carioca teams would not only interest spectators as a novelty, but would impress them with their technical skills.

In fact, women's teams traveled frequently, both in search of opponents and to play exhibition matches in places where women's football was less common. AC Independente's match against Valqueiro FC took them seventy-five kilometers by train from the northern Rio suburb of Bento Ribeiro to the town of Magé.[102] In the description of their trip, all eleven women's names and those of the reserve players were listed in the newspaper. This was a rare honor for even a national female athlete.[103] That year a women's football league, of at least ten teams, formed in Rio.[104] Certain players began to receive attention, including one woman identified as "Miss Targina" whose brothers played for América and Vasco da Gama. Scores between teams were increasingly less lopsided, which signaled regular play.[105]

Beyond Rio and São Paulo, a vibrant women's football scene emerged in Minas Gerais, although it is not entirely clear why the region tended to be a hotbed of the sport. Two Carioca clubs, Primavera FC and SC Oposição, traveled to Juiz de Fora, in Minas Gerais, to play an exhibition match at Tupy FC. *Jornal dos Sports* claimed that residents looked forward to the match with curiosity. The clubs were dubbed the "most prominent women's teams in the capital," with players who possessed both great skill and passion. Still, coverage appears contradictory, with one article on the match using the language of spectacle and sensationalism, remarking that town residents would "witness a rich spectacle of novelties."[106] The delegation for the match was impressive, including forty-five people. Along with the players and coaches, three journalists (Julio Gammarro, Octacilio Rezende, and Edyr Guimarães), a secretary, an assistant, and a nurse made the trip.[107] The goal of the organizer, Ernesto Costa, was to support women's football in whatever way possible and to introduce Mineiros to the sport.[108] Likely, Ernesto Costa was the trainer who went on to work with CR Vasco da Gama in the fabled period of the 1940s. One month later, another delegation of women's football players traveled to Petrópolis, about seventy kilometers north of Rio de Janeiro. The clubs Independente and Brasil Novo brought players who had "perfect control of the leather ball." Again, Ernesto Costa organized the events, which the media dubbed the first women's match in Petrópolis.[109]

At the same moment that women's football began to gain momentum, the men's game underwent intense scrutiny by pundits, politicians, and club leaders. Next to the brief notices of women's activities appear lengthy editorials on the corruption of men's football, supposedly ruined by too many foreigners and too much violence and immorality, as a result of professionalization.[110] The integration and success of working-class players brought a wave of Afro-Brazilian (both black and mixed-race) talent.[111] The association of the game with men of color fundamentally changed its social significance, challenging racial hierarchies and increasing its potential as a national symbol, but also increasing the transgression of women on the pitch. It is telling that promoting mixed-gender events was absolutely outside of the realm of possibility for these journalists, as it was with all sports with the exception of tennis. While mixed-gender contests were not a tradition in any part of Latin America, it is worth pausing to consider why gender integration was unthinkable. In politics or the household, women's supposed natural selflessness, at least some argued, would be helpful in the face of corruption. In football governance, it was not seriously considered. This both reflected the lack of appreciation for women's talents but also highlighted how important football had become in developing Brazilian masculinity. It also indicates that the social capital, leisure, and pleasure that players took away from football were privileged commodities that men were entitled to. Although journalists and club leaders did not go so far as to suggest women could play with men, they occasionally mentioned the possibility that women's amateurism could provide a model for men, whose game had been corrupted by money.[112]

Professionalism opened sports clubs to more black Brazilians in the late 1930s, and while by and large this meant more men of color joined, it also opened the doors to a select number of women players from beyond the sphere of the white elite.[113] Sports directors and journalists were influenced by the broader discussions of race sparked by intellectuals, especially Gilberto Freyre, that recast racial mixing of African, European, and indigenous people in a positive light. Indeed, the Vargas regime began to implement policies and adopt rhetoric that incorporated Freyre's idea of Brazil as a "racial democracy." Having suspended elections and political parties, Vargas positioned himself as the paternalist protector of the poor, and consequently of black and mixed-race Brazilians. The owner of *Jornal dos Sports*, Mário Filho, published the highly influential O *negro no futebol brasileiro* in 1947. In it, he celebrated pioneering black Brazilian players, such as Leônidas da Silva. This was not a coincidence; Filho and Freyre shared the same social circle and exchanged manuscripts.[114] Freyre wrote the preface to the first edition of Filho's book. Photographs of the Rio women's league demonstrate a racial diversity rarely found in tennis or swimming. Unfortunately, the brief notices on women players rarely provided details on their background.

The creation of the Rio women's football league in 1940 led one observer to declare that Brazil was at the vanguard of women's sports on the continent.[115] The sport began to seep into other parts of Brazilian cultural life. In one political cartoon, the potential growth of women's football was put in context of the war raging in Europe.[116] The woman in the cartoon is asked why she does not put together a team to play international matches, to which she responds that if the war continues as it was in 1940, "there would only be one team on the other side of the Atlantic."[117] While the cartoon was ostensibly about the war, it nevertheless highlighted the development of women's football: that a man would ask his female companion about an international squad suggests that the sport was entering the mainstream. According to journalists, in Rio there was strong enthusiasm for women's football; one editorial estimated that there were 1,001 women's games played each day.[118]

There is ample evidence that women began to play football in their workplaces and on union teams as well as in sports clubs. As mentioned earlier, the first recorded women's game took place under the auspices of the Tremembé Tramway Company in 1921. Companies, unions, and workplace friends developed teams at and around the job. For example, women players organized games during the company celebrations of the Cidade Light, a complex that included metal foundries and maintenance shops. The Cidade Light employed over two thousand workers.[119] Its exercise "fun day" featured boxing matches between amateurs and professionals, as well as women's and men's football tournaments.[120] Companies often sponsored athletic festivals and sports teams as a way to provide healthy leisure activities to their workers. These events could function as a form of capitalist paternalism, with management controlling workers' free time and building their loyalty to the company. In this regard, the goals of capitalists and the hygienic goals of the republic intertwined, each reinforcing the other. The inclusion of football in workplace festivals shows how deeply—and quickly—women's football integrated into Brazilian social life. The diffusion of women's football suggests that though it faced scorn, far from encountering universal ridicule, women's football briefly became a much more regular part of Brazilian life than has been thought.

The rapid expansion of women's football in the 1940 season concerned some politicians and journalists. However, it was not just how women's football was expanding that concerned them, but to *whom* it was expanding, namely to working-class women. At the very same moment, union and high school sports clubs promoted their women's volleyball and basketball teams. These sports did not occupy the central place in the construction of proper masculinity and national identity; therefore, they posed less of a challenge than football. By the end of May, the suburban football federation had three important standout women's teams—Casino de Realengo, Del Castillo, and Manufactura "Porcellana." Expectations were that the suburban league would hold a women's championship shortly, as the team "with the black stripes [Manufactura Porcellana]" raised its skill level.[121] Along with the exhibition match played in São Paulo as a preliminary to the Flamengo versus São Paulo match, the clubs Casino de Realengo and Brasileiro traveled to Belo Horizonte in June 1940. There, they played in the stadium of Club América, garnering twelve thousand reis in gate receipts.[122] In July 1940, SC Oposição faced off against Primavera FC in a night match at the SC Oposição grounds for the Santa Cruz cup. According to *Jornal dos Sports*, the second of three matches that night offered the chance for fans of the players Nicea, Sali, Morena, and Dirza to see the best examples of women's football.[123] Fans of Oposição, for their part, could see their stars, identified as Filinha, Neuza, and Tina, in action.

Tickets for the event were 2$000 for men and 1$000 for women. Women's football no longer appeared as a novelty. Rather, women's matches increasingly became marquee events.

As football, basketball, and volleyball gained popularity and offered women the opportunity to travel, women's participation in sports further pushed gender boundaries. If the notion of women traveling within the country broke with traditional confinements of gender, one should not be surprised that women traveling abroad caused significant controversy.[124] In December 1940, the police, and subsequently the second district court, prohibited women players of Primavera FC from traveling to Buenos Aires and Montevideo. Journalists assured readers who might have thought this unfair that the match was ridiculous and merely designed to make fun of women athletes. The writers thought the match would give the Argentine press fodder to mock Brazilian sports. Sportswriters urged the police to inspect all women's delegations going abroad in order to verify their true sporting intention. Writers suggested that Primavera FC belonged to one of Rio's "dens of perdition," or brothels.[125] Primavera's planned travel turned into a prolonged saga that revealed the surveillance of women athletes and the degree to which authorities suspected them of prostitution. In a rare instance of a signed newspaper article on women's football, the writer Ricardo Pinto criticized the proposed trip of the futboleras.[126] Pinto admitted that the team were the well-known champions of women's football. However, he doubted the players' legitimacy. According to Pinto, Rio police accused the team of activities unrelated to sports, including traveling with underage players. Police had, supposedly, received complaints early in 1940 that women football players gave "dances" in the red-light district of Rio. Yet Pinto's description left room for interpretation; was he insinuating the players were prostitutes, strippers, or generally involved in illicit activities? Suspicions of women players relied on the inaccurate assumption that Brazilian women's football was "unheard of." Pinto expressed anxiety over the racial identity of Brazilian players.[127] He assumed the Brazilian "morenas" would be ridiculed in Argentina and Uruguay. These types of anxieties reveal the worries about not only the players but the potential audience and the organizers of women's football. Articles portrayed organizers as sharks and charlatans. Some sportswriters could not imagine spectators who went to see the sport for its sake, but only as men hoping to ridicule or sexualize women players.

BACKLASH

The development of early feminist organizations, the passage of women's suffrage rights in 1932, and their enshrinement in Vargas's Constitution of 1934 exacerbated fears among socially conservative reformers who saw immorality increasing in lockstep with women's progress.[128] While Vargas positioned himself as a champion of these rights, he also sought approval from sectors quite opposed to them. Many feared that factory and office work—women's increasing participation in the public sphere—threatened women's "natural" virtue.[129] The number of women in the workforce increased rapidly. One estimate suggests that women accounted for more than half of the cotton spinners in São Paulo.[130] By the 1930s and 1940s, the number of women working in factories diminished, but the number of women—both proportionally and in total—working outside the home increased. Still, women only gained the right to work outside the home without their husband's consent in 1943.[131] The penal code of 1940 addressed concerns over women's increasing activities outside the home by redefining acceptable behaviors and policing women's behavior. One major concern was the impact that "modern women" would have on Brazil's morality, which revolved in large part around female chastity. As women's football was linked to women's modernity, solidarity, and freedom of movement, it was implicated as part of these threats. According to the historian Sueann Caulfield, thinkers of the 1920s and 1930s thought that the "sensual stimuli" of modern society threatened Brazil's social order.[132] For critics, the exhibition of female bodies on the football pitch qualified precisely as a form of these new sensual stimuli, which threatened to erode the moral fabric of society.

In the 1930s and 1940s, the Brazilian state became more involved in the administration and institutionalization of daily life through the heavy-handed policies of the Estado Novo.[133] This tendency shaped the expansion of physical education activities. Laws had been on the books regarding physical education since the late nineteenth century, with the educational reform of Rui Barbosa mandating girls' inclusion in 1882, but few reforms had been enforced or put into practice.[134] In the 1930s, however, the Brazilian government began to take physical education more seriously. Exercise became obligatory in secondary schools, for both boys and girls. In addition, the Ministry of Health created a section for physical education.[135] The goal of these new initiatives was "to train the new urban and industrial nation" with "sophistication and specialization."[136] A part of this effort, too, was the publication of the professional journal *Revista Brasileira de Educação Física* (Brazilian Journal of Physical Education). Being that it was concerned with the creation of the new Brazil, it should come as no surprise that the magazine focused on women's physical training. It was, after all, "strong mothers who created a strong nation."[137] One way that women could highlight their health was through beauty, and physical education experts described beauty as an outward sign of eugenic health and feminine strength.[138] Since physical health was so important for healthy mothers, women were expected, at least by state authorities, to be willing to submit to their patriotic duty to have their physical activity regulated in order to "protect the characteristics of their femininity, [and] preserve their fertility."[139] Too many muscles, too much strength, could impede women's path toward beauty and would "call into doubt . . . her sex and sexuality."[140] As in neighboring Argentina and Chile, heterosexuality was commonly believed to rely upon the most extreme expression of gender identification. Treatises written by psychologists and religious leaders usually focused on male homosexuality and assumed women's sexual development followed a similar path. The more one embodied the stereotypical attributes of gender, the more likely one escaped the "perversion" of homosexuality.

The increased scrutiny of women's sexuality, morality, and fertility led to more intense interest in their leisure activities. And those who saw women's football as detrimental to the well-being of the state found ready allies in the medical community to support their position. In 1940, one of the prominent experts who opposed women's football was Dr. Leite de Castro.[141] Castro wore many hats. Not only was he the chief doctor of the football league of Rio de Janeiro and of the clinic Beneficencia Portuguesa, but he also worked as a doctor in the civil police and was considered an expert on physical education, authoring over one hundred articles on the topic. He advocated reducing what he called the Brazilian obsession with football in favor of a diverse course of physical education that focused less on competition and more on the development of the individual body. In 1940, as the question of the effects of women's football became an important topic, numbers of men began to protest the sport, an act that some sportswriters characterized as "brave." When asked about women's football, Castro emphasized that he did not consider football to be an ideal sport when exclusively practiced by anyone, man or woman. Along with many of his peers, Castro emphasized the vital role of medical supervision of athletes.[142] This supervision ranged from strict nutritional regimens to sleep recommendations. While he suspected harm from playing too much football generally, he opposed the sport for women on public health grounds.

While the intense involvement of sports medicine in football has been cited as crucial to the rise of the Brazilian men's team to world prominence, the medical community hurt chances of broad-based support for women's football in the 1940s.[143] In particular, doctors—Castro among them—worried that football would cause harm to women's genital area, subsequently harming their fertility. Moreover, Castro and others claimed that football could alter women's endocrine balance and potentially cause uterine cancer. Beyond the pseudoscience, Castro showed contempt for female athletes, stating that futboleras could "be applauded as a grotesque display or theatre at the whim of popular curiosity."[144] He declared that men benefitted from struggle, but that violent sports diverted women from their biological destiny. What women gained as athletes, in other words, they lost as women. Their ovaries and uteri were simply too endangered by football. For health and beauty, he suggested, women could jog slowly or swim. Based on Castro's advice, one sportswriter begged women to flee football fields in favor of the swimming pool for the happiness of the nation, as well as for their own health and beauty.[145] Moreover, Castro's warnings disseminated from Rio to São Paulo, and beyond, causing distress among leaders in women's football.[146] His statements circulated in the midst of organizing the inaugural events at Estádio Pacaembu, as women football players prepared to play their biggest match.

PROHIBITION!

Dr. Leite de Castro's concerns found support beyond the medical community. On April 25, 1940, a concerned citizen named José Fuzeira wrote an open letter to the Brazilian minister of education criticizing women's football. Minister Campanema passed the letter on to President Getúlio Vargas.[147] In it, Fuzeira decried a "calamity" threatening the nation: girls and young women playing football. The danger in women playing football, according to Fuzeira, stemmed from the inherent violence in the game, which could "seriously damage the physiological equilibrium" of women's "organ functions." Perhaps influenced by Castro he suggested that football endangered girls' and women's reproductive capabilities. The game also had negative psychological effects, according to the letter. Players risked depression, which could lead to "rude and extravagant exhibitionism." Fuzeira worried that unless the government intervened to stop women's football, it could be ruinous to the country. If the game continued to expand from its base in the middle-class suburbs of Rio, São Paulo, and Belo Horizonte, he predicted that within the year over two hundred teams would form, destroying future mothers by jeopardizing their desire for and capacity to bear children.[148]

Contradictory reports appeared in the press regarding the opposition to women's football. According to the Rio de Janeiro newspaper *A Batalha*, for example, the impetus to stop the growth of women's football came from women themselves. The editorial argued that women showed their disdain for the game when they took up sports such as swimming, basketball, and golf. The newspaper outlined the moral failings of women football players and blamed them for the negative perception of the sport. The article claimed that the

Primavera FC team director, Carlota Alves Resende, was under investigation for walking young women, purportedly team members, to dance halls. The police considered prosecuting Resende for pimping, or *lenocínio*.[149] Some journalists applauded the announcement that the government was considering prohibiting women's football. In a small article, one Carioca sportswriter described the proposed ban as "magnificent" because the sport was a true danger, especially in its encouragement of lesbian relationships among players.[150] Other writers cast women's football as a public health threat, even linking the upsurge in the sport to an outbreak of whooping cough.[151] Regardless of the level of anxiety about women's football, the sport received surprisingly little press, considering its dynamism. Perhaps sports editors felt that the best way to stem the growth of women's football was to ignore it: the article implying lesbianism was little more than an announcement, taking as much space as a wire item on a polo match between Argentina and Chile. News of Brazilian women's football and the social conflict it sparked reached journalists abroad, even as far as Sweden. The reporters claimed that Brazilian women's football was well known and drew huge crowds. According to the country's largest sports newspaper, *Idrottsbladet*, the women were good-looking but violent, and the head of the association was under investigation for public disorder.[152]

The early 1940s brought significant changes to the relationship of government and sports, with major implications for women. The forces arrayed against women's football were tied closely to the state and thus possessed power, both in terms of access to the media and in terms of policy decisions. While women played with more vigor and had more support by 1940, so too they faced more criticism. In April 1941, Getúlio Vargas created the Conselho Nacional de Desportos (National Sports Council, or CND) with Decree Law 3199. According to the law, the CND fell under the auspices of the Ministry of Education and Health, directed at the time by Gustavo Capanema. The first secretary of the CND was João Barbosa Leite, director of the Division of Physical Education at the Ministry of Education and Health, which further underscored the links between the state and sporting practices. Vargas placed regulatory powers of sports in the hands of the council, and one of its roles was to determine which sports were "incompatible" with women's nature and to establish rules regarding their legality.[153] In the CND's first session, Capanema charged a military officer, Newton Cavalcanti, with creating the plan for regulating women's sports.[154] Cavalcanti identified with *integralismo*, a conservative doctrine that took moral direction from Catholicism. He had worked in the Ministry of War and had been sent by Vargas to extend the government's influence in Mato Grosso, Rio de Janeiro, and Minas Gerais. It is likely that Vargas sought to appease some of the *integralistas* who had remained loyal to him through measures such as giving them power over the CND. By August, Cavalcanti distributed a draft of the regulations for women's sports (and amateur sports) to his fellow CND members.[155] According to the new provisions, women were strictly forbidden from playing a variety of team sports, including "football, rugby, polo, and water polo, because they are violent sports and not adaptable to the female body." The law also prohibited women from participating in certain individual sports, including boxing, decathlon, and pentathlon.[156] The recommendations were unanimously approved by the CND and decreed by presidential order with immediate effect.[157] The decree also placed power with the president to abolish, maintain, or otherwise decide governance of sports confederations. Given the club directors' reticence to accept government interference, except in the case of financial support, Vargas's intrusion into the sports club world likely reflected his desire to control popular culture sectors, as well as to appease constituencies within the military and the Ministry of Education at once.

Jornal dos Sports published a part of the new regulations the following day, under the headline "A mulher não pode jogar o football nem o box!" (Women cannot play football nor box!).[158] The paper described Cavalcanti as an "illustrious soldier" in a seemingly derisive way. It pointed out that the decision came after very little deliberation and supposedly after the CND had reviewed studies on women's sports, though these were never named.[159] Track-and-field events (two-hundred-meter dash, four-by-one-hundred-meter relay, hurdles [with the hurdle height lowered and the length of the race shortened], long jump and high jump, discus and javelin [using lighter weights]), fencing, rowing, swimming, diving, field hockey, golf, skating, horseback riding, and pistol shooting were acceptable for women.[160] However, many of these sports came with restrictions. Along with the limits on the distance of footraces or the reduced weight of the discus, Cavalcanti and the CND circumscribed other activities. For example, women were banned from rowing regattas. Rather, rowing was to be used to "correct certain bodily deficiencies."[161] Team sports deemed acceptable for women included tennis, badminton, volleyball, and basketball (with court size and length of game diminished).[162] The CND's clarification might have been the result of efforts by some in Brazil to limit women's opportunity to swim as well. Some pools began to ban girls from swimming and from competition, even though the CND regulations clearly permitted women's swimming. This was likely harder to accomplish given the success of Brazil's female swimmers, such as Maria Lenk, who represented Brazil in the 1932 Olympics. At the same time that he worked to limit women's access to football, the CND and Cavalcanti supported an expansion of physical education practices among sports clubs in Brazil. The CND passed a resolution supporting the development of sports for both men and women, recommending to the member sports associations within professional sports that some money be spent on developing amateur and grassroots practices. Among the suggestions that the CND made was to develop sporting centers and a cadre of professional coaches, physical therapists, and others to train and control youth athletes.[163] The following year, in March 1942, Cavalcanti was promoted to General of Division.[164]

RESISTANCE

The idea of women's football as corruptive of national morals was far from universally supported. Instead of looking at the game as a site of perdition, many in the sporting world criticized those who attacked the virtue of the game. In an article celebrating the foundation of Primavera FC, *Jornal dos Sports* remarked that the team's inaugural event included the esteemed journalist Joaquím Inojosa.

Inojosa was the owner of the short-lived Rio newspaper *Meio-Dia*, and his presence, according to the article, was "an indication that women's football is gaining prestige in spite of the isolated elements seeking to distort it with insensitive propaganda."[165] Even more important, sportswomen defended themselves immediately. When José Fuzeira's 1940 letter criticizing women's football became public, women football players, and some in the press, lambasted his attitudes as outdated and sexist. For its part, *Jornal dos Sports* criticized Fuzeira in two ways: it published a rebuttal by the captain of one of Rio's most well-known teams, and it lampooned Fuzeira in its columns. On May 10, 1940, the newspaper ran an article entitled "Women's Football Players Defend Themselves." It reprinted, word for word with some commentary, a letter written by "Adyragram" in response to Fuzeira. The newspaper's prefatory remarks to the letter made it clear which side the publication was on. In describing Fuzeira, the paper noted that he was unknown in the sports community, thereby questioning his legitimacy and his expertise to comment on the topic.[166]

Jornal dos Sports presented Adyragram as a personal acquaintance of the writers, explaining that she stopped by their offices to provide a response to Fuzeira. In the weeks leading up to the controversy, the magazine had called meetings of the leaders of the women's clubs, while they were organizing tournaments, and created a *grêmio*, a loose social network of clubs. Adyragram saw the value in the social network that women's clubs were creating. She began her response by suggesting that Fuzeira come and see for himself if the players were worse off for playing football.[167] Adyragram not only questioned Fuzeira's knowledge on the topic, but broadly defended women's right to physical activity—football or otherwise. She agreed with Fuzeira that football should not be practiced by everyone, including those who couldn't participate in physical education. Throughout her article, Adyragram positioned herself and women's football as crucial to the construction of the nation: as physical education was a subject of national importance, and women's football was growing in popularity, it represented the healthy future of Brazil. She inverted Fuzeira's argument that women's football would destroy the moral center of the nation. Adyragram ended her piece sarcastically, saying Fuzeira "should concern himself with people playing ball games in the middle of the street . . . breaking windows."[168] Further, she questioned whether eventually Fuzeira would decide that women's swimming should be banned, since the "short clothes stuck to the competitors" might offend his ideal of future mothers.[169] Not only did Adyragram see Fuzeira's attack on women's football as arbitrary and threatening to the sport she loved, but she recognized that it could be part of a larger moralizing project based on efforts to enforce conservative gender norms. If women and their male supporters did not call Fuzeira out and stand up to him, women's ability to play any sport might someday be taken away. Little did she know that, as noted earlier, some clubs would indeed attempt to ban women's swimming less than a year later.

Writers for *Jornal dos Sports* depicted the ban as anachronistic and moralistic. Four days after the publication of Adyragram's letter, a sarcastic ode to Fuzeira appeared in "Off-Side," a regular commentary (often in poem form) in *Jornal dos Sports*. The poem mocked Fuzeira's rejection of women's football as a threat to women's decency as an antiquated view. The poem skewered him for believing the sport a novelty that would lead to "infertile ovaries," "sluts," and "sick women." The diatribe against Fuzeira described his campaign as a "holy and complete obsession," and, the author continued, "Fuzeira surely sees in his dreams the 11,000 virgins in an enormous stadium practicing bicycle kicks." While not explicit, the journalists placed Fuzeira's objections within a religious framework. The column then pointed out that women were doing all manner of tasks once perceived to be masculine. The piece referred to the British aviator Amy Johnson, the first woman to fly solo from England to Australia, and who would die transporting planes for the British Royal Air Force in World War II. Times, the poet noted, had changed. Attitudes about women's role in society had evolved, yet Fuzeira still expected a woman to be "a goddess, smelling of onions and salsa, and at night, a goddess of lace and perfume." Women, the commentary concluded, were becoming athletes who could play and dominate the sporting field. Not only did the author ridicule Fuzeira's argument, then, but the poet argued in favor of an evolution toward strong, athletic women. While critical of Fuzeira, however, one norm remained unchallenged in the pages of *Jornal dos Sports*: that of beauty and musculature. On the issue of football damaging the male-gaze feminine aesthetic, the poet noted that perhaps Fuzeira made a point. However, the author recommended these conversations should be kept private.[170]

While the ban no doubt curtailed women's football in Brazil, the action of women belied press reports of the sport's demise. Women's teams publicly resisted the ban on the sport that they loved. Primavera FC, pilloried in the press as a team of iniquity, as well as the teams Brasileiro, River, Independentes, Eva FC, and Oposição FC continued to play.[171] But with dwindling resources and no support from the media or clubs, the ban permanently damaged the women's game. As chapter 3 explores in depth, Brazilian women resisted the prohibition across the country by ignoring it and refusing to acknowledge its legitimacy. The state only intermittently sought to enforce the ban. Periodically, for the next forty years, this brought futboleras into conflict with the local police, government officials, teachers, and their own families.

The sport's effervescence was quickly forgotten. In 1948, a woman named Hayde Medeiros wrote a letter to a *Jornal dos Sports* column penned by the poet and journalist Manoel do Nascimento Vargas Neto.[172] Interestingly, Vargas Neto was the nephew of Getúlio Vargas, and one wonders about his access to the very administrators who imposed the ban. In her letter, Medeiros asked why sports clubs throughout Brazil had women's teams for volleyball, basketball, and fencing, but not women's football teams, which existed in other countries. Medeiros apparently had no knowledge of the sport's dynamism just seven years earlier. Vargas Neto's response placed the blame at the feet of the right person, General Newton Cavalcanti. However, Vargas Neto also indicated that he believed the accusations that women's football was a "dirty affair." Vargas Neto explained in his letter that the teams from a few years earlier were not clean and had provoked police intervention. Charges of "exploitation of minors, swindling, and *malandragem*," which could

mean any number of things in this context, had led to a general out-
cry and occasioned the banning of the women's game, according to
Vargas Neto.[173] He described Newton Cavalcanti as a sworn enemy
of women's football who had attempted to prohibit all women's
sports. Cavalcanti had "found medical opinions opposed to women's
participation," based on morphology and biology, and had opined
as well that football would make women ugly.[174] Vargas Neto made
clear—as another poet had done eight years earlier in mocking José
Fuzeira—that women were fighting in wars, working in factories,
and performing an array of male tasks, and thus should be allowed
to play any sport.[175]

Fans were not the only ones who seemed to have forgotten that
women's football had existed. In 1950, *O Dia* published an article
on women's football teams visiting Curitiba. The newspaper referred
to the women from Vila Hilda and Corinthians as curiosities, describing women's football as something never before seen. Only eight
years earlier, however, in December 1942, *O Dia* had rejoiced at the
government prohibition of the game.[176] In eight short years, the same
publication went from seeing women's football as a dangerous phe-
nomenon spreading quickly to a new and curious experiment. The
article explained that the women's game at Estádio Joaquim Américo
Guimarães had drawn one of the stadium's largest audiences in recent memory. Perhaps this perpetual amnesia helped illicit women
players from attracting too much scrutiny from the authorities. Or
perhaps the local authorities turned a blind eye because of women
players' supposed triviality. A different paper, also from Curitiba,
also seemed surprised at the large audience for women's football.
However, rather than expressing delight, the paper published a
writer who seemed scandalized by women's football.[177] This brief
editorial appeared in the "Catholic Column." The writer referred
to the players as "masculinized women" who were degraded by the
sport. Whereas one could find immorality in brothels or cabarets at
night, women's football provided ample opportunities for spectators
to indulge in the irresistible temptation of watching women running
on the field. The potential sexualization of players by spectators
troubled the Catholic columnist. In this regard, the moral basis to

criticize women's football echoed that of critics twenty years earlier.[178] Journalists and experts put forward a different version of the
prohibition in the 1950s. In 1953, the writer M. Mattoso recalled
that the police had banned women's football in 1939 after it had
already developed and disseminated.[179] Mattoso recalled both the
ban and the popular perception of it as being at the behest of a
medical doctor in Rio rather than because of police interest in the
matter and suspect morals.

If the media and the public seemed to have forgotten the brief
popularity of women's football, the state did not. The Brazilian educator Waldemar Areno confirmed the state's interest in restricting
women's access to certain activities when he attended the Second Pan-
American Conference on Physical Education, in 1945 in Mexico.[180]
Areno argued that individual sports such as badminton, tennis,
gymnastics, and track and field (with reduced distances and weights)
were fine for women's participation. However, women should not
attempt gymnastics with apparatus, such as the parallel bars and the
pommel horse.[181] Areno was concerned with women's stamina, and
along with shorter running races he advocated short bicycle races
with well-planned routes to prevent accidents. As with Dr. Leite de
Castro, team sports were less acceptable in Areno's eyes. Volleyball
and basketball were fine if they implemented new rules that prevented contact and collisions between players. Women's sports,
Areno concluded, should be rhythmic and fluid, since this type of
movement "has generally beneficial effects" on the female body.[182]
Yet he provided no studies to support this assertion. Areno hoped
for expanded physical education training for women in order to
oversee these activities. Like others who attacked women's football,
his rationale moved from pseudoscience to outright cultural bias.
He called women's football "absurd and harmful" without giving
any medical reason as to why. Then Areno switched to perhaps
the real reason—it was ostensibly offensive to the (male) observer.
"The spectacle it offers," he wrote, "besides being unsporting and
anti-physiological, degrades the good sense of the observers."[183]
Erasing the long history of women's football in the country, Areno

closed his remarks on women's football by saying that in Brazil women's football had never gained acceptance.

Despite the obstacles, women were ready to take to the field again by the 1950s. Brazilian women began organizing teams, coming into conflict with authorities who sought once again to repress women's football clubs. These struggles occurred on the pitch and in local courts. As discussed in the following chapter, in June 1959, the CND decided unanimously to renew the ban on women's football in response to efforts in the state of Minas Gerais to reinvigorate teams.[184] Even as the CND and the football establishment persecuted women's football, the national sporting council promoted more acceptable sports for women, especially tennis. Women's tennis grabbed the international spotlight in 1959. That year, the Brazilian Maria Esther Bueno won Wimbledon, a feat accentuated, in the international sports press at least, by Bueno's whiteness. When Bueno won the Associated Press Female Athlete of the Year award in 1959, _Jet_ magazine pointed out that Althea Gibson deserved the prize but had been snubbed because of racism. The contrast between public acceptance of women's tennis and suppression of women's football was stark. The same year, one of the first women's teams to escape the ephemerality imposed by the illegality of women's football emerged in Belo Horizonte. There, after eighteen years, the sport reemerged into the open in the provincial city of Araguari. Women athletes formed a team within the Araguari Athletic Club, traveled with the men's team, and drew national attention when they played matches in a mini tour of the country. A small notice appeared in a newspaper in Curitiba announcing that despite the ban on women's football, the writer had seen interesting matches every Sunday.[185] The notice was so vague and small as to give pause. It is difficult to ascertain if the writer was warning women that they had been spotted or encouraging them without alerting the authorities.

The fact that women's football resurfaced after nearly a generation suggests that perhaps it had never disappeared at all. Instead, while the CND ban restricted the growth of the sport, women continued to play under the radar until the late 1970s. The ban highlights the growing complicity between public health professionals and the state in regulating women's behavior outside the home. Through physical education curricula, sports regulations, and media focus on certain women's sports, the powers of Brazilian patriarchy successfully—on the surface, at least—outlined acceptable space for women in the mid-twentieth century. Defined by men, at the intersection of gender, race, and class, this sporting space included individual sports and those practiced primarily by the elite. Nevertheless, the diffusion of women's sports in the country remained largely outside of government control. If official sporting practice failed women, grassroots and subaltern organizations fostered women's continued play. This play, however, would be curtailed by autocratic regimes throughout the region before truly blossoming in the 1980s and 1990s.

3

BRAZILIAN SPORTSWOMEN DEFYING PROHIBITION

THE SUDDEN ERUPTION OF WOMEN'S FOOTBALL IN BRAZIL in the early 1980s would have taken the casual observer by surprise. Officially banned for forty years, women theoretically had very little opportunity to learn and play the sport. Though the state had long promoted physical education programs, the gender-differentiated curriculum only included football for boys. While women and girls around Brazil had continued to play in spite of the ban, government sanction had effectively stunted the sport's growth among women. Still, regardless of national efforts to regulate women's activities, regional and local federations supported women players. In other words, national goals collided with local realities. Among the latter was the continued desire of women to play football and other sports deemed too rough for them. Throughout the entire forty-year ban on women's football, women flouted both convention and legality and played anyway. In so doing they challenged the institutionalized sexism not only of Brazilian football but of Brazilian society as a whole. Their passion for football brought them into conflict with the justice system, their families, and sports organizations. Basketball, swimming, tennis, and volleyball escaped some of the scrutiny of football, and certainly the legal prohibition. Still, women's participation in these sports contributed to changing the long-standing prejudices about women's capacities.

Women's football had flourished before the ban, and women's participation in the sport was never limited to playing. After the ban was enacted, women appeared in sports media as foils to address a host of other issues in the national sporting scene. Sports magazines portrayed women as insufferable nags who stood in the way of male entertainment in the stadiums and at the clubhouse.

These caricatures reinforced gendered stereotypes about women and sports. "Femininity" was used to critique male football, further disconnecting women's football from acceptable sporting practices. If men who played poorly were considered "feminine," women's sports, by definition, lacked quality. Sports magazines and sports sections in newspapers also used women as vehicles to discuss male sports, particularly through the lens of class and race. At almost every turn, with perhaps the exception of elite sports such as tennis and swimming, discussions after the 1940s of women and sports cast aspersions on female athletes and placed women involved in sports in auxiliary roles. This shift altered perceptions of women in Brazilian sports in important ways. In earlier eras, female involvement as spectators and members in athletic clubs was commonplace and accepted. Now women began to be written out of Brazil's mainstream sporting scene.

No sooner was the ban on football printed than it was disobeyed. Brazilian women immediately came into conflict with authorities that sought to repress the growing organization of women's football clubs, both on the pitch and in local courts. At the same time that the Conselho Nacional de Desportos (National Sports Council, CND) and the Confederação Brasileira de Futebol (Brazilian Football Confederation) persecuted women's football, the CND promoted what it deemed more acceptable sports for women, especially tennis, gymnastics, and swimming. Moreover, the administrations of Getúlio Vargas (1930–1945) and Eurico Gaspar Dutra (1945–1951) expanded physical education, for both boys and girls, as part of their broader embrace of eugenics. Thus, physical education became part of a state vision of women as racial pioneers and vessels of future Brazilian racial improvement. Authors and physical education experts such as Fernando de Azevedo and Renato Kehl had ties to the eugenics movement in Brazil and published regularly in the well-respected journal *Educação Physica*.[1]

The state's increasing interest in physical education included making physical exercise mandatory in secondary school, creating a new division of physical education in the Ministry of Education, and founding the National School of Physical Education and Sport in Rio to educate future teachers.[2] Military personnel frequently led these new institutions and initiatives, underscoring the importance that the state placed on physical education for the defensive and reproductive capabilities of the nation. For example, as discussed in chapter 2, the military officer João Barbosa Leite was appointed the first head of the Division of Physical Education and Sport; at the same time he was secretary of the CND. Thus, it should not be surprising that military forms of discipline and strict gender segregation shaped the nation's programs in physical education. Physical education was also intimately tied to the projects of urbanization and industrialization. That physical education not only produced soldiers, but also trained industrial workers and protected citizens from the (racial) degradation of city life, was a central tenet of the government's interest.[3]

Women's increased participation in physical education was not inherently a feminist achievement. In physical education, women were taught that they were biologically inferior to men, more delicate and weak. Curricular materials sent the message that participation would increase their beauty and fitness for motherhood. At the same time, physical education experts issued dire warnings that too much athletic participation could result in "masculinization". As the professionalization of physical education evolved in the 1940s and 1950s, experts reinforced the immutable biological differences between men and women. To refute those who believed women could play any sport, Waldemar Areno, a professor of applied hygiene at the School of Physical Education and Sport at the University of Brazil and the chair of Human Anatomy, Physiology, and Applied Hygiene at the National School of Physical Education and Sport, explained that "women are profoundly different from men. All of their body is impregnated with chemical substances secreted by the ovaries."[4] This type of pseudoscientific statement, offered by credentialed "experts," appeared consistently in academic and popular literature of physical education and shaped both scientific and lay attitudes toward women's physical activities. Despite physical education's overtly sexist message, some scholars have found that it encouraged young women to occupy public spaces and helped to break down strict public and private gender separation.[5]

Physical education was not only a realm of government interest, but of academic debate as well. Beginning in the 1930s, the *Revista Brasileira de Educação Física* (Brazilian Journal of Physical Education) published articles related to women's physical activity, chiefly concerned with maternity and feminine "harmony." In the views of most physical education experts, beauty reflected a woman's good health just as strength expressed good health for men. The goals of women's exercise, according to these theorists, included building harmony, flexibility, and grace. Women, wrote one expert, were motivated by "the improvement of the race, of beauty, and of femininity."[6] Physical education experts correlated the physiological differences between women and men with acute psychological differences as well. Thus, they posited that women's lack of emotional control needed to be taken into account when designing class activities.

Given their belief that sports helped men's virility and strengthened their character, many experts worried that women would become more "masculine" through the practice of sports. As the scholar Silvana Goellner has shown, the persistent fears that tied women's exercise to masculinization, which in turn threatened their heterosexuality, surfaced and resurfaced in the academic literature on physical education from as early as the 1920s.[7] By the 1940s and 1950s, very little had changed. Whatever challenge to traditional womanhood had been posed by the *nova mulher*, or new woman, faded as the model of the nuclear family became reembedded as a middle-class Brazilian ideal of the Cold War. Physical education experts fully embraced the prohibition on women's football and attempted to erase the sport's previous popularity. For example, one article in the *Revista Brasileira de Educação Física* claimed that "football cannot be part of women's sport." According to the author, it was not only "antisporting" but "antiphysiological." Women's football was "absurd, harmful," and a "spectacle" that "offends the common sense of spectators."[8] The author concluded that "happily" women's football did "not have acceptance among us."[9] Even the most supportive physical education experts had a limited view of which females should participate in athletics. Given their interest in eugenics and belief in the importance of maternal health to the future of the race, physical education teachers nearly always assumed the profile of students to be white middle- or upper-class girls, who would otherwise be indolent and cloistered.

PLAY DURING PROHIBITION

The ban on women's football in Brazil, though incomplete, nevertheless affected the sport. While women *never* stopped playing football, certainly the press covered the sport much less than it had in the 1930s. Near the end of the 1940s, however, reports of women's football became more commonplace again. A 1950 article in the Curitiba newspaper O Dia highlighted the fact that women had likely been playing in the 1940s. It reported on Southern Brazil two famous women's teams from Rio Grande do Sul, Corinthians and Rio Grande, claiming that every Paranaense knew of them, which indicates the teams had likely been around for years. Moreover, the sports journalists' association Cronistas Esportivos do Paraná (Sportswriters of Paraná) sought permission from the regional Federação Paranaense de Futebol (Paranaense Football Federation) to host a game between the two teams of female "cracks," or top players. While O Dia promoted the match as a novelty and suggested that the match, to be played in Curitiba's main Joaquim Américo Guimarães stadium, provided the opportunity to gawk at attractive women, the journalists demonstrated a clear familiarity with the teams. Promotional articles assumed the audience would be "thrilled" to watch a game between twenty-two beauties, noting that the women players would be "parading in front of the curious eyes of thousands of [male] *futebolistas*."[10] That female athletes existed for the sexual fantasies of male onlookers could not have been stated much more obviously. At the same time, articles in advance of the match invited young women interested in playing to attend and learn the game.

It is not fully clear why Curitiba emerged as a center of women's football throughout the twentieth century. As with all sports, male or female, journalists played a key role in spreading news of and reporting on games, although in the case of women's football they often remained anonymous. *Diário da Tarde*, a daily paper in Curitiba, argued that women's football was "revolutionizing the sport of the masses: football."[11] It warned that the city of Curitiba would be shaken by the spectacle.[12] One can imagine some measure of journalistic embellishment coming from a desire to promote the event and generate paper sales. A few months later, another match was declared "unprecedented," though clearly precedent existed.[13] Even as they promoted the games in advance, Curitiba's journalists provided few details about the matches themselves, and offered even less information about the players. Perhaps this afforded the athletes some protection, and journalists might have wanted to keep details to a minimum, given that these activities were patently illegal. Clearly, however, the Paranaense Football Federation supported women's football, as it continued to approve matches in the face of the ban.[14]

Because of the ongoing interest in, and illicit support for, women's football, the CND was forced to reiterate the ban again and again. It sent representatives to the provinces regularly to ensure that its regulations regarding women's sports were being adhered to. In 1956, for example, *O Globo* published a very small notice announcing that the CND had reaffirmed its ban on women's football.[15] That same year, the CND sent a representative to reprimand the regional sports council of Bahia for allowing a game between two women's teams from SC Vitoria and SC Bahia.[16] The teams played in the Estádio Otávio Mangabeira, the largest stadium in Salvador da Bahia. The match was of such interest to the public that it headlined the night, superseding the men's regional championship game, and turned a profit of 350,000 cruzeiros, or roughly $12,000. Journalists remarked that the fans were highly enthusiastic. The photograph published of the Vitoria team shows a racially mixed team with proper football kits, including shorts rather than tennis skirts.[17]

In 1957, the CND acted once again to enforce the ban on women's football when the São Paulo businessman José da Gama Correia da Silva presented a petition to Brazil's governing body of sports to allow him to bring women's football teams to Europe.[18] Da Gama's plan was to give a portion of the tour's profits to the Pioneiras Sociais (Social Pioneers), a social welfare organization established in 1956 by the first lady, Sarah Kubitschek. Though no games were to be played in Brazil, the CND denied da Gama's request, citing Decree Law 3199 as its rationale. *O Estado de São Paulo* reminded readers that in addition to football, the law banned women and girls from participating in the triple jump, the high jump, rugby, polo, water polo, pentathlon, hammer throw, decathlon, wrestling, and boxing. Even outside the country, the CND sought to police Brazilian women and restrict their sporting activities.

Throughout the 1950s, futboleras persisted. Small announcements buried in newspapers attest to the ongoing vibrancy of women's football, particularly in Bahia, Minas Gerais, and Paraná. In May of 1959 one such note appeared announcing women's football in Belo Horizonte. *O Estado de São Paulo*'s note informed readers that two women's teams would be playing over the weekend in the Estádio Independência in the state capital. Enticing as the article is, the only information in the newspaper about the match notes that one of the teams, Araguari AC, comprised twenty-six women.[19] Similarly, in June of 1959 a very small notice explained that in Salvador, the women's football section of the Bahia Sports Club sent an invitation to Atlético Mineiro to play in "our capital."[20] The match, played between Baiana and Araguari in the Estádio Fonte Nova, had gate receipts of more than 300,000 cruzeiros.[21] Fans watched as Bahia defeated Araguari 4–2 in a "technically good" match, which was "interrupted constantly by the crowd applauding." So successful was the match that plans were made for additional games.[22]

In response to this match, the governor of Minas Gerais, José Francisco Bias Fortes, received a visit from Manuel Faria de Paula Ramos, the vice president of the CND, who ordered that the governor put a stop to women's football in the state.[23] According to the notice, Ramos was specifically charged with making sure the ban on women's football was adhered to.[24] At the same time, perhaps sensing a shift in public attitudes toward the women's game, the CND legal advisor Samuel Sabat suggested a study to consider revising the law.[25] However, the council decided against such a move. Instead, local officials issued their own ordinances that reinforced the law. In response to continuous rebellion of futboleras and the supposed permissiveness of the Paranaense football federation, a judge in Curitiba issued a new ordinance that specifically prohibited minor girls from joining football clubs.[26] So, while reporting on women's football had markedly diminished, the sport was clearly still being played. The ongoing legal actions testify to both the commitment and inability of the national government to stop women and girls from playing. Likely, the government's limited success stemmed from the sport's peripheral position. Officials' presence was relatively rare at the local level, and even more so when it came to girls' and women's athletics. The fact that most activity in the 1950s came from outside of Rio and São Paulo may also indicate that the ban had greater significance in preventing play in urban centers.

In 1959, the CND decided unanimously to renew the ban on women's football in response to efforts in Minas Gerais to reinvigorate teams.[27] But promoters continued to seek ways around the ban. By organizing women's football matches as charity events, they sought to take advantage of both loopholes in the prohibition and gendered norms in society: if women footballers were performing caregiving roles by playing for charity, then their activities would be more acceptable. The Brazilian state did not see it the same way. In August 1959, the CND took the promoter Lover Ibaixe to court in an attempt to stop a charity football match between women cabaret workers of Rio and São Paulo. In his defense, Ibaixe argued for an exception to the ban since all proceeds of the match would support the construction of a new retirement home for actors in São Paulo.[28] It was not an easy permission to obtain. Judge Julio Leal Fagundes of the Second Court of the Treasury allowed the match to take place, given its charity nature. Perhaps more important, Fagundes ruled that the CND had not adequately explained why it refused to allow the event.[29] After a series of appeals that dragged on for months, the court ruled that the game could go on.[30] However, Minister Afrânio Costa of the Federal Appeals Court briefly delayed the match again. A former Olympian in shooting, Costa agreed with the CND that the event was "circus-like" in nature and degraded sports' educational functions.[31] Strangely, in an evening meeting, the CND decided to allow the match to take place the following day.[32]

Defining women's games as charity partially undermined the prohibition against women's football. The logic of charity drew upon and reiterated the notion that women's activities were legitimate so long as they were for the benefit of others rather than their own enjoyment. Still, charity matches were untenable as a way to maintain a vibrant women's football league. At first glance, these games sound like they were more spectacle than anything else. However, photographs from the events indicate that the musical actresses who played took the endeavor seriously. While there were plenty of "pinup" photographs published of the women players, they played the game with intention. Moreover, the participation of the men's World Cup champions Pelé and Gilmar as "trainers" to help the young women lent an air of legitimacy to the proceedings.[33] Though these "novelty" matches continued to happen, efforts to close them down signaled that the patriarchal Brazilian sporting establishment continued to see women's football as a threat. As professional football played a larger and larger role in the national sporting organizations, the directors supported the ban, at least tacitly.

One of the chief opponents of women's football was José Augusto Cavalcânti Cisneiros, president and academic director of the School of Physical Education and Sport at the University of Brazil. He couched his opposition as concern for the futboleras, suggesting that the women were "like an instrument in the hands of unscrupulous exploiters making a clumsy business and infesting the national sport."[34] Cisneiros claimed to have consulted scholars who uniformly condemned the practice on "biological, physiological, and aesthetic principles."[35] He further explained: "We understand sports as a cult of the beautiful, for physical improvement, strengthening of a race, sociability of the individual, the seed of order, and the food

of liberty."[36] The discourse surrounding women's football emphasized that their play offended men. According to *O Globo*, the police stormed a celebrity match after it came to slaps and kicks. The
confusion was such that the spectators thought that the police were
part of the show.[37] The reports claimed that the Paulista Maria
Helena started the fight with a late kick, and it escalated into a brawl
from there. The article recommended that the women stop playing
and focus on their stage careers.[38] Yet the women remained unde-
terred, traveling after São Paulo to play in Rio at the Maracanã and
in Salvador.[39]

Following the celebrity match, *O Globo* declared that the CND
had lost its battle against women's football. Women's clubs began
to appear again in working-class neighborhoods, high schools, and
factories. Among the clubs that gathered strength was Ponta Preta
FC, from Jacareí, which had already organized a match against EC
Fazenda de São João de Meriti in the Estádio do Rio. The game was
part of the celebrations to honor Governor Roberto Silveira.[40] Just
a month later, a match in Conselheiro Lafaiete in Minas Gerais was
held between women of Meridional and Guarani, ending in a tie.
The notice claimed that the game had brought in a record profit of
Cr$160.500,00 in gate receipts.[41]

The following year, starlets from São Paulo challenged their
Uruguayan counterparts to two football matches in the Estádio
Pacaembu, São Paulo's municipal stadium. According to *Folha de
São Paulo*, the actresses demanded 50 percent of the gross in order
to play.[42] On the way to the stadium, the players for Uruguay and
Brazil paraded through the main streets of São Paulo. Despite the
excitement over the match, sportswriters did not take it seriously.
An anonymous author in *Caretas*, for example, mocked the celebrity
players, noting that their play "left everything to be desired," and
that any pay they received would be for "aesthetic compensation."[43]
The writer also noted that the juxtaposition of "playthings [*cria-
turas*] like that," on a football field, kicking at "the shins . . . of
their adversary," was "extremely bizarre."[44] Still, photographs of
the events in many ways normalized the idea of women footballers.
They showed the teams in uniforms with only slightly shorter shorts

ARAGUARI A. CLUBE 2 X FLUMINENSE F. CLUBE 1
(EQUIPE FEMININA)

FIGURE 3.1. Araguari football club, Minas Gerais, 1958. Courtesy of Museu do Futebol, Acervo Tereza Cristina.

than those worn by men, and also featured the women in action during a game.

One of the most stable women's football clubs during prohibition formed in the state of Minas Gerais. In 1959, the law banning women's football had been in place for nearly twenty years, when athletes formed a women's section in the Araguari Athletic Club in order to raise money for a local school. Comprising mostly middle-class students, the women's team occasionally traveled with the men's team from the same club. The women's team of Araguari drew national attention in May 1959 when they played a mini tour of Minas Gerais. The team also received an invitation to play in Mexico, but players recalled that the ban prevented them from pursuing the trip.[45] *O Globo* reported in 1959 that despite the prohibition, women's football was openly diffused throughout the city of Araguari.[46] Perhaps due to the distance from the state capital (more than 600 kilometers), Araguari AC had more leeway to support women's football. Throughout Minas Gerais, not only could teams be found in all of the "principal cities," but state institutions began to evade the ban. In Dores do Indaiá, a town located 255 kilometers from Belo Horizonte, two local schools—the Francisco Campos Normal School and the San Luis Business and Technical School—both began women's football teams in 1959. The coach of one of the teams explicitly recognized the ban and said that the school would ignore it.[47] In Paraná as well, in spite of the prohibition, one could find women's matches every Sunday in Curitiba, the state capital.[48]

Amazingly, despite the official ban on the sport, in February 1959 O Cruzeiro featured a five-page spread on the women's team of Araguari.[49] From the photographs, one can see that the matches were very well attended. In the stands the gender division was fairly equal and there was a significant representation of people of color. Still, the presentation of the sport was less than ideal. One photo showed two women, apparently players, posing on the field, with one holding a mirror and the other combing her hair. The caption stated that when the ball was not in play, the women could fix their hair and makeup, emphasizing the femininity of the players. The article claimed that Araguari AC began featuring women's football because it lost money on men's football and needed an attraction to bring people to the games. The article, which referred to players as the "bitter daughters of Eve," was partially humorous and partially ominous in tone.[50] According to the author, José Franco, it was only a matter of time before women would master the men's game. Still, the magazine focused part of its attention on the players' appearance. A caption that accompanied a photo of the goalkeeper read, "The goalie is in a poor technical position, but her hair looks pretty."[51] Even so, the article disrupted the visual repertoire of typical gender norms. Women wore standard kits, and the photographs showed women in positions of exertion and competition.

In reaction to the flagrant resistance to the women's football ban in Araguari, Válter Ferreira de Sousa led a group of sportsmen to protest their matches. Sousa and his fellow protestors reached out to O Globo for support against the futboleras.[52] The protestors accused the Mineiro football federation, the municipal league, and the regional sports council of neglecting to enforce the national decree.

Since Araguari AC was affiliated with the Federação Mineira de Futebol (Minas Gerais Football Federation), the club risked expulsion for violating the ban. But women had a long-term involvement in such clubs, and likely convinced directors that they would not face real sanctions. Sousa complained that the interest in women's matches stemmed from their novelty. At least, then, he recognized the financial value of women's football. A women's game, he noted, could have 200,000 cruzeiros in gate receipts, which benefited the club and its male players. Sousa also noted that although the Federação Goiana de Futebol (Goiás Football Federation) had prohibited all women's games in the state, a match had been planned for Palm Sunday in Tupaciguara. Though Tupaciguara is in Minas Gerais, it is close to the border with Goiana. It is possible that the match in Tupaciguara was supposed to include a team from nearby Itumbiara, in Goiás state. Sousa claimed that the population was incensed and had succeeded, with the help of the vicar, in getting the match canceled. Sousa enlisted the local newspaper in Araguari, *Gazeta do Triângulo*, as an ally in his campaign against women's football.[53]

Despite frequent editorials against women's football, newspapers continued to print notices of matches in the late 1950s and early 1960s, which clearly gave succor to the sport. The level of play in the interior led the newspaper *A Luta Democrática* to suggest that football clubs were "making a joke of the law" that banned the women's game.[54] New teams seemed to emerge and disintegrate on a weekly basis.[55] For example, *O Globo* reported a match between Fazenda FC and Iguaçu AA in the stadium of Volantes Sports Club, in the Rio de Janeiro suburb of Nova Iguaçu. The match fell within the allowable parameters for women's football: the charity match raised money for the Matriz de Nossa Senhora de Fátima in Rio. The women of Fazenda won 3–0. A photograph from the match showed the masseuse of Fazenda, notably Afro-Brazilian, treating the goalkeeper, Maria Augusta.[56] As other media outlets had done, *O Globo* again reported that despite the ban by the CND, women's football was growing each day during the 1959–1960 season. It pointed out that after matches between Belo Horizonte and the actresses from

São Paulo, Santos, and Salvador, enthusiasm for the sport spread like a wildfire.[57] Local students from Campinas also began to play and performed as the local rivals Guarani and Ponte Prêta, as a benefit for the Instituto Dom Nery, a nonprofit educational center. According to *O Globo*, the match, held at the twenty-thousand capacity Estádio Moisés Lucarelli, grossed 200,000 cruzeiros.[58]

Often, notices of women's matches listed a charitable cause as the recipient of the gate receipt, but at other times notices simply mentioned the teams and venue. Women's teams occupied stadiums throughout the country, which lent them a good deal of legitimacy. Stadiums had come to serve as centers of civic life, and fans regarded them as sacred spaces. However, by midcentury, Brazilian stadiums had also become a source of anxiety for social commentators because of increasing violence at football games. Organized fan groups attempted to keep the violence under control, but matches frequently descended into chaos.[59] For women to take to the pitch was a radical act in the late 1950s. The women who attended these matches would have had a fairly unique opportunity to see other women at the center of a spectacle, beyond film and theatre.

Evidence suggests that it was easier for women to organize in the provinces and suburbs than in major cities. And the fact that newspaper articles on women's football matches in the 1960s present them as somewhat normal suggests that the sport had continued more or less unabated. For example, in Paraná in April 1960, a festival to celebrate the anniversary of Fanático FC included a women's match between two neighborhood clubs, Vila Hauer and Vila Inah. The local newspaper commented that the public would excitedly wait to see the players' beautiful legs. While there can be little doubt that this story objectified women, it also provided a tiny space for women to read about the women's game.[60] While not the most far-flung location in Brazil, it is fair to say that Campo Largo, a suburb of Curitiba in Paraná, was quite distant from the Carioca and Paulista club scenes that dominated Brazilian football. The two clubs that presented the women's teams were from relatively middle-class organizations with a stable tradition and ties to European immigrants, which were prevalent in the region. Vila Hauer was organized in 1950 as a large sports club with a football division, while Vila Inah was a stable third-division team.[61]

In 1960, heartened by the proliferation of women's teams in disparate regions of the country, women launched an unsuccessful campaign to push the Confederação Brasileiro de Desportos (Brazilian Confederation of Sports) to revoke the ban.[62] One woman interviewed by *O Globo* estimated that more than thirty women's football teams played regularly in the Paraíba Valley alone. Identified as Luci, the young woman described the ban as "hateful discrimination."[63] The players defended the morality of women's football by noting that a major supporter of the women's game in the region was a Catholic school, where girls had the support of the priests. They also claimed to have the support of Vicente Feola, coach of the 1958 men's World Cup winning team.[64] Futboleras argued that they could bring grace and beauty back to football, which men had marred through brutality and rough play. Ultimately, conflict over women's football caused violence itself, which caught the attention of local media. In October 1960, women students in the School of Pharmacy and Dentistry in Belo Horizonte organized a football match. The game provoked social unrest. According to reports, fellow students attacked the players. The fighting escalated to the point where a soldier at the scene fired his gun, and the disturbance was such that the regional secretary of public safety considered posting an officer permanently at the university to restore order. The title of the news piece, "Futebol de mulhers causa conflito" (Women's football causes conflict), sent a clear message to readers that women's football—not opposition to it—was the problem.[65] Victoria Langland and others have written about the degree of police intervention in Brazilian university activities during the Cold War.[66] It is possible that increased surveillance hampered the development of women's football clubs at Brazilian universities. While neighboring Chile and Argentina had visible women's football clubs based at institutions of higher education, Brazil had none.

The 1964 military coup against President João Goulart ushered in an era of increased surveillance, repression, and state violence. While women's sports occupied a rather insignificant space in the social concerns of the military, defying any law could result in harrowing consequences. As the military assigned officers to positions within civil society and education, the chances for women's athletics to thrive within clubs and schools dimmed. Still, throughout the 1960s, women continued to play football, though small notices in major newspapers remain some of the only evidence of the sport. In March 1965, tucked at the bottom of the page, O *Estado de São Paulo* announced a match at Estádio Mansueto Pieroti in the São Paulo suburb of São Vicente. The match, between Comercial Futebol Feminino and Esporte Clube Emabaré, was played as a preliminary of the match between Santos and São Vicente. As minor as it might have been (the capacity of the stadium was around five thousand), the CND took notice.[67] That body's vice president, Anibal Pelon, later demanded an inquiry into Santos FC (home club of Pelé), accusing it of intentionally circumventing the ban on women's football.[68]

In fact, the CND launched a new offensive against women's football in 1965, less than a year after the military coup, by increasing pressure on provincial governors to stop women's games, particularly in Santos and Belo Horizonte.[69] In the latter case, organizers were forced to cancel a women's tournament because the vice squad of Belo Horizonte demanded that the municipality enforce the illegality of women's football.[70] Given the frequency with which notices of women's football matches appeared, with large headlines but virtually no information, they likely acted as warnings to women who might have had ideas about playing. The anti–women's football campaign also included new enforcement in Guanabara, which mainly comprised Rio de Janeiro. Its governor, Carlos Lacerda, a well-known conservative, received orders from the CND and committed to obliterate the women's game.[71] After the 1965 match between Comercial Futebol Feminino and EC Emabaré mentioned above, which between six and seven thousand people attended, the CND began to look at women's football in São Paulo as well.[72] That same year, an emergency committee of the International Federation of Association Football (FIFA) officially weighed in on women's football, recommending that federations "adopt 'prudent reserve' and . . . not encourage its development."[73]

Amidst renewed efforts to suppress the sport in the political context of dictatorship, women persisted in carving space for themselves in Brazilian sports.[74] Historical work has demonstrated the importance of policing gender difference to the military government's ideology. Benjamin Cowan, for example, has shown the right wing's conflation of Communism with the breakdown of gender binaries and diffusion of sexual licentiousness.[75] Given the climate of extreme political violence during the 1960s and 1970s, Brazilian women's refusal to obey the football ban, and their efforts in other sports, takes on a new meaning. In Catanduva, a northern municipality of São Paulo, a women's football match was held in 1969 to commemorate the founding of the city. Played as a preliminary to the men's match between Cantanduva and Rio, the Instituto de Educação Barão do Rio Branco faced off against Ginâsio Estadual Elias Nechar. That local secondary schools supported girls' football teams only highlights the conflicting attitudes about the sport. Due to the popularity and enthusiasm for the game, during the match regular substitution rules were suspended so that more girls would have the opportunity to play.[76] In addition, the match length was shortened to fifty minutes, ostensibly because the women were not in shape to play full games. These are fascinating examples of how women organizers changed the rules in order to create a different environment. At the same time, however, they highlight how organizers assumed that women had less ability than men, and both mimicked earlier efforts and presaged later ones to make the women's game less demanding. Following the game in Catanduva, the squad from Instituto de Educação Barão do Rio Branco was supposed to continue to Tabapuã, where they were scheduled to play another game in honor of that city's anniversary. The article made clear that the girls of the institute had been playing football for some time, practicing in the safe confines of the school.[77]

FUTBOLERAS BEYOND THE PITCH

Alongside playing, women created spaces for themselves within the *torcedores*, or organized fan groups, as well as within sports

Nº 164   S.Paulo, 28/10/1966

Aos Srs. Arrecadadores da F.P.F.

A portadora, Dna.SEMIRAMIS ALVES
TEIXEIRA, reportes da TV Tupi-Canal 4
tem livre ingresso nas praças desportivas, por ocasiao de jogos sob o pa-
trocinio desta Entidade, quando no e-
xercicio de suas funções para as Emis
soras Associadas.
          FEDERAÇÃO PAULISTA DE FUTEBOL

          Americo Egidio Pereira
          Secretario Geral

F.P.F. · 6 · 2.000 · 1/66

FIGURE 3.2. Figure 3.2. Press badge of Semíramis Alves Teixeira. Courtesy of Museu do Futebol, Coleção Semíramis Alves Teixera.

journalism. In 1956 Dulce Rosalina became the first female president of the Vasco da Gama *torcedores*, a position she retained for nearly twenty years.[78] Elisa Alves do Nascimento, from Corinthians, became one of the club's iconic fans, if not the actual president of a *torcida*. The Paulista Football Federation gave Elisa, as she was known, a pass to enter any field. These women, both working class and of color, knew male players personally, consulted with coaches over team strategy, and dined with club presidents. Thus, they wielded a notable amount of power. Club directors, players, and the media emphasized the maternal character of these women. Still, women at the top of the fan structure had power in orchestrating fan performances, influencing ticket sales, advising club trainers, and achieving community recognition. The historian Bernardo Buarque de Hollanda has discussed the important social relationships forged in fan clubs. Members organized complicated tours, working to pool resources.[79] They also created dances, songs, costumes, and placards in support of their teams. By the 1970s these relationships had dissipated. Scholars have shown that by then *torcidas* had become more hierarchical and violent, mirroring the military dictatorship's practices.[80]

The transition from the carnivalesque nature of fan groups in the 1940s and 1950s to the configuration along military lines made it difficult for women to participate in such groups.

The career of Semíramis Alves Teixeira, who became a pioneer in sports journalism, presents another window on women's involvement in sports and an important exception to women's public roles in the field. A young woman who was fashionable and assertive, Teixeira elbowed her way onto the field and into the locker rooms. According to the Brazilian media, she was a rarity, maybe the "only woman in the world" who could easily discuss techniques and tactics of football. By 1966 Teixeira was a regular on Brazilian television, commenting on men's football. Interestingly, she was not forced to present herself as a sex symbol. Female journalists that came after found it difficult to achieve a similar level of respect.

INTERNATIONAL INTEREST

Given Brazil's importance in global football, it is not surprising that women's football organizers from Europe sought to arrange matches with women's teams from the country. In the early 1960s, an English women's team promoted by Percy Ashley approached Brazilian officials in hopes of playing a match in Maracanã against a Brazilian team.[81] The CND turned down the proposal. Brazil's sports authorities rejected another proposed tour of British teams, spearheaded by the businessman José da Gama—who had earlier asked for permission to take a women's team to England—on the grounds that football was "incompatible" with women's nature. The CND described women's football as a "ridiculous" spectacle.[82] Da Gama sought to bring Nomad Ladies FC and Corinthians FC to play exhibition matches in Brazil. At least one of the British clubs, Corinthians, was accustomed to barnstorming in Latin America. In 1960 Corinthians—and a club called Northern Nomads—had played a four-team tournament in Venezuela.[83] Newspapers also briefly mentioned the effervescence of women's football in Sweden, which years later would become a premier destination for Brazil's most talented women players.

News of the first women's world championship in 1970 made it into the Brazilian papers, if only as small notices tucked away in the sports pages. Modest paragraphs here and there announced that Denmark had become the champions of women's football in Turin, defeating Italy 2–0. In third place figured Mexico, which had beaten England. The reports brought up the question of finances, and quoted the promoters' claims that profits had been "reasonable."[84] *O Globo* also briefly mentioned the tournament, giving its readers the barest of facts. Drawing from international news agency reports, *O Globo* informed its readers that the tournament had been organized in Italy and the teams attending included Italy, Austria, Switzerland, Mexico, England, France, Czechoslovakia, and Denmark.[85] Reports indicated that fans turned out in large numbers and that the teams had a high level of skill (with the exception of Austria and West Germany; Mexico defeated the former 9–0).[86] The media also reported that following the tournament, women's teams played throughout Italy.[87] The fact that the tournament was played in Italy surely raised eyebrows in Brazil, where Italian heritage was associated with whiteness and modernity.

The structure of the coverage of the women's world championship sheds light on the way that women's football was perceived in Brazil. Even as they were reporting on a world championship, Brazilian newspapers had a difficult time stepping out of the patriarchal norms about the sport and the women who participated. *Correio da Manhã*, for example, reassured its readers that the players did not exchange their shirts after the matches, at least not on the field.[88] The author highlighted at once that the sport did not transgress moral norms for women (stripping to bras to exchange shirts on the field) and that it represented the potential transgressing of sexual norms in suspected homosexual relationships among players (exchanging shirts in the privacy and intimacy of the dressing rooms). Thus, women's football was framed as sexualized—either with the titillation of the presumably male readership by suggesting female seminudity or the transgressive potential of the sport as a site of homosexuality. This sexualization was only magnified by comments that objectified players. One journalist mentioned that the masseur likely worked for free, presumably because it allowed him to touch women's legs at will.[89] *Correio da Manhã*'s coverage included photographs of the matches, including one of the "invincible" Mexican midfielder Cristina García.[90] Ideologies of ethnicity also played a role in framing conversations about the women's tournament and provided alluring titles, such as "Who will win in football: The blondes or the brunettes?"[91] In this case, the brunettes were Mexican and Italian, while the blondes were Danish and English. Importantly, the threat of the sport was brought home as well when local papers mentioned that a group of women in Rio was trying to organize weekly games in Aterro do Flamengo.[92]

The second world championship took place in 1971, in Mexico. According to one Brazilian newspaper, the tournament organizers asked Brazil to participate, but the Brazilian Football Confederation rejected the invitation.[93] Still, there were Brazilian supporters. *Diário da Noite*, for example, advocated that women take part in the tournament so that Brazil would not fall behind in developing any sports. The article mentioned that tournaments had been organized in various states of Brazil and that FIFA was changing its position on women's football, urging federations to take charge of the sport.[94] While Brazil did not send a team, the Brazilian media passively followed the planning and suggested that another Latin American team, perhaps Chile, Argentina, or Costa Rica, would participate.[95] In the end, Argentina sent a delegation and finished fourth. Some reports on the second championship criticized Mexican organizers for using starlets as prematch entertainment. The media criticized female athletes for lacking professionalism, despite the fact that they were by definition amateurs. One article called out Lena Schelke, the goalkeeper for Denmark, for taking pictures of the packed Estadio Azteca from midfield as her team was announced.[96] The article also complained that the English team took a day off from training in order to go sightseeing.[97] The reporting on these behaviors represented a persistent pattern of professional expectations placed on amateur players.

WOMEN'S FOOTBALL IN THE 1970S

To get a sense of Brazilian women's football in 1970, the example of Clube Atlético Indiano is illustrative. The club, which still exists today, was founded in 1930 on the outskirts of São Paulo in a newly settled middle-class neighborhood and named, if clumsily, after Gandhi and the Indian independence movement. Despite the ban on women's football, women of Indiano played the sport from the inception of the club and ignored the CND's ban.[98] Initially, the women's team organized charity matches, but by 1970 it had reorganized into a functional club, with over fifty women playing football. According to one newspaper article about the team, the women played with force and vigor, though their long nails could inflict serious injury. The article attempted to normalize women players by placing them into acceptable categories. That they grew their nails suggested femininity (and heterosexuality), as did reports that the team had a solid fan base, particularly among their boyfriends, husbands, and sons. The club's leader, Zuka, was the sister of José María Marin, a conservative politician and staunch supporter of the military government.[99] Zuka believed that concern over football affecting women's sexuality was nonsense. "True femininity," she told the reporter, "never disappears even in the heat of the contest." She suggested that players preferred "to clean the sweat from their faces than worry about their adversaries' shots."[100] Why would the military regime ignore the organization of women's football in some cases and persecute it in others? In the case of CA Indiano, Zuka's personal connections might have assuaged the government's fears about the demoralizing potential of the sport and reduced the chances of repression. Moreover, interviews with the players carefully toed the line of accepted feminine norms. And without concerted opposition, women's football thrived in a state of indifference.

The article on CA Indiano contained other insights into women's football culture. One woman stressed the joy and freedom she felt when playing, as if she could "forget everything."[101] But women's football also offered something else: a space where both men and

FIGURE 3.3. Women's football in Recife, Brazil, 1970s. Photo Narciso Lins. Courtesy of Museu do Futebol, Acervo da Cidade do Recife.

women could enjoy the game together. For example, Paulo Tanaka told the reporter that his wife attended his games to pick up pointers and that they were able to chat about what happened in matches in a friendly way.[102] The women's team included both married and single women, including pairs of mothers and daughters, which gave the team security. It was more difficult to attack the players as immoral since some were wives and mothers. The team benefitted from the support of the club board, which provided two fields with lights for the women to play on. The club also provided a coach, who said that women required special care because they were "sensitive and easily angered," and a masseuse.[103]

Not all women's efforts at organizing football were as well supported. That same year, the Rio newspaper *Correio da Manhã* published an article on what it claimed were "the only women playing football."[104] According to the article, a group in Aterro do Flamengo had organized four teams of futsal—a faster-paced, five-a-side derivative of football—which was not perceived to be as threatening as football itself. Though many of the players were quite talented, and one of the team's coaches had played for Brazil against Uruguay, they faced a good deal of opposition. The young women complained that "the world is against us" and noted that their mothers were the most opposed to their interest in the sport, fearing that their daughters would be harmed or "masculinized," which the players called "nonsense."[105] Perhaps Aterro do Flamengo, the largest public park in Rio, was too public of a site for women to fly under the radar.

In 1970 the club Santa Cruz, in Recife, created a women's football branch, and did so with CND permission. Although the military dictatorship was at its peak in terms of repression, the women took advantage of the brief window when Antonio Cordeiro was interim secretary of the CND.[106] Advocates believed that Brazil should model itself on the English women's league, which had adjusted the ball size and made other rule changes.[107] A supporter of women's football, Cordeiro granted permission for some women's institutions and matches. The request also received support from Alkindar Soares Filho, a local gynecologist who refuted claims that football caused breast cancer or was otherwise physically dangerous, as was popularly believed.[108] The new team was not without its detractors. *Correio da Manhã* surveyed Santa Cruz residents on the topic of women's football and found many opposed to the sport. The first interviewee, "Eneida," felt that women were too emotional to play football, while Irma Alvarez described the game as a "horrible thing." Although she had played three years of professional basketball in Argentina, Alvarez complained that football developed the wrong muscles and was an inappropriate sport for women. The wife of Mario Viana, a conservative radio journalist, said that her husband prohibited her from all sorts of things, including smoking, drinking, and playing football.[109] Pedro Valente, an ex–medical director of CR Vasco da Gama, concluded that women's physical state was incompatible with football. Still, a minority featured in the article expressed tepid support for women's football.[110] Claudio Marzo, a popular actor who played a football star, said he would love to see women play, mentioning his young daughter Alexandra's enthusiasm for a recent Brazil versus Peru match.[111]

THE END OF THE BAN

In 1970, while women's football grew all over the world, both in terms of organizing teams and developing the world championship, the CND reminded Brazilians that the ban on women's football remained in place. That year it sent a circular to all sporting authorities and institutions in the nation, informing them that regardless of shifting attitudes on women's football and the prohibition of it—which many had begun to treat as a joke—the CND intended to enforce the ban.[112] However threatening the circular, the CND did not increase its efforts to stymie futboleras. Throughout the 1970s, women's teams continued to play, and many garnered male support. The 1980s was the watershed decade for women's football, with teams gaining stability and momentum. By the time the final vestiges of the ban on women's football disappeared, in 1983, the sport had already experienced something of a boom.

One of the most notable features of the effervescence of women's football in the 1980s was its close relationship to the dynamic feminist movement in Brazil. Unlike in neighboring Argentina, in Brazil feminists made remarkable efforts to take up the banner of women's sports. Indeed, Brazilian feminists identified their exclusion from the national sport as an important part of their oppression. The magazine *Mulherio* took the lead in calling attention to the continued exclusion of women from football. It pointed to the fact that no woman served on the eleven-member council of sports, as well as to the profits that men gained from the sport.[113] Even after the ban was overturned, feminists noted that the governing bodies remained bastions of sexism. In 1982, feminists organized the first National Festival of Women in the Arts, in which football played a significant role.[114] The festival, held from September 3–12, featured international figures such as the singer Mercedes Sosa and the Bolivian activist Domitila Chúngara. The final event of the festival was a football match between women's select teams from Rio and São Paulo. The match was a preliminary to an official match between Corinthians and São Paulo, and was held at the Estádio de Morumbi. Even though it was highly irregular—the first half lasted eighteen minutes and the second half only ten—that it was officiated by the veteran referee Olten Aires de Abreu and played at an official stadium raised red flags with Brazilian sporting authorities.[115]

When the Confederação Brasileira de Futebol (Brazilian Football Confederation, CBF) found out about the festival, it attempted to stop the match. In late September 1982 the Federação Paulista de Futebol (Paulista Football Federation) sent a circular to member clubs explaining that the ban on women's football was still in force. Roseli Cordeiro Filardo, better known as Rose do Rio, took action. The circular stated that members could not allow games of affiliated clubs, could not cede fields or training grounds for women's matches, and could not permit women's matches to be played as preliminaries.[116] Rose had already organized another women's game to be played between select teams from Rio and São Paulo as a preliminary to a match pitting Palmeiras against Corinthians. When word of the memo reached the public, she hired two lawyers, who traveled to Brasília to meet with the minister of education and culture, Esther de Figueiredo Ferraz.[117] According to Rose, more than two hundred women's teams were already active in Rio.[118]

Among the clubs that formed and quickly gained momentum was the Paraná Esporte Clube of Curitiba, formed in the 1980–1981 season.[119] The team played eighteen games that season. In 1982, a select team of Futebol Amador de Luziânia played against the selection of Juniors de Brasília in Estádio Francisco das Chagas Rocha, near Brasília.[120] The match was well received, and one newspaper reported that women were no longer "mere spectators" for the people of Luziânia.[121] This sentiment was echoed by *Ultima Hora*, whose writer explained that women's football was losing its status as a spectacle and becoming respectable.[122]

The CND finally ended the ban on women's football with the publication of Deliberação do CND 01/83 on April 11, 1983. When the decision was made by the CND in 1983 to permit women's football, it referred to rules put in place by the Union of European Football Associations to govern the women's game. In Curitiba, *Diário da Tarde* published the decision in its entirety and commented that many women players and teams in Paraná had been awaiting

FIGURE 3.4. National Women's Festival, São Paulo, 1982. Courtesy of Museu do Futebol, Acervo Rose do Rio.

it.[123] Futboleras and their supporters organized a number of events in celebration. The neighborhood of Nova Orleans in Curitiba in particular had a vibrant community of futboleras. Jair de Lucca, president of the Associação Beneficente Esportiva Flamengo, or Flamengo (not to be confused with the Rio club of the same name), organized a women's championship in the city, which included the teams of Frigorífico Túlio, Vasquinho, Flamengo, Lojas Stival, Iguaçu, and Brasinha. This was the second tournament organized by Flamengo, and according to Lucca, the first had made a significant profit.[124]

Women athletes and their allies had pressured the Brazilian football institutions enough that 1983 saw what was incorrectly billed as the first women's football tournament in São Paulo, promoted by the municipal secretary of sports. In fact, the tournament highlighted the underground survival of the sport over the more than forty-year ban. When the tournament was announced, at least forty teams signed up for the cup.[125] More important, however, some sports institutions began to give tentative support to the women's game. In 1983, São

Paulo's Municipal Secretariat of Sports started a women's football school for girls fourteen years or older. The idea supposedly came from the municipal secretary, Andrade Figueira, though it was likely the ex-player Rose do Rio who came up with the plan. Rose was to run the school, which met twice a week in the afternoon at the Estádio Distrital da Aclimação.[126]

By 1984 there were 3,000 women's football teams scattered throughout the country and 1,615 players registered with the Football Federation of Rio de Janeiro. By 1987 the numbers would jump to 40,000 women and girls.[127] The most famous team was sponsored by Esporte Clube Radar of Copacabana, known simply as Radar. The club itself had been founded in 1931, but in 1981 the club president, the promoter Eurico Lira, organized a women's football section. Begun on the beaches of Rio de Janeiro, the team eventually borrowed practice fields inside the Casa de Marinheiro, a sports and recreation facility for Brazilian naval officers and their families. Given access to naval facilities at a time when the Brazilian Navy only hired women as secretaries, they practiced for five hours or more per day.[128] Radar toured Spain in 1982 and won every match, and their players were semiprofessional, although they earned only 60,000 cruzeiros per month.[129] Radar gained a good deal of press attention as women's football grew. From its founding in 1981 until 1983, the team went 76–0.[130] One of Radar's star players was an eighteen-year-old known as Pelezinha.[131] In many ways, her story was like that of many of her teammates. She began playing seriously at age ten with her brothers, two of whom played professionally, and then joined a futsal team at the Club Renascença in Andaraí at age thirteen before she started playing on the beach with Radar.[132] The club then gave her a job as a receptionist in order for her to be able to complete her education. Indeed, Radar sought to ensure that all of its players had job training and an education.[133]

Radar's players saw themselves as pioneers. Some, such as Cândida Levy Pestana, believed that they were the first women in Brazil to play football. The twenty-four-year-old Andréa Ribas explained that most of the players had begun playing as kids in the late 1960s and early 1970s, when it was considered even more taboo for girls to play. Rodrigues dos Santos, the Radar trainer, told the press he preferred coaching women because they played a purer form of the game.[134] Of course, players still had to contend with stereotypes about women footballers. Ribas defended herself against the male gaze by arguing that women were not masculinized by playing. Moreover, she called attention to the intelligence of the young women on her team.[135] Because of the belief that the game was too strenuous for women, in 1983 women still only played a seventy-minute game and used smaller balls. Radar, as a national and international women's football power, sought support from the state. The club's president, Eurico Lira, met with the secretary of tourism and sports, Trajano Ribeiro. Ribeiro helped Radar to secure patrons for the Brazilian championship.[136] Lira took the team to Spain, where they defeated a Madrid team 11–1. Radar also played in Castilha, Alicante. Lira called the Radar tour of Spain a historic moment, the first time that a South American women's team went to Europe to play.[137] The players were amazed at where football had taken them. Pelezinha remarked that she had "never dreamed that one day I would go to Europe," let alone as a football player.[138] The club planned to tour the United States in 1983, with stops in Tampa Bay, Orlando, Miami, Washington, and New York, for the first preliminaries of the American championship. Yet despite their success, Radar could not pay for their everyday expenses. In the end Banco BRJ sponsored the club, covering about half of its operating budget.[139]

In 1984, Eurico Lira of Radar and Fábio Lazzari, the sports promotion director of the São Paulo city sports department and the president of the Brazilian Association of Women's Football Clubs, claimed that João Havelange had become excited by the idea of a Brazilian national team.[140] Yet plans did not materialize. The player and activist Rose do Rio hoped to organize a national team in 1984, and to use the resources of Palmeiras as the team base.[141] The Palmeiras coach Oscar Paulino supported Rose's efforts, yet significant forces within football obstructed the project. While space was available at Parque Antárctica or Estádio Palestra Itália (where Palmeiras played, now known as Allianz Parque), the Palmeiras

FIGURE 3.5. Rose do Rio, the Brazilian football player and activist. Courtesy of Museu do Futebol, Acervo Rose do Rio.

director Hugo Palaia called women's football absurd and blocked the plan.[142] In the end, Lira used Radar players to compete and personally funded the Brazilian women's appearance at the 1988 FIFA Women's Invitation Tournament in China.[143]

Rose do Rio was among the most important advocates for women's football. Her playing career highlights the precarious nature of women's football in Brazil in the 1980s. She played for various clubs, including American Denim, Acisul, Radar, Beija Flor, and Roma EC. None of these clubs—with the exception of Radar—offered much in the way of stability. In 1986 she traveled to Spain, representing Brazil with Radar, and she continued her contributions to women's football after her playing career ended. She served as president of the Associação de Futebol Feminino do Estado do Rio de Janeiro (Women's Football Association of the State of Rio de Janeiro) and was the first woman to obtain a coaching license in Brazil, in 1989.[144] Rose mobilized support for candidates for directory positions, including the candidacy of Onaireves Nilo Rolim de Moura for president of the Paranaense Football Federation.[145] Rose was also friends with some male players and received key support from them. For example, Ubiraci Ferreira dos Santos went on the record with Rose calling for men to support women's football.[146] In 1985 Rose asked the former national team star Zico, at that time the secretary of sports, for help in developing women's football.[147] In large part, she was frustrated at every turn by leaders of sports associations.

Rose do Rio and Club Radar created the conditions for the first generation of professional women players. Among them, the star player Sisleide do Amor Lima, known as "Sissi," became one of the world's premier players in the 1980s and 1990s. Growing up in Esplenada, in the northeastern state of Bahia, Sissi began playing football while it was still prohibited. Her mother struggled to understand her daughter's passion for the game. In her adolescence Sissi fought for space on boys' teams, recalling, "They were mean to me. They told me that football was for men, not girls."[148] At fifteen years old, Sissi went to play for SC Bahia in the state capital of Salvador. The rumors of what Radar was starting in Rio excited her, and eventually she landed a spot on the first national team and subsequently played football for Radar, as well as futsal for Corinthians in São Paulo. She explained that the nature of professionalism under Lira's Radar meant the players did not receive salaries, but Radar provided their food, lodging, transportation, and clothing. Although Sissi remembered the excitement of that era, she also recognized the deep sexism and homophobia players faced. "There were consequences for being who you were," she explained. "The coaches told us to keep closeted, and if you were gay you might not be called up anymore because of that." When Sissi shaved her head, she faced outright hostility and could not play in the Paulista tournaments, because the federation required women to wear long hair. Despite winning the 1999 Women's World Cup Golden Boot award, Sissi's opportunities were bleak in Brazil. She found a home, alongside greats like Brandi Chastain, in the US professional league, the Women's United Soccer Association (WUSA), in the early 2000s, paving the way for the next generation of Brazilian futboleras.

The growth of women's football led to its increased, and considerably more positive, press coverage, again helped along by Andrade

Figueira. Television and radio began to broadcast women's games as well. For example, Rede Bandeirantes transmitted Isis POP's game against Internacional of Porto Alegre. Other women emerged alongside Rose do Rio as darlings of the sporting press, including Helen Cristiane of Isis POP. And, as with the 1930s era, the media helped grow the sport. Notices of matches often included information about where young women could play. One clipping from the press told women interested in the sport to head to Centro Educacional do Tatuapé.[149] Another article, from 1982, published a telephone number for interested players to call.[150] During interviews, players frequently mentioned the telephone calls between players and how important improvements in communication were to creating clubs. Still, gendered notions of women on the field persisted in some circles. A 1985 article about Radar in *Placar*, entitled "The Invincibles," detailed the strength of the team and their commitment to the game. At the same time, the article described some of the players, providing their weight, height, and bust size.[151]

The growth of women's football—and women's sports more generally—also led, in 1984, to the creation of the first sports section in a feminist magazine. That year *Mulherio* began a sports section that focused on women athletes, particularly those headed to the 1984 Olympic Games. The writers at *Mulherio* considered the rapid development of women's sports in the 1960s and 1970s as crucial to challenging pervasive medical concepts that categorized women's bodies as defective because they had a uterus, breasts that needed protection, and monthly menstruation.[152] The authors pointed to women athletes breaking records at the Olympic Games while menstruating, and highlighted the explosion of women athletes in Rio in 1984. In that year, there were nine thousand women swimmers in Rio, two hundred women registered with the Rio Judo Federation, and thirty women boxers. The magazine emphasized that football was the most sensitive sport, given that it had been prohibited by the CND until the year before. *Mulherio*'s sports page targeted a wide range of practices that disadvantaged women and perpetuated stereotypes about women's sports and women athletes. Physical education programs, for example, were singled out as being highly unequal.[153] So too sports journalism became a focus of feminist exposé. Female reporters, the magazine noted, were not allowed to enter locker rooms with the other journalists.[154] The magazine focused on how the lack of women's voices had contributed to the construction of a patriarchal media.

By 1984 women's football had developed enough that the former president of the CND, General Cesar Montagna, recognized the growth, diffusion, and benefits of women's football. Indeed, his own daughter played for the club Teresópolis. Although the daughters of Montagna and of Marcio Braga, the president of Flamengo, joined the ranks of women's football, according to contemporary press reports most female athletes came from poor families. The popular Pelezinha, the eighteen-year-old "queen of the beach," was from a working-class background.[155] Hortencia, who played for the Brazilian women's basketball team that won the bronze medal at the 1983 Pan-American Games, claimed that poor female athletes performed better because their parents had fewer preconceived notions and were more willing to let their daughters try to make a living outside "traditional" social norms. At the time, Hortencia received a good deal of press coverage and was forthcoming on feminist issues. Nonetheless, while defending women's right to play sports and criticizing those who opposed women athletes, she felt it necessary to defend her heterosexuality. She explicitly sought to change the standards of beauty in Brazil to allow for muscled women to be considered sexy, explaining that "no one believed I was a woman. The whole world called me a man." However, she continued, "it never humiliated me because I like myself the way I am."[156] She explained that men regularly tried to shame women basketball players by calling them *sapatões*, slang for lesbians. Yet while she criticized men for their sexist attitudes, she expressed a complex relationship with the stereotype. "I was never called that," she noted, "because I'm not."[157] In other words, she implied that there was justification for calling certain women lesbians, and it was derisive.

Not all female athletes embraced feminist ideas, even as the burgeoning feminist movement vocally supported them. Isabel, who played football for the Porto Alegre club Internacional, described the quest for gender equality as "silly."[158] This might have been part of a strategic discourse to increase support for women's sports, but it played a role in shaping the conversation around women's football. Isabel's attitude served as fodder for those who believed that women's football was a diversion rather than a serious sport. Sexism, of course, remained a part of women's football. From constant discussion in newspaper articles about the appearance and beauty of women players to hostility from fans, that much remained clear. Radar's Cenira, for example, recalled being told by a member of the crowd that she should be doing laundry and washing clothes instead of playing.[159] Further reinforcing the patriarchal stereotypes about women's football, the women's 1985 Taça Brasil de Futebol Feminino (Brazilian Women's Football Cup) included a "most beautiful player" award.[160]

Violence accompanied the women's sport—just as it did the men's—throughout the 1980s. According to some scholars, cheating and violence played a big role in the failure of women's football in the decade. In 1983, the Rio de Janeiro city football federation received forty-two lawsuits dealing with women's football. The clubs Radar and Bangú, in particular, were known for their violent rivalry. When Bangú lost to Radar in 1983, its manager, Castor de Andrade, beat up the referee Ricardo Ferreira.[161] Video from a 1983 match between Radar and Goiás shows the anger that the teams aimed toward the showman-referee Jorge Emiliano dos Santos, known as "Margarida."[162] When Margarida made a poor call against Goiás, the players physically threatened him until he left the field. In the film clip, one can see that both teams had passionate fans; male fans were also ready to fight the opponents. In 1989, the "folkloric" and "polemical" referee faced a two-year suspension for assaulting a player during the championship between Radar and Saad.[163] The referee punched a player named Elaine in the mouth after she complained about a penalty call. The CBF reviewed the case, but Elaine was displeased with the outcome and took the case to local court. When Elaine arrived in court she asked the judge for an apology from Margarida, which she eventually received.[164] The conflicts over women taking to the pitch involved physical confrontations, judicial actions, and personal arguments.

CONCLUSION

At first glance, it seems particularly strange that out of the most repressive institutional and cultural contexts, Brazilian women's football has dominated the continental game since the end of its prohibition. Once the continuity of teams in the provinces is taken into account, however, it starts to make more sense. In interviews with top Brazilian international players, almost all recalled playing on boys' teams until they traveled to Rio or São Paulo for Radar or the national team. The embedded nature of football in Brazilian society meant that women carved spaces for themselves to play in informal settings, in the neighborhood club, on the playground, and at family gatherings. Radar went on to win six Rio championships in the 1980s and to promote the sport internationally. Eurico Lira's club surprised everyone by placing third at the 1988 FIFA Women's Invitation Tournament in China. The 1991 World Cup team also relied almost exclusively on Radar players. Following that tournament, however, Lira faced charges of sexually harassing players and faded out of the women's football scene.

As the sport began to gain traction, however tenuous, backlash continued. Throughout the 1990s Brazilian women footballers were criticized as unfeminine. Some sought to highlight their femininity as a form of self-defense. Milene Domingues, who played for the national team and Corinthians, among other clubs, became—according to the *Jornal do Futebol*—the "symbol of women's football." With her blonde hair and blue eyes, she was the perfect pinup for those seeking to dispel notions of football as masculinizing. Domingues first signed up for Corinthians as a seventeen-year-old, and had already achieved fame for keeping a ball in the air over fifty-five thousand touches while juggling. An interview with the *Jornal do Futebol* presented Domingues to the broader Brazilian football world. She showed awareness of the struggle that women had gone through to play football in Brazil, and expressed the belief that the sport was on solid ground.[165] And in part, she was right. After all, Brazil had finished fourth in women's football at the 1996 and 2000 Olympic Games and finished second in 2004. The Canarinha, or women's national team, also won at the 2003 Pan-American Games. In other ways, however, she might have been overly optimistic. The fact that she was the symbol of Brazilian women's football suggests that the sport still needed to defend the heterosexuality of the players. That she was briefly married to Ronaldo further cemented her status. Domingues further raised the status of women's football in Brazil when she was transferred to Rayo Vallecano in Spain in 2002.[166]

The foregrounding of white, blonde Brazilian women players was only one way that the Brazilian media objectified women footballers. In 1995, *Placar*, the major Brazilian sports magazine, published an issue with women's football on the cover—only the cover was of four women in a hot pants version of the Brazilian national team uniform, pictured from behind. Rather than playing, they were touching each other suggestively. One woman was spanking another, while two others rubbed against each other. The cover text read: "The girls know how to play ball (and even exchange shirts after the game)."[167] The juxtaposition of the title's first and second halves, when combined with the image of sexualized women, only served to marginalize futboleras and to support men's fantasies rather than women's football.

Sadly, Brazilian women players have continued to face objectification, harassment, and neglect from the CBF and mainstream sports media throughout the 2000s. The federation consistently failed to provide necessary resources and training opportunities to the women's squad. In the 2011 World Cup, Brazil arrived in Germany with less time in camp than other squads and less time to acclimate. Fatigue and inadequate conditioning played a major role in the Canarinha's early exit. Three incidents since 2015 highlight how far the Brazilian sporting establishment still has to go. During the 2015 FIFA Women's World Cup, the CBF women's football director Marco Cunha applauded players for dressing more feminine. After the 2016 Olympic Games in Rio, when the Brazilian women had captured the attention of the nation like never before, playing to sold-out stadiums and rivaling the men's team in popularity, the CBF announced cuts to the women's program. And in 2017 Brazil fired its first woman head coach, Emily da Cunha Lima, after less than a year on the job. Her dismissal appeared to be a breaking point for many players: five senior players retired, and top stars wrote an open letter to the CBF demanding change. The pressure to market themselves, or to render women's football marketable, has resulted in the "femming up" of the national team, as well as the "whitening" and the "closeting" of players. Whereas in the late 1980s, the Brazilian national team fielded women with short hair, without makeup, and from diverse racial backgrounds, in the 2010s, the team had hardly any Afro-Brazilian players, and nearly all of the players sported long ponytails. None identified openly as gay. When we interviewed two former Radar and national team players, Sissi and Taffarel, they expressed astonishment that the situation for women's football in Brazil had not improved significantly since the 1980s.[168] Even with unprecedented fame, the Brazilian star Marta Vieira da Silva, better known simply as Marta, earned just about $45,000 with the Orlando Pride, while her counterpart with Orlando City SC, Kaká, pulled in $6.5 million. Thus, the field of Brazilian football, domestically and abroad, has continued to be awash in sexism.

Throughout Latin America in the twentieth century, women's involvement in football ran the gamut from acting as godmothers of clubs, to running fan clubs, to writing groundbreaking sports journalism. More than anything, though, women's involvement included playing the game. At every turn, men's football institutions, governments, and the media sought to suppress the sport. Perhaps nowhere were these efforts more explicit, and on the surface more effective, than in Brazil. Public health experts railed against the sport, claiming that it was too rough and thus unnatural for feminine harmony. Women whose bodies failed to develop softness and suppleness could not fulfill their "primordial duty" of motherhood. Thus, they risked the "extinction of their descendants," and by extension, the nation.[169]

Despite the institutional efforts to keep them out of the football world, women found a way to be engaged in the game. Women like

Elisa Alves do Nascimento and Dulce Rosalina worked their way to the top of fan organizations and wielded power and commanded respect. Semíramis Alves Teixeira, for her part, showed Brazil that women could conduct professional interviews and speak intelligently about football. However, the general public quickly forgot these pioneers. Players and supporters of women's football, too, played in the face of official sanction and threats. From the moment that the CND was formed and banned women from playing football, women ignored the ban. Moreover, they actively and knowingly resisted the prohibition. They wrote letters challenging the patriarchal attitudes of so-called experts, they petitioned the CND to change its decision on women's football, and, just as important, they continued to play. Realizing that they would receive little in the way of support from male-dominated institutions, women acted themselves. They established teams, organized games, and found allies willing to aid the sport.

Ultimately, the work of women football players like Rose do Rio and the associations she helped to create in São Paulo and Rio laid the groundwork for Brazil's participation in world football in the 1990s. That Brazil was able to build a competitive national team a mere decade after the prohibition on women's football was lifted highlights the fact that the ban was never effective in the first place. The efforts of generations of women who played illicitly eventually resulted in the first stable local, regional, and national women's associations. In the early 1980s, the relationship of futboleras to the feminist movement contributed to the discussion of women's rights in Brazil at the critical moment of democratization. Moreover, feminist leaders created an important set of arguments that placed sports within the broader claims for gender equality.

4

PHYSICAL EDUCATION AND WOMEN'S SPORTS IN MEXICO AND CENTRAL AMERICA

WHEREAS IN ARGENTINA AND CHILE THE DEMAND FOR physical education came from low-level bureaucrats, in Mexico and Central America governments played a heavier hand in shaping girls' exercise in schools. At the same time, however, advocates of women's sports also encountered stronger resistance, ranging from objections of conservative parents to congressional inquiries. While different political forces competed to control curricula in the Southern Cone, in Mexico the Institutional Revolutionary Party (PRI) and its predecessors, the National Revolutionary Party (PRN) and the Mexican Revolutionary Party (PRM), created a hegemonic apparatus that extended into the countryside. Mexican state officials understood sports, as did the Costa Rican governments of the midcentury, as an important diplomatic tool. They pioneered spectacle and sports events throughout the twentieth century. As revolutionary rhetoric of democracy began to dominate Mexican politics, there was an important reevaluation of the privileging of European culture. Still, however integrative the organizers hoped these events would be, in the end they still emphasized European sporting activities. This chapter attempts to balance a sensitive consideration of local historical conditions, while also connecting and comparing different national contexts.

Hand in hand with the changes sweeping Latin American economic and political systems in the late nineteenth and early twentieth centuries, including urbanization, immigration, and the development of export industries, came debates about proper gender roles. The new economic and social realities of many Latin American nations demanded women be active in the workforce simply for families to survive. Yet much of the drive for change came neither from society at large nor from the logic of capitalist development, but from women themselves. Aware of the possibilities afforded them by a more open political and social system, women began to advocate for increased rights.

At the same time, as discussed in relation to Argentina, Brazil, and Chile, the image of the ideal woman in Latin America shifted with the tenor of the times. For many in the region, the traditional roles of women—living a sheltered, more or less homebound existence—were outdated. In their place appeared new role models for "modern girls" or "new women." These were supposed to be more partners for men than mere servants, able to hold male interest as much for their intellect and engagement as for their appearance. To that end, the education of women and girls became an important element of creating modern citizens. Even for those who saw the rise of women working outside the home as a threat and who hewed to more "traditional" values, educating girls was seen as critical. But education was more than formal schooling (and indeed, across the region, advances in education for girls progressed unevenly). Rather, it included in an equally important role what we might call "informal education": reading newspapers and magazines, going to movies, attending sporting events, and being exposed, in other words, to a range of life outside the confines of the home. These experiences were, in the eyes of supporters of the new woman, part and parcel of improving women's happiness and the national health.

State officials, journalists, and other public figures who attempted to consolidate national identities in the early twentieth century spotlighted women's roles as mothers. To raise healthy, active citizens, women needed to be both educated and healthy themselves. Influenced by then-popular Social Darwinist ideas of race and evolution, the eugenic movement, and "scientific" racism, Latin Americans looked for ways to "improve" their "race," including the recruitment of immigrants from Europe, but also the redefinition of motherhood and femininity. They used eugenic ideas, which argued that selective breeding could create a stronger, more intelligent, and, important for national elites, whiter population. As mothers and care-givers, women formed the linchpin of these policies. No longer could they be confined to the home and sheltered from the realities of the world. To the contrary, women were expected to be educated and able to pass on to their sons and daughters the national values and norms.

Even before the rise of Porfirio Díaz in 1876, liberals in Mexico viewed the public education system as a way to modernize the nation, secularize society, and "civilize" its people. Mandatory primary education was suggested as early as 1867, when Mexico City made it obligatory. Roughly half of Mexican states adopted legal statutes requiring it by 1875. According to José Díaz Covarrubias, the minister of justice and public instruction from 1872 to 1876, the view of education as a vehicle for modernity reached back as far as the administration of Benito Juárez. As minister of education, Díaz Covarrubias outlined a detailed educational program in efforts to create modern Mexican citizens. His plan included physics, chemistry, mathematics, grammar, and, importantly, "hygienic gymnastics" for both boys and girls. In order to create well-educated youth, he argued, it was important to gain the "fundamental principles" of all subjects rather than to study one thing in isolation.[1] The goal of gymnastics was not to create "acrobats [*funámbulo*] and athletes," but rather "to develop . . . moderately, different parts of the body." Gymnastics, as Díaz Covarrubias saw it, consisted in "bodily movements regulated by strength and the use of muscles, taking advantage of the mechanical conditions of the human body."[2] Marching, jumping, running—all of these were to be practiced in moderation in order to "improve the race."[3] That other Latin American nations (which Díaz Covarrubias did not name) and much of Europe were using these techniques made the practice all the more important for "children and youth of both sexes."[4]

In this regard, the physical education landscape in Mexico prior to the revolution was not markedly different from that of Argentina, Brazil, or Chile. Concerns over the eugenic health of the nation and women's beauty surfaced in debates about women's physical activity. Public health experts and physical education teachers suggested gymnastics, swimming, and even baseball as ways to create women who were healthy but whose physical activity did not compromise their feminine beauty. The focus of physical education, and physical culture more broadly, was to maintain, according to Monica Chávez Gónzalez, the "differentiation and inequality between genders."[5] This attention to maintaining gender differences meant that physical education factored in the social uses of male and female bodies. Or, put more plainly by Porfirian thinkers in the education journal *La Enseñanza Primaria*, physical education such as gymnastics should "correspond exactly to [women's] delicate and fragile constitutions," as well as their "complex physiological functions."[6] Gender-specific physical education, in other words, was the norm.

Still, under the Porfiriato, the development of an educational system received crucial support, even if it remained strikingly underfunded in the countryside. Justo Sierra, Porfirio Díaz's secretary of education from 1905 to 1911, sought to model the Mexican system after that of France, believing it to be the ideal system for a modern republic. Though it would not be until after the Mexican Revolution that physical education became a part of the state educational curriculum, interest in physical culture gripped the country during the Porfiriato as well. The elite of Mexico City and larger towns in the central valley began riding bicycles, while baseball had entered the northern border region and the Yucatán Peninsula by the late 1800s. In other words, sports and physical education spread organically around the country. The institutional manifestation of the government's enthusiasm for gymnastics and modernity occurred in the Escuela Nacional Preparatoria (National Preparatory High School) and the Heroico Colegio Militar (Heroic Military College), as well as in elite private clubs such as the Porfirio Díaz Central Circle of Mexican Gymnastics. Through these institutions, Porfirian officials hoped to create a scientific physical culture that would create more racially fit men. At the grassroots level, police intervened in sports at an unprecedented level, regulating the use of the bicycle and shutting down boxing matches.[7]

The tie between modern life and physical culture came from both private institutions and the state. The Young Men's Christian

Association (YMCA) opened its first branch in Mexico City in 1902, ostensibly for the American community there.[8] By 1904 the Mexican YMCA had two branches in Mexico City, as well as one in Monterrey. A Chihuahua branch would open in 1907, and by the outbreak of the revolution, Tampico also boasted a YMCA. The YMCA made the link between organized physical activity, individual development, and national progress explicit, advertising programs that would help young men gain life skills. While there is little mention of women's activities in the YMCA, they did exist. For example, a 1910 excursion to Xochimilco featured races for boys and girls, as well as "indoor baseball for everyone."[9] But the YMCA appears to have had little influence in rural Mexico, at least until after the Mexican Revolution.

Beginning in the 1920s and continuing through the 1940s, successive governments sought to connect themselves to sports and physical education. With the former, they attempted to harness popular culture to their own ends. With the latter, they tried to engineer that culture and Mexican society more broadly. Although important distinctions separate the revolutionary and postrevolutionary governments of Venustiano Carranza (1917–1920), Álvaro Obregón (1920–1924), Plutarco Elías Calles (1924–1928), and Lázaro Cárdenas (1934–1940), all constructed stadiums, organized sporting events, and publicly connected themselves to sports, particularly baseball and football.

These sports had developed independent of state support or stimulus. In the case of baseball, the sport arrived in the Yucatán Peninsula with henequen production in the late 1800s and spread throughout the northern border territories. Football, on the other hand, developed as it did in much of the region—in elite sports clubs and in manufacturing towns. The Reforma Athletic Club was among the first places to see football played. The sport also caught on rapidly with miners in Pachuca and Real del Monte after being introduced by English engineers. Elsewhere in Mexico's central valley, textile workers and management in Orizaba formed a team at the beginning of the twentieth century.[10] Even before the revolution, in other words, football was popular, though by no means the hegemonic sport, in much of Mexico. The postrevolutionary state did support organized team sports such as baseball and football, however, lending legitimacy to the practices of the people and providing important official backing to them. In 1919, for example, President Venustiano Carranza granted an import tax exemption to all sporting goods entering the country. Two years later, President Álvaro Obregón provided federal funds for a football tournament to celebrate the centennial of Mexican independence in 1921, and gave the ceremonial first kick for the event. He also initiated a physical education regimen on all army bases in the country.[11] Obregón mandated that football be part of the curriculum, which had a twofold effect. On the one hand, it would create a sense of teamwork and camaraderie among the troops. On the other, it helped diffuse sports and physical education around the country—particularly to rural and heavily indigenous areas, which the government sought to homogenize. Mexican presidents began to attend sporting events such as football matches and baseball games on a regular basis, showing their approval for sports. The Copa Eliminatoria, the domestic football championship, renamed the Copa Lázaro Cárdenas in 1932, when the governor of Michoacán and future president donated a new trophy, pitted teams from around the country against each other. The cup brought players from different regions into contact with one another on a regular basis.[12] The state and national governments did not exclusively support football. In the physical education curricula, as well as in the cultural missions that sought to modernize the countryside, basketball, baseball, and volleyball received equal impetus. Sports became "a metaphor for the country's vitality and potential."[13]

POSTREVOLUTIONARY MEXICAN PHYSICAL EDUCATION

In Mexico, the revolution from 1910 to 1920 left a society with deep divisions between rural and urban, modern and traditional. Successive revolutionary governments sought to bridge these divides in a variety of ways, including through educational programs meant to "civilize" the rural and mostly indigenous populations, in order for them to conform to the goals of the modernizing state. To become active citizens in the "new" Mexico meant a focus on individual development, particularly adopting the dietary, physical, dress, and cultural habits of Europeans. These ideas were often modified and adapted to fit the needs of local politicians and daily lives of Mexicans. While the state sought to bring education to rural areas, in many ways rural Mexico came to the capital. Beginning in 1850, rural Mexicans began moving to Mexico City in ever larger numbers, so that by 1900 the city's population had doubled to 500,000, with fully 43 percent of that number being migrants.[14] By the start of the revolution the population of the city grew to 720,000, and over the next ten years another 200,000 would move to the Federal District as the population approached one million. The majority of these migrants were women. Starting in the 1910s and continuing throughout the course of the revolution, women from rural areas moved to the capital, believing it to be a safer alternative to life in the countryside. Such was the level of migration that by 1930, roughly 55 percent of the city's population was women.[15] Even with this migration, however, Mexico's population remained predominantly rural, which posed a challenge for the new government.

In the views of postrevolutionary state crafters, men and women, particularly those in rural areas, needed training in new modes of citizenship. Sports and spectacle were one way to co-opt preexisting pastimes to state-oriented ends, but education, both physical and intellectual, became a crucial tool in state efforts to create new, modern Mexicans. Starting with Álvaro Obregón's Secretaría de Educación Pública (Secretariat of Public Education, SEP) and its minister of education, José Vasconcelos, successive Mexican governments implemented physical education programs aimed at modernizing the nation. The national government took responsibility for diffusing education to the countryside, creating a system of rural schools, which it provided with technical training and support. Reception of these efforts in the countryside was mixed at best, as evidenced by the Cristero Rebellion in 1926.[16] The rebellion, in part a response to Plutarco Elías Calles's efforts to intensify the state's incursion into the countryside through education at the expense of the Church, would cost nearly one hundred thousand lives. It directly affected relations between many rural communities and the representatives of the SEP—be they teachers or members of cultural missions.[17] The Cristeros' antipathy for the teachers and their concern over state efforts to roll back the importance of the Church likely carried over to physical education as well, especially curricula that called for girls' and coed programs.

Nevertheless, the Mexican state persisted in its plans for rural schools, seeing an "urgent necessity to create a new race; strong, optimistic."[18] For the editors of *Educación Física*, there was only one "infallible way to attain this patriotic proposition: physical education."[19] This goal required extensive efforts at erasing ethnic difference and expunging indigenous roots, which the state believed could be done through the implantation of advanced educational and physical education programs, among other methods. Whereas the Chilean state physical education programs served elite public institutions first and foremost, the Mexican state showed a greater interest in bringing the state to the countryside in efforts to diffuse state power down to the local level. According to Keith Brewster, "mass sports formed part of a broader educational initiative designed to break down the insularity of the provinces and convert" the indigenous population into "useful members of society."[20]

The rural school acted as the nexus of local needs, daily routines, and state programs. Beginning in the 1920s, the revolutionary administrations of Álvaro Obregón and Plutarco Elías Calles strove to extend state authority into the far corners of the country. While Mary Kay Vaughan rightly suggests that the Mexican countryside was not as bereft of schools as the revolutionary government suggested at the time, nevertheless the state in the 1920s expanded opportunities exponentially.[21] Under Obregón, the SEP created a robust structure for education, including rural schools throughout the countryside. Elías Calles placed greater emphasis on constructing schools in the countryside. By 1928, for example, there were over 4,800 rural teachers spread throughout the country.[22] The national government took over administration of rural schools from the Mexican states and at the same time sought to disentangle the Church from education altogether.

As the main representatives of the state in the countryside, rural teachers were essential to SEP plans.[23] According to the minister of education, J. M. Puig Casauranc, teachers' "social action" would "overflow . . . from the poor little school and reaches the whole community, moving villagers to work for the collective good."[24] Social solidarity, glued by common culture and leisure such as sports, took on new importance in the late 1920s. The Mexican state augmented rural education by creating regional normal schools. Instead of having to travel to Mexico City for teacher training, students learned basic educational theory and practice in these rural normal schools. These teacher training facilities inculcated future teachers with the correct pedagogical and political messages. As part of the curricula, both female and male rural teachers received training in instruction on sports and physical education. Gender segregation in these lessons varied from place to place. For example, the rural normal school in Rioverde, San Luis Potosí, had no sports facilities when it was established. Future teachers had to level the land where barley fields and kilns once were in order to build basketball, volleyball, and tennis courts. Students did not form teams, preferring to practice all sports equally, and photographs show that these sports activities were mixed boys and girls. By contrast, in Tixtla, Guerrero, teams appear to have been gender segregated. Perhaps this was due to the opposition that the normal school faced from parents. Initially, many families refused to let their daughters go to classes with boys.[25]

Along with rural schools and regional normal schools, the SEP sent cultural missions around the country to reach further into Mexican society. Beginning in 1926, cultural missions traveled around the country, staying in rural villages for three weeks at a time in attempts to bring the state to the people. The missions worked with rural teachers, often lacking in training and resources, to provide assistance in pedagogy and in how to assess local educational needs.[26] The cultural missions also established local musical groups, crafts collectives, and sporting organizations, all of which were to be supported by local teachers when the missions left. While the explicit goal of the missions was to regularize teaching in rural Mexico, the underlying aims revolved around the desire to improve Mexico's "racial" stock, bring modern ideas of hygiene and family to the largely indigenous population, and increase the rural citizenry's attachment to the revolutionary state. For this task, women were crucial. And while the cultural missions, and rural schools more broadly, had elements of liberation in them, there were limits to what they could—or wanted—to do. As Jocelyn Olcott points out, while many within Mexican educational institutions sought radical change, upsetting the patriarchy proved difficult.[27] And so in many ways cultural missions also worked to reaffirm gender norms: they helped to establish communal kitchens, developed sewing workshops, and taught home economics classes as a way to both modernize Mexican women and keep them in their traditional roles. A physical education instructor traveled with each cultural mission, as physical well-being was considered a crucial part of uplifting the rural populations, and sports were a way of building modern citizens and communities.

According to Rafael Ramírez, the director of cultural missions in 1927, the role of the physical education teacher was "threefold." First, physical education instructors were charged with instructing rural teachers in sports, gymnastics, and games in order to create a "balance with the intellectual activities of the teachers," as well as to give them the skills they needed to introduce the activities to students. As a part of this role they were also supposed to organize rural sporting festivals. Second, physical education instructors were charged with "systematically" teaching sports, games, and gymnastics to students, both for their own education and as demonstrations of correct methods for the communities' permanent teachers. Finally, within the community the cultural missions established "sports organizations." The cultural missions trained teachers in physical education instruction methods and created sports clubs that were expected to carry on through local impetus.[28]

Instructions for community activities explicitly delineated activities "with men" and "with women," though no clarification on activities was provided.[29] To this end, physical education professors underwent refresher trainings in January 1927, not only on sports and gymnastics (calisthenic, rhythmic, and aesthetic) but also on physiology and hygiene.[30] In 1928 they received two hours of training per week, over four weeks, on football and basketball.[31] And the importance of physical education for the cultural missions and rural schools could not have been more explicitly expressed. The cultural missions were "creating habits of physical culture through games, gymnastics, dancing, singing, and sports" as part of the state's public health and hygiene efforts. Once the cultural mission left, the expectation was that the rural teachers would build on the work done by the mission. Teachers would help to establish athletic clubs for men, while women and women teachers would "practice rhythmic gymnastics." They would all feel part of the same movement toward improving public health, however, by wearing the same uniforms.[32]

Two aspects are striking when examining the regional reports of the cultural missions. The vast majority of rural teachers, the targets of training for the cultural missions and the rural normal schools, were women. Moreover, girls comprised at least half of members of the rural sports clubs founded by cultural mission programs. An examination of the cultural mission records from the late 1920s demonstrates that girls and women in rural areas participated in sports in large numbers. In Sonora, for example, fifty-five of sixty teachers were women.[33] Many sports clubs established by rural cultural missions appear to have been mixed gender, while others were all girls. In Sinaloa, Club Deportivo Anahuac, in Escuinapa, comprised roughly twenty people, all of whom (from the very grainy picture) appear to be girls. Photos of Club Deportivo Fenochio, in Magdalena, on the other hand, show twelve boys and fifteen girls. The club appears in two separate pictures, one of boys in tank tops and shirts, the other of girls in the de rigueur physical education attire: bloomers, white shirts, and ties. That the youth were segregated by gender suggests that they participated in different events. Their neighbors from Magdalena, Club Deportivo Femenil Excelsior, comprised twelve girls. There, the mission organized sports clubs, improved sports fields, and created facilities for tennis, volleyball, basketball, and baseball for boys and girls.[34] Other missions clearly helped to organize girls into athletic teams, as was the case in

Chihuahua and San Luis Potosí.[35] In Nayarit, the sports learned by local rural educators included those already mentioned, but also horseback riding, swimming, and football.[36]

Throughout Mexico, in all of the villages that the cultural missions visited, state officials sought to explain "the importance of Physical Education for children and youth," as well as the value of sports for the "evolution" and "awakening of ideals" among the population. At the same time, the Mexican government expressed the hope that physical education and sports would impart "moral customs" and the belief that they were "a sure agent of culture and moralization."[37] In the 1930s, educational experts in the SEP also sought to use sports to encourage sobriety of campesinos. Moreover, sports would ingrain the rural peasants with discipline and just the right amount of competitiveness.[38] The Mexican government sought to create more engaged and active citizenship, inculcated with the values of revolutionary Mexico. To that end, it sought a literate public, aware of its rights and attuned to its role as economic producers. Still, what the cultural missions meant by "morals" and "ideals" was so abstract that the idea evaded definitive descriptions. Clearly, through sports the missions sought to encourage temperance, physical stamina, and secularism. And women, according to many cultural missionaries, were the surest agents of social change. Women's physical education and physical culture were crucial for Mexico's development, according to Caterina Vesta Sturges, a feminist and cultural missionary. For Vesta Sturges, women were "called urgently to take part" in the regeneration of Mexico. As the caretakers of Mexico's future generations, the importance of mothers, and modern motherhood, could not be overstated. In order to integrate rural women into modern life, she argued, women needed to have opportunities for vibrant "recreation and social life," the benefits of which "favored physical and spiritual well-being." These activities would keep women from an "empty life" that would lead to "coquetry and malice" and distract them from their national duty.[39] The underscoring of coquetry reflected the policing of rural women's sexuality, a task the state readily assumed from the Catholic Church. In practice, both institutions increased their control over women's

bodies. Physical education molded girls' and young women's movements, their physical habits. To extend the limbs, to jump, to run in
public spaces must have felt liberating for many girls. Furthermore,
the mixed-gender structure of many clubs and physical education
activities would have been a radical departure from the norm for
much of rural Mexico.

Despite lofty state rhetoric, local communities needed persuasion
to convince them that girls needed physical education. In Tixtla,
for example, where physical education had gone "completely un-
attended," Rodolfo Bonilla, the head of the rural normal school,
initially encountered problems with the young women in the class.
Bonilla insisted that for physical education classes the students wear
special clothes, which were "considered an attack on [feminine] deli-
cateness." With some cajoling, including inviting mothers to observe
the class, Bonilla was able to convince the young women to wear
the gym uniforms. He also reported that he was very successful in
raising interest among girls and young women for physical fitness
and sports. Of the six basketball teams organized by the normal
school, two of them were teams of "señoritas." While there is no evidence that women played football, it is likely that they were at least
watching matches and kicking a ball with friends. There is evidence
that other nearby regional normal schools established women's basketball as well. Bonilla reported that the Tixtla women defeated the
corresponding team from Chilpancingo.[40] Still, while the state moved
to create new women, it did not want to go too far to overturn patriarchal norms. It is worth recalling the "War on the Pelonas" that
conservative young men waged in Mexico City at the same time.
The hairstyles, clothing, and habits of the "flapper" provoked some
young men to violence in order to put women back in their places.[41]
In the countryside as well, the conservatism of the peasantry had
not been wiped out by the suppression of the Cristero Rebellion, so
even with increased physical education, a strong social order based
on strict gender roles remained.

The impact of the rural normal schools and the cultural missions
that supported them was noted by many, including foreign visi-
tors. Elizabeth Curtiss, the general secretary of the Young Women's

Christian Association (YWCA), noted the effectiveness of the Mexican state's efforts to educate the rural population. "Never in all my travels," she wrote, "have I seen such efficacious constructive work in rural populations." Though she thought that the cultural missions should lengthen their stays (generally three weeks per community), she "hoped that no future circumstances" would "impede . . . the growth of this splendid program."[42] For the Mexican Jovita Boone de Cortina, president of the public health committee of the National Council of Women, the introduction of sports, such as basketball, gymnastics, and volleyball, was a "marvelous success."[43] Not everyone, however, believed team sports were optimal for girls. Luís F. Obregón, a physical education professor and a member of the SEP cultural missions, advocated a curriculum for girls' physical education limited to rhythmic gymnastics and "simple rhythmic dances." For boys and young men, on the other hand, Obregón recommended "calisthenic gymnastics, the formation of pyramids, and the initiation of athletic competition."[44]

This type of top-down organization in the countryside continued through the 1930s. Even with the work of the cultural missions and rural normal schools, the national government in Mexico City confronted challenges diffusing physical education in the countryside. In 1935, the government of Nuevo León published the *Manual de educación física* (Manual of physical education), by Miguel J. Ciriza, for the federal schools of the state. While the creation of a manual might not suggest the lack of diffusion, the very basic instructions of what each class would need, and how to instruct courses, suggests that physical education had not been fully embraced in the countryside. Ciriza had worked with the rural teachers of Nuevo León for two years in order to understand the problems they faced in implementing physical education programs, and the manual was an effort to help institutionalize practices. That the manual was published the year after Lázaro Cárdenas's inauguration might have had something to do with its goals. Among them, Ciriza noted that sports helped to "develop a clear sense of class consciousness," and that it should help fight "against fanaticism and religious prejudice."[45]

The manual offered detailed activity plans for physical education teachers, organized by age group, as well as descriptions of the age-appropriate activities. For "boys and girls" aged six to ten, Ciriza's plan included marches and children's games.[46] For children aged ten to twelve, Ciriza recommended teachers add dances, track-and-field activities, basic sports skills, and gymnastics. For track and field, the manual advised thirty-meter sprint, high jump, standing long jump, and four-by-thirty-meter relay. Introduction to sports included schoolyard baseball and volleyball.[47] The manual recommended increasingly challenging and complex versions of these activities for older boys and girls.[48] What is perhaps most surprising about Ciriza's manual is that even after the introduction of football as a sport for older children, he made no distinction as to what sports should be played by which gender. This could be read one of two ways. Either he failed to make these distinctions because he assumed that physical education teachers would already know that certain activities were not meant for girls and young women, or he saw no need to limit female physical education.[49] Indeed, in only one place in the manual did Ciriza make special mention of women and girls.

Toward the end of the publication, Ciriza laid out the relationship between rural schools and the development of peasant sports centers. These centers formed crucial support mechanisms for the physical education teachers in rural areas. The centers were the idea of the Departamento de Enseñanza Rural y Primaria Foránea (Department of Rural and Foreigner [Ethnic Outsider] Instruction) and were to be organized by local physical education teachers and constructed by local populations. The goal of the centers, according to the statutes created by the department, was "to foment and organize the practice of sports among peasant children, youth, and adults (men and women)."[50] That women were explicitly included suggests the state's interest in instilling in rural populations some sense of the necessity for women's physical activity. More than just noting the importance of female participation, however, the rural sports centers were charged with working to "interest and create enthusiasm [for sports] among women and girls." This was to be done in part by choosing "activities that are easy, attractive, and interesting to the female sex, and in part through a public education campaign, in "homes and among families in general in the towns," about the benefits of physical activity.[51] While the method for increasing women's participation in sports activities was patronizing, there was no mention of sports being inappropriate for Mexican women to play. It also belied the assumption that girls and women needed to be convinced and had no tradition of participating in sports activities. Still, the lack of gender segregation marked Mexico out as slightly different from its regional neighbors. This might have been due to the revolutionary government's continued efforts to reshape rural Mexico and root out vestiges of Catholic conservatism, but it remains an important aspect of Mexican physical education programming.

Nevertheless, women were not encouraged to play football by sporting institutions around the nation. They were pushed into other, supposedly less physical, sports such as volleyball and basketball. And Mexico would become a regional leader in these sports played by women, playing in circuits that included the southwestern United States. In the region of Tecamachalco, according to Mary Kay Vaughan, "the height of entertainment was the basketball game." Vaughan argued that although sports "celebrated male physical prowess and dominance," it did not overlap precisely with the state's efforts to "promote hygiene, sobriety, and productivity."[52] It is not far-fetched to imagine that women's enthusiastic embrace of basketball and exclusion from football increased the latter's popularity among men.

Another reading of the lack of gender specification in the manual is possible. Earlier texts focusing on physical education in Mexico differentiated between sports for girls and sports for boys, including the official *Plan de estudios de la escuela de educación física* (Plan of studies for the physical education school), which outlined the educational program for physical education teachers. The plan required courses in biology, English, physics, and ethics, alongside practical courses in how to teach various sports. The sports and physical activities covered included football, baseball, camping, calisthenics, gymnastics, and swimming, among others. While there did not appear to be any limitation on who might teach particular subjects, there was no gray area when it came to appropriate activities for students. After listing all of the curricula of the future students, the plan noted that "the practice of rhythmic [gymnastics] and dance will be especially for girls," and "baseball, apparatus, football, boxing, fighting, and handball will be specifically for boys."[53] In the following year, the revised plan contained a number of changes to the curricula, but the restrictions on girls playing baseball, football, and the other sports remained.[54]

The Mexican state further reinforced the work of the cultural missions and the physical education school through sporting institutions. There, too, administrators believed that the correct behavior of girls and young women was a linchpin in the evolution of Mexico and the Mexican people. In institutional terms, the establishment of the Confederación Deportiva Mexicana (Mexican Confederation of Sports, CODEME) in 1932 signaled Mexico's focus on sports and physical education as a development model for reforming Mexican society.[55] As Keith Brewster has noted, sports, "such as baseball and basketball," came to be seen as a "panacea for the political, social, and ethnic division that still beset the nation."[56] State agencies promoted team sports in tandem with an expanded physical education apparatus. The same year that CODEME was formed, the government also created the Consejo Nacional de Educación Física (National Council on Physical Education) in order to develop physical education programs throughout the country as a way to reach "the ideal patria."[57] Indeed, so important was the national council that among its members were representatives of all major ministries. The president's office, as well as the ministries of defense, foreign relations, health, and education all had seats on the council. The body was tasked with a series of responsibilities, among which were to help create the statutes that would govern all sports around the nation, to "choose the methods for teaching sports," and to "make all necessary efforts, both within and outside of government, to obtain the greatest success in sporting activities throughout the country."[58]

CODEME was a top-down organization, even if its programs prioritized local and grassroots athletics. Centralizing sports was seen as a way to "produce athletes who could bring honor to the nation and more importantly help to combat" vices that afflicted the country.[59] Loosely organized as a part of CODEME, the Departamento Autónomo de Educación Física (Autonomous Department of Physical Education) published the monthly journal *Educación Física* beginning in 1936. The journal heralded the importance of physical education for the broader health of the nation. There was scant, if suggestive, mention of women's sports in its pages, though its pages were full of images of female athletes. The Mexican physical education community sought to justify its existence through articles extolling the benefits of gymnastics and other activities that promoted a sound body and sound mind. Mexico, one anonymous author wrote in 1938, "needs healthy men with moral qualities like honor, mutual cooperation . . . etc." The author stressed that physical education practiced as an end in itself was harmful to "harmonic development." For women, the same held true. Women, the journalist wrote, "develop a spirit of moral happiness with sport." Exercises, however, differed for men and women. Those for women were especially designed to "strengthen . . . and make her happy and healthy."[60] In so doing, physical education helped a woman "become better suited to fulfill her physiological functions and run her house, help her parents, sustain herself, or be a good wife."[61]

Despite the abundance of state interest in regulating physical culture, there were also strange silences and practices that eluded state control. One development in this regard was the growth of athletic wear. Women in early twentieth-century Mexico used clothing choices to "articulate their social roles, to define their femininity, and to assert individual identity," according to the historian Joanne Hershfeld.[62] Shorter sleeves, exposed skin, and lighter fabrics, along with other fashion choices, offered women the chance to wear their gender politics. As a relatively new way to situate oneself in postrevolutionary Mexico, women's participation in sports may be conceived of in the same way. It could have been, to pick up Hershfeld's thought, "a way of rebelling against . . . patriarchal structures of femininity . . . [or] a way of promoting their sexuality."[63] Similarly, images of sportswomen proliferated in physical education journals

FIGURE 4.1. Women's basketball in Nayarit, Mexico, 1938. *Educación Física* 3, no. 21 (September 1938).

and the press. Perhaps these photographs were intended to compliment the advice, contained in physical education literature and women's magazines, that exercise was ultimately about wifely beauty and healthy motherhood. Since usually no commentary accompanied these images, it is difficult to ascertain their true intent. Still, the increased presence of sportswomen in the pages of Mexican newspapers and magazines in the 1930s helped normalize women's participation in sports. We must acknowledge that it is possible that these photographs were staged. Even so, however, they suggest the existence of significant numbers of sportswomen.[64]

Though the readership of a magazine such as *Educación Física* was specialized, the journal's reports on the national women's basketball tournament or on women participating in track-and-field events highlight the regularity of these activities among young Mexican women. Thus, that each issue of *Educación Física* contained at least four pictures of sportswomen mattered. For example, the image in this chapter of a young women's basketball team suggests that Mexican physical education teachers saw female participation in sports as crucial to their development. The caption to the photo reads: "The woman, devoted to physical education, has agility and [good] health."[65] Clearly this message was intended to show the positive aspects of women playing sports.

For the physical education community, concerned as it was with the development of the "new" Mexico, images of women had to walk the line between promoting physical culture and not overly sexualizing their subjects. The dominant images used in physical education magazines and in sports pages showed women in one of two ways: either they were in the process of participating in a sporting event—most often track-and-field events or gymnastics, but also basketball, and less frequently volleyball or softball (but never football)—or they were standing in uniform in a team photograph. Occasionally they were shown receiving awards for their participation in sporting events. These images were intended to be both inspirational and nonthreatening. They highlight the athletic prowess of women athletes rather than their appearance, as well as the healthfulness of the activity. For example, the cover of *Educación Física* in January 1939 featured a woman throwing a javelin. The article explained that the young woman practiced every day, one of the denizens who trained at the workers' sports fields in the capital. The woman appeared intensely focused on her task, and those who trained with her represented the "healthy and vigorous" young women of the "new" Mexico.[66] Yet it remained crucial to control the level of exercise for young women, lest they become overly muscled or too fatigued. In the same issue of *Educación Física*, the editors included an article on how to avoid fatigue. The accompanying photograph showed young women in a footrace at an interoffice meet. These were athletic competitions between the various ministries of the federal government. The caption with the photo read: "With women, principally, one needs to be very careful not to expose them to fatigue."[67] Strangely, in discussing how to avoid fatigue, the article makes no further mention of women or girls.

The images of women in Mexican print media had a profound effect on attitudes toward the modern woman. Perhaps nowhere was this truer than in coverage of sporting events. Still, while images of

FIGURE 4.2. Track and field in Mexico City. *Educación Física* 4, no. 24 (January 1939).

women in the Mexican media shifted remarkably over the period from 1920 to 1940, patriarchal ideas about womanhood and proper femininity persisted. Images of the modern girl were both alluring and threatening. Their independence could be read as both powerful and sexually open—and thus threatening to dominant norms. In many respects, for "traditional" Mexican society, the flapper and her more conservative, though no less public, office girl sister represented the threatening nature of modern life. They risked stripping women of her core responsibilities in the home. Some have suggested that the rise in representations of sportswomen in the Mexican media was less a function of increasing female participation than it was an effort of the state to suggest female participation in the revolutionary project. It was, in other words, merely one form of propaganda. While this may be the case, it seems a stretch. Based on the available evidence not only in Mexico but around Latin America, it would seem that images of sportswomen increased as a consequence of an increase in women's sporting activities.

Still, the inclusion and normalization of sportswomen in the media, both as individuals and as members of teams, played an important role in making physical activity and sports more acceptable for women in Mexico in the early twentieth century. Photographs of women's basketball teams, and discussion, however brief, of women's sports tournaments mattered. For example, beginning in 1936, CODEME organized a national women's basketball championship, with selected teams representing different Mexican states. A few images of women playing basketball in the 1939 tournament made the pages of *Educación Física*. Though there was not analysis of the games themselves, the top three teams appeared in uniform.[68] Another image shows the start of a basketball game in Morelia, with girls in midair for the jump ball. One team wore skirts, while the other is in long pants. In the picture, the crowd is visible, and it is possible to see people watching the game both at court level and in a balcony. This suggests that interest in women's sports was significant. Despite all of the tendencies to stress beauty and health, women at center court challenged a slew of other recommendations to girls and young women to be humble, demure, and self-effacing.[69]

In effect, according to Ageeth Sluis, "athleticism was encouraged as long as it enhanced and retained the female form," and once accepted, it proved difficult for even the most adamant physical education teacher to control.[70] Sluis ascribed notions of beauty as one of the main goals of female physical education, but it is important to recognize—as her work points out—that notions of beauty were always evolving. Thus, the feminine ideal might have had less to do with form, which was somewhat ephemeral, than with function, which was seen as unchanging. That is, changes in physiognomy were concerning to the physical education establishment only in as much as they signaled changes in physiology. A woman could be well toned and extremely athletic, for example, so long as she did not forgo her womanly duties as daughter, mother, or wife. Photographic evidence demonstrates that despite the advice of these experts on the beautifying potential of exercise, sportswomen remained focused on winning the games they played and promoting the sports they loved.

When women's football emerged in an organized way in Mexico, it would come from the ranks of physical education programs. Stable clubs appeared in the 1960s. This reflects in some part the later adoption of football as Mexico's national sport, and its ongoing competition with boxing and baseball for audiences. The history of Mexican women and sports changed dramatically during the

FIGURE 4.3. Woman javelin thrower, Mexico, 1939. *Educación Física* 4, no. 24 (January 1939).

mid-twentieth century, as discussed in chapter 5, culminating in the 1971 women's world football championship, the second edition of the tournament. Mexican women's sports did not exist in a vacuum. The growth of women's sports in the United States provided a ready-made rival and a well-trodden competition path through universities and high schools in the Southwest. The United States, however, was not the only important neighbor that played a role in the development of Mexican women's sports. Women in neighboring Central American countries, particularly Costa Rica, inspired sportswomen throughout the region.

COSTA RICA

Deportivo Femenino de Costa Rica FC played its first match on March 26, 1950. The team had been formed a little less than a year earlier. It might have been the brainchild of two brothers—both professional footballers—who concocted the idea with their sister and her friends at their father's wake. An alternate version of the club's origins holds that Nelly Coto Solano, one of the friends attending the wake, suggested a women's football team during a discussion about women's baseball.[71] Within months, over thirty young women were playing on the team, practicing at the Bonillas' uncle's property just outside of San José. Deportivo Femenino would go on to be, for its time, something of a missionary force for women's football in the region. Part of the reason for the sport's success in Costa Rica lies in the national context, which in 1949 was slightly different from other countries in the region.

As it did elsewhere in Latin America, the turn of the century brought rapid social changes to Costa Rica, particularly around women's education and women's roles outside the home. According to Roxana Hidalgo Xirinachs, Costa Rica's emergent identity in the late 1800s mixed rural and religious tradition with the "new values that accompanied modernization."[72] The ability to fuse, however unstable such a combination might have been, Catholic Church teachings with more modern, liberal philosophies, as evidenced with its early and earnest embrace of women's education, set Costa Rica apart from many of its neighbors. Women's education in Costa Rica began during the 1870s and 1880s. At that time, according to Steven Palmer and Gladys Rojas Chaves, demand for girls' education grew from the bottom up, and the number of girls in school approached that of boys.[73] The 1880s saw the passage of laws that were crucial to girls' education: the Ley Fundamental de Educación (1885) and the Ley General de Educación Común (1886). The latter made gymnastics for both boys and girls a part of the national curriculum.[74] Even before it became a required part of the day for students in public school, gymnastics appeared in the curricula of private schools, beginning in the 1860s. The aim of Costa Rican gymnastics was to "develop the physical strength and moral character" of the youth. From the outset, however, the desired strength and character differed based on gender. According to Ronald Díaz Bolaños, gymnastics aimed to prepare boys for life in the workplace, and in the public sphere more generally, by strengthening their upper body. At the same time, it helped girls get ready for life in the home, through exercises that "gave form to their pelvis and abdomen."[75] By the end of the following decade, the Instituto Nacional, a high school linked with the Universidad Santo Tomás, had taken up the practice of gymnastics, though only for boys.[76] With the passage of the Ley General de Educación Común and the creation of the Colegio Superior de Señoritas in 1888, girls' education, including physical education, became codified and regularized.

The Colegio Superior de Señoritas altered the shape of Costa Rican history. The school served not only as a training ground for generations of women teachers, but also as a seedbed of Costa Rican feminism and political activism. Teachers and students at the school helped lead the protests that ousted the Tinoco dictatorship in 1919, while the Liga Feminista (Feminist League), a leading voice not only for women's voting rights but for women's political mobilization more broadly, held its foundational meetings in the high school auditorium. Ana Rosa Chacón Gonzalez, a 1907 graduate of the Colegio Superior de Señoritas in physical education, was a founder of the Liga Feminista and also one of the first congresswomen in the country. The school also trained teachers, and by 1927, 71 percent of teachers in Costa Rica were women.[77] According to Roxana Hidalgo Xirinachs, "women teachers began to see their potential for action and decision in public and especially political spaces." This in turn broadened the horizons that women saw for themselves, and in a marked difference from much of the region, that men saw for them.[78] Throughout the 1920s and 1930s Costa Rican women lobbied for the right to vote, and some presidential candidates and other male politicians argued in favor of women's suffrage.[79]

At the same time, the 1920s saw a burgeoning media presence, which presented young *ticas* with European models to aspire to. Costa Rica's growing connections to the outside world, due to its growth as a coffee and banana exporter, as well as the almost simultaneous appearance of the flapper in the post–World War I era, made women's beauty a "public topic of discussion."[80] Modern clothes and hairstyles made their way into magazine articles and advertisements. Women were attending and graduating from secondary schools and universities (which were private at this time) in larger numbers.[81] And increasing numbers of women had income of their own to spend, further spurring the sense that women were becoming independent. These rapid changes caused disquiet in Costa Rica, as they did in Mexico and much of the region. The increased role of women in the public sphere, the state's role in education, and new "foreign" concepts of beauty played into fears that Costa Rica was losing itself to modernity. Women's newfound autonomy and the new ideas about women in the workplace and in the public sphere threatened traditional norms. The Church and other arbiters of morality used the trope of the modern woman as a stand-in for the perceived corruption of Costa Rican morality. Hidalgo Xirinachs argues that, when confronted with a state encroaching on its traditional bases of power, the Catholic Church cast the new norms in stark terms: secularization would lead to a degradation of honor and feminine virtue, as well as threaten the institution of marriage.[82]

It is in this context that state-run physical education and gymnastics grew—however slowly—in the country. Though the Colegio Superior de Señoritas initiated gymnastics for its students in 1888, the young women's gymnastics activities were limited to stretching and other movements that did not run the "risk" of building muscles. Swedish and rhythmic gymnastics became regular practices in the 1920s, at roughly the same time that physical education—the combination of gymnastics with sports and other activities—became established practice.[83] Even then, however, women were discouraged from being overly active. There had been earlier advocates of women's physical education, however. A 1915 article in *El Manantial*, a short-lived newspaper published in Heredia, sang the praises of physical culture for girls. The author, Gustavo Louis Michaud, played a major role in developing physical education in Costa Rica after the educational reform of the late 1880s. He noted the long-standing practice of physical education for girls in the United States, and focused on girls' ability to organize their own athletic league in New York State. They had established the league in the face of male resistance due to "customs . . . and conservative intransigence," he wrote, and by 1912 it included more than twenty-five thousand girls and nearly five hundred schools.[84] Since "prolonged exercise in the fresh air" were "indispensable activities for adolescent girls' health," Michaud called for Costa Ricans to leave "traditional ideas" behind for the good of the country.[85]

Even with recognition that physical education had moral and physical benefits for boys and girls, the Costa Rican state was slow to put its weight behind the practice. Though high schools and normal schools included it in their curricula in the 1920s, formalized physical education would not reach primary school curricula until 1942 as part of a broader effort to increase primary education. Still, according to Chester Urbina Gaitán, schools were encouraged to give students the opportunity to exercise outside whenever possible starting in the late 1920s.[86] Moreover, successive governments in the 1920s and 1930s funded the growth of sporting culture in other ways, including the construction of a national stadium in 1924. The state also created the Junta Nacional de Cultura Física (National Board of Physical Culture), a new government body composed of "[physical education] professionals, politicians, and public health specialists," charged with promoting sports in the country. Among other things, it began arranging tours of men's football teams from outside the country.[87] In other words, if Costa Rican governments were not proactive about physical education, they still saw the link between sports and the health of the nation.

That nation continued to change rapidly with regard to gender norms and expectations. The creation of the University of Costa Rica, in 1941, heralded a new moment in the country. From the outset, women were admitted to all courses of study, and by 1959, 36 percent of its students were women.[88] So too the civil war of 1948 altered the status of women. From political activists without voting rights, with the 1949 constitution women gained full suffrage, though they were not able to vote in national elections until 1953.[89]

Against this backdrop, women's football began in Costa Rica. Interest in the sport grew rapidly within the country, and football developed rapidly beginning in 1949. Manuel and Fernando Bonilla, both first-division professional players in the Costa Rican league, drilled their charges twice weekly in skills, explained tactics, and crafted a team. The founding players ranged in age from thirteen to mid-twenties. None of the girls and young women had ever played organized football before, though many had experience playing other sports, primarily basketball, which was wholly acceptable for women in the country.[90] According to Fernando Bonilla, one of the founders of the team, the first members of the team, including his sister, Dora Bonilla, and sister-in-laws Julieta Zúñiga and Carmen Morales, recruited their friends and acquaintances by "inviting them to join the team, but telling them it was basketball."[91] This is how Nelly Coto Solano recruited her friend Maria Eugenia Páez, asking her to come play basketball. Only when they arrived at the field did Coto Solano inform her friend that they were going to play football. Páez had to be convinced to stay, since she "didn't like football," but then she was a starting goaltender for four years.[92] Many of the young women lied to their families, saying that they were playing basketball, since women playing football was still considered scandalous. Irma Castillo Sánchez, another of the original players, remembered how on the bus on the way home from church, she saw a group of girls between the ages of fifteen and nineteen "who seemed confident, happy, and well mannered" sitting in the back of the bus talking loudly and laughing. After seeing them the following Sunday, she approached the group and was invited to play. She had never played before, but she quickly fell in love with the game. She, too, lied to her parents and said she was practicing basketball.[93]

Most of the young Deportivo Femenino players learned the game at the hands of the Bonilla brothers. Some players recounted that they had played football as long as they could remember, often with their brothers or fathers. But according to Fernando Bonilla, they all needed training in basic skills. Fernando Bonilla's wife, one of the founders of the team, had according to them never played before.[94] The very speed with which the club gathered enough women to field two teams suggests that women had some experience playing. Indeed, perhaps they had learned from mothers, sisters, or grandmothers. Recent research by Chester Urbina Gaitán has uncovered earlier traces of women's football in Costa Rica, dating back to the 1920s. According to Urbina Gaitán, women began joining La Libertad, a

FIGURE 4.4. Deportivo Femenino de Costa Rica FC, March 26, 1950. Courtesy of the family of Maria Elena Valverde Coto.

working-class sports club, as *socios*, in 1924.[95] By September 1926, enough interest existed that *La Prensa* published a small note that "a number of women" in San José were "engaged in forming a number of teams in order to have a series of games." Though the idea "caused great enthusiasm among the feminist element," no further news of the sport was reported. Perhaps the women could not find enough players, or perhaps the media failed to report further.[96]

Regardless of their past experience playing the sport, the team faced scorn when news of their existence reached the public. The Bonilla brothers were called crazy. Many of the girls and women faced opposition from family members when they began to play with Deportivo Femenino. Alice Quirós Alvarez's mother threatened to send her to a reformatory if she continued to play football, and began to cut her football uniform with scissors to keep Alice from practicing.[97] Other players recalled facing opposition as well. Zulay Loiza Martínez "had problems" with her father and brothers.

Carmen Morales's father told her that women should not play football, saying that the sport was "for *marimachos* [lesbians]."[98] The Araya sisters practiced with the team but did not get their parent's permission to play until eight days before the team's first exhibition. As it was, the Bonilla brothers, "accompanied by two or three players," would go to the team members' houses to try to win their families over, in order to be sure that the women and girls could play.[99]

Deportivo Femenino de Costa Rica played its first match at the national stadium in March 1950 in San José. The Bonilla brothers requested permission from Antonio Escarré, the director of sports, which was granted based on the brothers' football pedigree.[100] The Costa Rican president, José Figueres, was in attendance. Futboleras in Costa Rica faced audiences who were both skeptical that they could play and expectant that players would conform to feminine beauty standards while trying. In other words, the women were not taken seriously and they were objectified. Still, some in the Costa Rican sports media tried to be objective. On March 24, two days prior to the match, *La Prensa Libre* ran a small story about the match and included player names and positions for each team. The author urged spectators to go to the match and "leave their prejudices to one side."[101] One journalist admitted to believing before the match that women could not "assimilate this game," which is naturally masculine.[102] Too rough and too hard, the sport could never be mastered by women. However, he was surprised by their skill. While most of the women played well, the commentator wrote, some played excellently and "had nothing to envy" of male counterparts. Unable to step out of the patriarchal wonder at women athletes, the commentator wrote not only about the women's skill but of their beauty as well. The goalkeeper Maria Eugenia Páez, he wrote, "has a stupendous figure . . . a beautiful woman." However, he also noted that "tall and flexible," she "seemed more like an elegant male goalie."[103] Another reporter noted that the crowd was at first reticent, but as the match progressed they were "amazed" by the skill of the players.[104] The sportswriter for *Diario de Costa Rica* noted that "in synthesis" the match was "a complete success."[105] Journalists assumed that football masculinized women and ruined their pretty looks. That they played well *and* presented as traditionally feminine women caught many observers by surprise. After the game, Unión Deportiva de Escazú announced it would host a dance for the teams in April, "hoping to stimulate the brilliant work" done by Deportivo Femenino and to congratulate the team for "its brilliant debut."[106] A second game followed in June, given the "marked enthusiasm" for women's football created by the first exhibition match.[107]

Women's football was not universally well received. While some reporters for *La Nación* and *La Prensa Libre* commented on the quality of the Costa Rican players, other commentators did not. José Antich, a French tennis and swimming instructor at the Costa Rica Athletic Club, made his opinion known in a letter to *La Prensa Libre*. While it had not been his "intention to comment on any sporting theme" until he was well acquainted with Costa Ricans and "their idiosyncrasies," women's football caused him to break his silence. "Football," Antich wrote, "is a sport for men and should not be played by women." He believed that there were many reasons that they should not play, including "their physical, psychological, and sociological character." In addition, Antich argued that with "intense exercise . . . leg muscles would become too strong . . . [and] hips would become too wide." As if the connection between male expectations of feminine beauty were not clear enough, Antich continued, saying that women's "knee[s] would lose [their] normal roundness and would appear bony, like men's," while calves "would lose their attractiveness by becoming hard."[108] Further, Antich argued that women's pelvic bones were naturally weak and could not withstand the "kicking, frequent stopping, and collisions" of football, "let alone the mere fact of walking in cleats."[109] He argued that women "of whatever country" were not psychologically prepared to "resist the shock to the nerves of an opponent with hundreds of fans" cheering them on. But perhaps Antich's primary concerns were sociological. Women playing football harmed not only women, who "lost their femininity," but football in general. Were women to keep playing, he wrote, it would not be long until "the press and the radio compare the women's game with the men's and compare male players with women players." This, he argued, would be damaging to the men's game.[110] The Spanish newspaper *El Mundo Deportivo* called the game "a magnificent spectacle . . . though not precisely of football." Instead, it was a "disorganized mass chasing a leather ball." The article revealed other blemishes in the Costa Rican story as well: women players were apparently not always treated with respect, and the Costa Rican press had to remind spectators to mind their manners. Of course, the Spanish sportswriter was hardly surprised, since "even the coldest man would be pushed to his limits."[111]

A former player and a technical advisor to the Costa Rican general directorate of sport, Miguel Ángel Ulloa also thought that women could not play the game. "Football," he wrote, "is a sport of maximum mobility, [and is] fiercely strenuous, which makes it difficult for a certain category of men." Since even some men could not play the sport, women, he suggested, could not possibly be able to.[112] Not only did Ulloa's belief that women could not play football rest on the fallacy that the sport was too complicated, strenuous, and difficult, but also on a poor understanding of history. That countries "more advanced in football" than Costa Rica—"England, Italy . . . Argentina, Brazil . . . [and] Chile"—had not "opened their arms" to the women's game proved that the sport was "damaging and unsuitable."[113] Clearly, Ulloa had no knowledge of the long history of the sport in other countries. Ulloa attempted to legitimize his opinion on the grounds that as a former footballer, he knew how rough and tiring the sport could be. The ball was too hard, the shoes too dangerous, and the game too long. He did, however, suggest that the Costa Rican public health community study the issue and explore the "anatomical, psychological, and sociological" potential of women's football and the "indisputable risks" of the sport.[114]

Ulloa and *La Prensa Libre*'s sports page editor, known by his pen name, "Chutador," both argued for different-sized fields for women's football and suggested that women wear sneakers instead of cleats. Though they couched their concerns over both in technical terms, likely there were other motives. The field, both suggested, was too large and women players would tire quickly from the physical activity. The shoes also "complicated" the game, and to the extent that either accepted that women would play the game (Chutador was in favor, while Ulloa was not), they both believed that women should wear "keeds [*sic*]," meaning canvas sneakers, instead of cleats.[115] These justifications might have masked the deeper masculine concern that football would damage the feminine aesthetic. Running on a full-size field would tone women's muscles beyond male desires, while a clumsy challenge with cleats could scar women's legs. Indeed, the concern over the masculinizing potential of women's sports was made clear by Julio Mera Carrasco. Mera Carrasco, an author of multiple books on football and a physical education expert, argued that women's "physical constitution" was "too delicate," even for track and field. He suggested that women's physical activity "be an adornment of their beauty" based on "grace and style" rather than athletic perfection. He lamented that in Europe women athletes had begun to take on "masculine characteristics," to the extent that there were "real problems determining the sex" of some.[116]

In other words, though women's football received more support— or faced less criticism—in Costa Rica than elsewhere, along with support came controversy. As in Brazil and England, debate began about the healthfulness of the sport and whether it should be permitted for women at all. In 1950, the Costa Rican Senate convened a special hearing on public health and women's football. The panel did not discuss women's sports in general, just women's football, showing again that many viewed football as somehow different from other sports. Much like the earlier debates in England and Brazil, in Costa Rica discussion centered around whether the sport was too rough for women to play and whether it threatened girls' reproductive capacity. However, unlike the two football powers that had officially banned women and girls from playing, in Costa Rica the government refused to lend credence to unproven arguments about the game: women could play. But the conversation continued in the press. Chutador, the sports editor for *La Prensa Libre*, asked a number of male athletes, commentators, and doctors to opine on women's football. He offered prompts to the potential authors as well, such as: "Is football a sport for women"; "Do you think that women's football is good for the culture and manners" of those who play; "Can women's football affect the femininity of women players";

and "Physiologically, will women be harmed by playing such a rough sport."[117]

Responding to these questions, Luis Cartín Paniagua, a leading journalist of the day, defended women's right to play in no uncertain terms on the pages of *La Prensa Libre*, mocking those who called for the sport to be banned. To those who argued that the sport was bad for women, he pointed to the doctors who actually studied the game, noting that not one thought it unhealthy. To another objection, that so few nations played the sport that it must not be good, he replied that the diffusion of sports did not happen evenly: "We do not know . . . the game of rugby. . . . Does this mean that it is bad to play it?" Rather, he noted that women's football was played in Spain, Colombia, Guatemala, and Portugal. Cartín Paniagua proudly trumpeted that Deportivo Femenino had "broken the ridiculous chains of prejudice" that had kept Costa Rican women off the field. "We could almost qualify it," he continued, "as a call for the liberation of Costa Rican women."[118] Cartín Paniagua had coached the Costa Rican national men's side that year, and thus was a leading voice on football and well connected to communities across the Americas. A few days later, a commentator in *El Mundo Femenino* explained that sports did not compromise women's gender identity. The "brutal" sport of football would not make women "hard" or cause them to "lose their grace." A woman "who is sweet and delicate will never lose these qualities."[119] So too Deportivo Femenino's team physician, Dr. Coto Garbanzo, faced harsh criticism. He ignored colleagues who informed him of the potential damage to women's reproductive organs and counseled the women that playing would do them no harm whatsoever.[120]

In late April 1950, between its two exhibition matches in San José, Deportivo Femenino traveled to Panama City on the invitation of the Panamanian Football Federation. Thirty players and a staff of seven, including a doctor, a nurse, the Bonilla brothers, and three chaperones, left for Panama on April 29 for a match to be played on the thirtieth at the Olympic stadium. According to *La Prensa Libre*, Panamanians saw a good match, even though the field was in poor condition due to heavy rain the day before. The teams left a "magnificent impression" with the "enthusiastic fans" before returning to Costa Rica.[121] While women's football was not new to Panama, the sport did not grow quickly there. Furthermore, debates on the safety of women's sports raged in the 1950s. Deportivo Femenino returned to Costa Rica for its second exhibition match at home, on June 8. That match, in honor of former president José Figueres, also displayed the women's burgeoning skill for the game. The Costa Rican press reported that again the level of play was high, and that the match surpassed the first exhibition. Figueres presented medals to each member of the winning team.[122]

Deportivo Femenino de Costa Rica was soon off again, first to Curaçao, for a two-week tour in late August and early September. The tour almost started on a sour note: the club took two flights to Curaçao, one a commercial flight and one a charter, with the Salvadoran men's team on board. The second flight experienced trouble en route. Their delay caused a great deal of concern on the ground in Curaçao, and when the flight landed, the players cried and hugged each other. The rest of the tour went much better. The women of Deportivo Femenino played a series of exhibition matches that, according to press reports, were well attended and well received by the thousands of fans who packed into Rif Stadium in Willemstad to see "Azul" play "Rojo." The spectators' "shouts of admiration" apparently represented the "enormous friendship" between the two countries.[123]

The debate over women's football did not end, however. In 1951, a member of the National Council on Physical Education, José Francisco Carballo, gave a talk on the "much discussed topic" of women's football. Carballo, who sat on the national council with Miguel Ángel Ulloa and others, claimed the sport to be dangerous to girls' and women's health. Carballo had, apparently "on his own initiative," sent a request to the Congress on Pan-American Health to look into the sport further. An anonymous columnist for *La Nación* criticized the doctor, noting that he should have "tried to consult other doctors, at least those who have treated the women [players]," before looking to foreign intervention into the Costa Rican athletic scene. "We believe," wrote the author, "that this affair could have

FIGURE 4.5. Deportivo Femenino de Costa Rica FC, tour to Panama, 1950. Courtesy of the family of Maria Elena Valverde Coto.

been perfectly resolved in our own environment, without having to consult another country that has only heard of women's football."[124] Costa Rica, where the sport was played, the paper went on to argue, had plenty of expertise to draw on. Perhaps the article was referring to a medical panel, including the doctors Alfonso Acosta, Fernando Quirós, and Gonzalo González Murielo, which had been asked in 1950 by students at the University of Costa Rica to decide "if women's football is healthy or not." The goal of the request was to "develop a women's team . . . at the University."[125]

Regardless of the legal and public health debates, women continued to play. Deportivo Femenino de Costa Rica traveled outside the country for most of its matches, while other clubs formed in the country. The aforementioned La Libertad, the working-class-supported first-division Costa Rican club, formed a women's team, Club Sport Femenino La Libertad, on April 13, 1950.[126] The team held its first practice three weeks later. Deportivo Lourdes, a regional team based in Montes de Oca, had a women's team by the end of 1950, and two other clubs had formed in the San José area: Club Deportivo Eva de Perón, named for the powerful Argentine politician and supporter of sports; and Deportivo República de México.[127] With the addition of ODECA, by 1952 at least six women's teams, representing four clubs, played in the country. Both La Libertad and Deportivo Femenino could field two teams, which often played against each other in exhibition matches.

Foreign tours were common. Like Deportivo Femenino de Costa Rica, La Libertad traveled outside of the country. In 1950, the team received an invitation to travel to Guatemala, which apparently it did not accept. That same year, however, La Libertad traveled to El Salvador, playing two matches. On December 15, twenty thousand spectators in the Estadio La Flor Blanca in San Salvador watched an exhibition between "Blanquinegro" and "Azul y Rojo," two teams composed of La Libertad players. Two days later, a crowd witnessed a rematch in Santa Ana, site of the first football match in El Salvador. In April 1951, Deportivo Femenino played a one-match exhibition in Tegucigalpa, Honduras. The match, played on a "dry, dusty, hard, and poorly seeded" field at the national stadium, honored President Juan Manuel Gálvez and had, according to the Honduran newspaper *Diario Comercial*, a good attendance. What those who did not see the match missed was nothing short of a display of talented football players. In fact, the Honduran newspaper suggested that the level of play exceeded "what is offered in the same national stadium, afternoon to afternoon, by our male football stars." The women appeared to be "born with a ball between their feet," which was all the more surprising given the expectations of the crowd, who believed that the women would have no skill at all.[128]

One month later, Deportivo Femenino found themselves in Guatemala playing a match against a club from another nation. The tour, which lasted for twenty days and comprised twenty-three people, including coaches and chaperones, included three matches against the women's football club Cibeles.[129] Formed in Guatemala City in 1950, Cibeles was not the first to be formed in the country, but it was the first whose activities were recorded; thirty years earlier, Marta Padilla and Isabel Evans had founded a women's sports club called Club Deportivo Femenino.[130] Guatemalans expressed pride at being the site of what they thought was the first women's football international competition in the Americas, even if their team lost the series 2–1. And in June 1951, La Libertad traveled to Nicaragua to play an exhibition match in Managua against Costa Rican rivals Eva de Perón. *Diario de Costa Rica* reported on the match, noting that the 2–2 tie was an accurate reflection of the game. While La Libertad had more technical skill, the women of Eva de Perón played with more heart and speed.[131]

The women of both Deportivo Femenino de Costa Rica and La Libertad, with their travels overseas, not only acted as missionaries for women's football but also took on a role often reserved for men: acting as athletic ambassadors for the country. Cultural ambassadorship took on a new importance in Costa Rica with the abolition of the military. Deportivo Femenino "flew the national colors high" on their trip to Guatemala, comporting themselves like true emissaries and, of course, defeating the Guatemalan team.[132] The women met with the archbishop of Guatemala, making them the first "athletic ambassadors" to meet with the prelate. He gave the team silver medals inscribed with pictures of Santo Cristo de Esquipulas, the Black Christ of Esquipulas, and lauded them for showing a path to avoid immorality through sports.[133]

Morality played a much different role on the next tour made by Latin America's women's football missionaries. Scheduled to play a series of matches across Colombia over a two-month period, Deportivo Femenino de Costa Rica encountered serious opposition from the Colombian government and the League of Decency, a conservative women's group that had previously worked to ban "immoral" art. Though Colombia itself had a long history of women's football, the league successfully petitioned to deny the team entry visas on the grounds that the shorts worn by Deportivo Femenino represented an affront to decency. Initially slated to play seven games over three weeks, once the low-level diplomatic row was settled, the *ticas* remained in Colombia longer than expected, from September 9 to November 16, 1951. They traveled from Cúcuta on the Venezuelan border to Cali, playing as many as three games per week, and were planning to travel on to Ecuador.[134] By this time some members of the team had children, at least one of whom made the trip as team mascot.

As was the case in most places they played, in Colombia the women of Deportivo Femenino fought against preconceived notions of what women's football would be. In Cali, the public expected a game "without rhyme or reason," while in Manizales, spectators awaited a game of "little value." Yet everywhere they played, according to the press, they impressed. The Caleños witnessed a "good match" between futboleras who played "without fear and with decisiveness"—"true fútbol"—and spectators in Manizales "changed their opinion immediately" when they saw the speed and precision with which the women played. In Medellín, the audience saw that "women could master the ball" just as well as men. All the while, the *ticas* were able to maintain their beauty, grace, and femininity.[135] Nevertheless, while the team was generally well received, it continued to clash with "ridiculous Leagues and Societies" that argued that women's sports represented a threat to the morality of the nation. The League of Decency succeeded in prohibiting at least one match, when the rector of the national university in Bogotá ordered that the stadium remain closed on the day of a scheduled exhibition.[136] Millionarios, a men's team made up of stars from all over Latin America who were drawn to Colombia for its high wages (hence the name), played a match against an all-star professional team in honor of the women.

After its return from Colombia, Deportivo Femenino continued to play both nationally and internationally, as did the other women's clubs mentioned. Traces of the sport, however, became harder to find. In 1954 Deportivo Femenino traveled to Cuba, playing against the Cuban women's national team six times over three weeks in June and July. The Costa Ricans won five and tied one. In turn, the Cuban team visited Costa Rica in December and January, and again Costa Rican teams dominated.[137] *La Nación* occasionally noted women's games, such as that between the "distinguished young ladies" of Eva de Perón and La Libertad, who traveled to Golfito on the southern Pacific coast to play an exhibition match.[138] We know that the Costa Rican Women's Association of Football had formed at some point in the 1950s, only because *La Nación* reported in 1958 that its treasurer, Roberto Blanco Méndez, was stepping down from his post.[139] In 1960, ODECA and Independiente traveled to Caracas, Venezuela, where they participated in a four-team tournament against two English teams, Corinthians and Northern Nomads.[140] This tournament might have spurred the sport in Venezuela, which by 1966 had at least four women's teams and hosted the Colombian women's national team.[141] In 1961, Deportivo Femenino played its first game in three years, defeating Sanyo FC. And in late 1962 the team began a six-month tour of Mexico, which culminated in 1963. Deportivo Femenino played sixteen games in Mexico, playing in Tapachula, the Estadio Universitario, Veracruz, Morelia, León, Guanajuato, Puebla, and Jalisco, "among others." Only in Guanajuato did Deportivo Femenino encounter a preexisting team, but it was "in its infancy," according to Fernando Bonilla. Guillermo Cañedo, the president of the Mexican Football Federation and a member of the International Federation of Association Football (FIFA) executive committee, blocked the team from playing in "first level stadiums," due to his opposition to women's football.[142] With the exception of scattered references during the 1960s and 1970s, women's football disappeared from the Costa Rican press and from the historical narrative of the sport as well. Indeed, in a brief notice in 1971 on the sport outside the country, *La Nación* informed its readers that "Costa Rica had women's football too. Twenty years ago a group of enthusiastic young women formed teams, and brought their spectacle to North, Central, and South America."[143] It was as if the women's game had been played in 1950 and never again.

EL SALVADOR

Despite the clear differences between state development in Central American countries, girls' physical education in El Salvador took shape in much the same way as in Costa Rica. Elite Salvadorans' modernization projects targeted indigenous cultures and communities in hopes of reshaping the nation along European models. The expansion of public education comprised part of these visions. According to Chester Urbina Gaitán, El Salvador began promoting gymnastics in boys' secondary school curricula in 1885.[144] Soon after, then president Francisco Menéndez signed a law on public education that required boys to participate in "military exercises" in school, while girls would work on "handiworks." The stated goal of physical education programs was to "civilize the population."[145] By 1894, the national normal school for women teachers began a course on calisthenics and gymnastics. Still, it was not until the first decade of the twentieth century that physical education and hygiene became optional courses in primary school for both boys and girls. The very movements of students, the ways that they ran and jumped, could be controlled by the state through physical education. Thus, physical education developed as a way for the Salvadoran state of the early twentieth century to build a stronger military and adhere indigenous groups to national identity. However, in El Salvador, as elsewhere in Central America, the power of the state failed to reach into rural areas. This resulted in what Aldo Lauria-Santiago and Leigh Binford have described as "weak hegemony" in the country.[146] In other words, local educational institutions did not always adhere to national standards and did not create citizens with a strong national identity.[147]

That political elites were unable to create the population that they wanted does not mean that they did not try. To the contrary, throughout Central America women's and girls' physical education received greater attention in the 1920s and 1930s, in part in effort to police women's increased autonomy and independence. The *Revista Salvadoreña de Educación Física* (Salvadoran Journal of Physical Education), which began publication in 1922, stressed the need for women and girls to participate in physical education. In its second issue, the journal published a translation of a speech on the topic of women's physical education by Elie Mercier, a noted French specialist.[148] Mercier explained that "nature has imposed on women more deformations than men . . . destining them to a secondary role . . . in life." Physically, Mercier wrote, women's organs were "complex" and did not allow for "alterations."[149]

Women's fashions were defined as one of the vices that physical education could combat. Fashion kept women's muscles from developing correctly and freely; the corset weakened abdominal muscles and resulted in improper breathing, while high heels caused deformities of the spine. To rectify the damage done to women's bodies by fashion, Mercier held out the promise of proper physical education: games and dances in the fresh air. These, he said, would help to "create and maintain a healthy equilibrium in girls and adolescents."[150] Indeed, Mercier argued that physical activity was more important for girls aged seven to ten than it was for boys, since girls had a greater propensity for sedentary lifestyles and the related "fatal consequences."[151] Once girls entered puberty, however, Mercier cautioned, physical activity should be "avoid[ed] in order to create true women."[152] Yet he noted that French girls participated in all sports, with slight rules alterations. The risk for girls practicing sports, he suggested, lay not in sports itself, but rather in the fact that if girls suddenly took up sports without prior training, they might get injured.

Physical education was important not only to correct the mistakes of fashion, but also to create healthy, beautiful women with character, qualities that were "more appreciable than intended [for] intellectual value." Female intelligence was, according to Mercier, more like the "memory of a parrot than any true intellectual development."[153] Still, women, like men, faced daily stress, and for Mercier sports was a way to deal with the "nervous disturbances" that came with modern civilization.[154] Moreover, for improving the "racial" stock, physical activity helped to increase people's size. The sports that Mercier recommended for girls were those that "tend to straighten the spinal column, to increase breathing capacity, and do not stunt or shock the genital organs." Sports that fit these criteria included swimming, rowing, and cycling (in moderation), throwing sports, volleyball, basketball, tennis, "French boxing without attacks," and fencing. Footraces, he argued, should only be practiced by people who were "robust."[155] Hurdles and jumping were to be forbidden, due to the damage they could do to the ligaments of the stomach and breasts. In the end, Mercier hoped that limited physical activity and sports would beautify girls and help them realize that motherhood was the only true purpose of women.[156]

The recognition that physical education mattered for the future of the nation proved crucial for getting girls more physically active in the country. In 1917, the Salvadoran state created the National Commission on Physical Education, with the aim to regulate physical education and the regionally disparate spaces of physical education. Again, though no special mention of girls' activities was made, one can presume that female participation was on the minds of the officials. Not only were women participating in sports in the regional power Mexico, but in Costa Rica by the 1910s women and girls also played sports in school. Moreover, a scant two years later in 1919, the commission requested programs to teach physical education in girls' primary schools, in normal schools, and in secondary schools. The activities were primarily those popular in the era for women and girls: marching, gymnastics, jumping, and running.[157]

Little movement was made despite the high level of interest in government circles. The *Revista Salvadoreña de Educación Física* had begun publication, which would seem a step in the right direction, as was the arrival of four teachers to train the first group of Salvadoran physical educators. The four, according to numerous studies conducted in El Salvador, were the Frenchwoman Juanita Push and three American men. Push, who arrived in 1919 and taught at the Colegio Técnico de Señoritas (Girls Technical High School), a teacher training school, was "passionate about basketball" and began teaching the sport there.[158] From the scant references, it appears that at least some of the teachers remained in the country until 1939. State schools had clearly been teaching physical education and sports earlier, as by 1920 the national government sponsored a national sporting contest for all schools, including girls' schools, in the country. The events ranged from one-hundred-meter sprints to longer races, as well as long jump and high jump competitions.[159]

If the state did not invest the appropriate resources in sports and physical education, private clubs did. Despite the official proscriptions, women played an early role in the development of football in El Salvador. Though they might not have played on organized teams, they contributed directly in the formation and administration of football clubs in San Salvador and, importantly, in rural areas as well. Sporting activities in El Salvador began early in the twentieth century, as the philosophy of "mens sana in corpore sana" swept across the Atlantic from Europe. By 1921 there were seventy-three sports clubs in the country, some of which had activities for girls and women.[160] Women's tennis was promoted by the Salvadoran elite, with Margarita Alcaine and Tula Serra winning a championship in 1921.[161] In November 1921, the Salvadoran government sponsored a sports festival that had men's and women's sporting events, including women's basketball and tennis, along with men's baseball. On November 5, Lycee Francais defeated Colegio Santa Inez 24–2 in women's basketball. The following day Julia Meardy was crowned tennis champion.[162] Chester Urbina Gaitán even references a women's football team in Chalatenango in 1921, but only states that the women opted to stop playing due to their physical fitness.[163]

Physical education remained on the government docket into the military dictatorships of the 1930s and 1940s, with increasing regulation as to what sports women and girls could play. In 1939 the Ministry of Public Education was tasked with deciding what types of physical activities would be included in the physical education curricula at both public and private schools. The state mandated six hours of physical education per week, and required that certain sports be taught: "track and field, swimming, football (boys), basketball, baseball (boys), indoor [baseball] (girls)."[164] By 1937, the Central American and Caribbean Games included women's events and provided a major impetus for the development of programs for girls and women. Although the games did not include either baseball or football, the two events that contended for the title of "national sport," it opened opportunities for women to represent their respective nations.

CONCLUSION

The evidence from Costa Rica, El Salvador, and Mexico opens at least as many lines of questioning as it answers. As in the rest of the region, women's sports in Mexico and Central America had simultaneously controlling and liberating tendencies. On the part of the patriarchal state, efforts to inculcate correct physical education for girls and young women were part of larger efforts to educate modern citizens. Physical education programs comprised part of larger efforts of the state to police girls' movement and autonomy. As the caregivers for the next generation of citizens, women had to be healthy both physically and mentally. However, for women and girls themselves, the civilizing designs of the state often seemed to hold little import. Rather, they sought to play, to create community, and in some cases to fight against the stereotypes and boundaries that marked proper gender norms and behavior.

In Mexico, the revolutionary nature of the state afforded more opportunities for women to be both active participants and designers of physical education policy. In both El Salvador and Costa Rica, women had a smaller role in creating curricula but nevertheless played a part in the construction and dissemination of sports culture. Particularly in Costa Rica, where the girls' normal school was also a center of national feminism, women's physical education teachers were equipped not only with the teaching skills and curricula for physical education, but also with expectations to create a more egalitarian society, in part through sports. However, throughout the Americas, even when curricula included girls' physical education, it naturalized stark differences between genders. These differences were largely fictional and based on little or no accurate research. In the coming years, across the Americas, women athletes formed clubs outside of state institutions in increasing numbers and complexity. While impossible to quantify, the importance of girls' physical education in normalizing exercise and creating conditions for athletes to make connections cannot be underestimated. The comparative cases in Mexico and Central America illustrate the importance of educational institutions, national political events, and transnational networks. The success of Costa Rican futboleras suggests the importance of the confluence of those factors alongside an enormous amount of passion and effort from the players themselves.

5

THE BOOM AND BUST OF MEXICAN WOMEN'S FOOTBALL

GRAINY VIDEO SHOWS THE ESTADIO AZTECA PACKED WITH enthusiastic fans, cheering on their national team in the world championship finals.[1] For the second year in a row, the Azteca stadium hosted the finals of a major global tournament. The first, the 1970 men's World Cup, saw Brazil defeat Italy. Footage of this contest is legendary. Shown in color for the first time, the men's World Cup final changed the way that sports were seen. The second, the 1971 women's world championship, overseen by the Federazione Internazionale Europea Football Femminile (Federation of International and European Women's Football, FIEFF), also played in front of a capacity crowd of over 110,000 people. The finals pitted Mexico against defending champions Denmark. Though the home team would lose 3–0 to a superior opponent, the match represented the first time that any Mexican football team had reached the finals of a global tournament. Not more than three years earlier, many Mexicans would not have known that *fútbol femenil* existed. Women's football exploded in Mexico in the late 1960s, not only in Mexico City but also around the country. Journalists and physical education teachers saw an opportunity to create institutions around this energy. A few particularly supportive men began to set the groundwork for a women's football league around the capital, and within two years the number of leagues grew. During the period from 1969 to 1972, the Liga América and the other leagues formed rapidly, eventually consolidating under the auspices of the Mexican Federation of Women's Football in 1971. Mexican women's football represented one of the most vibrant arenas of women's sports in the Americas. And then it collapsed.

The story of women's football in Mexico and the country's partic-ipation in the 1970 and 1971 women's world championships offers a fascinating micro lens onto women's history and the politics of popular culture in Mexico. Without significant prior scholarship on Mexican women's football, and with a heavy reliance on spotty journalistic coverage, our arguments are tentative.[2] There is much that remains to be done. We explain that men, particularly the jour-nalists at *El Heraldo de México*, hoped to grow the sport, but with different motivations. Some sought to create a space for women to play football, others saw the sport as a business opportunity, while others believed it to be the best way forward for Mexican women's physical education. At the very moment of the women's football boom, men's professional clubs teetered on the brink of financial ruin due to mismanagement and corruption within the Mexican pro-fessional leagues and the Federación Mexicana de Fútbol (Mexican Football Federation, FMF). To differing degrees, promoters, club directors, and journalists hoped to compensate for declining revenue in men's football through the women's game. At the same time, the FMF and others saw the sport as a potential threat to the men's game. Moreover, the increasing recognition of women as consumers provided further impetus for imagining the possibilities of a women's football league. Women players, who had developed an extensive grassroots network of football teams, initially welcomed the sup-port of major newspapers and promoters. The relationship between women and the male organizers of the league soured rather quickly, we argue, because the two had distinct ideas about women's foot-ball. The players rejected attempts to market them as novelty acts and sought compensation from their sporting gains. This flew in the face of many male expectations that the futboleras would remain content as amateurs, playing for free while men reaped the financial rewards. Despite these conflicts, women players found validation on a new scale, opportunities to travel, and cherished camaraderie. At the same time, conflicts over the uses and misuses of women's football played a part in its disappearance from the historical record, as media outlets ceased covering the sport.

Global cultural currents, specifically second-wave feminism and the *jipis* (hippies), framed the conflicts and possibilities of women's football in the late 1960s. These movements were part of challenges to the Partido Revolucionario Institucional (Institutional Revolutionary Party, PRI), the party at the helm of Mexico's autocratic one-party state from the 1930s to the 1990s. Moreover, broader economic and demographic shifts changed women's lives. The Mexico of 1970 and 1971 was a vastly different place than it had been just fifty years earlier. At the end of the Mexican Revolution, as discussed in chapter 4, the government implemented a series of changes that attempted to alter society rapidly. While it faced resistance at every turn—notably with the Cristero Rebellion—the state successfully altered Mexico's economy and society. From a predominantly rural society in the 1950s, Mexico's urban population approached 60 percent in 1970.[3] And while women and girls entered education and the workforce in smaller numbers than their male compatriots, they did so at higher rates than their mothers and grandmothers. By 1970, roughly 18 percent of the formal workforce comprised women, and about 65 percent had at least some primary education.[4] Mexico's population soared between 1950 and 1970, nearly doubling from 28.5 million to 48.2 million.[5] This was made possible by increasing life expectancy, which had climbed from 39.8 years for women in 1940 to 63 years for women in 1970.[6]

The rapid urbanization and increase in living standards, particularly in the cities, had social and cultural ramifications as well. Cinema, sports, music, arts, and dance flourished in midcentury Mexico. At the time, Mexico was unique in the region in terms of the social forces unleashed by the revolution and the radical rhetoric it espoused. The postrevolutionary state set about the work of constructing a new national identity through nationalistic imagery and sporting events. This national identity hinged upon an idealized masculinity that defined proper men as breadwinners and benevolent patriarchs. Still, there were competing experiences and precedents. As Mary Kay Vaughan noted, the "revolution was not just an attack on property, social hierarchy, and exclusion; it assaulted Victorian morality and rules of sexual repression and brought women into public space in unprecedented ways."[7] Just as in the 1920s, when women with bobbed hair faced violent attacks by conservative neighbors, in the 1960s and 1970s women, particularly those defined as darker and lower class, continued to face persecution when entering the public sphere. Perhaps none of these spaces was as challenging as the sports stadium.

Women forayed into sports in greater numbers in the 1940s and 1950s, as the postrevolutionary state stressed physical education as a way to create healthy citizens. The Mexican state supported the development of a strong women's sporting culture around Olympic events such as swimming, track and field, and tennis. These tended to be sports practiced by the upper classes. Basketball and volleyball, which working-class clubs incorporated at a fast rate, also grew during the 1930s and 1940s. As with most other countries around the world, however, football was considered by Mexican sporting authorities to be too rough for women to play. As discussed in chapter 4, in 1929 the government instructed future physical education teachers that only boys should be taught baseball, football, and boxing.[8]

The PRI was notorious for its careful use of spectacle to promote Mexican nationalism and modernity. Sporting events provided the party with the opportunities to showcase its vision of Mexico. Beginning with the Central American and Caribbean Games in 1926, Mexico positioned itself as a sporting leader in the region. The 1955 Pan-American Games impressed delegations from across the Americas, establishing Mexico as a bridge between the United States and Latin America.[9] Moreover, these games included more women athletes from Latin America than had ever come together at once. They electrified sportswomen who saw themselves at center stage and enjoyed the opportunity to compete against the continents' best. In hosting the 1968 Olympic Games and the 1970 men's World Cup, the Mexican state mobilized its fullest resources to create a vision of modern Mexico through sports. Even though the Olympics were marred by the Tlatelolco massacre, both events highlighted Mexico's ability to plan a worldwide event and, to paraphrase the historian Eric Zolov, temporarily replaced the myth that Mexico was a land of *mañana*—where things could always wait until tomorrow—with the notion that it was the land of today.[10]

The Mexican state invested generously in popular culture, and by most accounts the PRI benefitted enormously from these endeavors.[11] Organizations affiliated with the PRI, such as the Sindicato Único de Trabajadores del Gobierno del Distrito Federal (Union of Federal District Government Workers), courted workers' children to attend events by offering free sports clinics. The regular inclusion of softball indicates that girls frequently participated.[12] The PRI directly intervened in cultural production, whether film, visual arts, or music. When advantageous, the government created bureaucratic institutions that could deflect archconservative demands for moral patrolling.[13] However, by the 1960s and 1970s the Mexican state's monopoly on popular culture had declined dramatically. At times, PRI officials tried to challenge social traditions that blatantly discriminated against women; however, feminist organizations found most of these PRI decrees to be empty gestures.[14]

The moment of the effervescence of women's football in Mexico coincided, not coincidentally, with the resurgence of the *nueva ola*, known in English as second-wave feminism. Given that suffrage remained a struggle for women's rights activists until 1953, there was somewhat less of a generational divide between the first and second waves of feminism in Mexico than in the United States. Feminists frequently point to the 1968 student movement as a benchmark in revitalizing the women's movement, although the sexist rhetoric of male leaders and the state's violent repression marginalized women active in the student movement.[15] Women cutting their maxi skirts into minis found their way into the Mexican media, which turned these symbolic events into calls for greater freedoms or restrictions on women's behavior.[16] Women transformed the student movement by infusing feminism into its ranks. Unlike their male counterparts, women activists were not sought out for co-optation by the government of Luís Echeverría.[17] However, his administration made symbolic overtures to women, notably by hosting the 1975 International Women's Year conference. Feminists in the 1970s created a pluralistic women's rights movement that organized consciousness-raising groups, nongovernmental organizations, and public events. Feminists recalled that the movement was distinctive from earlier eras in its emphasis on women's power over their own bodies, including abortion rights, sexual assault awareness, and positive sexuality.[18] The movement also sought to remain apart from formal political institutions or parties. It found organized expressions in Mujeres en Acción Solidaria (Women in Solidarity Action), which formed in 1971, and the Movimiento Nacional de Mujeres (National Women's Movement), which formed in 1973.[19] The emphasis on personal experience and bodily integrity connected profoundly with women's athletics, though the women athletes and feminists rarely connected in a formal way.

Structural changes, including mass migration and increased numbers of women in the formal labor sector, challenged traditional social relations in the 1960s and 1970s.[20] New economic imperatives created demands for low-wage labor, which women frequently filled. Some experienced the disruption to traditional family structures as traumatic, while others found it liberating. Women workers enjoyed participating in popular cultural practices as they carved out free time and some disposable income. Stories of women as consumers of globalized fashions like the miniskirt were sensationalized and used as cautionary tales.[21] Sportswear was limited to tennis outfits or bathing suits, and the makeshift football kits would have provided a comfortable, nontraditional look for players that likely raised eyebrows.

MEXICAN WOMEN IN SPORTS

Despite the fame of Mexico's female global icons like Frida Kahlo and Chavela Vargas, and women's contributions to national culture in Mexico more broadly, female public figures routinely experienced discrimination. In civic associations and leisure activities, women struggled to claim free time. As men's power rested on their control of women's time, labor, and bodies, women's athletics challenged all three. In the mid-twentieth century, tennis, gymnastics, swimming, track and field, basketball, and volleyball dominated the women's sports scene. These women's events, approved by the International Olympic Committee, developed further once they were included in the Pan-American and Central American and Caribbean Games.

This is not to say that women's inclusion in Mexican sporting activities was uncontroversial. In the 1951 Pan-American Games the Mexican team caused a scandal by including a woman, Eva Valdés, on the equestrian team. Her inclusion prompted vocal complaints from the Argentine team, and ultimately she was blocked from the competition. In the aftermath of the controversy, La Afición published a letter from an anonymous source lamenting the inclusion of Valdés, who was the sister of the team captain Alberto Valdés.[22] The letter expressed horror that the woman had tried to compete, as her efforts ignored the International Equestrian Federation's rules that prohibited women from competition. In fact, the shocked reader cited the specific article in the regulations, which stated, "Amazons are not allowed to participate."[23]

The 1955 Pan-American Games proved to be crucial to Mexico's sporting identity. Although Mexico had hosted the Central American and Caribbean Games, in 1955 the delegates from Argentina and Brazil were so impressed with the Mexican sporting facilities that they pushed Mexico to bid for an Olympics.[24] For Mexican sports, both women's and men's, the event was a success as well. Antonio Estopier y Estopier, president of the Confederación Deportiva Mexicana (Mexican Sports Confederation, CODEME) and head of the Mexican delegation to the games, rejoiced that Mexico won more gold medals in 1955 than it had four years earlier. That he mistakenly attributed a women's gold medal to the wrong athlete perhaps speaks to the amount of attention the sporting establishment actually paid to women's sports.[25]

Mexico's hosting of the Pan-American Games offered female athletes a special opportunity to compete internationally without travel, opening the door for larger numbers of women to compete. While Mexican women did not dominate the competition, they medaled in swimming and diving and won the gold medal in volleyball. Serving as host for the 1968 Olympics further increased funding and interest in amateur sports. While government entities allocated resources unevenly, women's sports benefitted significantly. For example, Mexico hired the Polish coach Stanislaw Poburka in 1966 to lead the women's volleyball team with an eye to winning the Pan-American Games and the Olympics.[26] Previously, the men's and women's teams had been coached by the same person. Thus, it appears that the Mexican Olympic Committee took the success of the women's team quite seriously.

Basketball, too, disseminated widely among women, despite the fact that it was criticized early on as "too rough" due to the level of contact between players.[27] Perhaps because basketball was not considered the national sport, women avoided some of the scrutiny they received when playing football. It might also have helped that the Young Men's Christian Association (YMCA) had promoted basketball in the Americas since the 1920s as a wholesome alternative to football. The general discourse on women's basketball in Mexico was that the Aztecas—as the national team was called—were very quick and talented, but always the underdog because of their height.[28] The national team toured Mexico extensively, and regular stops included Chihuahua and Ciudad Juárez. Northern Mexican cities in particular had strong ties to the clubs from the capital, as they were also convenient stops en route to the United States. Indeed, the growth of university women's basketball in the United States helped create opportunities for more talented sparring partners. In 1969, for instance, the Mexican women's national basketball team toured the United States, visiting Northern Arizona University and Philadelphia's Temple University.[29] Mexican teams did not compete against only educational institutions when they toured the United States. In Texas, they played against Union Furniture of El Paso, Williams Air Force Base, and the Phoenix Crusaders.[30] The Phoenix Crusaders likely represented a club affiliated with a Protestant church. Women also appeared more often as coaches in basketball than in other sports, perhaps reflecting their longer history of playing or their close ties to physical education institutes.

Indeed, the United States provided a significant network for women's sports to develop. Not only women's basketball teams, but also volleyball teams frequently traveled to the North for competition.

The Mexican national women's volleyball team often traveled with their male counterparts in the 1960s to Los Angeles in order to play tournaments.[31] These exchanges were cordial and exciting for players. However, the politics of the US-Mexican relationship were ever present within sports, as were broader geopolitics. For example, the United States denied a visa to Stanislaw Poburka, the Polish coach of the Mexican women's volleyball team, on the basis that he had not lived in Mexico long enough. In one stroke, the United States upheld its Cold War rivalry with the Soviet Bloc and its sporting rivalry with Mexico.[32]

Women's basketball and volleyball teams received considerable coverage when they represented Mexico in international tournaments. In 1970 the participation of the women's teams in the Central American and Caribbean Games sparked media coverage of female athletes.[33] Moreover, when women's teams outperformed their male counterparts, it drew attention.[34] Through players' biographies we can glean a bit about the history of women's basketball clubs. Sportswriters singled out Margarita Espinoza as particularly tall and talented.[35] Espinoza began to play in Chihuahua before she moved with her parents in 1965 to Mexico City. There, she began to play with the Universidad Nacional Autónoma de México (National Autonomous University of Mexico), where she was studying. By 1967 the university team was disintegrating and a new team called Leyes developed, which quickly made it into the top league of the city. Basketball provided an opportunity for Espinoza to travel to Texas and Arizona without her parents, a trip that would have been unheard of a generation earlier. Journalists demonstrated a long-term familiarity with women's basketball, which they had covered since at least the 1950s. When the veteran player Armida Guerrero was dropped from the national team, the press showed knowledge of her career years before. Guerrero had played for one of Mexico's most prominent clubs, Marina, since 1965, when she signed at seventeen. Her fiancé was a well-known cyclist who died tragically. Guerrero speculated that her personal problems could have interfered with her play.[36]

Occasionally, exceptional women captured the attention of the press and sports fans because of their international performances. Nuria Ortíz became a world champion in pigeon shooting in 1966.[37] Women sharpshooters were not uncommon in Mexico. Known as Adelitas, women fighters had played a prominent role in the Mexican Revolution, and the iconography of armed women in Mexico was particularly powerful when compared to other parts of Latin America, at least until the civil wars in Central America in the 1980s. However, Ortíz was hardly an Adelita, a mestiza, or an indigenous peasant fighter. Rather, Ortíz and sport shooting represented the upper echelon of Mexican society. A long way removed from the revolutionary fervor and practical needs of rural women sharpshooters, sport riflery was a leisure activity that Ortíz trained to master at a world-class level. Ortíz, a member of Club Golf México, belonged to a small circle of female athletes that belonged to exclusive sports clubs.[38] Florencia Hernández was a leading golfer in the 1970s and hoped to compete in the fourth world championship of amateur women golfers. She trained at Club Chapultepec.[39] At times, athletes and their supporters used these victories to press for more state support for women's sports. At the 1967 Pan-American Games in Winnipeg, for example, the gold medal performance by the fencer Pilar Roldán led the Mexican delegation's trainer to lament that a complete women's fencing team had not been sent.[40]

Indeed, while most of the time women's sports and women athletes received little attention in the Mexican media, coverage of them expanded during international competitions such as the Pan-American Games. Even still, attention paid to women's sports paled in comparison to that given to men's games. The sports magazine *La Afición* relied on wire services for information about particular events and then filled readers in about certain athletes. In the 1951 games, for example, it highlighted two female track-and-field athletes. Bertha Chiú, a javelin and discus thrower from Chihuahua, received attention after achieving surprising success. Concepción Villanueva, the national and Central American discus champion, was quickly dismissed after she underperformed and failed to make the finals.[41] One journalist asked, "Nerves? Poor conditioning? Who knows?"[42]

Hortensia "Tencha" López, a young woman from Ciudad Juárez, made the sports pages' headlines for winning the javelin throw, which came as a shock to sportswriters.[43] According to reports, López had never competed before in the javelin. The description of López is interesting and provides a window on the views of women athletes, at least in exceptional circumstances. The press explained that despite her supposed inexperience, the Mexican blood that coursed through her veins combined with the "decisiveness and traditional values of our race" meant that there "were no obstacles that could not be overcome."[44] After the tournament was over several athletes were invited to Brazil and Chile.[45] The brief mention of López highlights one of the more salient features of Mexican sportswriting at the time. Only when women performed well did they make the sports pages, and almost always their success was seen as coming out of the blue. Moreover, they disappeared from view just as quickly as they appeared.

THE RISE OF *FÚTBOL FEMENIL*

The rapid growth of women's football in Mexico was based in part on grassroots development and in part on the attention paid to the sport by journalists in the late 1960s and early 1970s. Based on scattered references in the magazines *La Afición* and *Esto*, Mexican women's football began in the late 1950s but remained relatively isolated. In Guadalajara, for example, women organized regular football matches beginning with the two teams El Nacional and Mayitas, in 1959.[46] One news report noted that the women put "seriousness and femininity into every play."[47] A league, organized by women from the city, emerged that year and played continuously until 1970. The league president, Clara Alicia Sepúlveda, was the sister of "Tigre" Guillermo Sepúlveda, a famous player on the Mexican men's national team. Armida Castellón and Estela Castellón also served on the executive board.[48] While locals in Guadalajara might have known of the league's existence, few others outside Jalisco's capital were aware. A 1963 tour by two Costa Rican teams might have changed that, spurring further interest in the game. From that point on women's football appeared to develop quickly in Mexico, though the sport had already been organized to a large extent. Indeed, the rapid growth of the sport after its supposed inception suggests that women had been playing organized football at an earlier date.[49] Whenever the sport actually began, however, by 1969 it emerged for good. Since then, whether in grassroots, women-organized leagues; as part of the formal Mexican Football Federation; or as something in between, women's football has been a part of the Mexican sports-scape.

In 1969, women fans from Club América organized two teams—"Azul" and "Crema"—and began playing exhibition matches. Their play rapidly attracted attention, and as new teams sprang up, the Liga América was born. In the first season of the league, seventeen teams competed in and around Mexico City. Games had thirty-minute halves and were played on municipal fields around the city. The FMF refused to recognize women's football, so the league received support from the city government. To the municipal authorities, the sport seemed to appear from almost nowhere. They believed that Mexican women were new to football and were following trends in Europe. The league, according them, "was created to open new horizons for the lovely sex inside sports, and is based on foreign countries who were instigators of women's football 5 or 6 years ago."[50] By 1970, Liga América had twenty-eight teams, coexisting uneasily with two other leagues: Escuela Nacional de Educación Física (National School of Physical Education) and Liga Iztaccíhuatl. All three leagues competed not only for players but also for referees, field space, and the scarce resources open to women's football. But leagues continued to form. The National Institute for Youth started a league, and the Liga de Xochimilco began as well.

The first national women's tournament, called the Copa Femenil Mexicano, also began in 1970, organized by the newly created Asociación Mexicana de Fútbol Femenil (Mexican Association of Women's Football, AMFF) and comprising sixteen teams. The popularity of the sport continued to grow, and by 1971 the Liga América had grown to forty-four teams. Its closest rival, Liga Iztaccíhuatl, had a further twenty-six teams. The hosting of the second women's football world championship provided both impetus for increased growth and cause for concern among the football institutions. As the International Federation of Association Football (FIFA) had not yet decided on whether to bring women's football under its auspices, any exhibition of it was deemed threatening not only to the gendered status quo, but also to its institutional oversight of all forms of the sport. When the FMF took over official control of the women's game in 1971, under instructions from FIFA, it gave women's football no resources. Effectively, in fact, the FMF takeover pushed the sport underground, where it survived relatively intact until the 1980s. After the world championship in Mexico, the sport quickly faded from the spotlight. Due to internecine squabbles among the mostly male league directors, including accusations of financial exploitation of the players after the event, the media turned on women's football and women football players. The world championship, though a cultural and sporting success, caused a good deal of consternation over who deserved the profit from the games and where women fell in terms of the professional and amateur categories.

THE FIRST LEAGUE

The "first" women's football tournament in Mexico City was played in November 1969, according to *El Heraldo de México*. It was contested between sixteen teams at the Estadio Municipal in the Ciudad Deportiva Magdalena Mixhuca. The matches had two halves of thirty minutes divided by a ten-minute rest. Efraín Pérez, a professor at the Escuela Nacional de Educación Física (National School for Physical Education), organized the tournament. Ten clubs came from the Federal District and six from nearby provinces. The roster included Club Delsa, of Cuautitlán; Universidad de Toluca; Universidad de Puebla; Deportivo Irapuato; Academia Fénix, of Cuautla; Gacelas, of San Juan; Progreso Industrial; Deportivo Coapa; Deportivo Tepito; Club Independiente; Unidad Morelos; Deportivo Financiera; Deportivo Cellini; Deportivo Karam; and

América teams A and B.[51] These clubs would form the basis for the first women's league. It is hard to determine the exact nature of these teams. Women and girls on the teams ranged in age from around thirteen to twenty. Judging from the club names and the brief descriptions, several represented small clubs from barrios, educational institutions, and workplaces. Tepito, a center of working-class sports, was represented, as was the watchmaker Cellini, and the dominant professional club América.[52]

In the first year, the only newspaper to cover the women's league with any regularity was *El Heraldo de México*, as its journalist Manelich Quintero became deeply involved in the organization and administration of the women's game. At the same time that *El Heraldo de México* promoted the women's game, however, it still relegated women's football to the margins, and gave much more column space to the Torneo de los Barrios (Tournament of the Barrios), which it sponsored. The Torneo de los Barrios was a male-only affair, bringing together local amateur teams from around the city and province for a massive competition. Moreover, while it supported both the women's competition and the Torneo de los Barrios, it separated them: there was no women's branch of the Torneo de los Barrios.[53] Women participated in the tournament in traditional roles: serving as godmothers of the teams and carrying flowers to the winners. Even in the most supportive of spaces, in other words, gender segregation in football was extreme.

Yet *El Heraldo de México*'s coverage of the Liga América took the sport seriously.[54] In 1969, the language and images used to describe women players were far less objectifying than those that would appear in the following years and, indeed, in the present day. Commentary on the matches included reports on women's skill and playing style. The newspaper also acted as something of a league promoter. It listed phone numbers so that interested players could call to join the league. It also commented that the public responded very positively to the matches. Photographs from games presented a great rupture to the visual landscape of the late 1960s. While certainly there were countercultural trends gaining popularity, such as long hair for men and miniskirts for women, images of women playing football represented a deviation from anything else in visual culture. Instead of suggestive images of posed women or of elderly women in domestic roles, futboleras' hair flew, their muscles strained, their elbows dug into opponents, and they sweat. Their faces grimaced, celebrated, and registered surprise. Still, alongside the constant references to women as the "weaker sex," even *El Heraldo de México*, which clearly wanted to support women's football, could not resist suggesting that women spent halftime primping.[55] However, the photographs that accompanied articles did not support the implication that women were concerned about the way they looked on the field. Moreover, in the era before women's sporting events were marketed on the basis of supposed sex appeal, one can see how different the optics of women's football in Mexico were in 1970. The players touched each other affectionately, and while it is impossible to know the inner workings of the women photographed, they appeared both happy and proud.[56]

The burst of attention on women's football provided a rare opportunity for women athletes to appear in major media outlets. Players' names, photographs, and small biographical details appeared in major newspapers of the city. In 1969, a match between América "Azul" and Ixtacalco was televised.[57] Media attention was paramount to attract spectators to games. In the league's first days, games attracted around two thousand people. From newspaper photographs of the first tournament, the crowds appear, as at men's games, to be mostly men. This appeared to change over the course of the tournament, with a greater number of women and young girls attending the matches.[58] *El Heraldo de México* published opinion pieces that argued women's teams deserved better fields. From the photographs, most of the matches were played on dirt. In addition, as the first season gained momentum, photographs show spectators watching from hills and trees surrounding the fields without bleachers.[59]

El Heraldo de México normalized women's football in other ways as well, at the same time that it mirrored larger debates around how women could reconcile work with motherhood. When the Swedish

women's player Yvonne Stelnert was offered a contract by Torino
to play professional football in Turin, Italy, *El Heraldo de México*
reported the news. The article title left little doubt as to the opinion
of the paper: "She's going to be a mother . . . and they want to sign
her in football!"[60] The brief story might not have had the desired
impact. Rather than shocking readers, it might have made the sport
seem more appealing. Shortly after publication, a young woman
named María Edith found her way to the offices of the newspaper
and asked for the address of the club in Turin in order to offer her
talents.[61] The newspaper took photos of María Edith, put together
a press package, and sent it along to Italy. The journalists tested her
out in the office. In its promotion of María Edith, the newspaper
included photographs of her in high heels. The paper explained that
she "did not lose her femininity due to football." "To the contrary,"
it wrote, "she is beautiful and charming."[62] The paper reported that
she immediately invited them for dinner to see that she cooked just
as well as she played. Nevertheless, María Edith admitted to the
newspaper that she lost boyfriends for playing better football than
they did.

Despite the canned narratives that framed many stories of women
footballers, their own opinions occasionally made it into print.
Women frequently noted the importance of the solidarity they felt
with other players, and solidarity represented one of the most threatening aspects of women's football. Given the patriarchal norms of
the country and the limited avenues for female solidarity, the unity
forged on the field represented a bridge too far for many men and
women. In religious practice, traditional political history, and popular culture, machismo meant that male satisfaction was of paramount importance. Yet futboleras frequently cited female friendship
as a central attraction to the sport. For example, María Edith explained her dissatisfaction with Club América, because of the team's
lack of *compañerismo*, or fellowship.[63] The pleasure of playing with
other women went beyond the pitch. It must have been a unique
opportunity to bond with other women over a shared passion and to
play competitively with them. Maria de la Luz Hernández, a forward

FIGURE 5.1. Dirt fields, Liga América, 1969. *El Heraldo de México*, December 1, 1969.

on the América team, explained that "the *compañerismo* of all the girls to be able do something and win if it is possible" was the most important part of the process.[64]

It is difficult to generalize about the women who played in the first league, given that only a handful captured the attention of the press. Some came from other sports. Elvira Aracén, for example, had never played a game of football before 1969. Her family were all fans of American football, so it was only when friends tricked her into playing that she set foot on the field. But she was an accomplished athlete who had represented Mexico in Jamaica at the ninth Central American and Caribbean Games in 1962, competing in the eighty-meter hurdles and the long jump.[65] Certainly, the young age of the participants is notable. Aracén, at twenty-two, was one of the older players, with many players between thirteen and fifteen years old, which was markedly different from the other teams in Latin America and Europe.[66] One exception was the club organized by the Escuela Nacional de Educación Física, which fielded multiple teams of physical education teachers and students studying to be physical education instructors.[67] Most players fit a common profile: they were Mexico City residents; most had migrated to the capital as children; many were students in vocational or secondary schools; and nearly all of them had a male family member who played football at some level. Some were recruited from other sports, such as track and field. Some futboleras worked. One, María Cristina, was a stenographer. Another, the captain of Club Independiente, worked as a bank secretary. Others were students, and one helped out at her family's fruit stand.[68] The club of Escuela Nacional de Educación Física seemed to receive at least some support from the school, as one journalist noted the players were "very coquettish with their new uniforms."[69] New clubs seemed to join the league in January, including one named after the intellectual forerunner of Mexican feminism, the seventeenth-century nun Sor Juana Inés de la Cruz.[70] By January 1970 there were fifteen teams regularly competing in what was dubbed the top league in the Federal District. *El Heraldo de México* described the movement as "football fever."[71]

The community of women's football attempted to create a civic association structure to stabilize and diffuse the leagues' activities, in line with international football regulations. An association, for example, had to include more than one league. In 1970, club leaders founded the Asociación Mexicana de Fútbol Femenil (Mexican Association of Women's Football, AMFF).[72] As with any governing body, this group set about creating rules for the sport. Liga América continued to thrive throughout the 1970 season. Yet despite the fashionable trend of women's football in 1970, reporters continued to have more familiarity and investment in volleyball.[73] Space posed a big challenge to teams that struggled for resources, in part due to increased urbanization. Fields were at a premium, and women's leagues were granted access to public—either municipal or CODEME—rather than private spaces. The fields made available, according to contemporary reports, were less than ideal.[74] They were dirt and rock. Some had broken glass mixed in with the rocks. In the words of Elvira Aracén, the fields "were not exactly like the Estadio Azteca."[75] There were neither bleachers nor dressing rooms. The women played six of the seven games of their tournament at the Ciudad Deportiva. Newspaper reports describe a festive environment, filled with optimism for the future of women's football. Again, photographs show a diverse crowd, and many children attended games, which was notably different from the men's game. When Progreso Industrial defeated América, fans rushed the field, but many

of the fans were children or were holding children.[76] It was a very
different scenario than América's usual pitch invaders. *El Heraldo
de México* reported that the interest in women's football had taken
everyone by surprise. Attendance had increased so substantially that
they needed a field with bleachers because fans crowded the sidelines
so tightly that they were nearly on the pitch.

Indeed, the sport's popularity seemed to grow every day. Celebrity
figures such as the television and film actor Chabelo agreed to be
godfathers of women's teams.[77] Local politicians also began to attend women's football events. The secretary of public works for
Querétaro, Alfonso Macedo Rivas, inaugurated a festival of wom-
en's football in San Juan del Río.[78] In the same festival, the municipal president, Raúl Olvera Aróstegui, captained one of the teams.[79]
According to *El Heraldo de México*, thousands of spectators attended. Women's increasing political activity might have influenced
politician's decisions to participate in women's football activities.
Nevertheless, the presence of local political leaders and cultural icons
lent credibility to the sport and made it more acceptable to play.

Women of the provinces paid keen attention to the women's
football tournaments in the Federal District. *El Heraldo de México*
received a letter from one Norma Ramírez, a football player from
Durango.[80] She sought a spot in Club Independiente and mentioned
that her parents had already given her permission to travel to the
city to pursue playing football. The newspaper published the telephone number of a hotline for women players, which they could call
between two and four in the afternoon to give their information.
The popularity of the league was such that it considered holding
open tryouts.[81] Men's teams, too, saw the opportunity in women's
football. Deportivo Reynosa de Azcapotzalco formed a women's
football section that apparently integrated many recent immigrants
to Mexico City from Tamaulipas.[82] Indeed, coverage of Mexican
women's football reflected the intense period of migration to Mexico
City, and many of the players—and sometimes entire teams—were
identified by their home states.[83] For instance, the women's team of
Independiente were nicknamed Las Poblanas.[84] Every day, it seemed,
new clubs formed and sought affiliation with the league, including

PUBLICO... La afición por ver en acción a las chamacas del futbol, está creciendo a pasos agigantados. María Elena López inicia un avance teniendo como marco a una multitud de aficionados.

FIGURE 5.2. Liga América, 1969. *El Heraldo de México*, December 28, 1969.

the squads Ciudad Madero, Tlacotal, Deportivo Perú, Doctores, and La Colmena.[85] Women's football grew in the provinces as well. In Cuernavaca, the sport was spearheaded by Textiles Morelos, which sought to organize more matches in the city.[86]

As the sport continued its rise, women's football relied on the regular coverage it received in the Mexican press. Manelich Quintero wrote almost daily features on the sport in *El Heraldo de México*. While increased press coverage gave women more exposure than ever, however, many pieces rested upon persistent commentary about women's bodies. Many descriptions focused on their legs, hair, breasts, and faces, noting how particular colors drew out their beauty.[87] Indeed, sexuality filtered into commentary on male players as well. As male players became part of a celebrity culture, writers patrolled the sexualization of players by using particularly heteronormative language. When *El Heraldo de México* featured two brothers, Carlos and Nacho Calderón, in a color photograph it stipulated that the photograph was for the "lady fans."[88] Thus, even while supporting women's football, *El Heraldo de México* reinforced the notion that women were more often fans than players. At the same time, it implied that lusting after male players was something exclusive to women. In the same vein, journalists constantly asked women athletes about their marital status, boyfriends, and even hopes for future mates.

The coach and president of the Liga América (which would soon change its name to the Liga Femenil de Fútbol Mexicana to reflect its independence from Club América and to broaden its appeal), Efraín Pérez, became a key leader in the organization of women's football. Pérez recognized the challenges that women players faced in Mexico, even if he was unaware of the longer history of the sport in the region. He argued that football was "a legitimate aspiration" for women and lamented the lack of support that the sport received, comparing women's struggles in sports to women's struggles in society more broadly.[89] "Women," he suggested, "have always felt— without being so—less than men; and through pride and eagerness have succeeded in overcoming their lack of support."[90] In every area of society, he argued, women were "if not surpassing, then becoming equal to men," including in sports "by way of football."[91] Pérez built upon his success in organizing the league to build the first women's national team in 1970.

The growth of women's football in Mexico and elsewhere made international institutions take note. Already in 1965, after the appearance of women's football in Costa Rica, Venezuela, Colombia, and around Europe, FIFA discussed the sport in an emergency meeting, encouraging member federations to discourage women's football.[92] But with the men's World Cup on the horizon, especially given the role of the FMF president Guillermo Cañedo in both FIFA and Telesistema, it was even more difficult to ignore the sport's explosion.[93] And so in 1970, just prior to the FIFA men's World Cup in Mexico, and before FIFA officially recognized that women's football existed, a group of wives of FIFA representatives toured Mexico City. One of their stops was at the Ciudad Vicentina, a center for the poor run by Vincentian nuns. The wives visited a workshop where young women produced clothing, and also attended a women's football match. *El Sol de México* sarcastically noted that the girls "would not raise the Jules Rimet Cup," but rather, "bruises on their beautiful extremities."[94] The tone of the article again highlights the difficulty some male sportswriters had with looking at women's sports as competition rather than spectacle. It also shows clearly that people connected to FIFA knew women's football existed.

If the world was coming to know Mexican women's football, so too the Mexican press informed its readers about the sport elsewhere. *El Heraldo de México* reported on the development of women's football in Europe, particularly Italy and France.[95] In Turin, it reported, over twelve thousand fans attended women's games. The game had become so popular in France that the Women's Football Federation of France considered requesting affiliation with FIFA. While this was clearly not the first time that European women's football was brought to the attention of the Latin American public, renewed interest in its popularity among European women provided legitimacy to the sport, at least in part, for Europhiles in Latin America.[96]

MEXICO AND THE FIRST WOMEN'S WORLD CHAMPIONSHIP

Media coverage of women's football in Mexico grew throughout 1969, but expanded exponentially by the middle of the following year as the AMFF readied a national team to compete in the first FIEFF world championship in Italy. Interest around the sport developed in tandem with increased exposure. From the outset of the endeavor, the press played an oversized role. The journalist Manelich Quintero claimed that he had received information about the tournament from Jorge Sandoval, a Mexican reporter based in Italy, and passed the information on to Efraín Pérez.[97] Quintero would also accompany the team to Italy in his capacity as secretary of the AMFF, at the expense of the team masseuse. In the end, the AMFF might have felt it was more important to control the media narrative of the team at the tournament, while *El Heraldo de México* might have seen unfettered access to the women's team as a marketing advantage.

The team that represented Mexico was chosen through the same method that men's teams were: a set number of women were on a preselection list, from which the final team was made. In the case of Mexico's 1970 women's team, the team director Efraín Pérez (also the AMFF president) and the coach José Morales gathered approximately one hundred of the best women players in the Mexico City area, and some from nearby states, and put them through a series of skill, speed, and conditioning drills, as well as tactical discussions. Eventually they whittled the team, after four separate selections, down to sixteen.[98] Tensions rankled the women's football world as the preselections approached, with rumors swirling that only players from the Liga América would be chosen for tryouts. In fact this was not the case, with players drawn from the Liga Iztacchíhuatl as well, including players from Cruz Azul, Naucalpan, Pachuca, Toluca, and Cuautla, and members of eleven teams from outside of the capital region called in for preselection.[99] The young women who were selected began training at 5:00 or 5:30 a.m. in Chapultepec Park, after which time the team would take a break in order for members to go to school or to work, followed by practice at whatever field the team had borrowed for the day. If no field was available, the squad found space at Chapultepec.[100] The women trained hard, in part because they had only two or three months to prepare. In the weeks prior to departure, the team played a series of friendly matches against local women's teams but faced little competition. As a result, the team approached a high school boys' team willing to play them.

As the media began reporting on the futboleras' upcoming trip, some likened the women's participation in the first world championship to Mexico's entrance into global football at the Olympics in Amsterdam in 1928.[101] Following this analogy, newspapers argued that Mexico should lower its expectations. After all, women had been playing the sport officially for less than a year, even if they had already formed recognized leagues and an association.[102] They reminded readers that Europe, as always, was well ahead of Mexico, especially because women's football was almost professional and had "true" athletes. José Morales, head coach of the Mexican team, was unconcerned about the European squads that his team would face, noting that he had "good material in the girls" to work with.[103] According to him, even though the "morenitas" lacked height, weight, and experience in comparison to their European opponents, they remained "undaunted."[104] Referring to the players as *morenitas*—a reference to their dark-skinned, lower-class backgrounds—highlights the nature of thinking about women's sports discussed earlier. Much in the same way that the press credited the javelin thrower Hortensia López's success to her Mexicanness rather than her training, here Morales stressed that the Mexican women would be undaunted because of their inherent *mexicanidad*. According to Elvira Aracén, Morales had no training and little tactical knowledge, though he was capable at directing players on the field.[105] Just before the departure for Italy, *El Sol de México* ran a photograph of the team member Rebeca Lara on the front page, spurring the team on and lauding its "good defenders" and "good forwards" who played "con ganas."[106] One week before the team's departure for Italy, the journalist Maria Guadalupe de Santa Cruz reinforced the notion of the Mexican underdogs, writing, "People have begun to become very interested in this committed little group of athletes who are ready to fight with unequaled passion in Italy."[107] While they were inexperienced, in other words, they still represented the nation. The image of Mexico as a smaller, darker, and scrappier team fighting against the Europeans was powerful and was used frequently in the press. Here, the players stood in for Mexico, often portrayed as competing in the world against the influence and wealth of Europe and the United States. In placing Mexicans as neophytes in the world of football, the press both preemptively excused any defeats and set the team up as heroic in case of victory.

But the press depiction of a team with little experience and resources was hardly a narrative meant to build up the team. To the contrary, players and coaches had much to worry about in regard to their lack of equipment. Just six days before the team left for Italy, Efraín Pérez put out a plea to "people and institutions of goodwill," through *El Sol de México*, asking for whatever help people could give in order to equip the team. Pérez estimated that the team needed roughly twenty thousand pesos to make the trip.[108] The team "lacked everything." Less than a week before departing, they had neither uniforms nor travel clothes. Many had no cleats, he said, due to the "scarcity of small sizes." This was not a new problem. According to Manelich Quintero, during the months of preparation for the championship, the women's team had no balls with which to practice. A men's national team player, Enrique Borja, lent the necessary equipment, while Dr. Arturo Heredia of the medical center of the national university offered medical care to the team for free.[109] In the end two institutional supporters came forward. General Alfonso Corona del Rosal, the regent of the Federal District, charged his office with providing uniforms and travel clothing, while the department of sports activities at the national university, headed by Gustavo Moctezuma, also helped outfit the team.[110] According to *El Heraldo de México*, Guillermo Cañedo, the president of the FMF, wanted to help the women's national team but could not because FIFA had not recognized women's football.[111]

Notwithstanding financial obstacles faced by the team, women faced individual challenges as well. The majority of the women playing on Mexico's first national team came from "humble backgrounds" and lacked the resources necessary to buy shoes, balls, and other equipment.[112] Some of them were workers, as was the case of Maria de la Luz Hernández, who assembled transistors, while others were students or helped their mothers with work (*quehaceres domésticos*) in their homes.[113] Given their economic backgrounds, traveling outside of Mexico—let alone to Europe to play football—was something that they had never expected.[114] Many had never thought of playing football outside of the relatively safe confines of the Liga América, though many had dreamed of wearing the Mexico jersey. All, save the reserve goalkeeper and self-described chaperone Elvira Aracén, were under twenty years old. Aracén was the only one who had been on a plane before—traveling to Cuba, Jamaica, and the United States to represent Mexico in track-and-field events.

Women players confronted disapproval from their parents, as elsewhere in Latin America. A number of women players recalled being punished for playing the sport. Maria Silvia Zaragoza's father beat her because he thought the sport "was made only for men." Alicia "La Pelé" Vargas faced opposition from her parents, who sometimes dragged her from games by her ears. Patty Hernández used

to argue with her sister over the appropriateness of playing football, until her sister started to play.[115] Elvira Aracén's family thought
that because Mexico was a *"machista* society" and football was a
man's game, a woman playing football was akin to "putting one's
nose where it didn't belong." Still, they did not try to stop her, perhaps because when she began to play she was already an adult.[116]
Nevertheless, in the run-up to Italy, the press focused on the support
futboleras received from their families. It made, after all, a much
better story. Many reports mentioned the importance of fathers and
brothers in encouraging the futboleras to play. In one case, Yolanda
Ramírez, the starting goalkeeper for the Mexican national team in
1970, actually taught her brothers how to play the game.[117] So,
whatever the parents of the first Mexican national women's team
actually thought about their daughters playing football, at least some
of them displayed pride. In an article just before the team left for
Italy, *El Sol de México* published a photo of "proud mothers of
families" and their "happy daughters."[118] The press offered assur-
ances that the girls never lost their femininity while playing football,
reporting, for example, that Elsa Salgado liked to knit in her spare
time.[119] According to press reports, as they prepared to board the
plane, some cried for fear of flying.[120] Once they arrived in Italy, the
young women showed their inexperience in other ways: the first sou-
venirs of the trip were packets of salt and sugar from the airplane;
and Maria Eugenia Rubio and Nila brought green chilies that their
families had stashed in their bags to the first dinner in Italy.[121]

The surprise of the Mexican sports press after Mexico's 9–0 defeat
of Austria in its first game can hardly be overstated. Articles noted
the futboleras' skills, complaining that "the encounter . . . lacked
interest due to the evident superiority of the winners."[122] An estimated ten thousand people attended the match to witness the "more
athletic" Austrians be overwhelmed due to their lack of "technical
faculties."[123] Indeed, across the board, press commentary noted the
"technique," the organization of the squads, and the "excellent impression" that the top teams made in the tournament.[124] Despite its
resounding victory over Austria, Mexico went on to lose to hosts
Italy 2–1 in the semifinals. According to press reports, the skill of

FIGURE 5.3. Elvira Aracén, goalkeeper for the
Mexican women's national team, 1971. *El
Heraldo de México*, September 1, 1971.

the Mexican players collapsed under the physicality of the Italian
squad. *El Sol de México* provided a full play-by-play of the match,
noting specifically the play of the Italian "diva," the left wing Elena
Schiavo, who scored both goals, one on a penalty and one with a
"precise shot, taken with very good style."[125] For *El Heraldo de
México*, however, it was not the skill but the strength of the Italian
squad that undid the *mexicanas*.[126] "The Italian defense," wrote *El
Sol de México*, was "composed of very strong girls who play quite
a rough game."[127] Still, while the physical play "demoralized" the
Mexican team, the "caserismo [favoritism]" of the Italian referee
was the "true basis" of Italy's victory.[128]

Mexico went on to play England in the third-place game, which made front-page headlines in *El Sol de México* on July 14. According to the media, Mexico "deservedly won" the hard-fought game 3–2. Journalists again took the efforts of the futboleras seriously, noting that they "confronted a solid English team whose reaction in the second half kept the outcome in constant doubt."[129] The photo that topped the sports section of *El Sol de México* noted that both Mexico and England "offered a good, technical game."[130] As with other matches, players' skills rather than appearance were analyzed. One author commented particularly on the speed and shot of England's Davies, who scored her team's first goal "with a magnificent shot from 25 meters."[131] In the summary of Mexico's victory, writers stressed English physical superiority—their height and strength, particularly. However, Mexico emerged victorious due to their speed and skill on the ball.[132] From the perspective of the Mexican media, the first women's football world championship was a total success in terms of its attendance. The Italian public turned up in large numbers to see the matches (with the exception of the Italy-Mexico semifinal, where three thousand attended a game played in extreme heat) and "responded with enthusiasm . . . rewarding the players with applause."[133] The games, particularly those involving Denmark, Mexico, and England, offered the "quality" expected by football fans of any gender, and the teams played at "an appreciable level . . . homogenous and well organized."[134] The level of play left no doubt that "women's football is as valid as men's."[135] In the face of FIFA and FMF reticence about the place of women's football, this was a strong conclusion, and one that still has not managed to penetrate the upper echelons of most footballing federations nearly fifty years later.

After their final match against England, the Mexican national team remained in Italy, where local officials treated them as visiting dignitaries. They received the symbol of the city of Turin, a bronze trophy on marble, during a visit to the Palace of Justice.[136] They were also given a tour of the Martini and Rossi factory and wine museum and visited the Basilica of Superga.[137] Italian "admiration" for the Mexican team also prompted organizers to schedule an exhibition match against Torino before returning home.[138] Other matches were offered, but the delegation turned them down for lack of funds.[139]

In retrospect, the significance of the experience in Italy, however brief, for women who played on this inaugural national team cannot be overstated. Many of the young women who played on the national team noted that it was their dream to play for their country. "We were truly," one former player from the 1971 team recalled, "representatives of Mexico."[140] Given that there were no prior women's national teams on which to model themselves, the futboleras had to work very hard to create their own universe. Prior to leaving for Italy, Silvia Zaragoza, a forward on the team, noted that football was her "only dream."[141] El Heraldo de México described the experience as a "dream converted into reality" for the women.[142] For Elvira Aracén, representing "the Mexico in which she was born and learned to live" was "the highest aspiration of any athlete."[143] Patricia Hernández concurred: "Upon being selected," she said, "what any player feels is a heavy weight and a responsibility that we have to fulfill."[144] Lupita Tovar, captain of the national team because of her "seriousness, calmness, and composure," told the press upon departing for Italy: "I don't have words to describe how I feel inside [and she raises her hand to her heart], but we're going with soul and life to do what is called a good job."[145]

On their return to Mexico City, the Mexican delegation was met with great fanfare, though the celebratory nature of their welcome papered over serious conflicts. The AMFF organized the twenty-eight clubs that belonged to the organization to greet the national team at the airport.[146] Mariachis were arranged, and groups from the players' neighborhoods showed up at the airport as well. Maria Eugenia "La Peque" Rubio arrived to a big banner from La Colonial El Alemán. So surprised were the women at the crowds waiting for their arrival that they thought someone famous had flown with them back to Mexico.[147] Not only did players receive a warm reception at the airport, but civic leaders and others sought to congratulate the team. The Mexico City Lions Club, for example, arranged a dinner for the coach and players, which was attended by the Italian ambassador.[148] Alfonso Corona del Rosal, the regent of Mexico City, met the team and promised them a field of their own.[149] Corona del Rosal made good on his promise, delivering a field in the Ciudad Deportiva Magdalena Mixhuca.[150] A dance at Salón Maxim was organized in honor of the team and featured the popular café singer Javier Batiz.

Still, before they even returned to Mexico, concerns arose over the place of women's football in the country, and of women's place in football. The success of the women's team occasioned little celebration on the part of the FMF. On the same day as it reported on the final of the women's world championship, *El Sol de México* published an article addressing the Mexican federation's attitude toward women's football. "In principle," it reported, "the Federation [FMF] is in favor of accepting the Association of Women's Football, but it first needs the authorization of FIFA, which will have the last word."[151] The FMF executive committee had "discussed the issue of women's football in its last meeting, without reaching definitive agreement."[152] Two days later, however, the headline of *El Sol de México*'s sports pages read, "No women's league has affiliated with the FMF."[153] The headline was accompanied on the first page by an opinion piece, "There should not be women footballers," with the subtitle, "The sport can cause disorders." In it, the author made clear that the FMF had not received any "indications" regarding the request that it had sent to FIFA, and as a result no women's league had been affiliated.[154] Joaquín Soria Terrazas, head of the amateur division of the FMF, summarized the federation's stance in regard to women's football:

Before we move forward with anything, we need to know under what situations we will have women's football. Until now we have only had informal discussions with the directors of the Liga Iztaccíhuatl, but only regarding the league's organization. It is also true that said league has requested affiliation [with the FMF] but the fact that they have made the request does not mean that they are affiliated.[155]

Soria added his personal opinion on the matter of women's football. "I consider," he told the reporter, "football to be unsuitable for women . . . as it is practiced, football can cause considerable disorders." He concluded this line of thinking with his final assessment. "I just do not believe," he said, "[football] is an appropriate sport for women." Soria Terrazas's view was hardly unique. Players recall being constantly criticized for playing football: "if you played women's football, it was almost as if you were thrown out of the female sex."[156] Still, Soria Terrazas implicitly acknowledged that the sport might have gotten too popular for the federation to stop, noting that should the sport continue, "it is imperative to create very different rules."[157]

As head of the amateur division of the FMF, Soria Terrazas wielded considerable influence both within and outside of the federation. At his urging, the FMF canceled a match between two women's teams from Guadalajara in Estadio Jalisco.[158] *El Heraldo de México* speculated that the FMF feared the women's match would draw spectators away from professional men's games, especially because it was free. In fact, Club Oro complained that fans would not attend their men's match Saturday for precisely that reason.[159] In other words, beyond the broader limitations of sexist structural and cultural conditions, the FMF and FIFA played an important role in impeding women's football.

The FMF sought to cut off access to fields for any games honoring the women's national team by claiming to be awaiting clarification on the status of women's football from FIFA. It instructed professional clubs not to permit women's football teams to use their fields under any circumstances, threatening to sanction those that did.[160] However, the organizers of the women's tribute match had already spent money and time in advertising the match, and supporters of the women's game took little interest in the FMF sanctions. Moreover, FMF regulations forbade professional clubs from using their fields for other purposes. Since the exhibition was sponsored by the national university's department of athletic activities, the football federation had no jurisdiction. On top of that, the journalist Flavio Zavala Millet questioned the premise that FIFA had a right to rule on the permissibility of women's football. Noting that FIFA regulations said nothing about women's football, he argued, "it is a general and universal legal principle that anything that is not expressly prohibited is permitted." What then, he asked, did FIFA have to decide on?[161] Much as in Brazil, where clubs flouted the government ban on women's football when it served their interests, so too in Mexico, those who supported the women's game did so anyway. Clubes Unidos de Jalisco (United Clubs of Jalisco) also decided to ignore the FMF circular and allowed the women to play, to a reported seven thousand spectators.[162]

Ultimately, the women who represented Mexico in the first women's world championship in Turin broke new ground in many ways. While they were hardly the first women in Mexico to play football, they certainly raised the profile of the sport in the nation. The narrative of the team, as *morenitas* facing off against the larger and more football-savvy Europeans, made them into heroes for many. The sport grew rapidly after the first world championship, with new teams and leagues developing around the country. One former player remembers being invited to play in different states around the country. The futboleras had gone to Europe with little in the way of institutional support and none from the Mexican Football Federation, and had come back the most successful Mexican football team to date. In fact, however, the response of the official football institutions, both in Mexico and internationally, portended a rocky future for the sport. Nevertheless, whether officials were in favor of the game or not, in July 1970 women's football seemed firmly embedded in the media and in the Mexican landscape as a result of the national team's success. More and more girls and women sought to play the game. The only path for the sport appeared to be toward growth and greater visibility.

CONTINUED GROWTH

In spite of the official resistance from the FMF, women's football met with a good deal of success in 1970, and the relationships between the Mexican women's federation and other women's organizations forged during the first women's championship flourished. A month after the world championship, the AMFF, still led by Efraín Pérez, sent a cable to the FIEFF inviting the Italian team to play a rematch in Mexico.[163] According to Manelich Quintero, Guillermo Cañedo, the FMF president and FIFA vice president, proposed the match and offered to pay all costs for the Italian team. He had apparently seen some potential in the sport and was hoping to curry favor with the Italians.[164] In the autumn of 1970 the Italian women's team arrived in Mexico to play a rematch with the home team. The rematch between the national women's teams of Mexico and Italy took place in Estadio Azteca and was broadcast nationally on Channel 2.[165] Mexico defeated Italy 2–0 in front of sixty thousand fans in Estadio Azteca.[166] As it aired on national TV, the game gave many more Mexicans the chance to see the futboleras play and the opportunity to make their own decisions about the quality of women's football. It also inspired a number of lengthy articles and commentaries as the sport moved in from the margins. While many remained positive in their evaluation of the women's skill, not all did. For example, Hugo Cisterna wrote an editorial for *El Heraldo de México* that followed a typically ignorant pattern of assumptions. He opined, "Although women are more flexible and coordinated than men, this is not the case when they are playing football."[167] Cisterna described the players as clumsy on the ball, which he excused since the women had (according to him) only recently taken up the sport. He clearly had not checked into the backgrounds of some of the players, many of whom had been playing since they were children. On the whole, however, he described the match favorably and suggested the men's game should play the more open, offensive game of the women's team.

Italy played Mexico in a second match, in Guadalajara's Estadio Jalisco, and also played against Club América. Channel 8 in Mexico City broadcast the match, with commentary from Lupita Olaiz and Addiel Bolio, though no footage of this match has been found.[168] The match was well publicized and fans were excited to see América's star player, Alicia "La Pelé" Vargas, who had been left out of the games with the national team for disciplinary reasons.[169] In their final match before returning home, the Italian side beat Club América 4–0.[170] Following the visit, Marco Rambaudi, the head of the Italian women's football delegation and the president of the FIEFF, was so impressed with the facilities in Mexico and the popularity of the sport there that he declared his support for Mexico hosting the next women's world championship. The site of the 1971 tournament had yet to be determined and would be decided during a meeting of the women's football federation in Geneva.[171] Still, it would not be an easy task to earn the rights to host the championship, as Switzerland, Luxembourg, and Spain had also expressed interest in hosting the event. After an inconclusive first round, Mexico won the rights in a second vote.[172]

Interest in women's football continued to grow steadily. A match was organized in homage to the national team's performance that was televised on Channel 4 and sponsored by the beer company Superior. The sponsors and promoters of women's football assumed that the marketing materials used in men's games would serve the same purpose in the women's game. As a result, Superior advertised the game featuring a blonde woman with her eyes closed and a foot on the ball in a sexy and submissive position.[173] *El Heraldo de México* ran color photographs of the reporters on the field and claimed it was the first women's match televised in full in the world. The match was a success. By August of 1970, women's matches were shown regularly on Channel 8. Matches were televised at least until October of that year.[174]

Women's leagues took off as well. Elvira Aracén recalled that on her return from Italy in 1970, "wherever you went, there were teams of [women's] football," likening it to an explosion of the sport.[175] As the 1970 season continued, *El Heraldo de México* increased its reporting on women's football, with more in-depth coverage from Manelich Quintero and "Ric Rac." *El Nacional* began publishing the schedules of women's games in its sports section, something earlier confined to men's amateur and youth football.[176] In addition, *Ovaciones*, *Esto*, and *Fútbol de México y del Mundo* began running regular articles on women's football. More biographical information appeared in the press, as well as descriptions of the athletes' achievements and, finally, their style of play.[177] The women's teams were moving into all kinds of interesting places, including a convent with an adjoining school. The Mexican press took interest in women's football in other Latin American countries as well. Taking no small measure of pride in the Mexican situation, the local press commented that "the environment for women's football" elsewhere was "adverse." The press reported on Brazilian women in recent months who had formed teams of "coristas y modelos" (chorus girls and models), and that they had great figures but did not play good football.[178] According to *El Heraldo de México*, João Havelange and the Brazilian Football Federation banned further matches by pinup girls.

The press also began to give nicknames to players. This and other quotidian practices began to alter the perception of the sport. Women players frequently acquired the nicknames of male players, which was oftentimes complimentary. Among these was the Mexican player Alicia Vargas, a.k.a. La Pelé. Born in 1954, Vargas began playing as a youth with her brothers and other boys in the street. Against the wishes of her parents, Vargas continued to play. Playing in the streets gave her great touch with both feet, a skill she used to dribble around opponents (à la her favorite player, Garrincha), to lay passes off to her teammates, or to unleash a powerful shot. Maria Eugenia Rubio acquired the name La Peque—the kid—and Silvia Zaragoza carried the nickname La Borjita, after the men's national team player Enrique Borja, while Araceli Aviña was known as Garrincha. For her part Rubio, La Peque, was one of the smallest players on the team, and one of the most skilled dribblers. She was known for her guile, with one story claiming that she ran through the legs of a taller Austrian defender while dribbling the ball.[179]

And the women of the national team helped the sport to grow as well. Along with playing on teams in Mexico City, they began something of a barnstorming tour. Every Saturday or Sunday the women of the national team were invited to different parts of Mexico to play against local teams. With food and lodging taken care of by the host town, the team was often able to play away from home, thereby bringing the sport around the country. Eventually, the team directors began to plan these excursions, taking a percentage of the ticket sales to pay for costs. The women, according to Aracén, didn't get "even a cent," but "for many of the girls it was great, because they didn't know many places in Mexico."[180] Moreover, towns went out of their way to "create the environment" for well-attended games. The players would speak to the local print media and give interviews on local radio in advance of matches in order to increase turnout. With these mini tours, the women's team "began to diffuse [women's] football around the country."[181] Moreover, after games the women of the national team would stay and offer advice and coaching to their erstwhile rivals. By stimulating more interest in the sport, the women of the national team hoped to diffuse it.

There was another interest in these trips around Mexico: recruitment. Whenever the national team played against a local or regional team, they would scout their opponents, looking for the best players. When the coaches saw someone with potential, the player would be given a two-week trial with the team, "to show that she could play." And so the team for the second world championship was strengthened and made "more complete" as a result of the games outside of Mexico City.[182] For the entire year between the two world championships, the team continued to train on Tuesdays and Thursdays and to travel around the country on weekends. All of the team had to be back in Mexico City by Monday to work or go to school. As evidence of the diffusion of the sport around the country, an open invitational tournament was held in August 1970 and included teams from Jalisco, Cuernavaca, Morelos, Guerrero, Veracruz, and the Federal District leagues. As preparation continued, Monterrey and Puebla registered with the women's football association in order to be able to play in the tournament. By this time, there were already two hundred women's teams in Monterrey alone.[183]

The sports press occasionally discussed feminism forthrightly. Sportswriters usually acknowledged that women were moving into spaces hitherto reserved for men, such as the workforce.[184] Sports, for example, lagged behind the workplace in terms of the integration of women. However, as in Brazil, the media never reflected on the possible reasons for this. *El Heraldo de México* positioned itself as the patron of the women's football league and also dedicated a fair number of articles to discussing women's activities in other sports, and even in coaching. One featured Elvira Jaime de Ferreira, who coached the Titanes of Monterrey, a men's team that played American football. *El Heraldo de México* described "Vira" as able to motivate the boys and as a coach who knew the rules perfectly. *El Heraldo de México* took a moderate editorial line in regard to women's liberation movements. While reassuring readers that changes to gender roles would not hasten the apocalypse, and that readers should accept them as part of modernity, the newspaper's pieces on women carefully avoided discussing recognition of women's rights or citizenship.[185] Similarly, the first woman football referee in Mexico, Grecia del Ángel, who graduated from the Colegio de Árbitros (College of Referees) and worked her first match in 1970, was also seen as a delightful exception to women's exclusion from sports. Ángel would go on to referee the France-England match in the 1971 women's world championship.[186] When describing women's advances in football, journalists frequently cast the process as a women's invasion of the sporting, political, and social spheres. However, *El Heraldo de México* pointed out that women had long played other sports, such as softball, basketball, track and field, and hockey. It was only football that was supposedly new.[187] Other papers took on the issue of women in sports as well. In August 1970, *El Nacional* published an article on the supposed danger of sports to femininity. While "much ha[d] been written" about "sports and the loss of femininity," the paper suggested that the latter was hardly the case. The anonymous journalist framed an article, ostensibly about women's field hockey, around debunking the myth of masculinization. The article noted that certain sports, such as football, basketball, and softball, were criticized for being defeminizing. Rosalinda Tripp, a field hockey coach, noted that "playing with women makes one more feminine," regardless of the sport.[188]

Whether to offset male readers' concerns about the demasculinizing of the sports pages or to stave off criticism of women's sports as defeminizing, in late 1970 and early 1971 different outlets began to run features on sportswomen. *Fútbol de México y del Mundo* paid attention to women football players, normalizing them for its readership. For example, the December 13 edition carried a brief interview with Silvia Zaragoza, forward for the national team. The magazine asked for her birthday, height and weight, and "something about football." Her answers, no doubt edited, included her zodiac sign, and the interview ended with Zaragoza saying, "I'm a romantic . . . but better if we stick to football."[189] The next installment featured the "preciosa" Graciela Patiño, "the best player in the Liga Iztaccíhuatl." The interview revealed that at age twenty, Patiño was already a physical education teacher, and that her future plans included "visiting, in the not too distant future, the marriage altar." The photo that accompanied the interview showed Patiño in a baseball cap, biting her lip in a coy smile.[190]

El Heraldo de México created a regular feature that profiled the most beautiful and eligible sportswomen.[191] However, if the newspaper hoped to take the "sports" out of the "women," the young interviewees did not focus their answers on their marital status or beauty. The first athlete featured in the series was the tennis star Elena Subirats. Subirats opened the interview discussing her studies and travels. The tennis players and sisters Patricia and Olga Montaño were interviewed in the following feature, and they tackled the question of gender equality directly.[192] Patricia asserted that women were equally as intelligent as men, and further that Mexican conservatives encouraged women to be cloistered and fostered an indolent life.[193] After traveling throughout Europe and the United States, she had concluded that Mexicans were still "green" when it came to women's rights. Moreover, they argued that "[p]arents put the brakes on any advance [toward women's independence] because of religion and its traditionalism."[194] The Montaño sisters no doubt spoke out with a degree of privilege not afforded to all women athletes. They were described as blonde, were clearly wealthy, and played a sport in which women had carved a secure space. Still, many working-class women expressed facing precisely the same obstacles.

The third installment of the "Beauties of Sports" series featured Lupita Tovar, the captain of the national women's football team. The description emphasized her well-formed body and feminine smile.[195]

Tovar's biography sheds light onto the experience of women athletes. She moved from Querétaro to Mexico City's Colonia Moctezuma at age eight. She told the reporter that as a child she had loved playing all sports, but that around age twelve or thirteen, she quit them. She was worried, she said, about the way that her playing with boys would be perceived. Without sports, however, she felt depressed and bored. Tovar explained that through a fan group of América, she saw a notification for girls to play football and signed up. She clearly saw the end to her playing career, however. Tovar explained that housework was essential to women's lives because "it gives them a solid foundation for marriage."[196] She explained, "[M]y end goal is to create a normal, harmonious home, and I believe that knowing how to do housework is indispensable for this happiness."[197] Tovar emphasized the exhilaration she felt at visiting Europe, a dream she had never thought would be realized. The journalists tried to make it a light piece, asking her if she read her horoscopes. "Yes," she replied, "but people make their own destiny."[198] Strangely, *El Heraldo de México* published pictures of Tovar, as well as the Montaño sisters, with dolls. Given that they were in their twenties, the women appear awkward holding their dolls, presumably from childhood. Indeed, dolls appeared often in the narratives surrounding women athletes. In popular culture, they indicated proper gender development. When interviewing Lupita Araceli, a basketball player for the team Guadalajara—named after Chivas de Guadalajara but based in Mexico City—*El Heraldo de México* inquired whether she was a "hogareña," or homemaker, to which she responded no.[199] Instead she had learned to work in the hotel industry with her father, perfecting her English along the way. While the series might have been intended as a forum to attract boyfriends for female athletes, the women interviewed expressed little interest in this angle. Instead, they reflected on the intense and varied relationships they had to sports and gender. In any case, both *Fútbol de México y del Mundo* and *El Heraldo de México* sought to feminize the women athletes for the publications' predominantly male readership.

By the end of 1970, women's football was a regular part of the sporting scene, both in terms of media coverage and play. In the Mexico

City area alone, the Liga América had over forty teams in three separate divisions.[200] The Valley of Mexico had its own league, with sixteen teams, while Cuernavaca had a fourteen-team championship. Naucalpan, Veracruz, Puebla, and Ciudad Juárez all had leagues, some of which began to affiliate with the AMFF. As mentioned earlier, Monterrey had over two hundred teams.[201] In Mexico City, the Liga Iztaccíhuatl had over fifty teams.

THE 1971 CHAMPIONSHIP

As discussed earlier, during its tour to Mexico in 1970 the Italian delegation, led by Marco Rambaudi of the FIEFF, realized that Mexico had the potential to host the second world championship. Mexico certainly had plenty of experience with large sporting events, as hosts of the 1968 Olympics and the 1970 men's World Cup, so facilities and infrastructure were of little concern. Mexican fans showed great enthusiasm, and large numbers attended both the Italy-Mexico matches and the regular league play of women's teams. Yet even after Mexico won the right to host the tournament, official Mexican football institutions were unwilling to help. At a FIFA executive committee meeting in January 1971, the world governing body recognized "the growing popularity of football for women" and instructed member associations to "follow the matter closely." Likely aware of the upcoming event in Mexico, the committee noted that FIFA could not organize a World Cup for women until such time that "this type of football is controlled by national associations."[202] Perhaps as a result of the meeting, at which Guillermo Cañedo was present, FIFA sent a directive to the Mexican federation in February of 1971 prohibiting it from organizing a women's tournament. In turn, the FMF threatened to fine clubs twenty-five thousand pesos for allowing women's teams to practice or play on their fields. *El Heraldo de México* judged that FIFA was trying to protect the male players, who were the intended stars of mega stadiums like the Estadio Azteca, as well as its own business interests.[203] Indeed, FIFA's concern in part rested on fears that women's football would "fall . . . into the hands of promoters—which could be detrimental to FIFA."[204]

In the face of FIFA and FMF resistance, the organizers of the various women's leagues met in the offices of CODEME and formed the Federación Mexicana de Fútbol Femenil (Mexican Federation of Women's Football, FMFF). Its purpose was to be the organizing body of the second women's world championship.[205] And, despite FIFA's warning, *El Heraldo de México* announced that the second world championship of women's football would be held in Mexico from August 8–29, 1971, though the dates would change as the event moved closer.[206] The games would take place in Estadio Azteca and Estadio Jalisco. As municipal stadiums, these fell outside the jurisdiction of the Mexican Football Federation. A mascot, Xochitl, which *El Heraldo de México* judged to be "better looking than Juanito," the 1970 men's World Cup mascot, had already been chosen as the symbol of the event.[207] Other Latin American teams apparently expressed interest, as the announcement mentioned that Brazil might participate in the event, although it lacked affiliation with the FIEFF.[208] As word of the tournament spread, directors from Argentina's Federation of Women's Football committed right away.[209] The federation also invited Mexico to tour Argentina in May 1971 and to play in the River Plate Stadium.[210] In the end, despite hopes that Brazil and Chile would participate, only Argentina was able to commit a team to the second world championship.

The open tryouts for the Mexican national team were underway by March and brought in many young players from Guadalajara, Morelos, and Monterrey. According to *El Heraldo de México*, Mexico boasted over one thousand women's football teams.[211] The FMFF chose the twenty-six-year-old Victor Manuel Meléndez, a physical education teacher, to be the national team's coach.[212] He had not coached in the women's leagues up until that point and was known to be somewhat temperamental. Meléndez held typical notions of gender difference. He explained to the reporters that women were "easier to manage" than men because of their "childish precocity."[213] Meléndez also explained that women obeyed with a better attitude than male athletes. Still, conflicts among the different leagues meant that tryouts continued even after the draw for the tournament in July.[214]

As a part of their preparations for the tournament, the Mexican women's team accepted an invitation from the Argentine women's federation and traveled to South America in July. After an emotional goodbye with family and fellow players, the Mexican women's team boarded Air Panama in July 1971 to Buenos Aires, Argentina. The Mexican embassy helped to organize a match between the Mexican team and its Argentine counterpart in Estadio de Gimnasia y Esgrima in Buenos Aires.[215] The team arrived in Buenos Aires on July 16, 1971. The scheduled match was rained out. In the meantime, the organizers sold so many tickets that they decided to move the venue to the stadium of Club Atlético Nueva Chicago because it had a capacity for fifty thousand spectators.[216] Ultimately, the game had a farcical nature to it. The game was marked with violence, as discussed in chapter 1, with the Mexican team walking off the field and losing 3–2. On their return to Mexico, the team stopped over in Lima, where it played a hastily organized match against the Peruvian national team. According to the Mexican press, the Peruvians were well prepared for the match against Mexico, which was organized by the Asociación de Cronistas Deportivos (Association of Sportswriters) and held in Lima's municipal stadium. After falling behind 0–2 in the first half, the Mexicans pulled out a 3–2 victory.[217] When the Mexican team arrived home, an even larger contingent of fans awaited them at the airport.[218]

The coverage of the 1971 world championship in Mexico provides the richest and most extensive view of global women's football in the period. Mainstream newspapers and sports magazines around Mexico ran color photographs of the visiting delegations and followed their daily activities.[219] Games were televised in prime time and in color, yet very little of the footage remains.[220] The frustrating aspect of this coverage is that it is difficult to gauge the comparative significance or development of the sport in different countries. Much of the media focused on turning the futboleras into sex symbols and celebrities. The draw for the second world championship was televised on the Televicentro program *Siempre en Domingo*. It slated Mexico to face Argentina in Estadio Azteca, followed by Denmark versus France in Estadio Jalisco.[221] Tickets went on sale soon thereafter at Sanborns, Borja Sports, and Almacenes Alvarez. The decision to sell tickets at Sanborns, a middle-class restaurant chain, indicates that organizers expected that many attendees would come from a privileged group, likely from the Federal District. It also meant that grassroots clubs, which could have distributed tickets, were not integrated into the tournament planning. Still, prices for a series of six games ranged from 330 pesos (roughly $24) to 30 pesos (approximately $2.40), meaning that even if tickets were sold in middle-class establishments, they were intended to be available to a broad cross section of Mexicans.[222] Four levels of single-game tickets ("populares," yellow, green, and orange) ranged from 5 to 50 pesos. Prices for general admission remained 5 pesos for the knockout round, but the three more expensive ticket prices rose. The second least expensive tickets went from 15 to 25 pesos, while the best seats went from 50 to 80. Three-game packages cost 15 to 180 pesos.[223]

During the 1971 championship, supporters prepared to cheer on their favorites. For example, Italian immigrants met before the tournament to make signage and costumes.[224] The press showered attention on Elena Schiavo, considered the world's most prominent women's footballer. Without a doubt *El Heraldo de México* understood the second world championship as its victory as well. The editors stated that they were "optimistic and think that the spectacle will be enjoyed." It placed women's football in the realm of "a 'show' . . . of color, beauty, and joy."[225] Indeed, the media played a major role in creating the excitement around women's football, just as it had decades before with the men's game.[226] The symbiotic relationship between the media and the men's sport developed in the early twentieth century and continues to this day. To that end, the draw to decide the team pools and the first-round games took place amidst a spectacle befitting a world championship. The draw was hosted by the sports commentator Ángel Fernandez and included a marching band. On hand for the draw were the Mexican women's team; Marco Rambaudi, vice president of the FIEFF; Jaime de Haro, head of the championship's organizing committee; Antonio Haro Oliva, president of CODEME; José Pérez Mier, head of Acción

Deportiva; and Efraín Pérez, president of the FMFF. The following day, the TV show *Puertas de Sorpresa* asked young women footballers to be part of the audience, stipulating that they wear uniforms and bring balls with them.[227]

As teams began to arrive in Mexico in early August, newspapers revved up their coverage of women's football. Articles on players, strategies, and off-field activities educated readership on the teams and their strengths. For example, the day that England and Italy landed in Mexico City—ten days before the start of the tournament—*Excelsior* published an article about the teams, including their hotel and training sites. England was housed for the length of their stay in the Hotel Royal Plaza and used the fields of Ciudad Deportiva to train. Italy, on the other hand, stayed at the Hotel Beverly and used the facilities of Club América while in Mexico City. Once in Guadalajara, the Bambinas, as the Italians were called, practiced at Club Deportivo Providencia, a private athletic facility.[228] That Club América allowed practices on its fields suggests that its president, Guillermo Cañedo, was either unafraid of the FMF sanction or at least unofficially interested in the women's tournament. As the immediate past president of the FMF and a member of the FIFA executive committee, his role is particularly intriguing. As an executive for Telesistema, the predecessor to Televisa, which controlled Channel 2, Channel 4, and Channel 5, his interest in a successful tournament might have been driven by motives outside his role as a FIFA executive. At times, Cañedo seemed intent to squash women's football, and at others, intrigued by its possible commercial value.

Information on the teams provided interesting insight as well. The seventeen women who made up the English team, for example, ranged in age from fourteen to twenty-four, with an average age of just over seventeen. Only two players were twenty or older, and three were fourteen years old.[229] *El Sol de México* provided its readers with information on team activities. One day after arrival, both Italy and England had "intensive practices" in Mexico City. The Italian team worked on technical skills, shooting, and general exercises for two hours in the morning before playing a scrimmage in the afternoon against a team of singers and actresses. England, for their part, began practice at 7:00 a.m., focusing on shooting and conditioning.[230] Indeed, *El Sol de México* reported regularly on team training activities, with articles nearly every day between August 10—when most teams had arrived—and the start of the tournament on August 15.[231] The Mexican media had experience with covering visiting national teams, as it had covered the 1970 men's World Cup in a similar manner.

For its part, *Ovaciones* began sensitizing its readership to the women's world championship in late 1970, but intensified coverage of the tournament in July 1971. That month saw articles and images surrounding women's football, and especially Mexico's South American tour. The "chamacas," or girls, received regular coverage of their tour of Peru and Argentina, from the day of departure on July 13 until the team's return. At the same time, however, *Ovaciones* spent more ink on highlighting the novelty of the tournament, focusing on the spectacle of women's football and the bodies of women footballers. Photographs of players resting in bikinis by the pool, with accompanying articles noting the catcalling and cheering by the "male public," highlight the attitude taken by the paper. Its additional focus on the actresses and singers who made up two teams that would play preliminary matches suggests that the newspaper did not take the women's championship seriously.

Media coverage exploded in the run-up to the tournament and during play. Six teams—Argentina, Denmark, England, France, Italy, and Mexico—were divided into two groups. Group A, which included Mexico, Argentina, and England, played its matches in Estadio Azteca, while Group B played in the Estadio Jalisco. The top two teams of each group advanced to the semifinals. All of the matches, whether in Mexico City or Guadalajara, received press attention worthy of a world championship event. Over the course of the two weeks, at least eight journalists covered the teams and reported on games for *El Heraldo de México*. Not only did the games receive attention, however, but as with coverage of the men's World Cup, correspondents wrote about how teams practiced, what they did during off days, and who their players were. Alongside Manelich Quintero's usual commentating, Nuria Basurto, Hugo Sanmontiel,

Hebert González, Juan Acevedo, José José (José Luis Jimenez), and Eduardo Morales, among others, wrote articles, including the following: "¡Golpeadas y cansadas, pero entrenar!" (Kicked and tired, but training!); "Fue más facil que esperabamos" (It was easier than we hoped); and "El fútbol femenil no puede ser amateur" (Women's football can't be amateur).[232] Photo spreads filled the sports pages as well, with images of the women both in action and at rest. *Excelsior*, Mexico's paper of record, had four correspondents covering the tournament, and like *El Heraldo de México*, it included game reports from both Mexico City and Guadalajara, reported on team tactics, and detailed the athletes' activities on off days.[233]

The success of the media coverage and promotional efforts could be seen in the crowd sizes. An estimated eighty-thousand-person crowd watched the inaugural match and saw Mexico defeat Argentina 3–1 at the Estadio Azteca.[234] Denmark played France in Jalisco in front of twenty thousand. The second match at the Estadio Azteca, England versus Argentina, drew roughly the same number.[235] While these numbers might not have been those desired by the organizers, nevertheless they suggest the popularity—or the curiosity—of the matches. Men's professional matches in 1971 rarely drew twenty thousand spectators. Moreover, the Mexican women's team played to almost full stadiums. Between eighty and ninety thousand people watched the England versus Mexico match, while the Denmark versus Argentina and Mexico versus Italy semifinals drew twenty-five to thirty thousand and eighty thousand, respectively.[236]

Not all media coverage was positive. Concern over the physicality of the games ran throughout the media, focusing particularly on the French, Italian, and Argentine teams, which were considered to be too rough. Photos showed French and Italian players kicking their opponents, while others showed the Argentines trying to slow the Danes through not-so-subtle arm and shirt grabs.[237] The Argentine coach suggested that his players would need armor to play against the Italians.[238] Additionally, some news sources stated that the players appeared like "men disguised as women."[239] Manuel Seyde, a commentator for *Excelsior*, regularly gave backhanded compliments to the women's game. In summarizing the tournament for his

FIGURE 5.4. Mexico versus Italy at the second women's world football championship, 1971. *El Sol de México*, August 30, 1971.

presumably male audience, Seyde could not contain his paternalism. It was, he wrote, "obligatory" to write one final column on the women's world championship. He noted that women played with more "imagination, daring, and sincerity" then men. But he could not keep from criticizing the game—and the players—as well. For Seyde, the tournament was a "sporting diversion," a spectacle that only the women who played took seriously. "You," he wrote, putting words in the mouths of his readers, "enjoyed it with sympathetic benevolence." The games offered "an attractive spectacle" that almost made men "forget the natural insufficiencies of women playing a man's game."[240] In his column, Sánchez Hidalgo explained that what old-timers didn't understand was that the crowds were not looking for an equal display of talent to the men's game. Instead, they sought a new spectacle.[241]

Despite the predictable sexism in much of the reporting on the second women's world championship, a few radically different perspectives emerged. Lourdes Galaz of *El Día* emphasized that women playing football in Mexico was no more exotic than women shopping or voting.[242] However nontraditional women's football was assumed to be from the outside, the Mexican team itself clung to some traditions. Players traveled together to the Basilica de Guadalupe to ask for God's blessing and prayed together as a team.[243] The representation of the team as traditionalists temporarily deflated arguments that women's football could be damaging to young women.

Nevertheless, girls playing football became considerably more visible in the city. *El Heraldo de México* ran a series of photos in September 1971 of girls in the street, with the title "Girls kick the ball now too." Inverting the trope of boys playing while girls watch, the photographs show boys sitting against a wall while girls play football in the middle of the street. One of the accompanying captions read: "In the streets of Mexico, playing in the streets is the classic game for boys. . . . Did I say boys? Now that girls are playing in the Estadio Azteca! They're also playing in the streets." Moreover, the author noted that "girls also scream before the game: 'I'm Peque,' . . . 'I'm Alicia Vargas,'" claiming the names of the star Mexican players.[244] That girls had begun playing in the streets highlights the level to which the sport had reached into the neighborhoods around Mexico City. Anecdotal evidence suggests that the sport permeated the countryside as well.

The effervescence of women's football in Mexico did not dissipate as a result of the national team's 3–0 loss to Denmark in the finals of the women's world championship. According to press reports, Mexico played its worst game of the tournament, but it did so in front of a packed Estadio Azteca. Fans eagerly awaited a Mexican victory that was not to be. But girls and women remained committed to the sport and played with as much, if not more, intensity in the immediate aftermath of the tournament. What changed was the perception of the sport and the attention it garnered from the press. If during 1970 and 1971 women's football had taken up increasing column space in Mexican newspapers, by the end of 1971 articles became more sporadic. By 1972 the sport disappeared almost completely from the media. Why?

One reason might have been the power of the Mexican Football Federation. Though there is little direct evidence to tie the decreasing visibility of women's football to FMF efforts, nevertheless the

FIGURE 5.5. Rough play at the second women's world football championship, 1971. *El Heraldo de México*, August 30, 1971.

federation did seek to take control of the sport after 1971. The sport received few, if any, resources.[245] Comparisons between women's and men's football at the time suggested that perhaps the women's game was purer. The Mexican men's professional game was in a state of decline and the men's national team were being called "ratoncitos," little mice, in the press. Diverting resources to the women's sport would have threatened the traditional structures of the men's sport. Another reason, however, might have begun during the tournament. Elvira Aracén recounted how "strange things happened" in the week between Mexico's semifinal victory over Italy and the final clash with Denmark.[246] Though it is not clear who first suggested it, the Mexican women's team went public with demands to be paid in order to play the final.[247] Lupita Tovar and Aracén informed the country that the team wanted 2 million pesos. The logic was simple— and frighteningly similar to the story of women's teams today: they had been training nonstop for the better part of two years and had received no income for their efforts. Most were juggling work or studies with team practice, and had not earned what they would have had they not been playing. For many of the young women and their families, this represented real sacrifice.[248] The team backtracked two days later, with Elvira Aracén suggesting that "applause was worth more than . . . pesos." Yolanda Ramírez agreed, saying that the team would play "for the public, which has always supported us."[249] While the team agreed to play the final for free, they had also secured promises of a benefit game. The women were to receive gate receipts and TV rights as compensation, along with "gifts" from various government agencies.[250]

The demand for pay turned some against the team. The Danish women players immediately spoke out against their Mexican counterparts, with Inger Pedersson expressing "total surprise" at the demand and accusing the *mexicanas* of "not acting like true amateurs."[251] For some it exposed the injustice of amateurism. Still others saw the manipulating hands of men behind the demand. The team "had almost become idols," wrote Carmen Anderson in *El Heraldo de México*, "especially [for] women who see in them their liberation." Yet they had betrayed the goodwill by being used as puppets by men's interests. Though she could not be sure of it, Anderson suggested that the women were not smart enough to make the demand on their own: "these girls . . . have a vocabulary of no more than 100 or 200 words," she wrote. Anderson called the women's team "pathetic" in its demands, even though she was sure that "behind them is the intellect of a man."[252]

That the women played for the applause, while organizers—from the international federation to Jaime de Haro and the organizing committee—earned from the players' sweat, was too much for the longtime promoter of women's football Manelich Quintero. Quintero, who had pioneered writing on women's football in the 1960s and who had formed part of the delegation to Italy in 1970, now turned on the leaders of the sport. An anonymous article in *El Heraldo de México*, published on September 21, 1971, criticized the FMFF in no uncertain terms. The federation "has given no signs of life, much less expressed any desire to reward its players or even host a meeting to officially disband the team." The paper wanted an answer for the mistreatment of the players, but received none.[253] Five days later, Quintero penned an article calling Efraín Pérez and Victor Manuel Meléndez "operators and gigolos." He also voiced the anonymous frustrations of the players, who claimed that the administration of the team and the FMFF had "exploited" them and "were making a grand living off of our backs." The root of the problem was that much of the money from the benefit game had disappeared, presumably into the pockets of the team directors.[254] Quintero's name does not seem to appear as author of any article on women's football after that date. He believed that to continue to promote the game would only benefit the "interests" that exploited the women's game, and so he stopped.[255]

CONCLUSION

The end of the women's world championship should have signaled a triumphant start for the FMFF and women's football in Mexico in general. The tournament was well marketed and attended. Women's football received television airtime and ample coverage in the print media. Over one hundred thousand spectators witnessed the final of the event. Instead of a beginning, however, it appears, on the surface, to have marked an end. Wrangling over money and the future of the sport caused many players to feel that they were being exploited by the organizers. And these disputes drove many supporters from the game. Manelich Quintero was one. He emphasized that "all the world rejected women's football, [while] I wanted to support them because of the respect and admiration I have for the women."[256] He noted that machismo held the sport back.[257] While the press supported the sport during 1971, with the end of the women's world championship and the sport's devolution into conflict, coverage slowly ceased.

Women's football as public spectacle receded into the background. This did not mean, however, that the 1971 championship was pyrrhic. In fact, the sport attained unprecedented publicity and for a brief moment became wildly popular. Even as the FMF embarked on a successful campaign to solidify men's football as Mexico's national sport, thereby shutting off official avenues for women to play, the women's sport continued to grow. Newspapers in Mexico City, from *Excelsior* to *El Sol de México*, from *Ovaciones* and *Esto* to *El Heraldo de México*, covered the sport throughout 1971 and into 1972. In October 1971, the first women's national championship took place, pitting seventeen different regional selected teams against one another. Women's teams from around the country, from Baja California to Veracruz, and from Sonora to Tamaulipas and Chihuahua, gathered to play at the Ciudad Deportiva in Mexico City. The first championship saw Guanajuato defeat the Federal District 1–0 in a game that had to be replayed due to a pitch invasion.[258] So too women's leagues continued to receive press coverage through 1971, though reporting became more sporadic.

Moreover, the championship spurred a boom in women's football throughout the nation. Mercedes Rodríguez Alemán, a futbolera from the 1970s and 1980s, recalled that her start in the sport was spurred by the events of 1971. There was, she explained, exponential growth in her hometown of Torreón as a result of the 1971 world championship. "Immediately after the tournament," she recounted, "the authorities . . . announced they would organize the first women's league in the city." According to Rodríguez Alemán, the first league had over sixty teams and formed the basis of a "boom" in the sport. On game days Avenida Presidente Carranza became clogged with traffic, and it was difficult to get to the fields since so many "trucks would pass full of people going to the sports complex to play or watch" the women's games.[259] "The whole city," she recalled, "would pour into the sports complex." As with most booms, the one in Torreón, Coahuila, was short lived. Shortly after the league formed, it split into two due to disagreements, and within a year or two the sport had almost completely disappeared. What remained, however, was the regional team of Lagunas, a territory comprising three cities—Ciudad Lerdo and Gómez Palacio in Durango and Torreón in Coahuila. That team "kept football alive" in the region. The team, which averaged in age from thirteen to fifteen years old, "trained and trained and played against men because there were no women's teams at the local level."[260] The Lagunas women's team participated regularly in the national football tournament, which continued through the 1970s. In 1976 Rodríguez Alemán was chosen for a team that played in Costa Rica. This, she recalled, was the final game that the Mexican national team played internationally until 1991.

Elsewhere in Mexico, too, the sport survived. According to Elvira Aracén, "there were many leagues after the world championship."

The problem was, she says, finding stadiums. Once CODEME no longer had women's football under its auspices, fields were harder to find. "We were like refugees," Aracén recalled; "you paid for a field, played, and the league had a record, and that was it."[261] But there were always fields. Aracén, for example, could use the stadium in Santa Cruz because she worked for the municipality of Iztapalapa. One group, the Liga de Cabeza de Juárez, was organized by Araceli Márquez. This league was regularly won by a team called the Mundialistas, comprising former world championship players and others (such as Mercedes Rodríguez Alemán) who were brought in later. The Mundialistas won the regional league from 1973 to 1980.[262] And when national tournaments happened, teams would host each other in their houses. Thus, the women's football community in Mexico became tight-knit and supportive.[263]

The world championship of 1971 remains a landmark in the history of Latin American women's sports. The event, in terms of both its popularity and its sporting success, disproves paternalist claims that women's sports are a recent development. So too it undercuts the suggestion that women's sports are unpopular and unmarketable. Even if they did not create a massive wave of women's football in Mexico, the Elvira Aracéns and Alicia Vargases, the Lupita Tovars and Peque Rubios, cleared a path for the women who came after them. In the words of Aracén, by continuing to play "as refugees," paying for a field, playing, and finding new fields the following week, they kept women's football in Mexico alive, so that at least "those who followed . . . had space" to play the game.[264] The generation who participated in the short boom of Mexican women's football continued their advocacy and helped to create the next moment of effervescence in the 2000s.

EPILOGUE

IN 1967, WHEN SISLEIDE DO AMOR LIMA, BETTER KNOWN AS
Sissi, was born, women's football was still banned in Brazil. As a
child, Sissi wanted to play for the Brazilian national team, which
was remarkable because, of course, there had never been a Brazilian
national women's football team. Perhaps her timing was right. Just
as she blossomed into a nearly unstoppable attacking midfielder,
the government repealed the prohibition on the sport, and women's
football exploded. Representing Brazil in the 1988 FIFA Women's
Invitation Tournament in China, Sissi recalled, meant "all my dreams
had come true."[1] However, if the 1980s marked a takeoff point for
women's football in Brazil, by the mid-1990s the sport had stag-
nated. This has been the case throughout the history of women's
sports in Latin America: brief periods of effervescence followed
by long periods of apparent inactivity. But under the surface, the
women remained active in the sport throughout the region. The
persistence and solidarity of sportswomen around the world helped
to pressure international governing bodies, such as the International
Federation of Association Football (FIFA) and the International
Olympic Committee, to organize tournaments and provide a minimum of support for development. The narrative of women's football
in Latin America may be on the verge of shifting permanently. New
configurations of capital, advertising, sexism, and corporate sponsorship have created fresh challenges. The days of medical warnings
about women's fragile psyches and bodies have mostly passed, but
gender-verification testing, market measures, corrupt federations,
and patriarchal restrictions on women's time and leisure continue
to inhibit the growth of women's sports. At the same time, the emergence of social media and a network of nongovernmental organizations, many of which have criticized exclusions in sports or sought to

use it as a vehicle for progressive social transformation, offers hope for longer term development.

The advent of the information society in the early 1990s gave women athletes and their fans new ways to connect with one another. Social media, cell phones, and widespread internet access meant that players could contact one another directly, as well as watch games, or at least highlights. In the 2010s, independent journalists emerged to fill the void from the lack of coverage provided by mainstream sports outlets. Today, fans can much more easily follow tournaments and athletes that they admire. Social media and alternative platforms for dissemination have been a boon for women's sports, particularly football, in the region, since federations are still loath to spend resources on broadcasting the sport. YouTube and other web-based platforms allow for broad diffusion of women's games and have helped to build a tighter network of women players and fans. Twitter has compressed the space between players and fans, and in some cases forced the hands of federations. The result has been a veritable explosion of interest in women's sports, particularly in women's football, around the world. This sharp increase in attention, however, has not been met with equivalent increases in resources or respect for women athletes. Though more attention is being paid to the sport by institutions ranging from federations to the media, more can be done for futboleras, and for women athletes in general. Perhaps, given the slow pace of change within sporting bodies, change will again require women athletes' collective action.

CONTINUED STRUGGLES

Despite large increases in state budgets for sports during the decades of the 2000s and 2010s, little of that money was allocated to girls' activities. Argentine and Chilean girls noted the lack of physical education and public programs for their development.[2] And perhaps it is not surprising, then, that in terms of national football teams, the disparity between the men's and women's teams is greatest, perhaps in the world, in those two countries. In December 2016 the Argentine men's team was ranked first in the world, and the Chilean team fourth.

The women's teams, on the other hand, were considered inactive. They had no ranking because they had not played a competitive match for at least eighteen months. The men's national teams received generous stipends and played a regular slate of events around the world, all paid for by the respective federations. Women barely practiced and received the equivalent of less than ten dollars per day for training. And Argentina and Chile were not anomalies. As of the end of 2016, seven of the ten South American women's teams, and two of the ten Latin American teams in the Confederation of North, Central America and Caribbean Association Football (CONCACAF), were considered inactive by FIFA. By September 2017, the situation had improved slightly in South America, with only four member nations of the South American Football Confederation (CONMEBOL) having inactive women's teams. In CONCACAF, however, the situation had worsened, with only four active teams out of ten.[3] Mainstream sports journalists and football directors seem uninterested in this crisis in international women's football. Until recently, CONMEBOL and national federations were reluctant to respond to demands, from both FIFA and grassroots groups, that more resources be spent developing and promoting women's football. They did little to explore the potential of linking promotion and sponsorship of the men's game to the women's. So the sport still relies heavily on the world governing body for funding.

The lack of adequate media coverage continues to plague the sport. When FIFA classified the Chilean women's national team as inactive, for example, no major sports media outlets reported the story. Chile's *El Gráfico* found space to discuss a sandwich named for Gonzalo Jara, the men's national team player, but not to expose the failure of the Chilean federation to provide the women's team with the bare minimum of resources. At the time, the Chilean women's team had not played a match in over eighteen months. CONMEBOL and FIFA representatives said little about the declassification of the women's team. In this sense, there is a systemic problem: the press cannot find any football authority to comment on the record about lack of interest in the women's game. Even when teams are active, the media fails. Television coverage for the 2014

Copa América Femenina began midway through the tournament, even though rights were free.

Women in sports media have been subjected to harassment, privately and publicly. Recently Vanessa Vargas Roja analyzed the coverage of the FIFA Confederations Cup, only to find the objectification of women fans and reporters repeated ad nauseam.[4] The debut of Grace Lazcano in August 2017 as a panelist on the Chilean television network Canal del Fútbol was announced with pride as a pioneering move by producers. However, fellow journalist Romai Ugarte ruined her debut. Sitting to Lazcano's left, as the panel and audience greeted her, Ugarte turned toward the cameras and audience, made a face of disgust, and gestured as if putting a penis in his mouth. Ugarte later apologized, but not before the Chilean men's team leaders Claudio Bravo and Gary Medel spoke out against his blatant sexism. Beyond the fact that Ugarte sought to humiliate Lazcano and ruin her debut, it is fascinating that he chose to do so by simulating performing oral sex on another man. Certainly, Ugarte expected the audience to understand his gesture not as homoerotic but rather as a "protest" to the inclusion of a woman on the panel. Despite his apology, Ugarte was fired from the program.

Misogyny is a major part of the sexism facing women's football and women's football players. Historically, homophobia has also been intimately tied to misogynistic efforts to suppress women's sports around the world. Since football has become consecrated as the national sport in many countries, it is perceived to develop proper masculinity. Thus, it has become a very important site for conversations around sexuality. Women players, from the early 1900s until today, have been regularly chastised for their sexuality (real or perceived). Brazilian and Mexican women players from the 1980s to the early 2000s recall being told that football is a "breeding ground" for lesbianism, and players continue to be called *marimachos* and *sapatões*.[5] Coaches have instructed national team players to avoid being seen with their girlfriends while wearing their jerseys. In men's football, misogyny and homophobia are constant as well: the obsession with wives and girlfriends of top male athletes reflects this reality. In Argentina, on the failure of the Boca Juniors women's team to reach the semifinals of the Copa Libertadores Femenina in 2015, sportswriters had no comment. Instead, the following day *El Gráfico* picked up a story that ranked the "hottest" girlfriends and wives of male players. In part this stems as much from the need to establish the heterosexuality of men players—whom we regularly see hugging, jumping into each other's arms, smacking butts, and kissing—as it does from a desire to objectify women.

The funding structure for women's sports continues to raise questions. While the men's game gains hundreds of millions of dollars through marketing and television rights, the women's game receives little. In football, many federations only spend the amount of money that FIFA gives them, if that, for girls and women, which is a small portion of the money that it distributes to each federation. From 2004 until 2016, a percentage of the money that FIFA provided to member associations as part of its Financial Assistance Program has been earmarked for women's football.[6] This amount has varied, but after 2008 "at least 15 percent" of disbursements were earmarked for women's football. In 2016 FIFA called this expenditure "an obligatory provision . . . of huge importance to the women's game."[7] As a result, between 2008 and 2016 FIFA set aside approximately $10 million per year for the development of women's football. Per federation, the program's requirements for women's football meant that roughly $37,500 went to the sport per year—hardly enough to build national programs on par with men's. Moreover, the program had no enforcement mechanism to ensure that federations spent the money on women's football. The lack of oversight and the paucity of audits meant that FIFA had no way of knowing if a federation spent money appropriately. Strictly speaking, this encouraged the underdevelopment of the women's game as funds could be distributed to the men's sides without retribution.

In 2017 FIFA altered the way it provided development funds to member federations. A new program, FIFA Forward, replaced the Financial Assistance Program. Instead of a $250,000 grant with 15 percent mandated for women's football, the new development project offered a guarantee of $100,000, with no requirements on expenditures, for federation running costs. However, it included an "incentivising payments policy" that could raise the amount of funding to $500,000 per federation.[8] Under these guidelines, each federation could receive an extra $50,000 for projects aimed at one of eight "essential elements." In order to be eligible for any of this additional money, at least two of the proposed elements must be for women's football. In other words, the new FIFA requirements mandated at least $100,000 per federation for women's-football-related projects—provided that federations requested the extra funding.[9] In addition to these monies, each federation could receive a further $750,000 for "tailor-made football development projects," including women's football. Alongside this funding, regional zones would be eligible for $1 million for "regional youth competitions (for girls and boys)." Importantly, the new program included development of multi-year strategies and oversight for all projects, including annual local audits, random selection for a central audit, and other compliance measures.[10] In other words, it appeared as of 2017 that FIFA had begun to take developing women's football more seriously.

Still, within CONMEBOL and CONCACAF, the institutional wheels have moved slowly. During the FIFA Women's World Cup of 2015, CONMEBOL scheduled the men's regional tournament, the Copa América, at precisely the same times. As of 2018, CONMEBOL had still held only one international tournament for women—the Copa América Femenina—which served as the World Cup, Olympics, and Pan-American Games qualifier. CONCACAF was only slightly more active, with separate tournaments for qualification to those events. The relative dearth of opportunities to play has had a clear impact on the teams. It reflected a lack of commitment to the sport, regardless of rhetoric to the contrary. The common pattern in Latin America is for federations to mobilize women's teams for brief moments around tournaments. In comparison, though CONMEBOL only organizes one tournament for men (the Copa América, held every two to four years), its system of qualifying for the FIFA World Cup ensures that men's national teams play on a regular basis during the four-year cycle. In addition, CONMEBOL organizes four tournaments for men's professional teams, as opposed to one for women. It was telling that in the midst of the Copa América Femenina in 2018, the CONMEBOL webpage had no information about the tournament on its homepage, though it did have scores for the men's Copa Libertadores. As the regional confederations spend few resources on the women's game, not surprisingly, few of the federations do either.

For the young women who worked for years to climb the world rankings without compensation or accolades, the lack of institutional support has been heartbreaking. "It hurts to become invisible, after working so hard to put Chile on the map," said Iona Rothfeld, who played for nine years on the Chilean national team.[11] Women's rankings spike in a qualifying year, then plummet when federations ignore the sport until the next cycle. Chile felt this effect most sharply. After organizing the FIFA U-20 Women's World Cup in 2008 and reaching a ranking of 41 in 2015, the women's national team has fallen into total disarray. Some Chilean players point to the departure of the former federation president Harold Mayne Nicholls in 2011 as a turning point. According to Christiane Endler, captain of the national team, women's football received sustained attention under Mayne Nicholls. His successor, Sergio Jadue, who later pled guilty to racketeering as part of the FIFA corruption scandal, neglected it entirely. The federation's complete silence on women's football continued under Jadue's successor, Arturo Salah. Between 2015 and 2017, players received no information about plans for training.

When Chilean players discovered they had been removed from the FIFA rankings, they decided to act. In the summer of 2016, they founded the Asociación Nacional de Jugadores de Fútbol Femenino (National Association of Women Football Players, ANJUFF), in response to not only the state of the national team but the extreme mismanagement of the roughly twenty women's clubs in the country. This marked one of the first efforts to unionize women athletes in Latin America. The goal of the organization, according to Iona Rothfeld, ANJUFF's first president, was to help create an environment of respect for women players. To strengthen its position, ANJUFF sought and received recognition from Chile's union of professional players and FIFPro, the international players' union. And the women's football community in South America took notice, as did the Chilean federation. Fernanda Pinilla and Iona Rothfeld both felt as though the interventions of ANJUFF played a major role in Chile deciding to host the 2018 Copa América Femenina. According to Christiane Endler, it was ANJUFF that proposed hosting the event in efforts to give Chile a chance at the FIFA World Cup.[12] As in the past, the work of women players themselves has continued to make changes, and international solidarity can help to shape CONMEBOL policy. Moreover, this generation of players has circulated around the region, among the collegiate ranks in the United States, and in European clubs. Those connections could be valuable when it comes to demanding accountability from the national federations, regional confederations, and FIFA.

But there remains little in the way of accountability, and women throughout the region routinely face both lack of support and outright humiliation within their clubs and federations. Directors tell players that women's football is an expense and an embarrassment. Homophobia is rampant, and many players report that coaches accuse them of being interested in football to meet sexual partners. South American federations organize women's football tournaments, but they do so begrudgingly. Major clubs, including Argentina's River Plate, have told players that the club will no longer provide them with medical insurance. In Chile, women players have been asked to pay their own transfer fees and travel costs. Corrupt federations magnify accounting problems for FIFA development monies earmarked for women. Thus, it's not surprising that the Argentine, Brazilian, and Chilean women's teams have seen such little economic support. In 2017, the entire women's team of Club Nacional in Uruguay accused their coach, Ignacio Chitnisky, of gender discrimination.[13] The accusations ranged from the coach making fun of women's football and commenting disrespectfully about the players' bodies, to taking advantage of the innocence of players and promising them trips abroad and salaries that never materialized. Chitnisky denied some of the allegations, but the conformity of stories from each player created a damning picture.

Until recently, the picture was much the same with Mexico. A long-tenured coach with little in-game success on his resume, Leonard Cuellar ruled over Mexican women's football for nearly twenty years. His supporters within the federation defended him, arguing that he had single-handedly built the support structure for women's football within Mexican footballing institutions. As a former Mexican men's national team player, and as a successful college coach in the United States, he had the pedigree to get the attention of the federation and sponsors. His detractors argued that although he had built the women's program, he failed to recognize when it was time to pass the baton to someone else. Over the course of his nineteen years in charge of the national team, Cuellar was dogged by accusations of favoritism for Mexican American players. A number of former players recalled that they never felt their place on the team was assured until they were on board the flight to a tournament. One expressed frustration that "we would spend months in training, three or four to a room," and then "at the end some *fresa* would arrive and be on the team."[14] While it is possible this type of complaint could be triggered by jealousy, the fact that it was reported multiple times suggests that the way in which Mexican American players were brought into the team created conflict. Some players felt that they were left off of the team for other reasons. Bianca Sierra, who had been a regular on the national team roster since 2010, was left off of the team for Olympic qualifying in 2016. In her opinion, this was because Cuellar disapproved of her romantic relationship with fellow Mexican national team player Stephany Mayor.[15] Whether coincidence or not, Sierra was called up to the national team in 2017, after Cuellar's departure. After the 2015 Women's World Cup, players began to speak out against Cuellar, suggesting that he was content to compete for second place in the region and would not invest the resources in trying to surpass the United States. More damning, perhaps, was the fact that from 1998 to 2016, the Mexican women's national team had a losing record. While Cuellar's teams had notable successes, including qualifying for the 2004 Olympics and back-to-back Women's World Cups, his teams nevertheless lost nearly twenty more games than they won, with an unofficial record of 87–22–104. It is hard to imagine the men's national team coach being given more than one year, let alone nearly two decades, to create a winning team.

In fact, the opportunity to oversee a team for such a long time is rarely given to women coaches of women's teams. After decades of men being in charge of the Brazilian women's team, for example, Emily da Cunha Lima was named coach of a *seleção* (national team) in November 2016. Like her predecessors, she oversaw a team short on resources and training opportunities. Even after the women's stellar performance—and massive popularity—at the 2016 Olympics, the Brazilian Football Confederation suggested that it would cut funding to the women's football program. Nevertheless, in her ten months on the job, her record was a respectable seven wins, five losses, and one draw. After her firing, in September 2017, five of the senior Brazilian women's team players, Cristiane Rozeiro, Francielle Manoel Alberto (Fran), Rosana dos Santos Augusto (Rosana), Maurine Dorneles Gonçalves (Maurine), and Andreia Rosa, retired in protest, each posting messages to their Instagram accounts excoriating the Brazilian federation for moving the women's program backward. Former players, led by Sissi and Marcia Tafarel (Tafa) from the Radar era, signed an open letter to the federation that demanded radical changes in governance to incorporate former women players. The Brazilian Football Confederation opened a commission in response to evaluate the conditions of women's football, only to summarily dismiss the body without explanation months later.[16]

The deterioration of women's football in Latin America, in other words, hurts even the most successful program in the region. Brazil, as one of the best women's teams in the world, can find opponents and travel to play, but has a difficult time finding quality regional opponents on a regular basis. The rest of the continental squads have less star power and fewer options. Colombia, Ecuador, and Venezuela have made strides in the past few years but suffer from the lack of quality opponents. Still, at least these teams exist. Inactive teams do not play or practice, and there is minimal communication between federations and athletes. Chilean and Paraguayan national team players often do not even know who their coaches are. The Argentine national team had no matches between a disappointing showing at the 2015 Pan-American Games and 2017. Their play should not have been surprising; the only preparation the team had prior to the Pan-American Games was one scrimmage against a boys' team. Yet they still have the depth of talent to send stars abroad to Spain, the United States, Sweden, and beyond to play in professional and collegiate leagues.

The state of affairs of women's football in Argentina was thrown into sharp relief in September 2017. In an open letter to Ricardo Pinela, head of the Argentine Football Association's women's committee, the national women's team players announced that they were going on strike and called attention to the lack of resources given to the team. Unlike other protests by women football players around the world, notably the US and Danish women's national teams, which threatened strikes over equal pay, the Argentine women highlighted the lack of even basic compensation. The women explained that they had not received the agreed-upon travel costs for the national team players to reach practice. Over the course of months, the women did not receive the 150 pesos (about $8.50) that they were owed for every day of training. They also protested having to play a friendly match in Uruguay the same day as traveling by bus for five hours. When they asked Pinela to meet with them, he did not show up. Only the coach Carlos Borrello appeared to represent the federation, but he could not give the players any information; he had been given none by the federation.[17] The players' strike came days before a scheduled friendly with the Uruguayan women's team and forced Borrello to play with the Argentine U-20 squad. Argentina lost 0–2 at home.[18]

SIGNS OF CHANGE

There are important exceptions to the mistreatment of women football players and the mismanagement of the sport in general. Women players and their supporters have managed to develop teams in clubs around Latin America. In Uruguay, there are well over one hundred clubs in all age ranges and a new committee on women's football. In Argentina, the women's team of UAI Urquiza, a third-division Argentine men's team, won the women's division three years in a row between 2015 and 2017 and made it to the semifinals of the Copa Libertadores Femenina in 2015. The goalkeeper, Gaby Gartón, who also plays for the Argentine national team when it is active, explained that UAI Urquiza is unique in helping players to complete their education, allowing women to train with the men's side, and busing them to training facilities.[19] Their coach, Carlos Borrello, had previously directed the women's national team and was named coach again in July 2017. When we asked Borrello how UAI Urquiza achieved its success, he answered pointedly, "by valuing them [the players] as human beings, offering them opportunities to study and to work seriously at football."[20] On the subject of the national team, Borrello concurred with FIFA's categorization of Argentina as "inactive." "The status of the women's team is very low," he said. "There is no work being done and no competition." After retaking the helm of the team in 2017, he recognized that there was much work to be done: "we have to put together all of the teams, especially the youth squads." There also needed to be rapid sensitization to women's football, as Argentina was selected to host the U-17 South American Championship. Through developing youth teams, Borrello hoped to lay the foundation for the future of the senior team, but he was not blind to the challenges that faced the latter in the present. Borrello suggested that Argentine senior women's football needed to address two deficiencies rapidly: it needed "permanent training" and "lots of competition."[21] The key was to change the mind-set of the federation toward women's football. People like Borrello who are in positions of authority in the women's sport suggest that change is possible.

In fact, throughout Latin America there is the sense that change is possible, if not already afoot. For example, Ecuador's Vanessa Arauz represents the face of change there. The head coach of the Ecuadorean women's national team has been on the job since 2014. Hired at age twenty-four, in 2015 at twenty-six she was the youngest person ever to coach at a FIFA World Cup, men's or women's. Ecuador finished last in the newly expanded tournament, scoring only one goal. While some federations might have fired the coach—especially a female coach—on the heels of such a performance, the Ecuadorean federation did not. Rather, the federation retained the young coach for the women's national program at all levels. By 2017 Arauz was coaching all women's teams for the federation and had been named an official instructor by CONMEBOL. In that position, Arauz traveled around South America providing training and assistance to women's programs.[22] Amelia Valverde took over the reins of the Costa Rican national team at twenty-eight years old and achieved notable results in the 2015 Women's World Cup.

The growth of women's football leagues, supported by member federations, is heartening. The Ecuadorean women's league has been in operation since 2013 under the auspices of the Ecuadorean federation's amateur wing. It has grown from one division with sixteen teams to two divisions with twelve teams each. Important for the long-term growth of the game, in November 2017 Servisky, an Ecuadorian television and communications company, purchased the television rights to the women's league for five years and transmitted the games on social media. The stated goal of the Ecuadorean federation was to "popularize women's football throughout the country."[23] The rights package was inexpensive, with Servisky paying $60,000 annually, to be split between the teams.[24] In Uruguay, FIFA funding is being used to start a professional league "in the medium term." The Uruguayan federation began using FIFA Forward money to train a cadre of women's coaches. CONMEBOL itself started a girls' development tournament in 2017, bringing together girls' teams from around the continent in U-14 and U-16 categories. CONMEBOL also passed a resolution in 2017 that requires all clubs to have a women's team for their men's team to compete in the Copa Libertadores.[25] A Paraguayan team won the 2016 Copa Libertadores Femenina, and a Venezuelan team finished second, marking the first time that a Brazilian team did not reach the finals. This parity can only help the game in the region.

Developments in Colombia created even more optimism for the future of women's football. Beginning in 2017, the Colombian Football Federation inaugurated a women's professional league with eighteen teams. From its inception, the women's league was placed under the División Mayor del Fútbol Profesional Colombiano, or Dimayor, Colombia's professional soccer division. The vast majority of teams were affiliated with men's clubs. In its second year the league expanded to twenty-three teams. Plans were in place for a further expansion, to thirty-six teams, in 2019. Equally important, as part of Colombia's professional division, the league benefited from sponsors such as Aguila beer, Golty, and Avianca, among others. After the first season, the women's league announced that it had reached a deal with FAN Network TV to broadcast 90 percent of the league's games in North America, Europe, and Asia.[26] Still, with all of the success of women's football in Colombia, much remains to be done to overcome stereotypes and failures to increase the visibility of the women's game in the country. For example, in November 2017, Adidas debuted the new Colombian national team jerseys with a well-publicized press conference. The former men's national team players Faustín Asprilla and Freddy Rincón modeled the new shirts for men. But instead of having Colombian futboleras introduce the women's kit, Adidas used the Colombian winner of the Miss Universe pageant, Paulina Vega. While the event was organized by Adidas, it is likely that the Colombian federation was involved in the kit unveiling. Notwithstanding the question of why the women's jerseys have plunging necklines, having women's national team players model the new jerseys would have been free publicity for the sport.[27] Adidas apparently failed to get the message: in April 2018, in the middle of the Copa América Femenina, it debuted the new Argentina jerseys—with male footballers and female models.

In Mexico, too, the women's professional league appeared to be taking hold. The Liga MX Femenil launched with a tournament called the Copa MX Femenil in 2017 after a failed attempt to insert national team players into the US-based National Women's Soccer League (NWSL). Under an agreement with the US league, the three North American federations (Mexico, the United States, and Canada) would allocate players to NWSL teams and pay their salaries. In 2013, the first year of the program, Mexico allocated sixteen players. In the second year that number was reduced by half, and in 2015 only four Mexican national team players were allocated to NWSL teams. After that season, in which none of the four saw playing time, Mexico pulled out of the program.[28] Perhaps not coincidentally, in late 2016 the Mexican federation announced plans for a women's professional league, the Liga MX Femenil. Twelve teams competed in the Copa MX Feminil, with sixteen teams entering the first full season of competition in 2017–2018. All women's teams were affiliated with clubs in the men's game, and by 2018–2019, eighteen women's teams comprised the Liga MX Femenil.

Mexico also led in other ways. The creation of nationwide amateur leagues in May 2015 for girls in the U-13 and U-16 categories was intended to help diffuse the sport and develop talent for the Mexican national team. These leagues coincided with the hiring of Lucia Mijares Martínez to became director of sports development for the amateur wing of the Mexican federation. Mijares Martínez admitted to being surprised when she was offered the job, as it remained "uncommon that a woman would direct anything within football."[29] In this role, Mijares Martínez oversaw all development in amateur football, for women and men and boys and girls. In its first year of the program, the federation affiliated U-13 and U-16 leagues and recognized 150 teams in fifteen states throughout Mexico. Many more teams existed, however, on a grassroots, unofficial level. "There are so many teams," Mijares Martínez admitted, "that we don't know how many there are."[30] Even with the support of the federation, creating the leagues was difficult. Due to the structure of the amateur division, all new projects needed the approval of the head of each state football association, and "there were many states that voted against it . . . [and] that said we will not vote for anything related to women's football."[31] Part of the reason might have been, as Mijares Martínez noted, that it would cut into the business interests of women's football promoters. Since the sport had been completely privatized, the creation of a national league within the Mexican federation threatened the profits of private league organizers.

The Clausura (closing tournament) of the Liga MX Femenil in 2018 saw disappointing results in terms of fans, with attendance down almost 80,000 from the Apertura (opening tournament). The latter had average attendance of 4,200 per match in the group stages, just under 11,000 per match for the semifinals, and over 60,000 total attendance for the two legs of the finals, won by Chivas. By comparison, the Clausura season saw an average of 2,000 fans per game. The playoffs, however, marked a major milestone in women's football in Mexico. Semifinal attendance stood at just over 42,000 for the four games. The finals however, far exceeded expectations. A total of nearly 90,000 people attended the two legs, with 51,211 fans at the last match, a world record for professional women's football.[32] The creation of both the national youth amateur leagues and the Liga MX Femenil nevertheless marked an important step in the Mexican sporting landscape. It also highlighted the strength of the grassroots work done to keep Mexican women's football alive. Mexican women's football survived on the margins over the years between the 1970s and the 2000s due to the initiative of players themselves as well as of league organizers. According to Fabiola Vargas, a former Mexican national team player, *fútbol rápido* (*fútbol sala*, or futsal) leagues, playing six a side, formed the base upon which Mexican women's football regrouped in the late 1980s and early 1990s. Just as Brazilian women embraced futsal, Mexican women's embrace of derivations on football helped to keep players active, interested, and skilled. The survival of women's football leagues depended on voluntary support networks.[33] As a young teenager, Ruby Campos Ramírez remembered playing with friends in the street and fantasizing about starting a team, only to see a woman walk by in a football uniform. After about a month of seeing the woman walk by at the same time every week, Campos Ramírez asked where she was going and if she could join her. In this way she discovered a women's league and a sport that would eventually take her to the Mexican national team.[34] The grassroots school and girls' programs started by women like Mercedes Rodríguez Alemán, Andrea Rodebaugh, and others in the 1980s and 1990s laid the groundwork for the growth of the sport. Mariana Gutiérrez Bernárdez and two friends organized a *fútbol siete* (seven a side) tournament in 2008 by finding a field and putting a call out on Facebook. In the first year the league had twenty teams. It doubled in size the following year. By 2010 over 150 teams participated in the Liga Kotex, which was sponsored that year by Kotex, Scotiabank, and Zwan.[35] Gutiérrez Bernárdez went on to become the supervisor of national leagues for the Mexican Football Federation—like Lucia Mijares Martínez, taking over a position that traditionally would have gone to a man.

In fact, more coaching, refereeing, and administrative positions seem to be opening up to women in Latin America. A strong cohort of women licensed by FIFA began to oversee men's and women's matches. The first women received federation training in the 1980s; however, it was nearly impossible to convince men to allow them into the programs. Officials denied the system was sexist, implying that women could not keep up with the pace of male players to properly do the job. The discrimination also comes from players. In 2004 Virginia Tovar became the first woman to arbitrate a first-division men's match. The legendary player Cuauhtémoc Blanco (currently mayor of Cuernavaca) yelled at her to go back to washing dishes.[36] The Argentine referee Salome di Iorio has been verbally abused, spat on, and threatened by players and fans alike. This hasn't stopped the interest of women in refereeing, as evidenced in FIFA's calculation that there are now over seven hundred women registered and qualified to referee professional matches.[37] Refereeing may be even more challenging to sexism in sports than playing, since it implies a combination of physical strength, technical knowledge, and authority of women on the pitch.

Women coaches, of course, are nothing new. For decades women have coached football and futsal in private clubs around the region. Now, however, players from the generation of the 1980s and 1990s have gone into coaching and have had an impact on the women's game both within their nations and internationally. For example, the former Mexican national team players Andrea Rodebaugh and Fabiola Vargas, who both represented the country in the 1990s and 2000s, completed their coaching training and have been working in various capacities. Rodebaugh was an assistant on Cuellar's staff and coached Mexico's U-20 women's team before becoming a roving coach for FIFA. In that capacity, she traveled around the world giving training and coaching clinics to national federations in order to better equip them to coach women and girls. For her, this was a part of a long-term development of women's football, not only in Mexico but worldwide. When the Liga MX Femenil formed, Rodebaugh left FIFA in order to coach Xolos de Tijuana Femenil. When named as coach, she brought her former teammate Fabiola Vargas onto the staff. Vargas became head coach of the Nexcaca women's team in 2018. Monica Vergara, who played for Mexico in the 1990s and 2000s, was on Leonard Cuellar's coaching staff and became the coach of the U-15 women's national team in 2014. Maribel Domínguez also began working with the women's national setup in 2017. These are hardly the only ex-players entering coaching. In Mexico alone, Fatima Leyva, Iris Mora, Monica Gonzalez, and Monica Gerardo have also attained licenses and have begun to work at different levels within the sport. In the inaugural season of the Liga MX Femenil, four of the sixteen head coaches were women. In the second season, the number of women coaches had increased by one. The rise in the coaching ranks of former players, who experienced firsthand the struggle for women's football, bodes well for the future of the sport.

With reason, women players are wary of the male-dominated sporting institutions. If the rhetoric from CONMEBOL, CONCACAF, and the national federations seems to point toward more resources for the women's game, the players have been down this road before. The Brazilian women's team, for example, experienced a wave of popularity during the 2016 Olympic Games as it cruised through the group stages of the tournament. It played a free-flowing, "Brazilian" style at a time when the men's team seemed to be playing in quicksand. Fans began buying Marta shirts. Political cartoons highlighted the hype around the women's team as well. Yet before the dust had settled after the games ended, the Brazilian federation announced cuts to the women's national team program. Brazil was not alone. Despite promises of more resources, women's teams—national and club level—rarely receive sufficient support. What is left for the women is collective action and grassroots mobilizing.

What else can improve the landscape of women's football? The history of the sport and its underdevelopment by FIFA, CONMEBOL, and national associations suggests that the Chilean ANJUFF may be on to something—a separate federation or a player's union and support from FIFPro. Like women players from more developed women's programs, Chilean, Argentine, and Brazilian women do not want to fight their federations. Unlike their peers, however, they are not fighting for equal treatment—or even equitable treatment. They merely want the basics: travel money, decent facilities, and better support networks. Given women's abuse at the hands of male-dominated national federations, perhaps they would be better served by organizing independently, as was done throughout the world into the 1970s. For example, the Federation of International and European Women's Football governed the sport in the late 1960s and organized the first two women's world championships (1970 and 1971), while in Mexico, Argentina, and Uruguay, women's leagues created their own national governing bodies. Now, however, players worry that the formation of independent federations will violate FIFA rules and put participants at risk of sporting exile.

Another way forward for women's football would be to change the dynamics of sports journalism. Indeed, a crucial obstacle to women's football is the media's continued objectification of women athletes and the wives and girlfriends of male players to the neglect of women athletes as athletes. The increased presence of women in the commentator booth and in postgame analysis will improve the place of women within football, though it remains to be seen if this will increase respect for women's football. Nevertheless, here too Mexico showed early leadership, with coverage of the Mexican women's national team including analysis and play-by-play from the former players Andrea Rodebaugh and Fabiola Vargas. Most Liga MX Femenil teams have television deals to air at least some games during the season. The spread of the internet has also aided the growth of grassroots media coverage and analysis of the world of women's football. FutFemenilMX, for example, hosts a weekly podcast to discuss the state of affairs of the sport inside (and occasionally outside) Mexico. Greater visibility for the sport, its players, and its history will only help to advance the game.

At the federation level, the directors of the national associations are almost entirely men. The South American confederation, CONMEBOL, in 2014 had the lowest percentage of women on executive committees, at 2 percent, according to a report by Moya Dodd and Sarai Bareman. Women need to be represented on executive committees. They should have their own representatives, with full voting rights, because otherwise women's football is completely ignored. So too should federations work with the sports media to promote women's football and to televise women's national team games. In today's landscape, the "market" is the actor responsible for success in sports. Fans and journalists frequently blame sexism and the lack of resources given to women's football on the "market." The standard justification is that if women's football sold more tickets or merchandise it would garner greater institutional support. But this argument is circular. Men's football did not become the national sport in much of Latin America on its own. As leagues developed, the sports media developed along with it in a symbiotic relationship. The explosion of men's football and the sports media was furthered by advertising and promotion in both print and radio. In other words, football did not grow into the sport it is today organically; it required support from outside. Moreover, most Latin American men's leagues struggle to stay afloat financially, as global football attention has turned to European leagues. Women's football has received far more scorn than support from the very same sources that made men's football—and men's sports in general—so pervasive. Furthermore, association directors claim that the women's game is new and underdeveloped. As this book has shown, these arguments lack historical and rational bases. Federations all over the world support terrible men's teams with public funds because the sport is seen as national patrimony, even as good women's teams languish.

Federations can also be inventive with their marketing and sponsorship. Federations can negotiate more money with the requirement that additional monies be spent specifically on women's football. Companies can take the lead as well by requiring that a part of sponsorship funds be spent on the women's game. In the Liga MX Femenil, sponsorship is club wide. So, for example, Huawei's sponsorship of Club América includes both the men's and women's teams. The league itself is sponsored by Coca-Cola, Voit, and Powerade.[38] Match attendance in the Brazilian women's league is growing, as is the level of competition and the number of games. There is not only a national Brazilian women's competition but also regional tournaments in Rio and São Paulo. The expansion of the women's Brasileiro has been a boon for clubs like EC Iranduba, in Manaus, which draws more fans than local men's teams. The team's semifinal loss to Santos in the Brazilian championship drew over twenty-five thousand people to the Arena da Amazônia, more than many men's clubs draw.[39]

In effect, what the history of women's sports—and particularly women's football—in Latin America suggests is that there is still a long way to go. Linked as it was to questions of national identity and the growth and development of healthy nations, women's physical activity was always going to be the source of vigilance on the part of families and the state. Thus, sports for women, much more so than for men, was never just about physical fitness. Rather, because women were the future mothers of the nation, patriarchal systems sought to ensure the healthfulness of women's activities. However, more often than not the purported experts worked more on the basis of their own sexism and prejudice than on any actual knowledge of either physical education or public health. Football, as a team sport that offered platforms for women's solidarity, and as the dominant male sport in the region, came under uniquely harsh criticism. With the support of public health "experts" who claimed that football damaged women's reproductive capacities, sports authorities systematically closed down options for women to play the game. But the development of physical education programs eventually opened the door for women's athletics.

Throughout the region, from football powers like Brazil to nations like Costa Rica, women's involvement in the sport dates almost back to its arrival. And there is much more to do. Peru and Colombia had vibrant women's football in the 1950s and 1960s, as recent research has shown. But for the most part, their involvement has been written out of the dominant history of the sport. Given the importance of football in Latin America, this is no minor elision: if the sport is essential to national identity, excluding women's football stories means excluding women from a crucial national construct. Women were not equally discouraged from playing all sports. Track and field, tennis, golf, basketball, and volleyball have enjoyed greater state and club support. After a century of playing, women's football faces particular scorn because it threatens the same male preserves: national identity, solidarity, leisure time, physical freedom, and athletic prowess. As shocking as the conditions are for some women athletes in Latin America when compared to the men's resources, sportswomen don't necessarily experience deprivation or bemoan their situation. After all of the treatment the Argentine futboleras endured, they still expressed their pride at wearing the national jersey. One player who made just $150 a month playing for Boca Juniors beamed when she described what it was like to represent the club she had adored since childhood.

Today's feminist movements in Latin America are struggling with urgent and immediate problems, such as poverty, femicide, workplace discrimination, and reproductive rights. The #NiUnaMenos (Not One [Woman] Less) movement in Argentina, originally emerging in 2015 in response to femicide, has broadened the definition of gender violence and spread throughout the region. It has organized successful national strikes, social media campaigns, and legal advocacy. The work of feminists such as the Brazilian politician Marielle Franco expanded the scope of these movements to include antiracism and socialism. Franco's assassination in 2018 was a painful reminder of the danger facing intersectional grassroots movements. In light of these struggles, sports equality is understandably lower on the agenda. Historically, however, sports has been a site of struggle over women's supposed inferiority, their rights to leisure and public spaces, their role in national identity, and their education. Insofar as gender differences are created and recreated on the pitch, by the media, and in school gymnasiums, understanding how these spaces have changed over time deepens our understanding of persistent inequalities. Hopefully, these histories, and the many sure to come, will be useful to those working to even the playing field. We also . hope they are a testament to the persistence of girls and women in Latin American sports, and their allies, who have fought for dignity and recognition for over a century.

ACKNOWLEDGMENTS

THIS BOOK HAS BEEN A LONG TIME IN THE MAKING. JUST as the book spans a lot of time and space, over the course of its creation the authors have too. From seemingly expected places, like Mexico, Costa Rica, Brazil, Chile, and Argentina, to less likely locales, like Athens, the complexities of writing while in a constant state of movement have been both challenging and fun. And there are many people to thank. First and foremost, Kerry Webb at the University of Texas Press. She signed on to the project from the outset and encouraged us at all points along the way. We would like to thank the Lozano Long Institute for Latin American Studies at the University of Texas at Austin and the staff at the Nettie Lee Benson Latin American Collection. Their knowledge and assistance cannot be overstated. Daniela Alfonsi, director of the Museu do Futebol, provided immeasurable assistance in the museum's archives. The Biblioteca Miguel Lerdo de Tejada is one of the most peaceful places to do research in Mexico City, and its staff are thoughtful and funny. Monica de la Vega cannot be thanked enough—not only for her research assistance, but for her sense of humor and instinct for great food. Dominik Petermann at the FIFA archive has now worked with both of us on two projects and for some reason continues to respond to our emails.

The network of futboleras also made our research much richer and warmer. To Fabiola Vargas, Andrea Rodebaugh, Elvira Aracén, Mercedes Rodríguez, and Ruby Campos, *abrazos*. Monica González offered information and guidance. Lucia Mijares and Mariana Bernárdez provided great insight into the workings of the Mexican football federation and its changes with regard to the women's game. Gaby Gartón, Ruth Bravo, "Marina," and Las Pioneras in Argentina; Siselaide do Amor Lima and Marcia Tafarel from Brazil; and Camila García, Fernanda Pinilla, and Iona Rothfeld in Chile have generously shared their stories with us. So too Fernando Bonilla Alvarado and Alice Quirós Alvarez deepened our understanding of the first women's football team in Costa Rica. Thanks to Xiomara Cubero, Veronica Bonilla Quirós, and John Henson for putting us in contact and facilitating our correspondence.

Many friends helped turn drafts of the manuscript into a much more polished book, in ways both direct and indirect. To Jean Williams and Shireen Ahmed, sisters-in-arms: your support and encouragement has meant the world to us both. Matthew Brown and James Green provided incredible insight on how to broaden our arguments. The anonymous readers of the manuscript pointed us toward important sources and helped sharpen our focus. Peter Alegi, Matt Andrews, Amy Bass, Claire Brewster, Keith Brewster, Bernardo Buarque, Laurent Dubois, Alex Galarza, Roger Kittleson, Lindsay Krasnoff, Belinda Monkhouse, Jaime Shultz, Rodrigo Soto, Shawn Stein, Diego Vilches, Jonathan Weiler, and David Wood all provided commentary at important moments.

* * *

FROM JOSH: I'd like to thank Brenda. It's pretty rare to find someone who is able to keep you more or less on task while still understanding that the vicissitudes of life sometimes create other priorities. I'm lucky to count you among my friends, and as a colleague you always make my work better. I'd also like to thank my colleagues at North Carolina Central University, both inside the history department and out, but especially Lydia Lindsey, Baiyina Muhammad, and the late Sylvia Jacobs. In the Triangle, both real and psychic, thanks to Matt and Lisa, Gustavo and Gracie, Todd and Erika, Ethan and Blain, Matthew and Leah, Layla and Josh, Claire and Jonathan, Mariola, Susan, Laura Wagner, the CSL crowd—especially Marc and Drew (or is it Drew and Marc?) and Ascary Arias—Randall, Lisa, Molly, Charlie, Jeff and Stephanie, Sam Amago, William Thomas, Sophie Adamson, Alchemy, and Neal's Deli. All of you play a big part in my sanity. The academy of Sporting Clube Portugal in Chalandri, Greece, gave me a place to work while my kids practiced a game they love and learned to swear in Greek. To the administration and coaches, much appreciation. Special thanks go to Mario Gavalas and Stavros Raptis. Ευχαριστω, Tzeni, for many great freddo cappuccinos. Patriarchy is strong in Greece, and that means that soccer dads are more common than moms. To all of the parents and friends there (too many to name individually) who patiently listened to me butcher Greek, thank you. Many went out of their way to help: Antonis Tzenes, Dino and Penny, Thanos and Ntina, Ariti and Giannis, Giannis and Dina, and Elias and Roma. Thanks to Victoria Kalonarou for a great place to live, think, and work, and to the cats of Kalisperi Sevastis, especially Isaiah, Steph, and Berry. To Eva's family in Greece—the Drellas, Zaxaropoulos, and Tiggelis families: ευχαριστουμε πολυ for taking such good care of us. And of course, to Evanthia, Sofia Ariadne, and Rafael Nikolaos: you have kept me focused and helped me to step away when it was time; without you, all of this would be a lot less fun. I love you. Finally, to Ginger and Helen: so much love . . . I wish Bill could have been around for this one.

* * *

FROM BRENDA: I would never have written this book without Josh. Over the last years, he has always reminded me of the contemporary implications of the work and kept me in it. I'm grateful for his intelligence, good nature, and friendship. At Hofstra, I would like to thank all of my colleagues in the history department and beyond, who have been incredibly supportive. Special acknowledgment to Benita Sampedro and Vimala Pasupathi. Simon Doubleday and Susan Yohn acted as chairpersons during the writing of this book and helped me to balance teaching and research whenever they could. There are so many friends whom I have leaned on and learned from over the years: Ernie Capello, Chandler Carter, Melissa Connolly, Enrique Garguín, Paul Gootenberg, Alberto Harambour, Liz Hutchison, Jorge Iturriaga, Zilkia Janer, Temma Kaplan, Ana Julia Ramírez, and Angie Thompson. To the shark crew, you know who you are, keep circling. J. Edward Durrett, thank you for making me laugh, almost daily, for so many years. Jessica Stites, for all kinds of reasons, has been a soul sister. The Bardfield-Mañons, the Kramers, and the Rose-Cortinas have made the Hudson Valley a beautiful place to live. Every week, Shireen Ahmed, Lindsay Gibbs, Jessica Luther, and Amira Rose Davis keep my spirits up and my brain working as part of the sports and feminism podcast *Burn It All Down*. I love you all.

Thanks to my family, the Browns, the Steeles, the Elseys, and their extensions, especially my mom, Joan, and my sister, Katie—a badass woman every week.

I can't say my children helped me write this book. But they brought me joy and laughter the rest of the time. All my love to Julieta, Luna, and Maya; three really is a magic number. And to their father, Enrique, I owe the biggest debt of all for his support. See you in the canoe, one way or another.

NOTES

INTRODUCTION

1. Marina Y., interview by Brenda Elsey, February 12, 2017.
2. Walter D. Mignolo, *The Idea of Latin America* (Malden, MA: Blackwell, 2005).
3. Examples include Gabriela Cano, "Género y construcción cultural de las profesiones en el Porfiriato: Magisterio, medicina, jurisprudencia y odontología," *Historia y Grafía* 14 (2000): 207–243; Mary Kay Vaughan, Gabriela Cano, and Jocelyn Olcott, eds., *Sex in Revolution: Gender, Power, and Politics in Modern Mexico* (Durham, NC: Duke University Press, 2006); Iana dos Santos Vasconcelos, "Mulher e mercado de trabalho no Brasil: Notas de uma história em andamento," *Examãpaku* 3, no. 2 (2010): 1–9, http://dx.doi.org/10.18227/1983-9065ex.v3i2.1497; Donna Guy, *Sex and Danger in Buenos Aires: Prostitution, Family, and Nation in Argentina* (Lincoln: University of Nebraska Press, 1991); Elizabeth Hutchison, *Labors Appropriate to Their Sex: Gender, Labor, and Politics in Urban Chile, 1900–1930* (Durham, NC: Duke University Press, 2001); Ann Farnsworth-Alvear, *Dulcinea in the Factory: Myths, Morals, Men, and Women in Colombia's Industrial Experiment* (Durham, NC: Duke University Press, 2000); Daniel James and John French, eds., *The Gendered Worlds of Latin American Women Workers: From Household and Factory to the Union Hall and Ballot Box* (Durham, NC: Duke University Press, 1997).
4. Karin Alejandra Rosemblatt, *Gendered Compromises: Political Cultures and the State in Chile, 1920–1950* (Chapel Hill: University of North Carolina Press, 2000).
5. Heidi Tinsman, *Partners in Conflict: The Politics of Gender, Sexuality, and Labor in the Chilean Agrarian Reform, 1950–1973* (Durham, NC: Duke University Press, 2000); Mary Kay Vaughan, *Cultural Politics in Revolution: Teachers, Peasants, and Schools in Mexico, 1930–1940* (Tucson: University of Arizona Press, 1997).
6. Much of this work is interdisciplinary in nature, and historiography has been enriched by anthropologists, sociologists, and others. See, for example, Antonia dos Santos Garcia, *Mulheres da cidade d'Oxum:*

Relações de gênero, raça e classe e organização espacial do movimento de bairro em Salvador (Salvador, Brazil: UFBA Editora, 2006).

7. See, for example, Brenda Elsey, *Citizens and Sportsmen: Fútbol and Politics in Twentieth-Century Chile* (Austin: University of Texas Press, 2011); Thomas Miller Klubock, *Contested Communities: Class, Gender, and Politics in Chile's El Teniente Copper Mine, 1904–1951* (Durham, NC: Duke University Press, 1998); Matthew C. Gutmann, *The Meanings of Macho: Being a Man in Mexico City* (Berkeley: University of California Press, 2006); Martha Santos, *Cleansing Honor with Blood: Masculinity, Violence, and Power in the Backlands of Northeast Brazil, 1845–1889* (Stanford, CA: Stanford University Press, 2012).

8. Kathya Araujo and Mercedes Prieto, eds., *Estudios sobre sexualidades en América Latina* (Quito, Ecuador: FLACSO, 2008); James N. Green, *Beyond Carnival: Male Homosexuality in Twentieth-Century Brazil* (Chicago: University of Chicago Press, 2000).

9. The field has grown enormously; some of the key volumes include: Pablo Alabarces, *Fútbol y patria: El fútbol y las narrativas de la nación en la Argentina* (Buenos Aires: Prometo, 2003); Matthew Brown, *From Frontiers to Football: An Alternative History of Latin America Since 1800* (London: Reaktion Books, 2014); Bernardo Buarque de Hollanda, *O clube como vontade e representação: O jornalismo esportivo e a formação das torcidas organizadas de futebol do Rio de Janeiro* (Rio de Janeiro: 7Letras; Faperj, 2010); Brenda Elsey, *Citizens and Sportsmen: Fútbol and Politics in Twentieth-Century Chile* (Austin: University of Texas Press, 2011); Julio Frydenberg, *Historia social del fútbol: Del amateurismo a la profesionalización* (Buenos Aires: Siglo XXI, 2011); Roger Kittleson, *The Country of Football: Soccer and the Making of Modern Brazil* (Berkeley: University of California Press, 2014); Roger Magazine, *Golden and Blue Like My Heart: Masculinity, Youth, and Power among Soccer Fans in Mexico City* (Tucson: University of Arizona Press, 2007); Joshua Nadel, *Fútbol! Why Soccer Matters in Latin America* (Gainesville: University Press of Florida, 2014); David Sheinin, ed., *Sport Culture in Latin American History* (Pittsburgh, PA: University of Pittsburgh Press, 2015); David Wood, *Football and Literature in South America* (New York: Routledge, 2017).

10. Andrea Stevenson Allen, *Violence and Desire in Brazilian Lesbian Relationships* (New York: Palgrave, 2015); Rosa Maria Oliveira, "Fronteiras invisíveis: Gêneros, questões identitárias e relações entre movimento homossexual e estado no Brasil," *Revista Bagoas*, no. 4 (2009): 160–172.

11. Anne Rubenstein, "The War on 'Las Pelonas': Modern Women and Their Enemies, Mexico City, 1924," in *Sex in Revolution: Gender,*

Politics, and Power in Modern Mexico, ed. Jocelyn Olcott, Mary Kay Vaughan, and Gabriela Cano (Durham, NC: Duke University Press, 2006): 57–80.

12. Valeria Manzano, *The Age of Youth in Argentina: Culture, Politics, and Sexuality from Perón to Videla* (Chapel Hill: University of North Carolina Press, 2014), 98.

13. Some sources list the name of the organization as the Independent Federation of Women's Football; see for example Jean Williams, *A Beautiful Game: International Perspectives on Women's Football* (Oxford, UK: Berg, 2007), 20. However, posters for the first world championship in Italy list the name as Federazione Internazionale Europea Football Femminile.

CHAPTER 1

1. Juana Gremler, *Monografía de Liceo No. 1 de Niñas* (Santiago, Chile: Imp. Cervantes, 1902).

2. Today the school is named Liceo Javiera Carrera. Chile's first female president, Michelle Bachelet; the writer Isabel Allende; and a number of prominent women attended the school.

3. Carola Sepúlveda Vásquez, "Esencias en fuga: Dime, mi bien, ¿quién me llorará, si me dan alas y echo a volar?" (thesis, Universidad de Chile, 2007), http://www.tesis.uchile.cl/tesis/uchile/2007/sepulveda_c/html/index-frames.html.

4. Macarena Ponce de León Sol Serrano and Francisca Rengifo, *Historia de la educación en Chile (1810–2010)* (Santiago de Chile: Taurus, 2012), volume 2.

5. Raúl Blanco, *Educación física, un panorama de su historia* (Montevideo, Uruguay: Imp. Adroher, 1948), 158.

6. Beatriz Sarlo, *La máquina cultural. Maestras, traductores y vanguardistas* (Buenos Aires: Ariel, 1998).

7. A key early influence was the US educational leader Catharine Beecher, who in the 1830s advocated for girls' and women's physical education. Beecher was the sister of Harriet Beecher Stowe, author of *Uncle Tom's Cabin*. In 1855, Catharine wrote the textbook *Physiology and Calisthenics for Schools and Families*.

8. Sepúlveda Vásquez, "Esencias en fuga."

9. François Martinez, "¡Que nuestros indios se conviertan en pequeños suecos! La introducción de la gymnasia en las escuelas bolivianas," *Andines* 28, no. 3 (1999): 364.

10. F. Martinez, "Que nuestros indios," 361–386, 372.

11. Blanco, *Educación física*, 118.

12. Blanco, *Educación física*, 119.
13. Roland Naul and Ken Hardman, eds., *Sport and Physical Education in Germany* (New York: Routledge, 2002).
14. Naul and Hardman, *Sport and Physical Education*, 96, 154.
15. "Y.M.C.A. Banned in Lima," *South American*, November 1919, p. 34.
16. Senda Berenson Abbott, *Spalding's Official Basketball Guide for Women* (New York: American Sports Publishing Company, 1916).
17. Jess Hopkins, "Basket Ball in South America," in *Spalding's Official Basketball Guide* (New York: American Sports Publishing Company, 1914), 181.
18. Jorge Iber et al., *Latinos in U.S. Sport: A History of Isolation, Cultural Identity, and Acceptance* (Champaign, IL: Human Kinetics, 2011), 95.
19. Jorge Saraví Rivière, *Historia de la educación física argentina* (Buenos Aires: Libros de Zorzal, 2012), 25.
20. Santiago Harispe, "Francisco Berra historiador: Aspectos de una biografía intelectual en el Río de la Plata a finales del siglo XIX," *Historia de la Educación* 16 (2015): 27–36.
21. Saraví Rivière, *Historia de la educación física argentina*.
22. Pablo Scharagrodsky, "El padre de la educación física argentina: Fabricando una política corporal generizada (1900–1940)," *Perspectiva* 22 (July–December 2004): 83–119.
23. Scharagrodsky, "El padre de la educación física."
24. Gisela Kaczan, "La práctica gimnástica y el deporte: La cultura física y el cuerpo bello en la historia de las mujeres. Argentina 1900–1930," *Historia Crítica* 61 (July 2016): 23–43.
25. Kaczan, "La práctica gimnástica."
26. Kaczan, "La práctica gimnástica."
27. *El Gráfico*, July 12, 1919.
28. *El Hogar*, January 28, 1929, cover.
29. Kaczan, "La práctica gimnástica"; and Andrés Horacio Reggiani, "Cultura física, performance atlética e higiene de la nación. El surgimiento de la medicina deportiva en Argentina (1930–1940)," *Historia Crítica* 61 (July–September 2016): 65–84.
30. Patricia Anderson, "*Mens Sana in Corpore Sano*: Debating Female Sport in Argentina: 1900–46," *International Journal of the History of Sport* 26, no. 5 (2009): 640–653.
31. Anderson, "Debating Female Sport."
32. Marcela Nari, *Políticas de maternidad y maternalismo político* (Buenos Aires: Biblos, 2004).
33. Arturo Raul Rossi, "La educación física en los canones biotipolo-gicos," *Anales de biotipologia, eugenesia y medicina social* 3, no. 64 (July 1936): 10–12.

34. "Dígame doctor," *Eva*, April 23, 1948, p. 31.

35. Blanco, *Educación física*, 107.

36. Blanco, *Educación física*; María Andrea Feiguin and Ángela Aisestein, "Diseño de sujetos morales, sanos y patriotas. Formación de profesores de educación física. Argentina, 1938–1967," *Pedagogía y Saberes*, no. 44 (January–June 2016): 12.

37. Congreso Panamericano de Educación Física, *Actas y Documentos Oficiales* (Montevideo, Uruguay: 1943).

38. Nikos Zaikos, "Ingeborg Mello: 'Two Lives' in Sport," *Nashim* 26 (Spring 2014): 5–34.

39. Zaikos, "Ingeborg Mello."

40. "En Buenos Aires, se practica football femenino," *Fray Mocho*, October 2, 1923.

41. See Mirta Zaida Lobato, "Afectos y sexualidad en el mundo de trabajo entre fines del siglo XIX y la década de 1930," in *Moralidades y comportamientos sexuales: Argentina, 1880–2011*, ed. Dora Barrancos, Donna Guy, and Adriana Valobra (Buenos Aires: Biblios, 2014), 155–174.

42. Biblioteca Nacional de Argentina, digital library, http://trapalanda .bn.gov.ar/jspui/handle/123456789/9021#prettyPhoto[iframes1]/3/ 1953 Union club of AOT.

43. Karina Ramacciotti and Adriana Valobra, "'Peor que putas': Tríbadas, satisfas y homosexuales en el discurso moral hegemónico del campo medico, 1936–1945," in *Moralidades y comportamientos sexuales: Argentina, 1880–2011*, ed. Dora Barrancos, Donna Guy, and Adriana Valobra (Buenos Aires: Biblios, 2014), 195–216.

44. Brenda Elsey, *Citizens and Sportsmen: Fútbol and Politics in Twentieth-Century Chile* (Austin: University of Texas Press, 2011).

45. See Sol Serrano and Rengifo, *Historia de la educación en Chile*, volume 2.

46. *Actividades Femeninas en Chile* (Santiago, Chile: Imp. Ilustración, 1928), 261.

47. Pedro Acuña, "Dribbling with the Left and Shooting with the Right: Soccer, Sports Media, and Populism in Argentina and Chile, 1940s–1950s" (PhD diss., University of California, Irvine, 2016), particularly chapter 5.

48. "Siguen los triunfos chilenos," *Estadio*, March 20, 1942.

49. *Los Sports.*

50. "Team Talca de Escuela Normal," photograph, 1900, Museo Histórico Nacional de Chile, PFA-240.

51. "Team Santiago de Escuela Normal de Talca," photograph, 1918, Museo Histórico Nacional de Chile, PFA-23.

52. Josafat Martínez, *Historia del fútbol chileno* (Santiago, Chile: Nacional, 1961), 12.
53. "A favor de la Estudiantina La Flor de Chile," *El Mercurio*, May 11, 1919, p. 13; and "Asociación Femenina de Football de Chile," *El Mercurio*, May 11, 1919, p. 13.
54. "Asociación Femenina de Football de Chile," *El Mercurio*, May 11, 1919, p. 13.
55. "La Flor de Chile—La Fiesta Sportiva de Hoy," *El Mercurio*, May 25, 1919, p. 19; and "El grán festival de las 8," *El Mercurio*, May 27, 1919, p. 7.
56. "Flor de Chile FC Femenino," *El Mercurio*, June 27, 1919, p. 19. The new executive board was: Srta. Carmela Hernández, president; Srta. Mariana Medina, vice president; Srta. Javiera Cárdenas, secretary; Srta. Teresa Arellano, vice secretary; Srta. Malvina A. De Escobar, treasurer; Srta. Emilio [*sic*(?)] Sepúlveda, vice treasurer; Srta. Quiteria Medina, "captain of the first team"; Srta. Inés Araneda, vice captain; and Srtas. Juana Romero, Doria Callardo, Juna Sepúlveda, and Marta Delgado, directors.
57. Blanco, *Educación física*, 218.
58. Acuña, "Dribbling with the Left," 47.
59. "Los deportes femeninos en Valparaíso," *Los Sports*, July 8, 1927, p. 2.
60. "Los deportes femeninos en Valparaíso," *Los Sports*, July 8, 1927, p. 2.
61. *Match* 1, no 1 (October 1928): 22.
62. Elcira Poblete, "La gimnasia y la mujer," *Justicia*, August 23, 1924, p. 4.
63. Elcira Poblete, "La gimnasia y la mujer," *Justicia*, August 23, 1924, p. 4.
64. "Club deportivo 'Aurora Porteña,'" Memorias del siglo XX, Ministerio de las Culturas, las Artes y el Patrimonio, Gobierno de Chile, n.d., http://www.memoriasdelsigloxx.cl/601/w3-article-51889.html.
65. "La mujer, los deportes y . . . el marido," *Match*, April 26, 1929, p. 5.
66. "La mujer, los deportes y . . . el marido," *Match*, April 26, 1929, p. 5.
67. "La mujer, el gimnasio y el prejuicio," *Los Sports*, December 20, 1929, p. 1.
68. Elcira Poblete, "La gimnasia y la mujer, *Justicia*, August 23, 1924, p. 4.
69. Elcira Poblete, "La gimnasia y la mujer, *Justicia*, August 23, 1924, p. 4.
70. "Deportes," *Unión Feminina de Chile*, April 1934.
71. "La mujer i los sports," *Sport i Actualidades*, May 4, 1913, p. 1.
72. "La mujer moderna y el deporte," *La Gaceta Deportiva*, June 14, 1930, p. 3.
73. "Sobre el lawn tennis," *Pacífico Magazine*, January 1916, pp. 25–28.
74. "Sobre el lawn tennis," *Pacífico Magazine*, January 1916, pp. 25–28, 26.
75. Susana Lenglen, "Táctica," *Los Sports*, June 11, 1926, pp. 6–7.

76. Don Pampa, "Nació estrella," *Estadio*, June 2, 1951, p. 4.
77. Inelia Casanova, "Síntesis histórica del basket-ball femenino en Chile," *Revista Chilena de Educación Física* 17, no. 67 (January 1951): 42–43.
78. Don Pampa, "Nació estrella," *Estadio*, June 2, 1951, p. 4. *Marimacho* is a term that can be translated as tomboy or butch lesbian, depending on the way it is used.
79. "Otro título para el norte," *Estadio*, April 21, 1944, p. 24.
80. Don Pampa, "El equipo viajero," *Estadio*, April 19, 1947, pp. 4–5, 22, 30, 5.
81. Don Pampa, "El equipo viajero," *Estadio*, April 19, 1947.
82. Colo-Colo FC, *Historia del Club Colo-Colo* (Santiago, Chile: Imprenta Arvas, 1953).
83. Tatanacho, "Chile doblo a Argentina," *Estadio*, May 25, 1946, pp. 16–21.
84. Tatanacho, "Chile doblo a Argentina," *Estadio*, May 25, 1946, pp. 16–21, 18.
85. "Confirmo excelencia," *Estadio*, May 28, 1949, pp. 8–9.
86. "Confirmo excelencia," *Estadio*, May 28, 1949, pp. 8–9.
87. "Natacha Méndez Cash, reina de la Primavera," Población Pedro Montt, March 4, 2009, http://poblacionpedromontt.blogspot.com/2009/03 /natacha-mendez-cash-reina-de-la.html.
88. "Ahora, una dama," *Estadio*, January 16, 1954, p. 3; Daniel Arellano, "Seleccionadas de la 'Época Dorada' del básquetbol femenino," *El Deportero*, December 5, 2016, https://eldeportero.cl/seleccionadas-de-la -epoca-dorada-del-basquetbol-femenino-recibieron-un-reconocimiento -a-su-trayectoria/.
89. José Contreras C., "Las sabrosas historias del dorado básquetbol femenino nacional," *La Tercera*, May 12, 2016, http://www.latercera.com/noticia /las-sabrosas-historias-del-dorado-basquetbol-femenino-nacional/.
90. "El basquetbol no es un deporte para mujeres," *La Nación*, November 22, 1948.
91. "Women in the World Sports Organisations," *Olympic Review*, no. 82–83 (September–October 1974): 401–414.
92. "Women in the World Sports Organisations," *Olympic Review*, no. 82–83 (September–October 1974): 401–414.
93. *Estadio*, December 31, 1943.
94. Track and field was one of the most popular sports in the early Pan-American Games, with the number of athletes doubling from two thousand at the 1951 games to four thousand in 1955.
95. Stephanie Elias, "Las mujeres de oro," *Ya: El Mercurio*, July 28, 2015, pp. 16–20.

96. Elias, "Las mujeres de oro"; Alexis Jeldrez, "Marlene Ahrens: Una ganadora en serie," *Caras*, November 27, 2013, http://www.caras.cl /deportes/marlene-ahrens-una-ganadora-en-serie/.

97. "Migajas," *Estadio*, May 14, 1949, p. 30.

98. Pepe Nava, "Cosas de gringos," *Estadio*, August 27, 1949, pp. 20–23. Pepe Nava, which sometimes appeared as Pepe Navas, was the pseudonym of José María Navasal.

99. As of this writing, we have been unable to find evidence of these organizations.

100. Pepe Nava, "Cosas de gringos," *Estadio*, August 27, 1949, pp. 20–23.

101. Pepe Nava, "Cosas de gringos," *Estadio*, August 27, 1949, pp. 20–23.

102. Pepe Nava, "Cosas de gringos," *Estadio*, August 27, 1949, pp. 20–23.

103. Jeldrez, "Marlene Ahrens."

104. Jeldrez, "Marlene Ahrens."

105. Elias, "Las mujeres de oro," 16–20.

106. Zvonimir Ostoic, "Adolescencia y gimnasia," *Revista Chilena de Educación Física* 22, no. 86 (October 1955): 1095–1100.

107. Ostoic, "Adolescencia y gimnasia."

108. Luis Bisquerit, "Charlas en torno a la II Lingiada," *Revista Chilena de Educación Física* 18, no. 70 (October 1951): 187–193.

109. *La Tribuna* (La Cisterna), July 23, 1950, p. 6.

110. *Gol y Gol*, June 19, 1963, p. 20.

111. *Gol y Gol*, March 6, 1963, p 4.

112. "Migajas," *Estadio*, May 24, 1952, p. 32.

113. Don Pampa, "Nació estrella," *Estadio*, June 2, 1951, p. 4.

114. *Gol y Gol*, January 9, 1963, p. 5.

115. *Gol y Gol*, June 12, 1963, p. 21.

116. Leontina Gallardo, "Iquique," *Gol y Gol*, December 11, 1963, p. 21.

117. Juan Aparo, "Vallenar," *Gol y Gol*, October 9, 1963, p. 21.

118. Marta Briceño, "Debe preocuparnos la educación física femenina," *Revista Chilena de Educación Física* (January 1951): 40–42.

119. "Partió el voleibol," *Gol y Gol*, June 5, 1963, p. 22.

120. "[P]uso un hermoso marco en la inauguración del presente torneo." "Partió el voleibol," *Gol y Gol*, June 5, 1963, p. 22.

121. "Rostro pálido," *Estadio*, February 3, 1966, pp. 16–18.

122. "Minicosas," *Estadio*, April 2, 1970, p. 25.

123. "El tesoro atlético," *Estadio*, June 4, 1970, pp. 12–13.

124. "De natación femenina entre los colegios extranjeros," *Estadio*, November 28, 1941.

125. "Brillante festival acuatico," *Estadio*, February 20, 1942.

126. Jaime Drapkin S., *Historia de Colo Colo, club de deportes 1925–1952* (Santiago, Chile: 1952), 8.
127. Colo-Colo FC, *Estatutos y reglementos 1930* (Santiago, Chile: Electra, 1930), 6.
128. Club de Deportes Green Cross, *Estatutos y reglamentos* (Santiago, Chile: Imparcial, 1940).
129. María Graciela Rodríguez, "The Place of Women in Argentinian Football," *International Journal of the History of Sport* 22, no. 2 (March 2005): 231–245.
130. Gabriela Binello et al., "Mujeres y fútbol: ¿Territorio conquistador o a conquistar?," in *Peligro de gol: Estudios sobre deporte y sociedad en América Latina*, ed. Pablo Alabarces (Buenos Aires: CLACSO, 2000), 33–56.
131. "La Gorda Matosas," *El magazine electrónico del recuerdo* 1, no. 5 (February 2005), http://archive.is/20121209180332/jof13.tripod.com/revista/Latinos_Inolvidables_nro_005.doc.
132. "El Torino femenil jugará en Argentina," *El Heraldo de México*, January 17, 1970, p. 4B. Manuel Corbatto is listed as the head of Boca's women's section. Imagine a female fan chanting the beginning of the University of Chile's hymn in 1948: "Ser un romántico viajero y el sendero continuar, ir más allá del horizonte de remonta la verdad, y en desnudos de mujer contemplar la realidad."
133. Mariana Conde and María Graciela Rodríguez, "Mujeres en el fútbol argentino: Sobre prácticas y representaciones," *Alteridades* 12, no 23 (2002): 93–106.
134. Conde and Rodríguez, "Mujeres en el fútbol."
135. Conde and Rodríguez, "Mujeres en el fútbol."
136. Pablo Alabarces and María Graciela Rodríguez, "Football and Fatherland: The Crisis of Representation in Argentinian Football," in *Football Culture: Local Contests, Global Visions*, ed. Gerry Finn and Richard Giulianotti (London: Frank Cass, 2000), 118–133.
137. Unión Española, *Bodas de oro 1897–18 Mayo 1947* (Santiago, Chile: Imparcial, 1947).
138. Unión Española, *Bodas de oro*, 13.
139. Unión Española, *Bodas de oro*.
140. Unión Española, *Memoria* (Santiago, Chile: El Comercio, 1936), 6.
141. Unión Española, *Memoria*.
142. Fernando Larraín Mancheño, *Fútbol en Chile, 1895–1945* (Santiago, Chile: Molina y Lackington, 1945).
143. *La Voz del Cristalero*, May 10, 1944, p. 3.
144. *La Opinión de Conchalí* 1, no.1 (June 1954): 12.

145. *La Voz del Poblador*, September 15, 1954, p. 4.
146. René Mera Pineda, "Lanco," *Gol y Gol*, May 29, 1963, p. 20.
147. *Ritmo*, September 21, 1965, p. 18.
148. Antonino Vera, *El fútbol en Chile* (Santiago, Chile: Editora Nacional Quimantú, 1973).
149. Vera, *El fútbol en Chile*, 5.
150. Vera, *El fútbol en Chile*, 43.
151. *Sport i Actualidades*, June 28, 1912, p. 1.
152. "Mercado Persa," *Estadio*, February 11, 1971, p. 50.
153. "Mercado Persa," *Estadio*, February 11, 1971, p. 50.
154. *Estadio*, November 18, 1971, p. 45.
155. "Fútbol femenino," *Estadio*, March 11, 1965, p. 7.
156. "Triangular de México, Argentina y Chile?," *El Heraldo de México*, May 21, 1971, p. 2B; "Futbol femenil," *El Heraldo de México*, March 16, 1971, p. 4B. A Chilean representative of the Central Association of Women's Football, Julio Cazor Arlegui, contacted the Mexican organizers to express interest. While *El Heraldo de México* reported on Brazilian interest, it made no mention of women's football being illegal in Brazil.
157. "En definitiva," *El Heraldo de México*, June 23, 1971, p. 2B.
158. "Argentina quiere participar en el II Mundial Femenino," *El Mundo Deportivo* (Barcelona), April 12, 1971, p. 15; "Perú quiere ver a la selección de México," *El Heraldo de México*, May 6, 1971, p. 2B; Marina Y., interview by Brenda Elsey, March 22, 2017.
159. "Las argentinas," *El Heraldo de México*, July 3, 1971, p. 3. This article lists Miguel Harrington and Félix Menaldi as the heads of the delegation.
160. "Las argentinas," *El Heraldo de México*, July 3, 1971, p. 3; the names mentioned include Maria Fiorelli and Marta Soler. "Son muy solicitados las mexicanas en radio y TV," *El Heraldo de México*, July 18, 1971, p. 4B; the article mentions Betty Garcia, Angelica Cardoso, and Susana Lopertto.
161. "En Buenos Aires Anunica se jugará el 16," *El Heraldo de Mexico*, July 8, 1971, p. 2B.
162. "Perú quiere ver a la selección de México," *El Heraldo de México*, May 6, 1971, p. 2B; "Quieren que la selección femenil juegue en Caracas," *El Heraldo de México*, July 15, 1971, p. 3B.
163. "Llegaron a Lima," *El Heraldo de México*, July 14, 1971, p. 4B.
164. "México-Perú en fútbol femenil," *El Heraldo de México*, July 21, 1971, p. 2B; "Las mexicanas salieron entre aplausos," *El Heraldo de México*, July 22, 1971, p. 8B. Players listed include Zoila León, Raquel Antaihua, Rosa Hurtado, Rosario Constantini, Nelly Sánchez, Norma Rodríguez,

Ana Proaño, Olga Pinto, Maritza Teresse, Norma Bernal, and Ana Sánchez. The match was sponsored by the Peruvian Sportswriters Association.

165. "México-Argentina, suspendido por lluvia," *El Heraldo de México*, July 17, 1971, p. 2B.

166. "Argentina venció a México 3–2 en futbol femenil," *El Heraldo de México*, July 19, 1971, p. 2B. The players listed are as follows. Mexico: Yolanda Ramírez, Irma Chávez, Berta Orduña, Marta Coronado, Paula Pérez, Guadalupe Tovar, Sandra Tapia, Patricia Hernández, Silvia Zaragoza, and Maria Eugenia Rubio. Argentina: Marta Soler, Zulma Gómez, Ofelia Fleitas, Maria Fiorelli, Zunilda Troncoso, Angelica Cardozo, Virginia Andrade, Eva Lenbesis, Betty García, Elba Selva, and Blanca Bruccoli. The referee was Guillermo Nimo.

167. Hugo Sanmontiel, "Avanzada Argentina," *El Heraldo de México*, August 10, 1971, p. 1B.

168. Manelich Quintero, "Ya están aquí diez argentinas más," *El Heraldo de México*, August 13, 1971, p. 5B.

169. "Mundial (Women) 1971," Rec.Sport.Soccer Statistics Foundation, last updated February 29, 2004, http://www.rsssf.com/tablesm/mundo-women71.html.

170. Facebook page for Las Pioneras del Fútbol Femenino ARG, https://www.facebook.com/laspionerasdelfutbolfemenino/.

CHAPTER 2

1. See Sueann Caulfield, *In Defense of Honor* (Durham, NC: Duke University Press, 2000), 26–33, 80.

2. Caulfield, *In Defense of Honor*, 27.

3. Alfredo G. Faria Júnior, "Futebol, questões de gênero e co-educação: Algumas considerações didáticas sob enfoque multicultural," *Pesquisa de Campo* 2 (1995): 21.

4. Faria, "Futebol, questões de gênero."

5. Lívia Bonafé d'Ávila and Osmar Moreira de Souza Júnior, "Futebol feminino e sexualidade," *Revista das Facultades Integradas Claretianas* 2 (December/January, 2009): 32.

6. *O Paiz* (Rio), October 10, 1922, p. 3.

7. This comes from a review by the authors of the use of the term "violent sport" in *Jornal dos Sports* from the 1930s through the mid-1940s.

8. Mario Filho's *O negro no foot-ball brasileiro* was influential in creating this notion; see Gregg Bocketti, *The Invention of the Beautiful Game: Football and the Making of Modern Brazil* (Gainesville: University Press of Florida, 2016).

9. Carmen Lucía Soares, "Da arte e da ciência de movimentar-se: Primeiros momentos da ginástica no Brasil," in *História do esporte no Brasil*, ed. Mary del Priore and Victor Andrade de Melo (São Paulo: UNESP, 2009), 133–178.

10. Inezil Penna Marinho, *Contribuição para a história da educação física no Brasil* (Rio de Janeiro: Imp. Nacional, 1943).

11. *Jornal dos Sports*, June 21, 1931, p. 1.

12. Jeffrey Dávila, *Diploma of Whiteness: Race and Social Policy in Brazil, 1917–1945* (Durham, NC: Duke University Press, 2003).

13. Lacerda Nogueira, "De como devemos educar as nossas gerações," *O Fluminense*, May 23, 1920, p. 1. Nogueira was a medical doctor who went on to become a senator from Rio de Janeiro.

14. Madeiros e Albuquerque, "Um Brazil mais forte," *A Noite*, November 26, 1929, p. 1.

15. Mônica Raisa Schpun, *Beleza em jogo: Cultura física e comportamento em São Paulo nos anos 20* (São Paulo: SENAC, 1999).

16. Schpun, *Beleza em jogo*, 35.

17. Schpun, *Beleza em jogo*, 38.

18. Schpun, *Beleza em jogo*, 43.

19. Joshua Nadel, *Fútbol! Why Soccer Matters in Latin America* (Gainesville: University Press of Florida, 2014), 83.

20. Dávila, *Diploma of Whiteness*.

21. Dávila, *Diploma of Whiteness*, 49–50.

22. "Futebol feminino," *A Cigarra*, March 1926, p. 36.

23. "Sport Club Mangueiras," *Sport Ilustrado*, September 18, 1920, p. 21.

24. See Eriberto José Lessa de Moura, "As relações entre lazer, futebol e gênero" (MA thesis, Universidade Estadual de Campinhas, December 2003), 9–11, 16–17.

25. James N. Green, *Beyond Carnival: Male Homosexuality in Twentieth-Century Brazil* (Chicago: University of Chicago Press, 2001).

26. "O sport e a mão da mulher," *Sport Ilustrado*, August 7, 1920, p. 14.

27. "O sport e a mão da mulher," *Sport Ilustrado*, August 7, 1920, p. 5.

28. "O sport e a mão da mulher," *Sport Ilustrado*, August 7, 1920.

29. *Sport Ilustrado*, August 14, 1920, p. 6.

30. *Sport Ilustrado*, August 14, 1920, p. 17.

31. "Carnet mundano sportivo," *Sport Ilustrado*, November 6, 1920, p. 14.

32. *Sport Ilustrado*, February 26, 1921, p. 13.

33. *Sport Ilustrado*, September 18, 1920, p. 19.

34. *Sport Ilustrado*, September 18, 1920, p. 19.

35. Barbara Weinstein, *For Social Peace in Brazil: Industrialists and the Remaking of the Working Class in São Paulo, 1920–1964* (Durham, NC: Duke University Press, 1997).

36. Rachel Soihet, "A conquista do espaço público," in *Novas histórias das mulheres do Brasil*, ed. Carla Bassanezi Pinsky and Joana Maria Pedro (São Paulo: Editora Contexto, 2012), 219.

37. Hilary Owen, "Discardable Discourses in Patricia Galvão's *Parque Industrial*," in *Brazilian Feminisms*, ed. Solange Ribeiro de Oliveira and Judith Still (Nottingham, UK: University of Nottingham Monographs in the Humanities, 1999), 68–84, 69.

38. Soihet, "A conquista do espaço público," 222. Prior to 1922, only private schools prepared women for university. Public schools were a path to normal school.

39. Maria Inacia d'Ávila Neto, *O autoritarismo e a mulher: O jogo da admoniação macho-fêmea no Brasil* (Rio de Janeiro: Achiamé, 1980), 15.

40. *Correio da Manhã*, November 23, 1930, p. 16.

41. *Diário da Noite*, November 26, 1930, p. 16.

42. Luiz Guilherme Veiga de Almeida, *Ritual, risco e arte circense* (Brasília: UNB), 2008.

43. *Diário da Tarde*, January 6, 1934, p. 7.

44. "Os maiores espectaculos circenses que Curityba já," *Correio de Paraná*, January 5, 1934, p. 5.

45. "Futebol no Circo Irmãos Garcia," *O Dia*, November 3, 1940, p. 10.

46. *O Dia*, February 15, 1943, p. 5.

47. *Visibilidade por futebol feminino*, exhibition, Museu do Futebol, São Paulo, December 15, 2015.

48. Adriano Wilkson, "1ª maria-chuteira do Brasil fez poesia para conquistar o goleiro da seleção," *Folha*, February 10, 2014, http://esporte.uol.com .br/futebol/ultimas-noticias/2014/10/02/1-maria-chuteira-do-brasil-fez -poesia-para-conquistar-o-goleiro-da-selecao.htm#fotoNav=1.

49. Anna Amélia de Queiróz Carneiro de Mendonça, *Alma* (Rio de Janeiro: Empreza Brasil, 1924).

50. Mendonça, *Alma*, 156–157.

51. Ronald Hilton, ed., *Who's Who in Latin America* (Stanford, CA: Stanford University Press, 1948).

52. See an excellent analysis of these poems and other women writers on football by David Wood, *Football and Literature in South America* (New York: Routledge, 2017).

53. "Amor e futebol," *O Paiz*, January 26, 1920, p. 7.

54. *O Globo Esportivo*, May 7, 1939, p. 11.

55. Bernardo Buarque de Hollanda, "The Competitive Party: The Formation and Crisis of Organized Fan Groups in Brazil, 1950–1980," in *Football and the Boundaries of History*, ed. Brenda Elsey and Stanislao Pugliese (New York: Palgrave, 2016), 295–311.

56. FIFA archive, Correspondence with National Associations, Brazil 1935–1950, folder 1, Federacão Brasileira de Football.

57. Carlos Alberto Cocchi, *Cuatro centros del fútbol mundial* (Montevideo, Uruguay: 1963), 91–94.

58. *Rush: Revista del Deporte Uruguayo* occasionally published articles on women's tennis in the 1930s.

59. Green, *Beyond Carnival*, 26.

60. "O team de Eva," *Revista da Semana*, September 1, 1923.

61. "Futebol não é esporte só para homens," *Correio de S. Paulo*, May 21, 1935, p. 5.

62. Estadio Gran Parque Central was the original home of the Uruguayan club Nacional, with a capacity of 26,500. It was one of the stadiums used in the first men's World Cup.

63. "O association está empolgando as nossas patricias," *Jornal dos Sports*, November 28, 1931, p. 3.

64. "O association está empolgando as nossas patricias," *Jornal dos Sports*, November 28, 1931, p. 3. The referee named was Sylvio Vinhaes de Viterbo, who was the secretary of the Asociação Metropolitana de Esportos Athleticas.

65. "Um sonho dentro da vida," *Sport Ilustrado*, May 11, 1938, p. 7.

66. Carmen Lúcia Soares, *As roupas nas práticas corporais e esportivas: A educação do corpo entre o conforto, a elegância e a eficiência (1920–1940)* (São Paulo: Autores Associados, 2017).

67. "Proclamando una verdade," *Sport Ilustrado*, May 18, 1938, p. 3.

68. *Correio Sportivo*, March 9, 1916, p. 6.

69. "Proclamando una verdade," *Sport Ilustrado*, May 18, 1938, p. 3.

70. "Proclamando una verdade," *Sport Ilustrado*, May 18, 1938, p. 3.

71. "Taça *Sport Ilustrado*," *Sport Ilustrado*, May 18, 1938, p. 7.

72. "Taça *Sport Ilustrado*," *Sport Ilustrado*, May 18, 1938, p. 7.

73. *Sport Ilustrado*, May 18, 1938, p. 8.

74. *Sport Ilustrado*, May 18, 1938, p. 9.

75. "Quarto poderosas equipes femininas em desfile," *Diario de Noticias*, May 1, 1940. "N'um match feminino, houve pancada a valer," *Jornal dos Sports*, May 19, 1931.

76. *Jornal dos Sports*, August 18, 1931. Brasil Suburbano FC was located in the Piedade neighborhood of Rio. The men's team began playing in the second division of the Associação Metropolitana de Esportes Athleticos in 1931, winning the league title in 1934. See "Rio de Janeiro—Segunda Divisão—1932," Rec.Sport.Soccer Statistics Foundation, last updated August 11, 2007, http://www.rsssfbrasil.com/tablesr/rj1932l2.htm.

Ypiranga FC in this case could refer to teams based either in Niterói or Macaé and should not be confused with the Ypiranga FC still in existence today, which is based in Erechim, in Rio Grande do Sul. The Niterói team played in the Asociação Fluminense de Esportes Athleticos (Fluminense Association of Athletic Sports) and in the Asociação Nitheroyense Esportes Athleticos (Niteroi Association of Athletic Sports). The Macaé team joined the Associação Metropolitana de Esportes Athleticos in 1929. While either is a possibility, the likelihood of a women's team making the 181 kilometer trip from Rio to Macaé in 1931 is slim. Thus it is our conclusion that Ypiranga FC was from Niterói.

77. *Jornal dos Sports*, September 4, 1931.
78. *Jornal dos Sports*, February 25, 1940.
79. *Jornal dos Sports*, February 25, 1940. Cruzeiro FC in Rio was founded in 1932 and remains in the Carioca league's third division.
80. *Jornal dos Sports*, March 3, 1945, p. 6.
81. "Nove annos que apontama conciencia de um dever cumprida," *Jornal dos Sports*, March 13, 1940, pp. 1, 4.
82. *Jornal dos Sports*, March 13, 1940, p. 4.
83. *Jornal dos Sports*, March 13, 1940, p. 5.
84. "Football feminino," *A Noite*, March 30, 1940, p. 7.
85. *Jornal dos Sports*, April 27, 1940.
86. "Football feminino no Campo de Bomsuccesso," *Jornal dos Sports*, May 1, 1940.
87. "Football feminino no Campo de Bomsuccesso," *Jornal dos Sports*, May 1, 1940, p. 6.
88. "Football feminino no Campo de Bomsuccesso," *Jornal dos Sports*, May 1, 1940.
89. *Jornal dos Sports*, May 19, 1940, p. 3.
90. *Jornal dos Sports*, August 8, 1940, p. 7.
91. *Jornal dos Sports*, September 7, 1940, p. 6.
92. *Jornal dos Sports*, September 20, 1940, p. 5
93. *Diário de Noticias*, November 12, 1940, p. 1.
94. "Minas têm um clube de futebol feminino," *O Momento* (Caxias do Sul), April 15, 1940, p. 1.
95. *Jornal dos Sports*, May 14, 1940, p. 6.
96. *Jornal dos Sports*, May 16, 1940, pp. 1, 4.
97. *Jornal dos Sports*, May 14, 1940, p. 6.
98. *A Noite* (Rio), April 24, 1940, p. 1.
99. Salathiel Campos, "Ao correr da penna," *Correio Paulistano*, May 5, 1940, p. 16.
100. Salathiel Campos, "Ao correr da penna," *Correio Paulistano*, May 5, 1940, p. 16.

101. "O novo confronto," *Correio Paulistano*, May 17, 1940, p. 8.
102. "Futebol feminino em Magé," *A Batalha*, August 10, 1940, p. 1.
103. "Quatro poderosas equipes femininas em desfile," *Diário de Noticias*, May 1, 1940.
104. *Correio Paulistano*, March 31, 1940, p. 14.
105. *Correio Paulistano*, May 5, 1940, p. 17. The four teams participating were Casino de Realengo, SC Brasileiro, SC Valqueiro, and Eva FC. Brasileiro won with goals from Margarida and Zizinha. It is plausible that Targina's brother was Alfredo Brilhante da Costa, who played for Vasco da Gama and Bangu in the 1930s.
106. *Jornal dos Sports*, September 27, 1940, p. 5.
107. *Jornal dos Sports*, September 27, 1940, p. 5.
108. *Jornal dos Sports*, September 27, 1940, p. 5.
109. *Jornal dos Sports*, October 19, 1940, p. 5.
110. "Ao correr da penna," *Correio Paulistano*, March 31, 1940, p. 17.
111. Excellent analyses of this process include: Roger Kittleson, *The Country of Football: Soccer and the Making of Modern Brazil* (Berkeley: University of California Press, 2014); and José Sergio Leite Lopes, "Da usina de açúcar ao topo do mundo do futebol nacional: Trajetória de um jogador de origem operária," *Cadernas AEL Esportes e Trabalhadores* 16 (2010): 13–40.
112. "Ao correr da penna," *Correio Paulistano*, March 31, 1940, p. 17.
113. *Sport Ilustrado*, May 18, 1938, p. 28.
114. Fernanda Ribeiro Haag, "Mario Filho e *O negro no futebol brasileiro*: Uma análise histórica sobre a produção do livro," *Esporte e Sociedade* 9, no. 23 (2014): 6, http://www.uff.br/esportesociedade/pf/es2306.pdf.
115. "Ganha terreno," *O Dia Sportiva*, April 3, 1940, p. 4.
116. *O Dia* (Curitiba), April 16, 1940, p. 1.
117. *O Dia* (Curitiba), April 16, 1940, p. 1.
118. "Ao correr da penna," *Correio Paulistano*, March 31, 1940, p. 17.
119. Oliver Dinius, *Brazil's Steel City: Developmentalism, Strategic Power, and Industrial Relations in Volta Redonda, 1941–1964* (Stanford, CA: Stanford University Press, 2010).
120. *Diário de Noticias*, September 6, 1940, p. 1.
121. *Jornal dos Sports*, May 31, 1940, p. 4. Manufactura Nacional de Porcelanas FC was founded in 1932 and played in the Federação Atlética Suburbano until the league was replaced by the Departamento Autônomo in 1949.
122. *Jornal dos Sports*, June 16, 1940, p. 4.
123. "A noitada sportiva de Hoie," *Jornal dos Sports*, July 18, 1940, p. 4.
124. "Quatro poderosas equipes femininas em desfile," *Diário de Noticias*, May 1, 1940, p. 1.

125. *Diário de Noticias*, December 1940.
126. Ricardo Pinto, "Futebol feminino," *Diário de Noticias*, January 22, 1941, sec. 2, p. 1.
127. Ricardo Pinto, "Futebol feminino," *Diário de Noticias*, January 22, 1941, sec. 2, p. 1.
128. Moema Toscano and Mirian Goldenberg, *A revolução das mulheres: Um balanço do feminismo no Brasil* (Rio de Janeiro: Editora Revan, 1992), 28–29.
129. Caulfield, *In Defense of Honor*, chapters 2 and 3.
130. Maria Izilda Matos and Andrea Borelli, "Espaço feminino no mercado produtivo," in *Novas histórias das mulheres do Brasil*, ed. Carla Bassanezi Pinsky and Joana Maria Pedro (São Paulo: Editora Contexto, 2012), 129.
131. Matos and Borelli, "Espaço feminino no mercado produtivo," 134, 142.
132. Caulfield, *In Defense of Honor*, 85. Here Caulfield is quoting Roberto Lira, "a young socialist reformer"; see 241n19.
133. Alcir Lenharo, *A sacralização da política* (São Paulo: Papirus, 1989).
134. Alfredo G. Faria Júnior, "Futebol, questões de gênero e co-educação: Algumas considerações didáticas sob enfoque multicultural," *Pesquisa de Campo* 2 (1995): 22–23.
135. Marcelo Moraes e Silva and Mariana Purcote Fontoura, "Educação do corpo feminino: Um estudo na *Revista Brasileira de Educação Física* (1944–1950)," *Revista Brasileira de Educação Física* 25, no. 2 (April/June 2011): 264.
136. Silva and Fontoura, "Educação do corpo feminino," 265.
137. *Revista Brasileira de Educação Física* 2 (1944), p. 41, quoted in Silva and Fontoura, "Educação do corpo feminino," 266.
138. Silva and Fontoura, "Educação do corpo feminino," 266.
139. Silva and Fontoura, "Educação do corpo feminino," 267.
140. Silva and Fontoura, "Educação do corpo feminino," 267.
141. "O futebol é improprio para moças," *O Dia* (Curitiba), June 26, 1940, p. 1.
142. "Basketball," *Sport Ilustrado*, May 18, 1938, p. 12.
143. Kittleson, *Country of Football*.
144. "O futebol é improprio para moças," *O Dia*, June 26, 1940, p. 1.
145. "O futebol é improprio para moças," *O Dia*, June 26, 1940, p. 1.
146. "De tudo um puoco," *Correio Paulistano*, May 9, 1940.
147. "Notas cariocas," *Correio Paulistano*, May 11, 1940, p. 12.
148. In the primary and secondary literature on the ban on women's football, José Fuzeira's letter is cited extensively as crucial to the prohibition. But who was Fuzeira? He is identified as merely a citizen, and apparently has left no other paper trail.

149. "Esplendor e decadencia do futebol feminino," *A Batalha*, January 12, 1941, p. 3.

150. "O futebol feminino vai acabar," *Diário de Noticias*, February 12, 1941, p. 1.

151. "Esplendor e decadencia do futebol feminino," *A Batalha*, January 12, 1941, p. 3.

152. *Idrottsbladet*, May 7, 1941, p. 9.

153. Article 54 of Law 3199 reads: "Às mulheres não se permitirá a prática de desportos incompativeis com as condições de sua natureza, devendo, para este efeito, o Conselho Nacional de Desportos baixar as necessárias instruções às entidades desportivas do país." See http://www.planalto. gov.br/ccivil_03/decreto-lei/1937-1946/Del3199.htm.

154. "Instalado o Conselho Nacional de Desportos," *Jornal dos Sports*, July 8, 1941, pp. 1, 4.

155. "Autorizado O América a contratar mais dois players estrangeiros," *Jornal dos Sports*, August 20, 1941.

156. "A mulher não pode jogar o football nem o box," *Jornal dos Sports*, September 4, 1941, p. 4.

157. "Tomou posse o Sr. Luiz Aranha," *Jornal dos Sports*, September 3, 1941, p. 4.

158. "A mulher não pode jogar o football nem o box," *Jornal dos Sports*, September 4, 1941, p. 1. The subtitle of the article is: "Establecidos pelo Conselho Nacional De Desportos os esportos que as filhas de Eva podem praticar, restringidas as condições de algumas modalidades desportivas permitidas ao sexo fragil."

159. "Esportes que a mulher pode praticar," *Jornal dos Sports*, September 26, 1941, p. 6.

160. "Esportes que a mulher pode praticar," *Jornal dos Sports*, September 26, 1941, p. 6.

161. "Esportes que a mulher pode praticar," *Jornal dos Sports*, September 26, 1941, p. 6.

162. "Esportes que a mulher pode praticar," *Jornal dos Sports*, September 26, 1941, p. 6.

163. "Educação física paralelmente à prática desportiva," *Jornal dos Sports*, September 12, 1941, p. 4.

164. *Jornal dos Sports*, March 14, 1942, p. 6.

165. "Mais um club de football feminino," *Journal dos Sports*, May 9, 1940, p. 6. *Meio-Dia* ran from 1939 to 1942 and had openly fascist sympathies, even though figures associated with Brazil's leftist movements—such as Jorge Amado and Oswald de Andrade—were affiliated with the newspaper until the Nazi invasion of the Soviet Union. See João Arthur

Ciciliato Franzolin, "Joaquím Inojosa e o jornal *Meio-Dia*" (MA thesis, Universidade Estadual Paulista, 2012), 1–14. Franzolin calls the paper a "mouthpiece" for Nazi propaganda.

166. *Jornal dos Sports*, May 10, 1940, p. 6.
167. *Jornal dos Sports*, May 10, 1940, p. 6.
168. *Jornal dos Sports*, May 10, 1940, p. 6.
169. *Jornal dos Sports*, May 10, 1940, p. 6.
170. "Off-Side," *Jornal dos Sports*, May 14, 1940, p. 6.
171. "Esplendor e decadencia do futebol feminino," *A Batalha*, January 12, 1941, p. 3.
172. Manuel do Nascimento Vargas Neto was a poet and journalist from Rio Grande do Sul. He wrote a column for *Jornal dos Sports* entitled "A Crónica de Vargas Neto."
173. "A Crónica de Vargas Neto," *Jornal dos Sports*, April 30, 1948, p. 4.
174. "A Crónica de Vargas Neto," *Jornal dos Sports*, April 30, 1948, p. 4.
175. "A Crónica de Vargas Neto," *Jornal dos Sports*, April 30, 1948, p. 4.
176. Joao Ribeiro, "Comentarios," *O Dia* (Curitiba), February 14, 1942, p. 6.
177. "Espetaculo degradante," *A Tarde* (Curitiba), March 21, 1951, p. 1. It is not clear if the author is Rubeca Padilha Mendes or Rubena Padilha Mendes.
178. *O Dia*, December 14, 1950, p. 7.
179. M. Mattoso, *A Manhã* (Rio), April 14, 1953, p. 1 (esporte amador).
180. Waldemar Areno, "Desportos para a mulher," *Jornal dos Sports*, December 1, 1946, p. 7. The second Pan-American Congress was held in Montevideo, Mexico, in March 1945. See *Journal of Health and Physical Education* 16, no. 2 (1945): 81.
181. Waldemar Areno, "Desportos para a mulher," *Jornal dos Sports*, December 1, 1946, p. 7.
182. Waldemar Areno, "Desportos para a mulher," *Jornal dos Sports*, December 1, 1946, p. 9.
183. Waldemar Areno, "Desportos para a mulher," *Jornal dos Sports*, December 1, 1946, p. 7.
184. "Proibido futebol feminino," *Correio do Paraná*, June 13, 1959.
185. "Mosaico da," *Correio do Paraná* (Curitiba), September 25, 1959, p. 5.

CHAPTER 3

1. See Tarciso Alex Camargo, "A revista *Educação Physica* e a eugenia no Brasil (1932–1945)" (MA thesis, Universidade de Santa Cruz do Sul, 2010), 71–95.

2. Silva and Fontoura, "Educação do corpo feminino," 263–275.
3. Silva and Fontoura, "Educação do corpo feminino," 263–275.
4. Silva and Fontoura, "Educação do corpo feminino," 270.
5. Silva and Fontoura, "Educação do corpo feminino," 263–275.
6. Waldemar Areno, "Considerações médico desportivas sobre atletismo feminino," *Arquivos de Escola Nacional de Educação Física e Desportos* 1, no. 1 (October 1945): 24.
7. Silvana Vilodre Goellner, *Bela, maternal e feminina: Imagens da mulher na revista "Educação Physica"* (Ijuí, Brazil: Unijuí, 2003).
8. Waldemar Areno, *Revista Brasileira de Educação Física* 34 (1947): 32; quoted in Silva and Fontoura, "Educação do corpo feminino," 272.
9. Waldemar Areno, *Revista Brasileira de Educação Física* 34 (1947): 32; quoted in Silva and Fontoura, "Educação do corpo feminino," 272.
10. *O Dia*, November 26, 1950; *O Dia*, December 10, 1950, p. 11.
11. "Futebol feminino," *Diário da Tarde* (Curitiba), December 12, 1950, p. 3.
12. *Diário da Tarde*, December 11, 1950.
13. *O Dia*, March 16, 1951, p. 7.
14. *O Dia*, March 16, 1951, p. 7.
15. "Notícias de *O Dia*," *O Globo*, October 24, 1956, p. 12.
16. "O futebol feminino na Bahia," *O Globo*, October 22, 1956, p. 6. The games were played in the Estádio Otávio Mangabeira, which is also known as the Estádio Fonte Nova. It is the main stadium in Salvador da Bahia.
17. "O futebol feminino na Bahia," *O Globo*, October 22, 1956, p. 6.
18. "Futebol feminino," *O Esatado de São Paulo*, October 1, 1957, p. 22. José da Gama Correia da Silva was a Portuguese businessman who arranged a number of tours of Europe and the Americas by Brazilian teams in the 1950s and 1960s. He was president of Club Madureira from 1959 to 1960 and helped to organize the team's tour of Cuba in 1963.
19. "Futebol feminino em Belo Horizonte," *O Estado de São Paulo*, May 9, 1959, p. 13.
20. "Futebol feminino," *Correio do Paraná*, June 31, 1959.
21. "Futebol feminino em Salvador," *O Globo*, 1959.
22. "Futebol feminino em Salvador," *O Globo*, 1959.
23. "Providencias contra futebol feminine," *O Estado de São Paulo*, June 4, 1959, p. 17.
24. "Poy deverá," *O Estado de São Paulo*, June 13, 1959, p. 14.
25. "Poy deverá," *O Estado de São Paulo*, June 13, 1959, p. 14.
26. "Menores não poderão integrar equipes de futebol feminino," *Diário da Tarde*, April 29, 1959, p. 1.

27. "Proibido futebol feminino," *Correio do Paraná*, June 13, 1959.
28. *Futebol Feminino*, exhibition, Lover Ibaixe collection, Museu do Futebol, São Paulo, November 2015. The actors' home received 15 percent of the proceeds from the match and a guaranteed Cr$50.000,00.
29. "Haverá futebol feminino no Pacaembu," *O Estado de São Paulo*, July 23, 1959, p. 16.
30. "Futebol feminino só depois da sentence," *O Estado de São Paulo*, August 13, 1959, p. 9.
31. *O Estado de São Paulo*, August 13, 1959, p. 14.
32. "O CND decidiu," *O Estado de São Paulo*, August 16, 1959, p. 23.
33. "Futebol de Vedetas," *O Globo*, July 1959.
34. "Evitemos," *O Globo*, 1959, Acervo O Globo, Museu do Futebol.
35. "Evitemos," *O Globo*, 1959, Acervo O Globo, Museu do Futebol.
36. "Evitemos," *O Globo*, 1959, Acervo O Globo, Museu do Futebol.
37. "Evitemos," *O Globo*, 1959, Acervo O Globo, Museu do Futebol.
38. *O Globo*, September 1, 1959.
39. *O Globo*, September 1, 1959.
40. Silveira, a member of the Brazilian Labour Party, was governor of Rio from 1959 until his death in a helicopter accident in 1961.
41. "Dos estados," *O Estado de São Paulo*, September 10, 1959, p. 15.
42. *Folha de São Paulo*, July 20, 1960, p. 5. According to *Folha*, three players met in the house of Maril Marley: Marley, Taluama, and Irene Betal. The other players included Mary Jane, Maria Helena, Cirene Portugal, Belo do Prado, Denise Paiva, Vilma Palmer, and Lurdinha.
43. "Futebol feminino," *Caretas*, August 20, 1960.
44. "Futebol feminino," *Caretas*, August 20, 1960.
45. Lucas Reis, "Primeiro time feminino brasileiro é reativado em Minas," *Folha de São Paulo*, December 6, 2011, http://www1.folha.uol.com.br /esporte/2011/06/928856-primeiro-time-feminino-brasileiro-e-reativado -em-minas.shtml.
46. "Protestos em Araguari," *O Globo*, 1959.
47. "Continua em Minas o futebol feminino," *A Luta Democrática*, May 26, 1959, p. 7.
48. "Mosaico da," *Correio de Paraná* (Curitiba), September 25, 1959, p. 5.
49. José Franco, "'Glamour' usa Chuteira," *O Cruzeiro*, February 28, 1959, pp. 124–129.
50. José Franco, "'Glamour' usa Chuteira," *O Cruzeiro*, February 28, 1959.
51. José Franco, "'Glamour' usa Chuteira," *O Cruzeiro*, February 28, 1959, p. 127.
52. "Protestas em Araguari contra a prática do futebol feminino," 1959, Acervo O Globo, Museu do Futebol.

53. "Protestas em Araguari contra a prática do futebol feminino," 1959, Acervo O Globo, Museu do Futebol.

54. "Apesar da proibição: Continua o futebol feminina en Minas," *A Luta Democrática*, May 8, 1959, p. 7.

55. "Futebol feminino em Campinas," Acervo O Globo, Museu do Futebol.

56. "Futebol feminino em Campinas," Acervo O Globo, Museu do Futebol. The article notes that Didi, a defender from Iguaçu, committed a horrible penalty. It was common that female players adopted the nicknames of male players. While this could be a tribute to their position or type of play, at other times it was based on their appearance.

57. "Futebol Feminino em Salvador," *O Globo*, Acervo O Globo, Museu do Futebol.

58. "Futebol feminino em Campinas," Acervo O Globo, Museu do Futebol.

59. Bernardo Buarque de Hollanda, "The Competitive Party: The Formation and Crisis of Organized Fan Groups in Brazil, 1950–1980," in *Football and the Boundaries of History*, ed. Brenda Elsey and Stanislau Pugliese (New York: Palgrave, 2017): 295–311.

60. "Sensação hoje em Campo Largo," *Correio do Paraná*, April 5, 1960.

61. *Paraná Esportiva*, August 28, 1952, p. 5.

62. The confederation preceded the Confederação Brasileiro de Futebol (Brazilian Football Confederation) as the governing body of football in the country. Why *O Globo* would claim that the confederation and not the CND had jurisdiction at this time is unknown. It might have been a mistake on the part of the newspaper, showing its unfamiliarity with the women's game.

63. "Môças defendem direito de jogar bola," *O Globo*, folder 1959–1961, Acervo O Globo, Museu do Futebol.

64. "Môças defendem direito de jogar bola," *O Globo*, folder 1959–1961, Acervo O Globo, Museu do Futebol.

65. "Futebol de mulhers causa conflito," *O Estado de São Paulo*, October 25, 1960, p. 6.

66. Victoria Langland, *Speaking of Flowers: Student Movements and the Making and Remembering of 1968 in Military Brazil* (Durham, NC: Duke University Press, 2013).

67. "Jôgo feminino," *O Estado de São Paulo*, March 1, 1965, p. 23. The stadium holds around five thousand people and was inaugurated in 1958.

68. "Comissão técnica," *O Estado de São Paulo*, September 1, 1965, p. 12.

69. "Proibido para mulher," *Diário da Tarde* (Curitiba), January 12, 1965, p. 1.

70. "Proibido futebol feminino em Minas," *Diário da Tarde*, May 7, 1966, p. 6. The phrase translated as "vice squad" is "delegacia de jogos diversões."

71. "Govêrno agirá contra futebol feminine," *O Estado de São Paulo*, February 4, 1965, p. 18.

72. "Jôgo feminino," *Estado de São Paulo*, March 1, 1965, p. 23.

73. "FIFA aplica planes," *O Estado de São Paulo*, February 28, 1965, p. 16.

74. Mario Julio, "Cronista de futebol," September 5, 1964, Fondo Semiramis Alves, Museu do Futebol.

75. Benjamin Cowan, *Securing Sex: Morality and Repression in the Making of Cold War Brazil* (Chapel Hill: University of North Carolina Press, 2016).

76. "Cantanduva terá futebol femenino," *O Estado de São Paulo*, June 28, 1969, p. 29.

77. "Cantanduva terá futebol femenino," *O Estado de São Paulo*, June 28, 1969, p. 29.

78. Leda Maria da Costa, "O que é uma torcedora? Notas sobre a representação e auto-representação do público feminino de futebol," *Esporte e Sociedade* 2, no. 4 (November 2006–February 2007).

79. Bernardo Buarque de Hollanda, "The Competitive Party: The Formation and Crisis of Organized Fan Groups in Brazil, 1950–1980," in *Football and the Boundaries of History*, ed. Brenda Elsey and Stanislao Pugliese (New York: Palgrave, 2017).

80. On *torcedores* and women, see Costa, "O que é uma torcedora?" See also Mauricio Murad, "Futebol e violência no Brasil," in *Futebol: Síntese da vida brasileira*, ed. Mauricio Murad et al. (Rio de Janeiro: UERJ, 1996); Bernardo Buarque de Hollanda, "The Competitive Party."

81. "Em Maio," folder 1959–1961, Acervo O Globo, Museu de Futebol. Ashley was the manager of the Manchester Corinthians, which he organized in 1949. The Manchester Corinthians played a four-team tournament in Caracas in 1960.

82. *Diário da Tarde* (Curitiba), May 10, 1962, p. 1.

83. Eliézer Pérez in correspondence with Joshua Nadel, July 10, 2010; and Eliézer Pérez, "Las inglesas al mando en la Copa Banco de Sangre," eliezerperez, March 12, 2016, https://eliezerperez.wordpress.com /2016/03/12/inglesas-y-ticas-le-dieron-vida-a-la-copa-banco-de-sangre -en-la-ucv/.

84. "Dinamarca campea," *O Estado de São Paulo*, July 16, 1970, p. 30.

85. "Começa o mundial feminine," *O Globo*, July 16, 1970, Acervo O Globo, Museu de Futebol. The newspaper report was incorrect: France and Czechoslovakia did not participate in the tournament, while Germany did.

86. "Futebol de qualidade no Mundial Feminino," *Diário da Noite*, July 10, 1970, p. 11.

87. *Diário de Noticias*, 1970, Acervo Biblioteca Nacional, Museu de Futebol.
88. "Elas também são boas de bola," *Correio da Manhã*, July 8, 1970, p. 15.
89. "Elas também são boas de bola," *Correio da Manhã*, July 8, 1970, p. 15.
90. "Quem vence no futebol: As louras ou as morenas?," *Correio da Manhã* (Rio), July 15, 1970, p. 13.
91. "Quem vence no futebol: As louras ou as morenas?," *Correio da Manhã* (Rio), July 15, 1970, p. 13.
92. "Elas também são boas de bola," *Correio da Manhã*, July 8, 1970, p. 15.
93. "Elas, as boas de bola no II Mundial," *Diário da Noite*, January 16, 1971, p. 3.
94. "Elas, as boas de bola no II Mundial," *Diário da Noite*, January 16, 1971, p. 3. In fact, FIFA had just discussed women's football at a meeting of its executive committee in Athens. At the meeting, associations were encouraged to suggest that clubs create women's teams. See minutes of the fifteenth meeting of the Executive Committee, Athens, Greece, January 10, 1971, Executive Committee, FIFA Archives.
95. "As boas de bola," *Correio da Manhã*, June 19, 1971, p. 19.
96. "Ninguém leva a sério o Mundial Feminino de Futebol," *Diário da Noite* (São Paulo), August 12, 1971.
97. "Ninguém leva a sério o Mundial Feminino de Futebol," *Diário da Noite* (São Paulo), August 12, 1971. It should be noted that coverage of the 1970 men's World Cup included vast spreads of players lounging poolside, going on excursions, etc.
98. José Goes, "O jogo do esmalte e do batom," *Diário da Noite*, December 29, 1970.
99. Marin served as deputy for São Paulo State and vice governor of São Paulo. He became president of the Brazilian Football Confederation in 2012, a position he held until his indictment and arrest on corruption charges related to FIFA in 2015.
100. José Goes, "O jogo do esmalte e do batom," *Diário da Noite*, December 29, 1970.
101. José Goes, "O jogo do esmalte e do batom," *Diário da Noite*, December 29, 1970.
102. José Goes, "O jogo do esmalte e do batom," *Diário da Noite*, December 29, 1970. Walter Abrahão, a television commentator, visited and came away impressed. The president of the club appears to have been Walter Maria Laudisio.
103. José Goes, "O jogo do esmalte e do batom," *Diário da Noite*, December 29, 1970.
104. "As feras femininas," *Correio da Manhã*, June 22, 1970, p. 4.
105. "As feras femininas," *Correio da Manhã*, June 22, 1970, p. 4.

106. "As feras femininas," *Correio da Manhã*, June 22, 1970, p. 4.
107. "As feras femininas," *Correio da Manhã*, June 22, 1970, p. 4.
108. "As feras femininas," *Correio da Manhã*, June 22, 1970, p. 4.
109. "As feras femininas," *Correio da Manhã*, June 22, 1970, p. 4.
110. "As feras femininas," *Correio da Manhã*, June 22, 1970, p. 4.
111. "As feras femininas," *Correio da Manhã*, June 22, 1970, p. 4.
112. *Tribunal da Imprensa*, 1970, Acervo Biblioteca Nacional, Museu do Futebol.
113. "Desportes," *Mulherio*, November/December 1981, p. 23.
114. Leonor Amarante, "Gols de placa," September/October 1982, p. 47, in folder "Enviado pela Rose," Acervo Rose do Rio, Museu do Futebol; "Fora de campo," *Mulherio*, November/December 1982, p. 21, Acervo Radar, Museu do Futebol.
115. "Rio goleia SP," *Jornal do Brasil*, October 1982; "Publico vibrou com as meninas no campo," *Gazeta Esportiva*, September 13, 1982, folder "Enviado pela Rose," Acervo Rose do Rio, Museu do Futebol. Abreu was a referee in the 1962 World Cup in Chile. The lawyers who represented Rose do Rio were Zulate Cobra Fernandez and Fernando Marques.
116. Federação Paulista de Futebol, circular no. 115/82, signed Waldemar Bauab, Acervo Radar, Museu do Futebol. There is a good deal of debate surrounding the end of the ban in women's football. Some suggest that the ban ended as early as 1976, and others 1979, when Law 3199 was repealed. However, state federations and the national confederation continued to uphold the ban until 1983. See Katia Rubio, Helena Altmann, Ludmila Mourão, and Silvana Vilodre Goellner, "Women and Sport in Brazil," in *Women and Sport in Latin America*, ed. Rosa López D'Amica, Tansin Benn, and Gertrud Pfister (Abingdon, UK: Routledge, 2016), 69–78; Ludmila Mourão and Marcia Morel, "As narrativas sobre o futebol feminino," *Revista Brasileira de Ciências do Esporte* 26, no. 2 (January 2005).
117. "Futebol feminino," *Notícias Populares*, October 29, 1982, p. 17. Figueiredo Ferraz was the first woman to serve as a minister in the Brazilian government, from 1982 to 1985.
118. "Fora de campo," *Mulherio*, November/December 1982, p. 21, Acervo Radar, Museu do Futebol.
119. "Mulheres no futebol," *Diário da Tarde* (Curitiba), May 13, 1982, p. 7.
120. "Futebol feminine é atração," *Voz de Luziânia*, October 1982, p. 16.
121. Sérgio Noronha, "A mulher tem razão," *Ultima Hora*, October 1983.
122. Sérgio Noronha, "A mulher tem razão," *Ultima Hora*, October 1983.
123. The meeting in which the CND overturned the ban on women's football occurred on March 25, but the decision was published on April 11.

"Vigora o regulamento do futebol feminino," *Diário da Tarde* (Curitiba), April 14, 1983, folder "Manchete com foto," Acervo Biblioteca Nacional, Museu do Futebol.

124. "Mulheres preferem as competições amistosas," *Diário da Tarde* (Curitiba), April 9, 1983, folder "Manchete com foto," Acervo Biblioteca Nacional, Museu do Futebol.

125. "Futebol feminino," *A Gazeta Sportiva*, May 31, 1983, p. 8. The clubs were Clube Atlético Paulistano, Clube de Regatas Brasil, Unicos do Burgo Paulista Feminino, Associação Desportiva da Policia Militar do Estado de São Paulo, Gremio Esportivo São João do Tatuapé, Esporte Clube Corinthians Paulista, Café Futebol Feminino, Unidos Futebol Feminino, AS Cacadors Futebol Feminino, Centro Esportivo [illegible], Clube de Regatas Juvenil, Vasco da Gama, Cafum Futebol Clube, Internacional Futebol Clube, União Esportiva Edu Chaves, Centro Educacional e Esportivo Edson Arantes do Nascimento, Gremio Esportivo Palmeiras, Brasilhas Tricolor FC, Isis EC, Panterinhas EC, A Seme CEE Mané Garrincha, São Paulo FC, SE Pameiras, Lacta [illegible], Virgina FC, Jardim São Bernardo, AS [illegible], EC Nely, FC Estrela da Vila da Paz, Philco Radio e Telivisão, EC [illegible] Maria, Feminino EC Jardim Palmira, Venus Spopemba Clube, Linhas Correntes FC, Estrela da Ilha Futebol Feminino, Sociedade Esportiva Olaria, Clube Atlético Expedicionários, Gremio Esportivo Malory, Legionarios EC, Nacional EC, and others.

126. Clipping, Acervo Radar, Museu do Futebol.

127. Adélia Borges, "De Atenas a Los Angeles," *Mulherio*, May/June 1984, pp. 14–15, 15; Ramon Missias Moreira, "A mulher no futebol brasileiro: Uma ampla visão," *EFDeportes* 13, no. 120 (May 2008), http://www .efdeportes.com/efd120/a-mulher-no-futebol-brasileiro.htm.

128. Maria Elena Araújo, "As Invencíveis," *Placar*, February 1, 1985, pp. 26–28.

129. Roughly $28–32 in 1984 US dollars. See https://www.measuringworth .com/datasets/exchangeglobal/result.php; http://www.historicalstatistics .org/Currencyconverter.html; and http://documents.worldbank.org /curated/en/427451468019765396/text/multi-page.txt.

130. Sérgio Noronha, "A mulher tem razão," *Ultima Hora*, October 1983.

131. Sérgio Noronha, "A mulher tem razão," *Ultima Hora*, October 1983.

132. Sérgio Noronha, "A mulher tem razão," *Ultima Hora*, October 1983.

133. Sérgio Noronha, "A mulher tem razão," *Ultima Hora*, October 1983.

134. "Feminismo é isso," *Uh Revista* (Rio), April 7, 1983, p. 1.

135. "Feminismo é isso," *Uh Revista* (Rio), April 7, 1983, p. 1.

136. "Feminismo é isso," *Uh Revista* (Rio), April 7, 1983, p. 1.

137. "Feminismo é isso," *Uh Revista* (Rio) April 7, 1983, p. 1.

138. Sérgio Noronha, "A mulher tem razão," *Ultima Hora*, October 1983.

139. Sebastião Votre and Ludmila Mourão, "Women's Football in Brazil: Progress and Problems," in *Soccer, Women, Sexual Liberation: Kicking Off a New Era*, ed. Fan Hong and J. A. Mangan (London: Frank Cass, 2004): 254–267. Wellman de Queiroz and Julio Singer were the main forces in BRJ in favor of sponsoring Radar.

140. Votre and Mourão, "Women's Football in Brazil."

141. "Rose do Rio," *Popular da Tarde*, April 3, 1984.

142. See clippings and news from Acervo Rose do Rio, Museu do Futebol.

143. "O dono do Radar," *Placar*, September 1996, p. 52.

144. Eliane Benicio, "Rose do Rio: O futebol feminino no Brasil," *Teresópolis*, July 13, 1996, p. 12.

145. "Rose do Rio," *O Estado do Paraná*, January 4, 1985, p. 16.

146. "Para o experiente Ubiraci," *A Gazeta Sportiva*, May 21, 1986.

147. "Futebol feminino agoniza e pede ajuda para Zico." See Acervo Rose do Rio, Museu do Futebol.

148. Sissi, interview by Brenda Elsey and Joshua Nadel, June 24, 2015.

149. See clippings and news from Acervo Radar and Acervo Rose do Rio, Museu do Futebol.

150. "Futebol feminino na Justiça Comum," *A Gazeta Esportiva*, October 16, 1982.

151. Maria Elena Araújo, "As Invencíveis," *Placar*, February 1, 1985, pp. 26–28.

152. Adélia Borges, "De Atenas a Los Angeles," *Mulherio*, May/June 1984, pp. 14–15.

153. *Mulherio*, April/May/June 1985.

154. Rosali Figueiredo, "Mulher não entra," *Mulherio*, May/June 1987, p. 19.

155. Sérgio Noronha, "A mulher tem razão," *Ultima Hora*, October 1983.

156. Adélia Borges, "De Atenas a Los Angeles," *Mulherio*, May/June 1984, pp. 14–15.

157. Adélia Borges, "De Atenas a Los Angeles," *Mulherio*, May/June 1984, pp. 14–15.

158. Votre and Mourão, "Women's Football in Brazil," 257.

159. Follow-up in *A Gazeta Esportiva*, October 1984. Votre and Mourão, "Women's Football in Brazil," 254–267.

160. Votre and Mourão, "Women's Football in Brazil."

161. Votre and Mourão, "Women's Football in Brazil."

162. The match made the news program *Fantástico*, https://www.youtube.com/watch?v=Ao7A-P4A4FY.

163. "'Margarida' pode sofrer suspensão," *O Liberal* (Belém), January 10, 1989, p. 15. Margarida had something of a history: he had assaulted a player during a Radar match in 1983 as well.

164. "'Margarida' se desculpa," *O Liberal*, January 12, 1989, p. 12.
165. "Milene: Símbolo do futebol feminino," *Jornal do Futebol*, June 1997, p. 3, in Fondo Juliana Cabral, Museu do Futebol.
166. Carmen Pérez-Lanzac, "Meet Mrs. Ronaldo," *Guardian*, February 2, 2003, https://www.theguardian.com/football/2003/feb/02/newsstory .sport4.
167. *Placar*, August 1995.
168. Sissi and Tafferal, interview by Brenda Elsey, October 12, 2017.
169. Hollanda Loyola, "Pode a mulher praticar o futebol," *Revista Educação Physica* 46 (1940): 41; Orlando Rangel Sobrinho, *Educação Physica Feminina* (Rio de Janeiro: Typografica do Patronato, 1930), 7, quoted in Silvana Goellner, "'As mulheres fortes são aquelas que fazem uma raça forte': Esporte, eugenia e nacionalismo no Brasil no início do século XX," *Revista de História do Esporte* 1, no. 1 (June 2008): 15.

CHAPTER 4

1. José Díaz Covarrubias, *La instrucción pública en México* (Mexico City: Imprenta del Gobierno, 1875), cxviii.
2. Díaz Covarrubias, *La instrucción pública*, xxxvi.
3. Díaz Covarrubias, *La instrucción pública*, xxxviii.
4. Díaz Covarrubias, *La instrucción pública*.
5. Monica Lizbeth Chávez Gónzalez, "Construcción de la nación y el género desde el cuerpo. La educación física en el México posrevolucionario," *Desacatos* 30 (May–August 2009): 44. By physical culture here, we mean the various practices that emerged in the late nineteenth and early twentieth centuries that encouraged physical activity in the service of both individual and collective healthfulness. Though Chávez Gónzalez was here discussing the postrevolutionary era, twentieth-century educators embraced the philosophies of Covarrubias and others from the Porfiriato.
6. Quoted in Georgina Ramírez Hernández, "Educar al cuerpo en el Porfiriato: Una mirada a través las revistas pedagógicas," paper given to XI Congreso Nacional de Investigación Educativa, http://www.comie .org.mx/congreso/memoriaelectronica/v11/ponencias.htm.
7. David LaFevor, "Prizefighting and Civilization in the Mexican Public Sphere in the Nineteenth Century," *Radical History Review* 125 (May 2016): 137–158.
8. Though the YMCA was (and remains) headquartered in Geneva, the Mexico branch was under the umbrella of the North American YMCA. See Glenn Avent, "A Popular and Wholesome Resort: Gender, Class, and the Young Men's Christian Association in Porfirian Mexico" (MA

thesis, University of British Columbia, 1996); and William Beezley, *Judas at the Jockey Club and Other Episodes of Porfirian Mexico* (Lincoln: University of Nebraska Press, 1987), 47–59. However, David LaFevor found YMCA centers that held boxing exhibitions by the 1890s. See LaFevor, "Prizefighting."

9. Avent, "Popular and Wholesome," 35.

10. Javier Bañuelos Renteria, *Crónicas del fútbol mexicano: Balón a tierra (1896–1932)* (Mexico City: Editorial Clio, 1998), 64–65.

11. Bañuelos Renteria, *Crónicas del fútbol mexicano*, 64–65.

12. Carlos Calderón Cardoso, *Crónicas del fútbol mexicano: Por amor de la camiseta (1933–1950)* (Mexico City: Editorial Clio, 1998), 46.

13. Keith Brewster, "Redeeming the 'Indian': Sport and Ethnicity in Post-Revolutionary Mexico," *Patterns of Prejudice* 38, no. 3 (2003): 223.

14. Alan Knight, *The Mexican Revolution, Volume 1: Porfirians, Liberals and Peasants* (Omaha: University of Nebraska Press, 1990); Robert McCaa, "The Peopling of Mexico from Origins to Revolution," in *The Population History of North America*, ed. Richard Staeckel and Michael Haines (Cambridge, UK: Cambridge University Press, 2000).

15. Joanne Hershfeld, *Imagining la Chica Moderna: Women, Nation, and Visual Culture in Mexico, 1917–1936* (Durham, NC: Duke University Press, 2008), 27.

16. The Cristero Rebellion (1926–1929) pitted the new revolutionary state against peasants eager to protect traditional relations between church and community. The constitution of 1917 contained a number of anticlerical articles, which went unenforced until Plutarco Elías Calles came to power in 1924. At that point the government began to accelerate efforts to weaken the clergy, which responded by calling for Catholics to boycott government institutions. Tensions between Church affiliated groups and the state continued into 1927, when a rebellion broke out in several western states. By 1929, nearly one hundred thousand people had died.

17. See Alicia Civera Cerecedo, "Respuestas comunitarias a un proyecto educativo: El caso de una misión cultural en México de los años treinta," *Revista Interamericana de Educación de Adultos* 4, no. 2 (July–December 1996); Alicia Civera Cerecedo, *La escuela como opción de vida: La formación de maestros normales rurales en México, 1921–1945* (Mexico City: Secretary of Public Education for Mexico City, 2013); and Mary Kay Vaughan, "Nationalizing the Countryside: Schools and Rural Communities in the 1930s," in *The Eagle and the Virgin: Nation and Cultural Revolution in Mexico, 1920–1940*, ed. Mary Kay Vaughan and Stephen Lewis (Durham, NC: Duke University Press, 2006).

18. "La importancia de educación física," *Educación Física*.

19. "La importancia de educación física," *Educación Física*.

20. Brewster, "Redeeming the 'Indian,'" 214.
21. Vaughan, "Nationalizing the Countryside," 157–158. For more on rural education and its impact on women, see Mary Kay Vaughan, *Cultural Politics in Revolution: Teachers, Peasants, and Schools in Mexico, 1930–1940* (Tucson: University of Arizona Press, 1997); Lucía Martínez Moctezuma, ed., *Formando el cuerpo del ciudadano. Aportes para una historia de la educación física en Latinoamérica* (Cuernavaca: Universidad Autónoma del Estado de Morelos, 2016); and Jocelyn Olcott, *Revolutionary Women in Postrevolutionary Mexico* (Durham, NC: Duke University Press, 2006).
22. Secretaría de Educación Pública, *Las misiones culturales en 1927: Las escuelas normales rurales* (Mexico City: Secretaría de Educación Pública, 1928), 6.
23. Puig Casauranc was minister of education from late 1924 to 1928, and again from 1930 to 1931.
24. J. M. Puig Casauranc, "Los caracteres del verdad maestro rural. Sus virtudes y los peligros que hay que evitar," speech given February 18, 1928, reprinted in Secretaría de Educación Pública, *Las misiones culturales en 1927*, 211–220, 217.
25. Secretaría de Educación Pública, *Las misiones culturales en 1927*, 268, 270, 320–322.
26. Lucía Martínez Moctezuma, "Desencuentros en el desarrollo de la escuela rural mexicana en las primeras decadas del siglo XX: El caso de los institutos de mejoramiento en el estado de Morelos." *Revista Brasileira de História da Educação* 16, no. 2 (2016): 293–295. Martínez Moctezuma notes that in Morelos, of 111 teachers who attended an Instituto de Mejoramiento, only 20 had attended normal school for at least one year. The vast majority of the teachers had only a primary school education.
27. Olcott, *Revolutionary Women*, 93–122.
28. Secretaría de Educación Pública, *Las misiones culturales en 1927*, 34.
29. Secretaría de Educación Pública, *Las misiones culturales en 1927*, 34.
30. Secretaría de Educación Pública, *Las misiones culturales en 1927*, 30–31.
31. Secretaría de Educación Pública, *Las misiones culturales en 1927*, 12–13.
32. Secretaría de Educación Pública, *Las misiones culturales en 1927*, 47–48.
33. Secretaría de Educación Pública, *Las misiones culturales en 1927*, 91.
34. Secretaría de Educación Pública, *Las misiones culturales en 1927*, 78, 75.
35. Secretaría de Educación Pública, *Las misiones culturales en 1927*, 67–71, 78, 151, 203.
36. Secretaría de Educación Pública, *Las misiones culturales en 1927*, 95.
37. Secretaría de Educación Pública, *Las misiones culturales en 1927*, 103, 122.

38. Vaughan, "Nationalizing the Countryside," 160.
39. Vesta Sturges, "Algunas aspectos del trabajo social realizado por las misiones culturales," in Secretaría de Educación Pública, *Las misiones culturales en 1927*, 442.
40. Secretaría de Educación Pública, *Las misiones culturales en 1927*, 327–328. Bonilla also noted, without reference to gender, that the students played volleyball and football "with little skill."
41. Anne Rubenstein, "The War on 'Las Pelonas': Modern Women and Their Enemies, 1924," in *Sex in Revolution: Gender, Power, and Politics in Modern Mexico*, ed. Jocelyn Olcott, Mary Kay Vaughan, and Gabriel Cano (Durham, NC: Duke University Press, 2007), 57–80.
42. Secretaría de Educación Pública, *Las misiones culturales en 1927*, 399. The YWCA first established itself in Mexico in 1921.
43. Secretaría de Educación Pública, *Las misiones culturales en 1927*, 401.
44. Luís Obregón, "La labor del educador físico en las misiones culturales," in Secretaría de Educación Pública, *Las misiones culturales en 1927*, 451.
45. Manuel J. Ciriza, *Manual de educación física para las escuelas federales de Nuevo León* (Monterrey, Mexico: Gobierno del Estado, 1935), 6, 71.
46. Ciriza, *Manual de educación física*, 7.
47. Ciriza, *Manual de educación física*, 8.
48. Ciriza, *Manual de educación física*, 9–10.
49. Ciriza, *Manual de educación física*, 6–9, 65–68.
50. Ciriza, *Manual de educación física*, 71.
51. Ciriza, *Manual de educación física*, 73.
52. Vaughan, "Nationalizing the Countryside," 165.
53. Secretaría de Educación Pública, *Plan de estudios de la escuela de educación física* (Mexico City: Talleres Gráficos de la Nación, 1928), 6.
54. Secretaría de Educación Pública, *Plan de estudios de la educación física* (Mexico City: Talleres Gráficos de la Nación, 1929).
55. The founding of CODEME is the subject of some disagreement. Some scholars put its foundation in 1933 and others in 1932. We fall in the latter camp, largely as a result of the publication of the regulations of the Consejo Nacional de Educación Física, which was the council charged with creating the structure and regulations of CODEME. This body was created in October 1932 and published its bylaws, in the name of CODEME, in November 1932.
56. Brewster, "Redeeming the 'Indian,'" 223.
57. Confederación Deportiva Mexicana, *Consejo Nacional de Educación Física* (Mexico City: Imprenta Mundial, 1932), 4.
58. Confederación Deportiva Mexicana, *Consejo Nacional de Educación Física*, 5–6.

59. Brewster, "Redeeming the 'Indian,'" 224.
60. "Educación física democrata," *Educación Física* 3, no. 22 (October 1938).
61. "Educación física democrata," *Educación Física* 3, no. 22 (October 1938).
62. Hershfeld, *Imagining la Chica Moderna*, 71. On the development of lighter fabrics for sporting women, see also Jaime Schulz, *Qualifying Times: Points of Change in U.S. Women's Sports* (Champaign: University of Illinois Press, 2014).
63. Hershfeld, *Imagining la Chica Moderna*.
64. Ageeth Sluis, "Building Bodies: Creating Urban Landscapes of Athletic Aesthetics in Postrevolutionary Mexico City," in *Sports Culture in Latin America*, ed. David Sheinin (Pittsburgh, PA: University of Pittsburgh Press, 2015), 124.
65. *Educación Física* 3, no. 23 (November 1938).
66. *Educación Física* 4, no. 25 (January 1939).
67. César Juarros, "La fatiga, como evitarla," *Educación Física* 4, no. 25 (January 1939).
68. *Educación Física* 4, no. 29 (May 1939).
69. *Educación Física* 4, no. 32 (August 1939).
70. Sluis, "Building Bodies," 125.
71. Fernando Bonilla Alvarado, in correspondence with Joshua Nadel, July 12, 2018; and Julieta Muñoz Coto, in Elías Zeledón Cartín, *Deportivo Femenino de Costa Rica, FC: Primer equipo de fútbol femenino en el mundo* (San José, Costa Rica: Ministerio de Cultura, Juventud y Deportes, 1999), 188. Coto is the niece of Nelly Coto, who was an original member of Deportivo Femenino de Costa Rica.
72. Roxana Hidalgo Xirinachs, *Historias de las mujeres en el espacio público en Costa Rica, ante el cambio del siglo XIX al XX* (San José, Costa Rica: FLACSO, 2004), 23.
73. Steven Palmer and Gladys Rojas Chaves, "Educating Señorita: Teacher Training, Social Mobility, and the Birth of Costa Rican Feminism, 1885–1925," *Hispanic American Historical Review* 78, no. 1 (February 1988): 56.
74. Hidalgo Xirinachs, *Historias de las mujeres*, 47.
75. Ronald Díaz Bolaños, "'Quiero que la gimnástica tome bastante incremento': Los orígenes de la gimnasía como actividad física en Costa Rica (1855–1949)," *Diálogos* 12, no. 1 (February–August 2011): 6–7.
76. Díaz Bolaños, "Los orígenes de la gimnasía," 10. The Instituto Nacional changed its name to the Instituto Universitario in 1883.

77. Palmer and Rojas Chaves, "Educating Señorita," 49–50; Hidalgo Xirinachs, *Historias de las mujeres*, 47.

78. Hidalgo Xirinachs, *Historia de las mujeres*, 47–49; and Teresita Cordero Cordero, "Mujeres y la Universidad de Costa Rica (1941 a 1950)," paper given at VIII Congresso Iberoamericano de Ciência, Tecnologia e Gênero, 3, http://files.dirppg.ct.utfpr.edu.br/ppgte/eventos/cictg /conteudo_cd/E2_Mujeres_y_Universidad_de_Costa_Rica.pdf.

79. Sara Sharratt, "The Suffragist Movement in Costa Rica, 1889–1949: Centennial of Democracy?," in *The Costa Rican Women's Movement: A Reader*, ed. Ilse Abshagen (Pittsburgh, PA: University of Pittsburgh Press), 73–76. See also Eugenia Rodríguez S., "Visibilizando las facetas ocultas del movimiento de mujeres, el feminismo y las luchas por la ciudadanía femenina en Costa Rica (1890–1953)," *Diálogos 5*, nos. 1–2 (2005): 36–61, https://revistas.ucr.ac.cr/index.php/dialogos/article /view/6230/5933; and Eugenia Rodríguez S., "Cronología: Participación socio-política femenina en Costa Rica (1890–1952)," *Diálogos 5*, nos. 1–2 (2005): 695–722, https://revistas.ucr.ac.cr/index.php/dialogos/article /view/6254/5956.

80. Virginia Mora Carvajal, "Moda, belleza y publicidad en Costa Rica (1920–1930)," *Boletín AFEHC* 45 (June 2010), http://afehc-historia -centroamericana.org/index.php?action=fi_aff&id=2445.

81. Iván Molina Jiménez, "Educación y sociedad en Costa Rica: De 1821 al presente (una historia no autorizada)," *Diálogos* 8, no. 2 (August 2007–February 2008): 246.

82. Hidalgo Xirinachs, *Historias de las mujeres*, 19.

83. Díaz Bolaños, "Los orígenes de la gimnasía," 19.

84. "Educación física de las mujeres," *El Manantial* 1, no. 3 (July 1915): 1. Gustavo Louis Michaud is credited with introducing basketball to Costa Rica in 1905. According to Adrián Antonio Echeverría Ramírez, Michaud was part of a group of foreign physical education teachers who came to Costa Rica as a result of the educational reform of 1888. He was also instrumental in creating the first track for athletics events in the country. See Echeverría Ramírez, "Análisis legal de las federaciones deportivas de representación nacional e internacional" (thesis, University of Costa Rica, 2012), 26–27.

85. "Educación física de las mujeres," *El Manantial* 1, no. 3 (July 1915): 2.

86. Chester Urbina Gaitán, "Orígenes de la política deportiva en Costa Rica (1887–1942)," *EFDeportes* 7, no. 34 (April 2001), http://www. efdeportes.com/efd34/crica.htm.

87. Urbina Gaitán, "Orígenes de la política"; and "Historia del fútbol cubana," http://www.elblogdelfutbolcubano.com/p/historia-del-futbol -cubano-1_11.html, webpage no longer active.

88. Cordero Cordero, "Mujeres y la Universidad de Costa Rica," 3.

89. See Hidalgo Xirinachs, *Historias de las mujeres*; and Sharratt, "Suffragist Movement."

90. See interviews with players in Zeledón Cartín, *Deportivo Femenino*, 182–209.

91. Fernando Bonilla Alvarado, correspondence, July 12, 2018.

92. Gaetano Pandolfo, "Las pioneras del fútbol fueron ticas," *Semanario Universidad*, http://163.178.170.36/index.php/mainmenu-deportes/671 -las-pioneras-del-futbol-fueron-ticas.html; and Alejandro Fonseca Hidalgo, "Que se den su lugar," *Diario Extra*, July 9, 2010, http.www.diarioextra .com/2010/Julio/09/deportes09.php.

93. Irma Castillo Sánchez, in Zeledón Cartín, *Deportivo Femenino*, 195.

94. Fernando Bonilla Alvarado, correspondence, July 12, 2018.

95. Chester Urbina Gaitán, "El fútbol femenino en Costa Rica (1924–2015)," *EFDeportes* 21, no. 221 (October 2016), http://www.efdeportes .com/efd221/el-futbol-femenino-en-costa-rica.htm.

96. "El foot-ball en el element femenino," *La Prensa*, September 22, 1926, p. 2.

97. Fernando Bonilla Alvarado, correspondence, July 12, 2018. Alice Quirós married Fernando Bonilla.

98. Zulay Loiza Martínez and Carmen Morales Sequiera, in Zeledón Cartín, *Deportivo Femenino*, 204, 185.

99. Fernando Bonilla Alvarado, correspondence, July 12, 2018.

100. Fernando Bonilla Alvarado, correspondence, July 12, 2018.

101. "El domingo veremos futbol femenino en el Estadio Nacional," *La Prensa Libre*, March 24, 1950, p. 8. See also "22 jugadoras de fútbol se enfrentará mañana en el estadio," *La Prensa Libre*, March 25, 1950, p. 8.

102. "Las futbolistas la dieron ayer una gran lección a los futbolistas," *La Prensa Libre*, March 27, 1950, p. 9.

103. "Las futbolistas la dieron ayer una gran lección a los futbolistas," *La Prensa Libre*, March 27, 1950, p. 9.

104. *La Nación*, March 28, 1950, in Zeledón Cartín, *Deportivo Femenino*, 22–25.

105 "Brillante result el encuentro de fútbol femenino el domingo," *Diario de Costa Rica*, March 28, 1950, p. 7.

106. *La Prensa Libre*, April 4, 1950, p. 8.

107. *La Nación*, June 3, 1950, p. 14.

108. "Deportes del dia," *La Prensa Libre*, March 28, 1950, p. 8.

109. "Deportes del dia," *La Prensa Libre*, March 28, 1950, p. 8.

110. "Deportes del dia," *La Prensa Libre*, March 28, 1950, p. 8.

111. "La mujer costarricense juega al fútbol," *El Mundo Deportivo*, January 4, 1954, p. 3.

112. Miguel Ángel Ulloa Z., "Si de mi dependiera no permitiría que se llevara a cabo un partido más de fútbol femenino," *La Prensa Libre*, April 12, 1950, p. 6.

113. Miguel Ángel Ulloa Z., "Si de mi dependiera," *La Prensa Libre*, April 12, 1950, p. 6.

114. Miguel Ángel Ulloa Z., "Si de mi dependiera," *La Prensa Libre*, April 12, 1950, p. 6.

115. Chutador, "Con el mayor respeta, a una futbolista," *La Prensa Libre*, April 14, 1950, p. 8. "Keeds" (Keds) was a common word for sneakers.

116. Julio Mera Carrasco, "La mujer en el atletismo," *AS*, June 21, 1952, p. 15.

117. Chutador, "El fútbol femenino y sus consecuencias personales," *La Prensa Libre*, March 29, 1950, p. 5.

118. Luis Cartín Paniagua, *La Prensa Libre*, April 19, 1950, p. 10.

119. *El Mundo Femenino*, April 24, 1950, in Zeledón Cartín, *Deportivo Femenino*, 34.

120. Fernando Bonilla Alvarado, in correspondence with the author, July 12, 2018.

121. "Las futbolistas gustaron en Panama," *La Prensa Libre*, May 2, 1950, p. 9. According to Fernando Bonilla, chaperones were parents of players and traveled with the team on all tours. Fernando Bonilla Alvarado, correspondence, July 12, 2018.

122. "Maginifica fue la segunda presentación que ayer hicieron las señoritas futbolistas," *La Prensa Libre*, June 9, 1950, p. 11.

123. In Zeledón Cartín, *Deportivo Femenino*, 80.

124. "Invitación a los médicos para que asistan hoy a la conferencia del Dr. Carballo," *La Nacion*, April 4, 1951, p. 14.

125. Universidad de Costa Rica, Consejo Universitario, Acta de la Sesión no. 51, October 9, 1950.

126. "El Femenino Libertad eligió directiva," *Diario de Costa Rica*, June 30, 1950, p. 7.

127. "Duelo en las filas del Deportivo Lourdes," *Diario de Costa Rica*, August 22, 1950, p. 7.

128. *La Nación*, April 19, 1951. The article in *La Nación* reprints, in its entirety, an article from the Honduran paper *Diario Comercial*; Zeledón Cartín, *Deportivo Femenino*, 87.

129. "Embajada de belleza deportiva llegó procedente de Costa Rica," *El Imparcial*, May 12, 1951; and "Sensacional match de fut femenino internacional: Guatemala–Costa Rica," *El Imparcial*, May 12, 1951; in Zeledón Cartín, *Deportivo Femenino*, 88–91.

130. Chester Urbina Gaitán, "Génesis del fútbol en Guatemala (1902–1921)," *EFDeportes* 14, no. 135 (August 2009), http://www.efdeportes.com /efd135/genesis-del-futbol-en-guatemala-1902-1921.htm.

131. "La prensa niacarguense y nuestras futbolistas," *Diario de Costa Rica*, June 21, 1951, p. 11.

132. In Zeledón Cartín, *Deportivo Femenino*, 98.

133. In Zeledón Cartín, *Deportivo Femenino*, 99–100.

134. In Zeledón Cartín, *Deportivo Femenino*, 100–103. It is unclear why the trip to Ecuador failed to materialize.

135. *Relator*, September 13, 1951; *La Patria*, September 21, 1951; and *El Colombiano*, September 24, 1951; in Zeledón Cartín, *Deportivo Femenino*, 105–106, 109–112.

136. *Radar Deportivo*, October 6, 1951; and *El Espectador*, September 29, 1951; in Zeledón Cartín, *Deportivo Femenino*, 112–114.

137. Zeledón Cartín, *Deportivo Femenino*, 115–126.

138. "Fútbol Femenino," *La Nación*, February 14, 1952, p. 20.

139. "Renuncia irrevocable del Sr. Blanco Mendez directivo del fútbol femenino," *La Nación*, October 3, 1958.

140. Eliézer Pérez, correspondence, July 17, 2010; and Eliézer Pérez, "Femenino," eliezerperez, https://eliezerperez.wordpress.com/category/femenino/.

141. Eliézer Pérez, correspondence, July 17, 2010; and Eliézer Pérez, "Femenino," `https://eliezerperez.wordpress.com/category/femenino/.

142. Fernando Bonilla Alvarado, correspondence, July 12, 2018.

143. *La Nación*, 1971.

144. Chester Urbina Gaitán, "Origenes del deporte moderno en El Salvador," *Realidad y Reflexión* 17, no. 6 (May–August 2006): 20.

145. Adan Benjamin Cuellar Martínez, Jairo Gerardo Flores Díaz, and José Saúl Romero Barrera, "Análisis histórico de la educación física en relacion a sus tendencias pedagogicas, en la República de El Salvador desde el año 1920 al año 2010" (thesis, Universidad de El Salvador, 2011), 40.

146. Aldo Lauria-Santiago and Leigh Binford, "Local History, Politics, and the State in El Salvador," in *Landscapes of Struggle: Politics, Society, and Community in El Salvador*, ed. Aldo Lauria-Santiago and Leigh Binford (Pittsburgh, PA: University of Pittsburgh Press, 2004), 2.

147. Victor Hugo Acuña Ortega, "The Formation of the Urban Middle Sectors in El Salvador, 1910–1944," in *Landscapes of Struggle: Politics, Society, and Community in El Salvador*, ed. Aldo Lauria-Santiago and Leigh Binford (Pittsburgh, PA: University of Pittsburgh Press, 2004), 39–49.

148. Mercier would go on to be the first director of France's National Institute of Sport, from 1945 to 1948.

149. Elie Mercier, "La mujer y los deportes," *Revista Salvadoreña de Educación Física* 1, nos. 2–3 (February–March 1922): 32.

150. Mercier, "La mujer y los deportes," 32.

151. Mercier, "La mujer y los deportes," 32.

152. Mercier, "La mujer y los deportes," 35.
153. Mercier, "La mujer y los deportes," 35.
154. Mercier, "La mujer y los deportes," 35.
155. Mercier, "La mujer y los deportes," 35.
156. Mercier, "La mujer y los deportes," 36.
157. Cuellar Martínez, Flores Díaz, and Romero Barrera, "Análisis histórico," 42.
158. There is some debate as to when Push arrived in El Salvador. Some works suggest 1919, while others cite 1922. See Beatriz Eugenia Avalos Sánchez, Elba Georgina Berroterán De Rivera, Concepción Del Carmen Cruz De González, "La educación física y su incidencia en el desarrollo integral de niños y niñas párvulos del sector público del Distrito 06-01 de la ciudad de San Salvador" (thesis, Universidad Francisco Gavida, 2003), 9; Atilio Antonio Arévalo Campos, Luis Remberto Hernández Grande, and Josué Ernesto Recinos, "La practica de juegos tradicionales que beneficien el desarrollo de las capacidades motrices basicas en la clase de educación física en los alumnos de segundo ciclo del centro escolar de Huizúcar, Distrito 0523, Zona 3 del departamento de la libertad, durante el año lectivo 2010" (thesis, Universidad de El Salvador, 2011), 16; Adan Benjamin Cuellar Martínez, Jairo Gerardo Flores Díaz, and José Saúl Romero Barrera, "Análisis histórico de la educación física en relacion a sus tendencias pedagogicas, en la República de El Salvador desde el año 1920 al año 2010" (thesis, Universidad de El Salvador, 2011), 42.
159. Urbina Gaitán, "Origenes del deporte moderno en El Salvador," Realidad y Reflexión 17, no. 6 (May–August 2006): 40.
160. Urbina Gaitán, "Origenes del deporte," 38.
161. Urbina Gaitán, "Origenes del deporte," 42.
162. Urbina Gaitán, "Origenes del deporte," 45.
163. Chester Urbina Gaitán, "Fútbol, estado e identidad nacional en El Salvador (1897–1943)," Realidad y Reflexión 17, no. 6 (May–August 2006): 60. Urbina Gaitán here cites Diario de El Salvador, August 29, 1923, p. 3.
164. Cuellar Martínez, Flores Díaz, and Romero Barrera, "Análisis histórico," 43–45.

CHAPTER 5

1. Personal collection of Joshua Nadel.
2. To date, the most exhaustive prior work on the topic is a bachelor's thesis. See Maritza Carreño Martínez, "Fútbol femenil en México, 1969–1971" (thesis, Universidad Nacional Autónoma de México, 2006).

3. "Urban Population (% of Total)," World Bank, https://data.worldbank.org/indicator/SP.URB.TOTL.IN.ZS?locations=MX.

4. *Mujeres y hombres en México* (Mexico City: Instituto Nacional de Estadística, Geografía e Informática, 2007), 322; "Mexico: Social and Economic Aspects of the Status of Women (1970–2003)," Refworld, Immigration and Refugee Board of Canada, November 13, 2003, http://www.refworld.org/docid/403dd20214.html.

5. *Mujeres y hombres en México*, xxvii.

6. *Mujeres y hombres en México*, 87.

7. Mary Kay Vaughan, "Introduction," in *Sex in Revolution: Gender, Power, and Politics in Modern Mexico*, ed. Jocelyn Olcott, Mary Kay Vaughan, and Gabriela Cano (Durham, NC: Duke University Press, 2006), 25.

8. Secretaría de Educación Pública, *Plan de estudios de la educación física* (Mexico City: Talleres Gráficos de la Nación, 1929), 5.

9. Brenda Elsey, "Cultural Ambassadorship and the Pan-American Games of the 1950s," *International Journal of the History of Sport* 33, nos. 1–2 (2016): 105–126. Women's events were included in the Central American and Caribbean Games beginning in 1938.

10. Eric Zolov, "Showcasing the 'Land of Tomorrow': Mexico and the 1968 Olympics," *Americas* 61, no. 2 (October 2004): 163. See also Keith Brewster and Claire Brewster, "Cleaning the Cage: Mexico City's Preparations for the Olympic Games," *International Journal for the History of Sport* 26, no. 6 (May 2009): 790–813; and Kevin B. Witherspoon, *Before the Eyes of the World: Mexico and the 1968 Olympic Games* (DeKalb: Northern Illinois University Press, 2008).

11. Gilbert Joseph, Anne Rubenstein, and Eric Zolov, eds., *Fragments of a Golden Age: The Politics of Culture in Mexico since 1940* (Durham, NC: Duke University Press, 2001), particularly Mary Kay Vaughan, "Transnational Processes and the Rise and Fall of the Mexican Cultural State: Notes from the Past," 471–472.

12. "Clases gratuitas," *La Afición*, February 17, 1951, p. 3.

13. Anne Rubenstein, *Bad Language, Naked Ladies, and Other Threats to the Nation: A Political History of Comic Books in Mexico* (Durham, NC: Duke University Press, 1998).

14. Marie Sarita Gaytán and Ana G. Valenzuela Zapata, "Mas alla del mito: Mujeres, tequila y nación," *Mexican Studies* 28, no. 1 (Winter 2012): 183–208.

15. Elaine Carey, *Plaza of Sacrifices: Gender, Power, and Terror in 1968 Mexico* (Albuquerque: University of New Mexico Press, 2005).

16. See, for example, *El Heraldo de México*, October 10, 1970, pp. 1A, 13A; and Agustín Barrios Gómez, "Comentarios de hoy," *El Heraldo de México*, October 1, 1970, p. 3D.

17. For PRI efforts to co-opt the student movement, see Jaime Pensado, *Rebel Mexico: Student Unrest and Authoritarian Political Culture during the Long Sixties* (Stanford, CA: Stanford University Press, 2013).

18. Eli Bartra, Anna M. Fernández Poncela, and Ana Lau, *Feminismo en México: Ayer y hoy* (Mexico City: Universidad Autónoma Metropolitana, 2000).

19. Estela Serret, "El feminismo mexicano de cara al siglo XXI," *Cotidiano* 16 (March–April 2000), http://www.redalyc.org/articulo.oa.

20. María Patricia Fernández-Kelly, *For We Are Sold, I and My People: Women and Industry in Mexico's Frontier* (Albany, NY: SUNY Press, 1984). For an important analysis on the recent historiography, see also Fernández-Kelly, "Reading the Signs: The Economics of Gender Twenty-Five Years Later," *Signs* 25, no. 4 (2000): 1107–1112.

21. Alexander Dawson, "Salvador Roquet, María Sabina, and the Trouble with *Jipis*," *Hispanic American Historical Review* 95, no. 1 (2005): 103–133.

22. "Es casi seguro," *La Afición*, March 15, 1951, p. 12.

23. "Es casi seguro," *La Afición*, March 15, 1951, p. 12.

24. Guillermo Salas, "México cuenta con lo necesario para celebrar una Olimpíada," *La Afición*, March 27, 1955, p. 6.

25. Alfonso Roldan P., "Estopier jefe de la delegación," *La Afición*, March 25, 1955, p. 11.

26. "Llegó el polaco Poburka, entrenador de la selección de volibol femenil," *El Heraldo de México*, January 5, 1966, p. 20.

27. Luis Jordá Galeana, reproduced in "Fútbol femenil," *Fútbol de México y del Mundo* 9, no. 424 (December 13, 1970), 23.

28. "México se batió en grande ante Brasil," *El Heraldo de México*, August 4, 1967, p. 2.

29. "La preselección femenil empezará su gira el 22," *El Heraldo de México*, November 19, 1969, p. 8B.

30. Pancho Dorado, "Las 'Adelas' esperan con ganas a la preselección," *El Heraldo de México*, November 22, 1969, p. 4B.

31. "Voli en Los Angeles," *El Heraldo de México*, January 15, 1966.

32. "Voli en Los Angeles," *El Heraldo de México*, January 15, 1966.

33. "Segunda victoria de los cuadros mexicanos," *El Heraldo de México*, March 3, 1970, p. 4B.

34. "Vamos por el primero," *El Heraldo de México*, March 12, 1970, p. 4B.

35. Jaime Castillo, "Gracia y femeninidad," *El Heraldo de México*, July 26, 1970, sports supplement, p. 7.
36. Jaime Castillo, "Extraña a Armida Guerrero," *El Heraldo de México*, September 13, 1970, p. 2B.
37. *El Heraldo de México*, February 28, 1966, p. 1.
38. Hugo Ceron-Anaya, "Golf, habitus y elites: La historia del golf en México (1900–1980)," *Esporte e Sociedade* 5, no. 15 (July–October 2010), http://www.uff.br/esportesociedade/index.html?ed=15.
39. "Al mundial de golf femenil," *El Heraldo de México*, January 31, 1970, p. 2B.
40. "Dos medallas de oro," *El Heraldo de México*, August 1, 1967, p. 1.
41. *La Afición*, February 27, 1951, p. 2.
42. "Una Argentina," *La Afición*, February 28, 1951, p. 2.
43. *La Afición*, March 1, 1951, p. 1.
44. Antonio Pineda, "Joaquín Capilla," *La Afición*, March 16, 1951, p. 4.
45. *La Afición*, March 9, 1951, p. 2.
46. "Se integró ya una liga," *El Heraldo de México*, July 10, 1970, p. 2B.
47. "¿Tomará auge el fut femenil?," *Esto*, June 2, 1959, p. 8B.
48. "¿Tomará auge el fut femenil?," *Esto*, June 2, 1959, p. 8B.
49. Carreño Martínez, "Fútbol femenil en México," 9.
50. *El Sol de México*, June 29, 1970, p. A12.
51. "Empieza hoy el torneo de futbol femenil," *El Heraldo de México*, November 16, 1969, p. 2B.
52. "Choque de los 2 Américas," *El Heraldo de México*, November 29, 1969, p. 5B.
53. "Fue una fiesta," *El Heraldo de México*, October 7, 1970, p. 1B.
54. Se inauguró ayer la liga femenil de fut," *El Heraldo de México*, November 17, 1969, p. 2B.
55. "El América 'A' goleó 4–0," *El Heraldo de México*, November 30, 1969, p. 5B.
56. "Golearon," *El Heraldo de México*, January 12, 1970, p. 2B.
57. Manelich Quintero, "Equipos cremas hacen el 1–2," *El Heraldo de México*, December 22, 1969, p. 5B.
58. "También en femenil," *El Heraldo de México*, December 28, 1969, p. 1B.
59. "Multitud," *El Heraldo de México*, March 23, 1970, p. 6B.
60. "¡Va a ser mamá . . . y quiere que la contraten en futbol!," *El Heraldo de México*, November 6, 1969, p. 8B. See also "Calcio femminile: Straniere in arrivo," *L'Unità*, November 6, 1969, p. 11.
61. "¡María Edith quiere jugar con Torino!," *El Heraldo de México*, November 16, 1969, p. 2B.

62. "¡María Edith quiere jugar con Torino!," *El Heraldo de México*, November 16, 1969, p. 2B.

63. "¡María Edith quiere jugar con Torino!," *El Heraldo de México*, November 16, 1969, p. 2B.

64. *El Sol de México*, June 28, 1970, p. A6.

65. Elvira Aracén Sánchez, interview by the author, December 17, 2015; and Confederación Deportiva Mexicano, *Historia* (Mexico City: CODEME, n.d.), 87. Manelich Quintero, in "Futbol femenil," *El Heraldo de México*, January 24, 1970. Aracén played for the team Guadalajara in the Liga América. She grew up in a small village in Veracruz and moved to Mexico City when she began high school.

66. Elvira Aracén Sánchez, interview, December 17, 2015.

67. Manelich Quintero, "América, líder en fut femenil," *El Heraldo de México*, December 8, 1969, p. 4B.

68. "Fútbol femenil," *El Heraldo de México*, January 5, 1970, p. 2B; and Elvira Aracén, interview, December 17, 2015.

69. Manelich Quintero, "En medio de una Tolvanera," *El Heraldo de México*, December 29, 1969, p. 2B. The Spanish is "muy coquetas con sus uniformes nuevas."

70. "ENEF venció 2–0 a la CFE," *El Heraldo de México*, January 12, 1970, p. 2B.

71. Manelich Quintero, "Hoy la octava jornada femenil," *El Heraldo de México*, January 11, 1970, p. 6B.

72. "Femenil: Reglamentado," *El Heraldo de México*, February 25, 1970, p. 3B.

73. "Carolina Mendoza," *El Heraldo de México*, January 14, 1970, p. 5B.

74. *El Heraldo de México*, January 4, 1970, p. 5B. Also retold in interviews with Elvira Aracén, December 17, 2015, and Mercedes Rodríguez Alemán, December 11, 2015. Rodríguez told of a slightly later date, and both Fabiola Vargas and Andrea Rodebaugh told of playing on dirt fields in the 1990s.

75. Elvira Aracén, interview, December 17, 2015.

76. *El Heraldo de México*, January 5, 1970, p. 2B.

77. "Con 'Chabelo,'" *El Heraldo de México*, February 6, 1970, p. 1B. Chabelo (Xavier López Rodríguez) was the *padrino* for the Chivas women's team.

78. "Así fue la fiesta," *El Heraldo de México*, February 10, 1970, p. 2B.

79. "Así fue la fiesta," *El Heraldo de México*, February 10, 1970, p. 2B.

80. Manelich Quintero, "Un teléfono par alas que deseen jugar en un equipo," *El Heraldo de México*, January 17, 1970, p. 4B.

81. Manelich Quintero, "Un teléfono par alas," *El Heraldo de México*, January 17, 1970, p. 4B.
82. Manelich Quintero, "Un teléfono par alas," *El Heraldo de México*, January 17, 1970, p. 4B.
83. "Futbol femenil," *El Heraldo de México*, January 26, 1970, p. 2B.
84. "Los poblanas," *El Heraldo de México*, February 2, 1970, p. 4B.
85. Manelich Quintero, "Futbol femenil," *El Heraldo de México*, January 30, 1970, p. 2B.
86. *El Heraldo de México*, March 25, 1970, p. 4B.
87. Manelich Quintero, "Futbol femenil," *El Heraldo de México*, January 30, 1970, p. 2B.
88. *El Heraldo de México*, November 18, 1969, p. 2B.
89. *El Sol de México*, June 29, 1970, p. A1.
90. *El Sol de México*, June 29, 1970, p. A1.
91. *El Sol de México*, June 29, 1970, p. A12.
92. "FIFA aplica planes," *O Estado de São Paulo*, February 28, 1965, p. 16.
93. In 1970, Cañedo was the vice president of Club América, the president of the Mexican Football Federation, and the vice president of FIFA. Ahead of the 1970 World Cup he was also made head of football broadcasting for Telesistema Mexicana, which would become Televisa in 1972. In 1971, Cañedo was no longer officially president of the Mexican federation, but retained his other posts. See Keith Brewster and Claire Brewster, "'He Hath Not Done This for Any Other Nation': Mexico's 1970 and 1986 World Cups," in *The FIFA World Cup, 1930–2010: Politics, Commerce, Spectacle, and Identities*, ed. Stefan Rinke and Kay Schiller (Gottingen, Germany: Wallstein Verlag, 2014), 199–219.
94. *El Sol de México*, June 24, 1970, p. C1.
95. "El futbol femenil," *El Heraldo de México*, November 22, 1969, p. 3B.
96. The Argentine sports magazine *El Gráfico* included stories on women's football in England and France in the 1920s. For more on the sport in England, see Jean Williams, *A Game for Rough Girls? A History of Women's Football in Britain* (London: Routledge, 2003).
97. Manelich Quintero, personal correspondence, November 4, 2012. For the controversy, see *El Sol de México*, June 30, 1970, p. B3. In what might have been a journalistic spat over access, *El Sol de México* took the masseuse Alma Estela Ramírez's side. In the end, Elvira Aracén, the backup goalie and a student at the National School for Physical Education, took on the role of *preparadora física*.
98. *El Sol de México*, June 28, 1970, pp. A1, A6; and Elvira Aracén, interview, December 17, 2015. Aracén suggested that she was the one who came up with the idea for the preselection process and then helped

with selection. In the end, Morales would not make the trip with the team; he was replaced by Efraín Pérez. Though he coached a team in the Liga América, Morales, according to Aracén, was not trained as a coach.

99. Manelich Quintero, "Futbol femenil," *El Heraldo de México*, March 25, 1970, p. 4B.

100. *El Sol de México*, June 28, 1970, p. A6; and Elvira Aracén, interview, December 17, 2015.

101. Manelich Quintero, "Futbol femenil," *El Heraldo de México*, April 15, 1970, p. 5B.

102. Manelich Quintero, "Futbol femenil," *El Heraldo de México*, April 15, 1970, p. 5B.

103. *El Sol de México*, June 28, 1970, p. A6.

104. *El Sol de México*, June 28, 1970, p. A6.

105. Elvira Aracén, interview, December 17, 2015. It is also possible to interpret *morenitas* as pejorative, slang for "little dark ones." However, given the context of the article, this use seems unlikely.

106. *El Sol de México*, June 29, 1970, p. A1.

107. Maria Guadalupe de Santa Cruz M., "El equipo femenino de fútbol," *El Sol de México*, June 30, 1970, p. A1.

108. *El Sol de México*, June 29, 1970, p. A12.

109. Manelich Quintero, personal correspondence, December 23, 2014; "Maletas," *El Heraldo de México*, June 28, 1970, p. 3B.

110. Manelich Quintero, "Ya tiene equipo," *El Heraldo de México*, July 2, 1970, p. 2B.

111. Manelich Quintero, "Ya tiene equipo," *El Heraldo de México*, July 2, 1970, p. 2B.

112. *El Sol de México*, June 29, 1970, p. A12.

113. *El Sol de México*, June 29, 1970, p. A12.

114. *El Sol de México*, June 28, 1970, p. A6.

115. Carreño Martínez, "Fútbol femenil en México," 42, 38, 36.

116. Elvira Aracén, interview, December 17, 2015.

117. *El Sol de México*, June 28, 1970, p. A6.

118. *El Sol de México*, June 28, 1970, p. A6.

119. "México en Italia," *El Heraldo de México*, July 25, 1970, p. 2B.

120. "Homenaje al once," *El Heraldo de México*, July 22, 1970, p. 3B.

121. "Homenaje al once," *El Heraldo de México*, July 22, 1970, p. 3B.

122. "En el 1er. Tiempo recibió Austria cinco anotaciones," *El Sol de México*, July 8, 1970, p. B1. Manelich Quintero and Elvira Aracén both give different scores of the game. Aracén notes that the score was 15–0 but that six goals were disallowed.

123. "En el 1er. Tiempo recibió Austria cinco anotaciones," *El Sol de México*, July 8, 1970, p. B1.

124. "Exito total ha sido el Mundial de fut femenil," *El Sol de México*, July 10, 1970, p. B1.
125. "Italia derrotó 2–1 a México en futbol femenil," *El Sol de México*, July 12, 1970, p. B6.
126. Manelich Quintero, "México cayó ante Italia, 2–1," *El Heraldo de México*, July 12, 1970, p.1B
127. *El Sol de México*, July 12, 1970, pp. B1, B6.
128. *El Sol de México*, July 12, 1970, p. B6.
129. "En buen juego vencieron a Albión 3–2," *El Sol de México*, July 14, 1970, p. B1.
130. "En buen juego vencieron a Albión 3–2," *El Sol de México*, July 14, 1970, p. B1.
131. *El Sol de México*, July 14, 1970, p. B6.
132. Manelich Quintero, "México ganaba 3–10," *El Heraldo de México*, July 14, 1970, p. 5B.
133. "Exito total ha sido el Mundial de fut femenil," *El Sol de México*, July 10, 1970, p. B1; "Italia derrotó 2–1 a México en futbol femenil," *El Sol de México*, July 12, 1970, p. B6.
134. "Exito total ha sido el Mundial de fut femenil," *El Sol de México*, July 10, 1970, pp. B1, B6.
135. *El Sol de México*, July 10, 1970, p. B1.
136. Manelich Quintero, "Desde Turín," *El Heraldo de México*, July 14, 1970, p. 5B.
137. "Exhibición," *El Heraldo de México*, July 18, 1970, p. 3B.
138. "Que no debe haber damas futbolistas," *El Sol de Mexico*, July 18, 1970, p. B5.
139. Carreño Martínez, "Fútbol femenil en México," 68.
140. "Profesor Meléndez uno de los organizadores de la selección femenil 1971," Liga Premier del Fútbol Femenil Mexicano, YouTube video, September 6, 2016, https://www.youtube.com/watch?v=-1vr9gzUZZ8.
141. *El Sol de México*, June 28, 1970, p. A6.
142. "Futbol femenil," *El Heraldo de México*, July 4, 1970, p. 2B.
143. *El Sol de México*, June 28, 1970, p. A6.
144. *El Sol de México*, June 28, 1970, p. A6.
145. Manelich Quintero, "Ultimo encuentro," *El Heraldo de México*, June 26, 1970, p. 5B; *El Sol de México*, June 28, 1970, p. A6.
146. "Preparativos para el sábado próximo," *El Heraldo de México*, July 15, 1970, p. 4B.
147. Elvira Aracén, interview, December 17, 2015.
148. "Un heraldo," *El Heraldo de México*, July 16, 1970, p. 5B.
149. Manelich Quintero, "Darán una cancha," *El Heraldo de México*, August 8, 1970, p. 2B.

150. Manelich Quintero, "Inaugura cancha el fut femenil," *El Heraldo de México*, August 23, 1970, p. 4B.

151. "En prinicipio acepta la FMF a elementos del sexo femenino," *El Sol de México*, July 16, 1970, p. B1.

152. *El Sol de México*, July 16, 1970, p. B1.

153. *El Sol de México*, July 18, 1970, p. B1.

154. *El Sol de México*, July 18, 1970, p. B1.

155. "Que no debe haber damas futbolistas," *El Sol de México*, July 18, 1970, p. B5.

156. Elvira Aracén, interview, December 17, 2015.

157. "Que no debe haber damas futbolistas," *El Sol de México*, July 18, 1970, p. B5.

158. Raul Sanchez Hidalgo, "Ogros . . . del futbol," *El Heraldo de México*, July 26, 1970, p. 1B.

159. Club Deportivo Oro was in the first division of Mexican football at the time.

160. Guillermo Aceves, "También les suspendieron," *El Heraldo de México*, July 26, 1970, p. 1B.

161. Flavio Zavala Millet, "La federación trato de impedir un homenaje a la selección femenil," *Ovaciones*, July 24, 1970, p. 2.

162. Guillermo Aceves, "Sí jugaron en el Estadio Jalisco," *El Heraldo de México*, July 27, 1970, p. 5B. Like the Estadio Azteca, at the time Estadio Jalisco was administered by the local government, which limited FMF jurisdiction over its usage.

163. "¡Invitan a México a la selección femenil italiana!," *El Heraldo de México*, August 22, 1970, p. 3B.

164. Manelich Quintero, personal correspondence, November 4, 2012.

165. *El Heraldo de México*, October 18, 1970, p. 1B.

166. "Magnífica demostración," *El Heraldo de México*, October 19, 1970, p. 1B.

167. Hugo Cisterna, "El fut femenil como platillo," *El Heraldo de México*, October 19, 1970, p. 2B.

168. *El Heraldo de México*, November 5, 1970, Ocho TV supplement, p. 8.

169. "Italia contra el América," *El Heraldo de México*, October 23, 1970, p. 4B. It is unclear what, precisely, the disciplinary reasons were. Officially, Vargas had issues with members of the team Guadalajara. Some suggested that she was left off the team for complaining that coaches earned money off the games, while the players did not even get paid the travel costs to attend practice. See *Ovaciones*, October 17, 1970, p. 8.

170. "Italia goleó 4–0," *El Heraldo de México*, October 28, 1970, p. 4B.

171. "Que el II Mundial Femenil sea aquí," *El Heraldo de México*, October 29, 1970, p. 3B.

172. Manelich Quintero, personal correspondence, November 4, 2012.
173. *El Heraldo de México*, July 25, 1970.
174. "Canal Ocho," *El Heraldo de México*, November 5, 1970, Ocho TV supplement, p. 8; Carreño Martínez, "Fútbol femenil en México," 80.
175. Elvira Aracén, interview, December 17, 2015.
176. See, for example, *El Nacional*, August 14, 1970, sec. 2, p. 3; August 21, 1970, sec. 2, p. 3; August 28, 1970, sec. 2, p. 2.
177. Manelich Quintero, "Futbol femenil," *El Heraldo de México*, January 24, 1970, p. 4B.
178. "Selección de futbol femenil," *El Heraldo de México*, August 7, 1970, p. 3B.
179. Elvira Aracén, interview, December 17, 2015. Rubio's brother Sergio went on to play for Cruz Azul and Chivas in the Mexican professional leagues and was known as "El Peque." See also *El Heraldo de México*, January 5, 1970, p. 2B.
180. Elvira Aracén, interview, December 17, 2015.
181. Elvira Aracén, interview, December 17, 2015.
182. Elvira Aracén, interview, December 17, 2015.
183. Manelich Quintero, "Ahora se reportan," *El Heraldo de México*, August 13, 1970, p. 2B.
184. "Una mujer," *El Heraldo de México*, August 27, 1970, p. 4B.
185. Agustin Barrios Gomez, "Comentarios de hoy," *El Heraldo de México*, October 1, 1970, p. 3D.
186. "Se llama Grecia del Angel," *El Heraldo de México*, December 13, 1970, p. 3B; *El Heraldo de México*, August 29, 1970, p. 3B. Ángel worked in the Liga Naucalpan de Fútbol Femenil.
187. Teodoro Cano, "Llegará a arbitrar en primera división," *El Heraldo de México*, April 9, 1971, p. 7B.
188. "La mujer que es deportista jamás pierde su femineidad, manifestó Rosalinda Tripp," *El Nacional*, August 7, 1970, sec. 2, p. 2.
189. "La entrevista," *Fútbol de Mexico y del Mundo*, December 13, 1970, p. 18. Zaragoza's full name was Maria Silvia Zaragoza Herrera.
190. "Mini-entrevista," *Fútbol de Mexico y del Mundo*, December 20, 1970, p. 18.
191. Jose Luis Jimenez, "Las bellas del deporte," *El Heraldo de México*, January 10, 1971, p. 1B.
192. Jose Luis Jimenez, "Las bellas del deporte," *El Heraldo de México*, January 16, 1971, p. 6B.
193. *El Heraldo de México*, January 16, 1971, p. 6B.
194. *El Heraldo de México*, January 16, 1971, p. 6B.
195. Jose Luis Jimenez, "Las bellas del deporte," *El Heraldo de México*, January 19, 1971, p. 6B.

196. *El Heraldo de México*, January 19, 1971, p. 6B.

197. *El Heraldo de México*, January 19, 1971, p. 6B.

198. Jose Luis Jimenez, "Las bellas del deporte," *El Heraldo de México*, January 19, 1971, p. 6B.

199. Jose Luis Jimenez, "Las bellas del deporte," *El Heraldo de México*, February 16, 1971, p. 6B.

200. *El Heraldo de México*, January 10, 1971, p. 3B.

201. *El Heraldo de México*, December 20, 1970, p. 4B; December 22, 1970, p. 3B; December 12, 1970, p. 5B; October 13, 1970, p. 4B; and Manelich Quintero, "Ahora se reportan de Monterrey y Puebla," *El Heraldo de México*, August 13, 1970, p. 2B.

202. FIFA, minutes of meeting no. 15 of the Executive Committee, January 10, 1971, p. 9.

203. Sánchez Hidalgo, "La FIFA . . . y las novias," *El Heraldo de México*, February 25, 1971, p. 5B.

204. FIFA, minutes of meeting no. 15 of the Executive Committee, January 10, 1971, p. 9.

205. José José, "Se formó la federación de futbol femenil," *El Heraldo de México*, February 28, 1971, p. 2. It is unclear why CODEME went against the FMF on hosting the tournament. It is possible that the two organizations worked together to bring the championship to Mexico, seeing the potential economic benefit. Cañedo could not officially go against FIFA rulings, but CODEME was under no restrictions. As a television executive, Cañedo stood to benefit personally.

206. The tournament was held from August 15 to September 5.

207. "En Augusto, el Mundial Femenil," *El Heraldo de México*, February 28, 1971, p. 5B.

208. *El Heraldo de México*, February 28, 1971, p. 5B.

209. "Futbol femenil," *El Heraldo de México*, March 16, 1971, p. 4B.

210. *El Heraldo de México*, April 24, 1971, p. 4B.

211. "4 'bellos' prospectos para la preselección," *El Heraldo de México*, March 23, 1971, p. 4B.

212. Juan Acevedo, "'Vamos, niña, juega como tu sabes,' dice el Profe Meléndez," *El Heraldo de México*, June 1, 1971, p. 2B.

213. *El Heraldo de México*, June 1, 1971, p. 2B.

214. *El Heraldo de México*, July 27, 1970, p. 1B.

215. "En Buenos Aires anuncia se jugará el 16," *El Heraldo de México*, July 8, 1971, p. 2B.

216. "México-Argentina, suspendido por lluvia," *El Heraldo de México*, July 17, 1971, p. 2B.

217. "México-Perú en futbol femenil," *El Heraldo de México*, July 21, 1971, p. 2B.

218. *El Heraldo de México*, July 23, 1971, p. 3B.

219. *El Heraldo de México*, August 7, 1971, p. 1B.

220. Personal collection of Joshua Nadel. Brief footage of the women's world championship, from the opening ceremonies and the championship game, can be found online. In his personal collection, Joshua Nadel has some of this footage along with Mexico's game with Argentina and the Mexican team's trip to Buenos Aires. Televisa reportedly retains footage of the entire final, but the authors were unable to verify this.

221. *El Heraldo de México*, July 26, 1971, p. 4B.

222. "A la venta boletos del Mundial Femenil," *El Heraldo de México*, July 28, 1971, p. 3B.

223. *El Heraldo de México*, August 24, 1971, p. 3B. See also *Ovaciones*, August 8, 1971, p. 12.

224. *El Heraldo de México*, August 5, 1971, p. 10B.

225. Sanchez Hidalgo, "Quien creía," *El Heraldo de México*, August 15, 1971, p. 1B.

226. For more on this relationship between media and sports, see Eduardo Archetti, *Masculinities: Football, Polo and the Tango in Argentina* (Oxford, UK: Berg, 1999), especially chapter 2; Jeffrey William Richey, "Playing at Nation: Soccer Institutions, Racial Ideology, and National Integration in Argentina, 1912–1931" (PhD diss., University of North Carolina at Chapel Hill, 2013); Matthew Karusch, "National Identity in the Sports Pages: Football and Mass Media in 1920s Buenos Aires," *Americas* 60, no. 1 (2003): 11–32; Brenda Elsey, "The Independent Republic of Football: The Politics of Neighborhood Clubs in Santiago, Chile, 1948–1960," *Journal of Social History* 42, no. 3 (Spring 2009): 605–630; and Joshua Nadel, *Fútbol! Why Soccer Matters in Latin America* (Gainesville: University Press of Florida, 2014), 82–84. For non–Latin American perspectives, see Alan Tomlinson, Christopher Young, and Richard Holt, eds., *Sport and the Transformation of Modern Europe: States, Media, and Markets, 1950–2010* (Abingdon, UK: Routledge, 2011); Brian Carrol, *The Black Press and Black Baseball, 1915–1955: A Devil's Bargain* (New York: Routledge, 2015); Michael Oriard, *King Football: Sport and Spectacle in the Golden Age of Radio and Newsreels, Movies and Magazines, the Weekly and the Daily Press* (Chapel Hill: University of North Carolina Press, 2001).

227. *El Heraldo de México*, July 27, 1971, p. 1B; July 28, 1970, p. 3B.

228. *Excelsior*, August 5, 1971, p. 3D.

229. *Excelsior*, August 6, 1971, p. 6D.

230. "Prácticas intensivas de Italas e Ingleses," *El Sol de México*, August 7, 1971, p. B12.

231. See *El Sol de México*, August 10, 1971, p. B7; August 11, 1971, p. B9; August 12, 1971, p. B9; August 13, 1971, p. B10; August 14, 1971, p. B9.

232. *El Heraldo de México*, August 28, 1971, p. 2B; September 6, 1971, p. 5B; September 5, 1971, p. 3B.

233. Correspondents for *Excelsior* were José Garduño, José Barrenechea, Rose Maria Roffiel, and Jorge Escobosa.

234. "Ahora ya hay ¡Idolos femeniles de fútbol!," *El Heraldo de México*, August 16, 1971, p. 3B. Other newspapers placed the attendance at just under eighty thousand. See, for example, José Barrenechea Jr., "México derrotó a Argentina 3–1 al iniciarse el Mundial Femenil," *Excelsior*, August 16, 1971, p. 1D.

235. *El Sol de México*, August 18, 1971, p. B1.

236. *Excelsior* and *El Heraldo de México* had slightly different numbers for the Denmark-Argentina match. *Excelsior* estimated the crowd at thirty thousand while *El Heraldo de México* went to press with the number of fans at twenty-five thousand. Teodoro Cano, "México goleó . . . ¡Pero tiene que mejorar!," *El Heraldo de México*, August 23, 1971, p. 2B; Teodoro Cano, "5–0 . . . ¡Dinamarca es gran campeón!," *El Heraldo de México*, August 29, 1971, p. 2B; José Barrenechea Jr., "Dinamarca clasificó ayer para la final: Goleó a Argentina 5–0," *Excelsior*, August 29, 1971, p. 29A; and Teodoro Cano, "¡Las italianas perdieron la cabeza y el partido!," *El Heraldo de México*, August 30, 1971, p. 2B.

237. *El Heraldo de México*, August 22, 1971, pp. 1B, 6B; "La violencia amenaza al fútbol femenil," *El Heraldo de México*, August 23, 1971, pp. 3B, 4B; and *El Heraldo de México*, August 29, 1971, p. 1B.

238. Nuria Basurto, "Quieren armaduras para jugar contra las bambinas," *El Heraldo de México*, September 1, 1971, p. 3B.

239. Manuel Seyde, "Temas del día," *Excelsior*, September 6, 1971, p. 1D.

240. Manuel Seyde, "Temas del día," *Excelsior*, September 7, 1971, p. 1D.

241. "Era el fin y no se iban," *El Heraldo de México*, August 16, 1971, p. 1B.

242. Fausta Gantús and Martha Santillán Esqueda, "Fútbol femenil en México: Una percepción de género a través de la prensa al inicio de los años setenta," *Esporte e Sociedad* 5, no. 15 (July–October 2010), http://www.uff.br/esportesociedade/index.html?ed=15.

243. *El Heraldo de México*, August 15, 1971, p. 1B.

244. "Las niñas patean ahora el balón," *El Heraldo de México*, September 1, 1971, p. 1B.

245. Unfortunately, all FMF records from this era were destroyed in a fire.

246. Elvira Aracén, interview, December 17, 2015.

247. See, for example, "En caso contrario, México no jugará contra Dinamarca," *Excelsior*, September 2, 1971, p. 1D; "O les dan dinero o no se presentan a jugar," *El Sol de México*, September 2, 1971, p. B1; "¡Dos millones de pesos o no juegan!," *El Heraldo de México*, September 3, 1971, p. 1B; Eduardo Morales, "El fútbol femenil no puede ser amateur," *El Heraldo de México*, September 3, 1971, p. 3B.

248. Eduardo Morales, "El fútbol femenil no puede ser amateur," *El Heraldo de México*, September 3, 1971, p. 3B.

249. Carlos Trapaga, "¡Vale mas un aplauso que dos millones de pesos!," *Esto*, September 4, 1971, p. 5. See also José Barrenechea Jr. and Jorge Escobosa, "Accedió la selección a jugar mañana en la final," *Excelsior*, September 4, 1971, p. 1D; Enrique Valencia, "El domingo; México contra Dinamarca," *El Sol de México*, September 4, 1971, p. B2; and Eduardo Morales, "¡Valen mas los aplausos que millones!," *El Heraldo de México*, September 4, 1971, pp. 3B, 5B.

250. Jorge Escobosa and José Barrenechea Jr., "El comité ofreció un juego de beneficio a las mexicanas, ayer," *Excelsior*, September 4, 1971, p. 1D; Eduardo Morales, "Ganen o pierdan, ¡Inundarán de regalos a las mexicanas!," *El Heraldo de México*, September 5, 1971, p. 1B. Among those offering gifts were the governor of the state of Mexico, Carlos Hank González; the president of the municipality of Toluca, Alfonzo Gómez de Orozco; and a group of actors and actresses. On TV rights and the benefit game, see José José, "¡Recibieron 245 mil pesos las futbolistas mexicanas!," *El Heraldo de México*, September 13, 1971, p. 3B; *Excelsior*, September 9, 1971, p. 1D; José José, "Hasta placas para taxi obsequió Hank González, a las mexicanas," *El Heraldo de México*, September 14, 1971, p. 2B.

251. Rosa Maria Roffiel, "Las danesas reprueban la actitud de las mexicanas," *Excelsior*, September 3, 1971, p. 1D.

252. Carmen Anderson, "El diario acontecer," *El Heraldo de México*, September 4, 1971, p. 5C.

253. "Despues de una cena en su honor, se disintegra hoy la seleccíon femenil," *El Heraldo de México*, September 21, 1971, p. 6B.

254. There is some debate as to how much money the benefit game raised. Quintero says 415,000 pesos, while other sources cite 245,000. Manelich Quintero, "Contra sus 'explotadores,' las futbolistas pedirán ayuda al jefe del DDF," *El Heraldo de México*, September 26, 1971, p. 2B. See also José José, "¡Recibieron 245 mil pesos las futbolistas mexicanas!," *El Heraldo de México*, September 13, 1971, p. 3B; Arturo A. del Castillo, "El profesor Meléndez Trinqueteó a las futbolistas con treinta mil pesos," *Ovaciones*, September 25, 1971, p. 4; and "Las seleccionadas dicen que les 'birlaron' 55 mil pesos," *Esto*, September 25, 1971, p. 7.

255. Manelich Quintero, personal correspondence, December 26, 2014.
256. Manelich Quintero, personal correspondence, December 26, 2014.
257. Manelich Quintero, personal correspondence with Joshua Nadel, July 2, 2010.
258. *El Heraldo de México*, November 1, 1971, p. 5B; *Excelsior*, October 24, 1971, p. 3D; and *El Sol de México*, November 2, 1971, p. B1. All of these newspapers had complete coverage of the tournament.
259. Mercedes Rodríguez Alemán, interview, December 11, 2015.
260. Mercedes Rodríguez Alemán, interview, December 11, 2015.
261. Elvira Aracén, interview, December 17, 2015.
262. Mercedes Rodríguez Alemán, interview, December 11, 2015.
263. Elvira Aracén, interview, December 17, 2015.
264. Elvira Aracén, interview, December 17, 2015.

EPILOGUE

1. Sisleide do Amor Lima, personal interview with Brenda Elsey and Joshua Nadel, April 2016. The team that represented Brazil at the 1988 Women's Invitational was actually the women's team Radar, of which Sissi was a member.
2. Elisa Araya Cortez and Karin Lofstrom, "Women and Sport in Chile," in *Women and Sport in Latin America*, ed. Rosa López de D'Amico, Tansin Benn, and Gertrud Pfister (London: Routledge, 2016), 79–92.
3. In 2016 the South American nations with inactive women's teams were Argentina, Bolivia, Chile, Ecuador, Paraguay, Peru, and Uruguay. The Central American and Caribbean teams were Panama and Honduras. By 2017, Chile and Peru had "active" women's teams, according to FIFA, while Guatemala, Cuba, the Dominican Republic, and Puerto Rico had joined the ranks of the inactive squads. See http://www.fifa.com/fifa-world-ranking/ranking-table/women/.
4. Vanessa Vargas Roja, "Sexismo y cosificación: Cómo trata la prensa deportiva las mujeres en la cobertura de la Copa Confederaciones," *El Desconcierto*, www.eldesconcierto.cl/2017/06/22/sexismo-y-cosificacion-como-trata-la-prensa-deportiva-a-las-mujeres-en-la-cobertura-de-la-copa-confederaciones/; Fernanda Pinilla, interview, August 2017.
5. Ruby Campos Ramírez, interview, December 12, 2015; Fabiola Vargas Curiel, interview, December 14, 2015; Sisleide do Amor Lima, interview, April 2016; Andrea Rodebaugh, correspondence, March 11, 2010.
6. FIFA circular no. 1246.
7. FIFA circular no. 1512, November 25, 2015.
8. FIFA circular no. 1541, May 31, 2016.

9. FIFA circular no. 1545, June 8, 2016. This circular includes the FIFA Forward regulations.

10. FIFA circular no. 1545, June 8, 2016. At the time this book went to press, no annual audits had been released. The first round of audits were due by June 30, 2018.

11. Iona Rothfeld, personal interview with the authors, August 2016.

12. Fernanda Pinilla, personal correspondence, March 2018; Iona Rothfeld, personal correspondence, March 2018.

13. "Escandalo en el femenino de Nacional," *Referi*, January 21, 2017, http://www.referi.uy/escandalo-el-femenino-nacional-n1022566.

14. Ruby Campos Ramírez, interview, December 12, 2015. This story was confirmed by other observers of women's football in Mexico. *Fresa*—literally "strawberry"—is slang for elite, although in this context it carries the additional connotation of American born or raised.

15. Raúl Vilchis, "For Teammates in Love, an Island Oasis," *New York Times*, July 6, 2017, https://www.nytimes.com/2017/07/06/sports/soccer/iceland-soccer-stars-in-love-find-acceptance.html?mcubz=1&_r=0.

16. Silvana Goellner, interview, March 2018.

17. Olivia Díaz Ugalde, "La crisis de la selección femenina de fútbol: De la ilusión de volver a entrenar a un paro por falta de pago," *La Nación*, September 21, 2017, https://www.lanacion.com.ar/2065217-seleccion-femenina-de-futbol-de-la-ilusion-de-volver-a-entrenar-al-paro-acordado-por-falta-de-pago.

18. "Uruguay le ganó 2:0 a Argentina," Tenfield.com, September 27, 2017, http://www.tenfield.com.uy/uruguay-le-gano-20-a-argentina/.

19. Gaby Gartón, personal interview with Brenda Elsey and Joshua Nadel, July 2016.

20. Gaby Gartón, interview, July 2016.

21. Deborah Puebla, "Carlos Borrello, el regreso que trae esperanza al fútbol femenino," *MDZ*, July 20, 2017, http://www.mdzol.com/nota/745011-carlos-borrello-el-regreso-que-trae-esperanza-al-futbol-femenino/.

22. "DT Vanessa Aráuz será nueva instructora en la CONMEBOL," *El Telégrafo*, September 18, 2017, http://www.eltelegrafo.com.ec/noticias/futbol-nacional/23/dt-vanessa-arauz-sera-nueva-instructora-en-la-conmebol.

23. "27,000 aficionados observaron el inicio del torneo nacional de fútbol femenino," Federación Ecuatoriana de Fútbol, December 6, 2017, http://ecuafutbol.org/web/noticia.php?idn=41990&idc=.

24. "Servisky adquirió los derechos de televisón del torneo femenino," *El Telégrafo*, December 1, 2017. For comparison, Servisky's losing bid for the rights to the men's professional league was for at least $21 million per year.

25. Martín Fernandez, "Clube sem futebol feminino ficará fora da Libertadores a partir de 2019," *Globoesporte*, January 26, 2017, http:// globoesporte.globo.com/futebol/noticia/2017/01/clube-sem-futebol -feminino-ficara-fora-da-libertadores-partir-de-2019.html; "A partir de 2019, time sem futebol feminino não joga Libertadores," *Catracalivre*, January 28, 2017, https://catracalivre.com.br/geral/cidadania/indicacao/ partir-de-2019-time-sem-futebol-feminino-nao-joga-libertadores/. In commenting on the development, however, Marco Cunha—head of women's football for the Brazilian Football Confederation—said that "with just 5 percent of the resources of a men's team, it is possible to start a women's team."

26. "La Liga Femenina de Colombia será transmitida en Norteamérica, Europa y Asia," FeminasdeTacon.com, May 24, 2017, http:// feminasdetacon.com/la-liga-femenina-de-colombia-sera-transmitida-en -norteamerica-europa-y-asia/ (site discontinued); see also "Fan Network, el nuevo patrocinador de la Liga Femenina de Fútbol," *El País*, May 22, 2017, http://www.elpais.com.co/deportes/fan-network-el-nuevo -patrocinador-de-la-liga-femenina-de-futbol.html. With the exception of short analyses, it is unclear whether Fan Network actually broadcast any games.

27. "No entiendo por qué inviter a modelos y no a una jugadora a lucir la camiseta," RCNRadio.com, November 8, 2017, https://www.rcnradio .com/deportes/no-entiendo-por-que-invitar-modelos-y-no-a-una-jugadora -a-lucir-la-camiseta-nicole-regnier; "Polémica por discriminación a selección femenina en presentación de camiseta de Colombia," RCNRadio.com, November 8, 2017, https://www.rcnradio.com/deportes /polemica-por-discriminacion-a-seleccion-femenina-en-presentacion -de-camiseta-de-colombia.

28. Jeff Kassouf, "Mexico No Longer Allocating Players to NWSL," *Equalizer*, January 11, 2016. https://equalizersoccer.com/2016/01/11/ mexico-stops-allocating-nwsl-player-salaries/.

29. Lucia Mijares Martínez, interview, December 14, 2015.

30. Lucia Mijares Martínez, interview, December 14, 2015.

31. Lucia Mijares Martínez, interview, December 14, 2015.

32. Jorge González, "Liga MX Femenil, con 40% menos de asistencia en el Clausura," *AS*, March 1, 2018, https://mexico.as.com/mexico/2018/03/02 /futbol/1519967885_706441.html; "Noticias #Asistencia," Liga MX Femenil, http://www.ligafemenil.mx/cancha/hashtag/asistencia; "Liga MX Femenil revela impresionantes números de asistencia," CONCACAF, November 25, 2017, http://www.concacaf.com/es/article /liga-mx-femenil-revela-impresionantes-numeros-de-asistencia.

33. Fabiola Vargas Curiel, interview, December 14, 2015.

34. Ruby Campos Ramirez, interview, December 12, 2015.

35. Mariana Gutiérrez Bernárdez, interview, December 14, 2015.

36. AFP, "The dangers of being a female referee in Latin America," May 6, 2017, https://www.news.com.au/sport/sports-life/the-dangers-of-being -a-female-referee-in-latin-america/news-story/4d9f6e31f4247ac325a14 e6956bbe7f5.

37. AFP, "The dangers of being a female referee in Latin America," May 6, 2017, https://www.news.com.au/sport/sports-life/the-dangers-of-being -a-female-referee-in-latin-america/news-story/4d9f6e31f4247ac325a14 e6956bbe7f5.

38. Rodrigo González, "Comienza el fútbol femenil en México con la Liga MX," Deportes Inc., May 2, 2017, https://deportesinc.com/torneo -de-liga-mx-femenil/.

39. Joshua Law, "EC Iranduba—The Women's Team Putting Amazonian Football on the Map," The Set Pieces, http://thesetpieces.com/features /ec-iranduba-womens-team-putting-amazonian-football-map/.

BIBLIOGRAPHY

PRIMARY SOURCES

Archives, Museums, and Libraries

Biblioteca Miguel Lerdo de Tejada, Mexico City
Fédération Internationale de Football Association (FIFA), Zurich
Museu do Futebol, São Paulo
Museo Histórico Nacional de Chile, Santiago
Benson Latin American Collection, University of Texas at Austin

Magazines and Newspapers

ARGENTINA
Crítica
El Gráfico
La Nación
La Razón

BRAZIL
A Batalha
A Cigarra
A Gazeta Sportiva
A Luta Democrática
A Manhã
Anales de Biotipologia, Eugenesia y Medicina Social
A Noite
Arquivos de Escola Nacional de Educação Física e Desporto
A Tarde
Correio da Manhã
Correio de S. Paulo
Correio do Paraná
Correio Paulistano
Correio Sportivo
Diário da Noite
Diário da Tarde
Diário de Noticias

Folha de São Paulo
Educação Physica
Jornal dos Sports
Mulherio
O Cruzeiro
O Dia
O Dia Sportiva
O Estado do Paraná
O Estado de São Paulo
O Fluminense
O Globo
O Globo Esportivo
O Liberal
O Momento
O Paiz
Paraná Esportiva
Placar
Revista Brasileira de Educação Física
Revista da Semana
Sport Ilustrado
Uh Revista
Ultima Hora
Voz de Luziânia

CHILE
Actividades Femeninas en Chile
Estadio
Gol y Gol
Justicia
La Gaceta Deportiva
La Opinión de Conchalí
La Tribuna
La Voz del Cristalero
La Voz del Poblador
Los Sports
Match
Pacífico Magazine
Revista Chilena de Educación Física
Ritmo
Sport i Actualidades
Sport Ilustrado
Unión Feminina de Chile

COSTA RICA
Actas del Consejo Universitario, 1949–1960
AS
Diario de Costa Rica
El Manantial
El Mundo Deportivo
La Nación
La Prensa
La Prensa Libre
Revista Médica de Costa Rica

EL SALVADOR
Cultura Física
Revista Salvadoreña de Educación Física

HONDURAS
Revista Médica Hondureña

MEXICO
Educación Física
El Heraldo de México
El Hogar
El Nacional
El Sol de México
Esto
Excelsior
Femina
Fútbol de México y del Mundo
La Afición
Ovaciones

PANAMA
Lea Deportes

URUGUAY
Rush: Revista del Deporte Uruguayo

Club Documents

Club de Deportes Green Cross. *Estatutos y reglamentos*. Santiago, Chile: Imparcial, 1940.
Colo-Colo FC. *Estatutos y reglementos 1930*. Santiago, Chile: Electra, 1930.

Colo-Colo FC. *Historia del Club Colo-Colo*. Santiago, Chile: Imprenta Arvas, 1953.

Unión Española. *Bodas de Oro 1897–18 Mayo 1947*. Santiago, Chile: Imparcial, 1947.

Unión Española. *Memoria*. Santiago, Chile: El Comercio, 1936.

Interviews and Correspondence

Aracén Sánchez, Elvira
Bonilla Alvarado, Fernando
Borrello, Carlos
Campos Ramírez, Ruby
Gartón, Gabriela Nicole
Goellner, Silvana
Gutiérrez Bernárdez, Mariana
Lima, Sisleide do Amor
Mijares Martínez, Lucia
Quintero Hernández, Manelich
Quirós Alvarez, Alice
Pinilla, Fernanda
Rodebaugh Huitrón, Andrea
Rodríguez Alemán, Mercedes
Rothfeld, Iona
Tafarel, Marcia
Vargas Curiel, Fabiola
Y., Marina

Pamphlets and Other Published Primary Sources

Berenson Abbott, Senda. *Spalding's Official Basketball Guide for Women*. New York: American Sports Publishing Company, 1916.

Blanco, Raúl. *Educación física, un panorama de su historia*. Montevideo, Uruguay: Impresora Adroher, 1948.

Castillon, Oscar F. "Physical Education in Mexico." *Journal of Health and Physical Education* 5, no. 5 (May 1934): 11–12, 54.

Ciriza, Manuel J. *Manual de educación física para las escuelas federales de Nuevo León*. Monterrey, Mexico: Gobierno del Estado, 1935.

Confederación Deportiva Mexicana. *Consejo Nacional de Educación Física*. Mexico City: Imprenta Mundial, 1932.

Congreso Panamericano de Educación Física. *Actas y documentos oficiales*. Montevideo, Uruguay: 1943.

Consejo Nacional de Educación Física. *Llamamiento a los deportistas de toda la república*. Mexico City: Imprenta Mundial, 1932.

Díaz Covarrubias, José. *La instrucción pública en México*. Mexico City: Imprenta del Gobierno, 1875.

Educación física y social. Bogotá, Colombia: Ministerio de Educación Pública, 1908.

Gallindo y Villa, Jesús. *La educación de la mujer mexicana al través del siglo XIX*. Mexico City: Imprenta del Gobierno Federal en el Ex-Arzobispado, 1901.

Gremler, Juana. *Monografía de Liceo no. 1 de Niñas*. Santiago, Chile: Imp. Cervantes, 1902.

Hopkins, Jess. "Basket Ball in South America." *Spalding's Official Basketball Guide*. New York: American Sports Publishing Company, 1914.

Ichaso Vásquez, Rachel. *La enseñanza nacional femenina*. La Paz, Bolivia: Imprenta Intendencia de Guerra, 1927.

Jerez Alvarado, Rafael. *La educación de la mujer en Honduras*. Tegucigalpa, Honduras: Publicaciones del Ministerio de Educación Pública, 1957.

Obregón, Luís. "La labor del educador físico en las misiones culturales." In Secretaría de Educación Pública, *Las misiones culturales en 1927: Las escuelas normales rurales*. Mexico City: Secretaría de Educación Pública, 1928.

Programa de estudios para la educación secundaria, ciclo pre-vocacional. Educación física. Guatemala City: Editorial del Ministerio de Educación Pública, 1956.

Prospecto de la escuela industrial para señoritas "Malinalxochitl." Mexico City: Editorial "Cultura," 1926.

Puig Casauranc, J. M. "Los caracteres del verdad maestro rural. Sus virtudes y los peligros que hay que evitar." Speech given February 18, 1928, reprinted in Secretaría de Educación Pública, *Las misiones culturales en 1927: Las escuelas normales rurales*, 211–220. Mexico City: Secretaría de Educación Pública, 1928.

Rodrigo, Saturnino. *La educación física en Europa (Bélgica, Francia, Alemania, Checoeslovaquia, Suecia y Suiza)*. La Paz, Bolivia: Imprenta Renacimiento, 1929.

Rosada y Avila, Encarnación. "La educación física. Su importancia. Acción que puede ejercer el maestro en la educación física de sus alumnos." Escuela Normal de Profesoras, 1912.

Schmidt de Alvarez, Adela. *Enseñanza artística de la mujer: Informe presentado al Ministerio de Instrucción Pública*. Santiago, Chile: Encuadernación i Litografía Esmeralda, 1903.

Secretaría de Educación Pública. *Las misiones culturales en 1927: Las escuelas normales rurales*. Mexico City: Secretaría de Educación Pública, 1928.

———. *Plan de estudios de la educación física*. Mexico City: Talleres Gráficos de la Nación, 1929.

―――. *Plan de estudios de la escuela de educación física*. Mexico City: Talleres Gráficos de la Nación, 1928.

Sturges, Vesta. "Algunas aspectos del trabajo social realizado por las misiones culturales." In Secretaría de Educación Pública, *Las misiones culturales en 1927: Las escuelas normales rurales*. Mexico City: Secretaría de Educación Publica, 1928.

Tanco, Rafael. *Educación física*. Bogotá, Colombia: Imprenta Nacional, 1935.

Terra Núñez, Guillermo. *Educación física*. Montevideo, Uruguay: Imprenta Militar, 1942.

Toledo, Francisco. *Algunas consideraciones que la dirección de educación física y salud someterá al seminario de planeamiento de la educación*. Guatemala City: Ministerio de Educación, 1969.

SECONDARY SOURCES

Acuña, Pedro. "Dribbling with the Left and Shooting with the Right: Soccer, Sports Media, and Populism in Argentina and Chile, 1940s–1950s." PhD diss., University of California, Irvine, 2016.

Acuña Ortega, Victor Hugo. "The Formation of the Urban Middle Sectors in El Salvador, 1910–1944." In *Landscapes of Struggle: Politics, Society, and Community in El Salvador*, edited by Aldo Lauria-Santiago and Leigh Binford, 39–49. Pittsburgh, PA: University of Pittsburgh Press, 2004.

Alabarces, Pablo. *Fútbol y patria: El fútbol y las narrativas de la nación en la Argentina*. Buenos Aires: Prometo, 2003.

―――. *Héroes, machos y patriotas: El fútbol entre la violencia y los medios*. Argentina: Aguilar, 2014.

Alabarces, Pablo, and María Graciela Rodríguez. "Football and Fatherland: The Crisis of Representation in Argentinian Soccer." In *Football Culture: Local Contests, Global Visions*, edited by Gerry P. T. Finn and Richard Giulianotti, 118–133. London: Frank Cass, 2000.

Allen, Andrea Stevenson. *Violence and Desire in Brazilian Lesbian Relationships*. New York: Palgrave, 2015.

Almeida, Luiz Guilherme Veiga de. *Ritual, risco e arte circense*. Brasília: UNB, 2008.

Anderson, Patricia. "*Mens Sana in Corpore Sano*: Debating Female Sport in Argentina: 1900–46." *International Journal of the History of Sport* 26, no. 5 (2009): 640–653.

Araujo, Kathya, and Mercedes Prieto, eds. *Estudios sobre sexualidades en América Latina*. Quito, Ecuador: FLACSO, 2008.

Araya Cortez, Elisa, and Karin Lofstrom. "Women and Sport in Chile." In *Women and Sport in Latin America*, edited by Rosa López de D'Amico, Tansin Benn, and Gertrud Pfister, 79–92. London: Routledge, 2016.

Archetti, Eduardo. *Masculinities: Football, Polo and the Tango in Argentina.* Oxford: Berg, 1999.

Arellano, Daniel. "Seleccionadas de la 'Época Dorada' del básquetbol femenino." *El Deportero*, December 5, 2016. https://eldeportero.cl/seleccionadas-de-la-epoca-dorada-del-basquetbol-femenino-recibieron-un-reconocimiento-a-su-trayectoria/.

Armus, Diego, and Stefan Rinke, eds. *Del football al fútbol/futebol: Historias argentinas, brasileras y uruguayas en el siglo XX.* Madrid: Iberoamericana, 2014.

Avent, Glenn. "A Popular and Wholesome Resort: Gender, Class, and the Young Men's Christian Association in Porfirian Mexico." MA thesis, University of British Columbia, 1996.

Ávila, Lívia Bonafé d', and Osmar Moreira de Souza Júnior. "Futebol feminino e sexualidade." *Revista das Facultades Integradas Claretianas* 2 (December/January 2009): 30–41.

Ávila Neto, Maria Inacia d'. *O autoritarismo e a mulher: O jogo da admoniação macho-fêmea no Brasil.* Rio de Janeiro: Achiamé, 1980.

Barney, Robert. *Rethinking the Olympics: Cultural Histories of the Modern Games.* Morgantown, WV: Fitness Information Technology, 2010.

Barrancos, Dora. *Mujeres, entre la casa y la plaza.* Buenos Aires: Penguin Sudamericana, 2012.

Bartra, Eli, Anna M. Fernández Poncela, and Ana Lau. *Feminismo en México: Ayer y hoy.* Mexico City: Universidad Autónoma Metropolitana, 2000.

Beezley, William. *Judas at the Jockey Club and Other Episodes of Porfirian Mexico.* Lincoln: University of Nebraska Press, 1987.

Benicio, Eliane. "Rose do Rio: O futebol feminino no Brasil." *Teresópolis*, July 13, 1996.

Binello, Gabriela, Mariana Conde, Analía Martínez, and María Graciela Rodríguez. "Mujeres y fútbol: ¿Territorio conquistador o a conquistar?" In *Peligro de gol: Estudios sobre deporte y sociedad en América Latina*, edited by Pablo Alabarces, 33–56. Buenos Aires: CLACSO, 2000.

Bocketti, Gregg. *The Invention of the Beautiful Game: Football and the Making of Modern Brazil.* Gainesville: University Press of Florida, 2016.

Boykoff, Jules. *Activism and the Olympics: Dissent at the Games in Vancouver and London.* New Brunswick, NJ: Rutgers University Press, 2014.

Brewster, Claire, and Keith Brewster. *Representing the Nation: Sport and Spectacle in Post-Revolutionary Mexico.* Abingdon, UK: Routledge, 2010.

Brewster, Keith. "Redeeming the 'Indian': Sport and Ethnicity in Post-Revolutionary Mexico." *Patterns of Prejudice* 38, no. 3 (2003): 213–231.

Brewster, Keith, and Claire Brewster. "'He Hath Not Done This for Any Other Nation': Mexico's 1970 and 1986 World Cups." In *The FIFA World Cup, 1930–2010: Politics, Commerce, Spectacle, and Identities*, edited by

Stefan Rinke and Kay Schiller, 199–219. Gottingen, Germany: Wallstein Verlag, 2014.

———. "Cleaning the Cage: Mexico City's Preparations for the Olympic Games." *International Journal for the History of Sport* 26, no. 6 (May 2009): 790–813.

Bromberger, Christian. "Deportes, fútbol e identidad masculina. Los deportes, un revelador de la construcción de los géneros." *EFDeportes* 12, no. 111 (August 2007). http://www.efdeportes.com/efd111/deportes-futbol-e -identidad-masculina.htm.

Brown, Matthew. *From Frontiers to Football: An Alternative History of Latin America since 1800.* London: Reaktion Books, 2014.

Brown, Matthew, and Gloria Lanci. "A Transnational Investigation of Football and Urban Heritage in São Paulo, 1890–1930." In *Global Play: Football between Region, Nation, and the World in Latin American, African, and European History,* edited by Stefan Rinke and Christina Peters, 18–39. Stuttgart, Germany: Heinz, 2014.

Caffrey, Kevin. *The Beijing Olympics: Promoting China: Soft and Hard Power in Global Politics.* London: Routledge, 2011.

Cahn, Susan K. *Coming on Strong: Gender and Sexuality in Twentieth-Century Women's Sport.* New York: Free Press, 1994.

Callcott, Wilfrid Hardy. *Liberalism in Mexico, 1857–1929.* Hamden, CT: Archon Books, 1965.

Camargo, Tarciso Alex. "A revista *Educação Physica* e a eugenia no Brasil (1932–1945)." MA thesis, Universidade de Santa Cruz do Sul, 2010.

Cano, Gabriela. "Género y construcción cultural de las profesiones en el Porfiriato: Magisterio, medicina, jurisprudencia y odontología." *Historia y Grafía* 14 (2000): 207–243.

Cardona Álvarez, Lina María, Juan Cancio Arcila Arango, and Juan Carlos Giraldo García. "Influencia sociocultural en la mujer futbolista de Medellín." *EFDeportes* 17, no. 171 (August 2010). http://www.efdeportes .com/efd171/influencia-sociocultural-en-la-mujer-futbolista.htm.

Carey, Elaine. *Plaza of Sacrifices: Gender, Power, and Terror in 1968 Mexico.* Albuquerque: University of New Mexico Press, 2005.

Carpentier, Florence, and Jean-Pierre Lefèvre. "The Modern Olympic Movement, Women's Sport and the Social Order during the Inter-War Period." *International Journal of the History of Sport* 23, no. 7 (November 2006): 1112–1127.

Carreño Martínez, Maritza. "Fútbol femenil en México, 1969–1971." Thesis, Universidad Nacional Autónoma de Mexico, 2006.

Carrera, Isabel. "¿Qué pasa con las mujeres que viven apasionadamente el fútbol en el ecuador?" In *El jugador número 12: Fútbol y sociedad,* edited by Fernando Carrión M., 155–172. Quito, Ecuador: FLACSO, 2006.

Carrol, Brian. *The Black Press and Black Baseball, 1915–1955: A Devil's Bargain*. New York: Routledge, 2015.

Castañeda, Luis. *Spectacular Mexico: Design, Propaganda, and the 1968 Olympics*. Minneapolis: University of Minnesota Press, 2014.

Castañón Rodríguez, Jesús. "Mujer, idioma y fútbol en España (1904–2004)." *EFDeportes* 12, no. 107 (April 2007). http://www.efdeportes.com/efd107/mujer-idioma-y-futbol-en-espana-1904-2004.htm.

Caulfield, Sueann. *In Defense of Honor: Sexual Morality, Modernity, and Nation in Early-Twentieth-Century Brazil*. Durham, NC: Duke University Press, 2000.

Ceron-Anaya, Hugo. "Golf, habitus y elites: La historia del golf en México (1900–1980)." *Esporte e Sociedade* 5, no. 15 (July–October 2010).

Chávez Gónzalez, Monica Lizbeth. "Construcción de la nación y el género desde el cuerpo. La educación física en el México posrevolucionario." *Desacatos* 30 (May–August 2009): 43–58.

Civera Cerecedo, Alicia. *La escuela como opción de vida: La formación de maestros normales rurales en México, 1921–1945*. Mexico City: Secretary of Public Education for Mexico City, 2013.

———. "Respuestas comunitarias a un proyecto educativo: El caso de una misión cultural en México de los años treinta." *Revista Interamericana de Educación de Adultos* 4, no. 2 (July–December 1996).

Cocchi, Carlos Alberto. *Cuatro centros del fútbol mundial*. Montevideo, Uruguay: n.p., 1963.

Conde, Mariana, and María Graciela Rodríguez. "Mujeres en el fútbol argentino: Sobre prácticas y representaciones." *Alteridades* 12, no 23 (2002): 93–106.

Confederación Deportiva Mexicano. *Historia*. Mexico City: CODEME, n.d.

Contreras C., José. "Las sabrosas historias del dorado básquetbol femenino nacional." *La Tercera*, May 12, 2016. http://www.latercera.com/noticia/las-sabrosas-historias-del-dorado-basquetbol-femenino-nacional/.

Cordero Cordero, Teresita. "Mujeres y la Universidad de Costa Rica (1941 a 1950)." Paper given at VIII Congresso Iberoamericano de Ciência, Tecnologia e Gênero, April 5–9, 2010. http://files.dirppg.ct.utfpr.edu.br/ppgte/eventos/cictg/conteudo_cd/E2_Mujeres_y_Universidad_de_Costa_Rica.pdf.

Córdova, Martha. "El fútbol es un deporte machista." In *Con sabor a gol: Fútbol y periodismo*, edited by Kintto Lucas, 75–80. Quito, Ecuador: FLACSO, 2006.

Cosse, Isabella. *Pareja, sexualidad y familia en los años sesenta*. Buenos Aires: Siglo XXI, 2010.

Costa, Leda Maria da. "O que é uma torcedora? Notas sobre a representação e auto-representação do público feminino de futebol." *Esporte e Sociedade* 2, no. 4 (November 2006–February 2007).

Cowan, Benjamin. *Securing Sex: Morality and Repression in the Making of Cold War Brazil*. Chapel Hill: University of North Carolina Press, 2016.

Cuellar Martínez, Adan Benjamin, Jairo Gerardo Flores Díaz, and José Saúl Romero Barrera. "Análisis histórico de la educación física en relacion a sus tendencias pedagógicas, en la República de El Salvador desde el año 1920 al año 2010." Thesis, Universidad de El Salvador, 2011.

Daniels, Stephanie, and Anita Tedder. *"A Proper Spectacle": Women Olympians, 1900–1936*. Houghton Conquest, UK: Walla Walla Press, 2000.

Dávila, Jeffrey. *Diploma of Whiteness: Race and Social Policy in Brazil, 1917–1945*. Durham, NC: Duke University Press, 2003.

Dawson, Alexander. "Salvador Roquet, María Sabina, and the Trouble with *Jipis*." *Hispanic American Historical Review* 95, no. 1 (2005): 103–133.

Díaz Bolaños, Ronald E. "'Quiero que la gimnástica tome bastante incremento': Los orígenes de la gimnasía como actividad física en Costa Rica (1855–1949)." *Diálogos* 12, no. 1 (February–August 2011): 1–33.

Dinius, Oliver. *Brazil's Steel City: Developmentalism, Strategic Power, and Industrial Relations in Volta Redonda, 1941–1964*. Stanford, CA: Stanford University Press, 2010.

Drapkin S., Jaime. *Historia de Colo Colo, club de deportes 1925–1952*. Santiago, Chile: 1952.

Dunn, Carrie. *Female Football Fans: Community, Identity, and Sexism*. Houndmills, UK: Palgrave Macmillan, 2014.

Echeverría Ramírez, Adrián Antonio. "Análisis legal de las federaciones deportivas de representación nacional e internacional." Thesis, University of Costa Rica, 2012.

Elias, Stephanie. "Las mujeres de oro." *Ya: El Mercurio*, July 28, 2015.

Elsey, Brenda. *Citizens and Sportsmen: Fútbol and Politics in Twentieth-Century Chile*. Austin: University of Texas Press, 2011.

———. "Cultural Ambassadorship and the Pan-American Games of the 1950s." *International Journal of the History of Sport* 33, nos. 1–2 (2016): 105–126.

———. "The Independent Republic of Football: The Politics of Neighborhood Clubs in Santiago, Chile, 1948–1960." *Journal of Social History* 42, no. 3 (Spring 2009): 605–630.

Faria Júnior, Alfredo G. "Futebol, questões de gênero e co-educação: Algumas considerações didáticas sob enfoque multicultural." *Pesquisa de Campo* 2 (1995): 17–39.

Farnsworth-Alvear, Ann. *Dulcinea in the Factory: Myths, Morals, Men, and Women in Colombia's Industrial Experiment*. Durham, NC: Duke University Press, 2000.

Feiguin, María Andrea, and Ángela Aisestein. "Diseño de sujetos morales, sanos y patriotas. Formación de profesores de Educación Física. Argentina, 1938–1967." *Pedagogía y Saberes* 44 (January–June 2016): 9–20.

Fernández-Kelly, Patricia. "Reading the Signs: The Economics of Gender Twenty-Five Years Later." *Signs* 25, no. 4 (2000): 1107–1112.

Fernández-Kelly, María Patricia. *For We Are Sold, I and My People: Women and Industry in Mexico's Frontier*. Albany, NY: SUNY Press, 1984.

Fonseca Hidalgo, Alejandro. "Que se den su lugar." *Diario Extra*, July 9, 2010. http.www.diarioextra.com/2010/Julio/09/deportes09.php.

Franzolin, João Arthur Ciciliato. "Joaquím Inojosa e o jornal *Meio-Dia* (1939–1942)." MA thesis, Universidade Estadual Paulista, 2012.

Fraser, Nancy. *Fortunes of Feminism: From State-Managed Capitalism to Neoliberal Crisis*. London: Verso, 2013.

Frydenberg, Julio, ed. *Fútbol, historia y política*. Buenos Aires: Aurelia Rivera Libros, 2010.

———. *Historia social del fútbol: Del amateurismo a la profesionalización*. Buenos Aires: Siglo XXI, 2011.

Gallo Cadavid, Luz Elena, Olga Lucia Mosalve Tamayo, Julia Adriana Castro Carvajal, Herbert Hopf, Luz Dary Agudelo Florez, and Verónica Ochoa Patiño. "Participación de las mujeres en el deporte y su rol social en el área metropolitana del Valle del Aburra, Medellín." *EFDeportes* 5, no. 27 (November 2000). http://www.efdeportes.com/efd27a/mujerm.htm.

Gallo Cadavid, Luz Elena, and Luis Alberto Pareja. "Fútbol femenino en Colombia. Relaciones con la identidad y la salud." *EFDeportes* 10, no. 78 (November 2004). http://www.efdeportes.com/efd78/femenino.htm.

———. "A propósito de la salud en el fútbol femenino: Inequidad de género y subjetivación." *EFDeportes* 6, no. 33 (March 2001). http://www.efdeportes.com/efd33a/futfem.htm.

Gantús, Fausta, and Martha Santillán Esqueda. "Fútbol femenil en México: Una percepción de género a través de la prensa al inicio de los años setenta." *Esporte e Sociedad* 5, no. 15 (July–October 2010). http://www.uff.br/esportesociedade/pdf/es1501.pdf.

Garcia, Antonia dos Santos. *Mulheres da cidade d'Oxum: Relações de gênero, raça e classe e organização espacial do movimento de bairro em Salvador*. Salvador, Brazil: UFBA Editora, 2006.

Gaytán, Marie Sarita, and Ana G. Valenzuela Zapata. "Mas alla del mito: Mujeres, tequila y nación." *Mexican Studies/Estudios Mexicanos* 28, no. 1 (Winter 2012): 183–208.

Goellner, Silvana Vilodre. "'As mulheres fortes são aquelas que fazem uma raça forte': Esporte, eugenia e nacionalismo no Brasil no início do século XX." *Revista de História do Esporte* 1, no. 1 (June 2008): 1–28.

———. *Bela, maternal e feminina: Imagens da mulher na revista "Educação Physica."* Ijuí, Brazil: Unijuí, 2003.

———. "História e cultura do movimiento olímpico." In *Ética e compromisso social nos estudos olímpicos*, edited by Roberto Mesquita, Katia Rubio,

Alberto Reppold Filho, and Nelson Todt, 203–216. Porto Alegre, Brazil: EDIPUCRS, 2007.

———. "Imagens da mulher no esporte." In *Historia do esporte no Brasil*, edited by Mary del Priore and Victor Andrade de Melo, 269–292. São Paulo: UNESP, 2009.

Green, James N. *Beyond Carnival: Male Homosexuality in Twentieth-Century Brazil*. Chicago: University of Chicago Press, 2000.

Gutmann, Matthew C. *The Meanings of Macho: Being a Man in Mexico City*. Berkeley: University of California Press, 2006.

Guy, Donna. *Sex and Danger in Buenos Aires: Prostitution, Family, and Nation in Argentina*. Lincoln: University of Nebraska Press, 1991.

———. *Women Build the Welfare State: Performing Charity and Creating Rights in Argentina, 1880–1955*. Durham, NC: Duke University Press, 2009.

Harispe, Santiago. "Francisco Berra historiador: Aspectos de una biografía intelectual en el Río de la Plata a finales del siglo XIX." *Historia de la Educación* 16 (2015): 27–36.

Henderson, Simon. *Sidelined: How American Sports Challenged the Black Freedom Struggle*. Lexington: University Press of Kentucky, 2013.

Hershfeld, Joanne. *Imagining la Chica Moderna: Women, Nation, and Visual Culture in Mexico, 1917–1936*. Durham, NC: Duke University Press, 2008.

Hidalgo Xirinachs, Roxana. *Historias de las mujeres en el espacio público en Costa Rica, ante el cambio del siglo XIX al XX*. San José, Costa Rica: FLACSO, 2004.

Hill, Christopher. *Olympic Politics*. 2nd ed. Manchester, UK: St. Martin's Press, 1996.

Hollanda, Bernardo Buarque de. "The Competitive Party: The Formation and Crisis of Organized Fan Groups in Brazil, 1950–1980." In *Football and the Boundaries of History*, edited by Brenda Elsey and Stanislao Pugliese, 295–311. New York: Palgrave, 2017.

———. *O clube como vontade e representação: O jornalismo esportivo e a formação das torcidas organizadas de futebol do Rio de Janeiro*. Rio de Janeiro: 7Letras; Faperj, 2010.

Hutchison, Elizabeth. *Labors Appropriate to Their Sex: Gender, Labor, and Politics in Urban Chile, 1900–1930*. Durham, NC: Duke University Press, 2001.

Iber, Jorge, Samuel O. Regalado, José Alamillo, and Arnoldo De León. *Latinos in U.S. Sport: A History of Isolation, Cultural Identity, and Acceptance*. Champaign, IL: Human Kinetics, 2011.

James, Daniel, and John French, eds. *The Gendered Worlds of Latin American Women Workers: From Household and Factory to the Union Hall and Ballot Box*. Durham, NC: Duke University Press, 1997.

Jeldrez, Alexis. "Marlene Ahrens: Una ganadora en serie." *Caras*, November 27, 2013. http://www.caras.cl/deportes/marlene-ahrens-una-ganadora-en-serie/.

Joseph, Gilbert, Anne Rubenstein, and Eric Zolov, eds. *Fragments of a Golden Age: The Politics of Culture in Mexico since 1940*. Durham, NC: Duke University Press, 2001.

Kaczan, Gisela. "La práctica gimnástica y el deporte: La cultura física y el cuerpo bello en la historia de las mujeres. Argentina 1900–1930." *Historia Crítica* 61 (July 2016): 23–43.

Kane, Mary Jo. "Sex Sells Sex, Not Women's Sports." *Nation*, July 27, 2011. https://www.thenation.com/article/sex-sells-sex-not-womens-sports/.

Kane, Mary Jo, and Heather D. Maxwell. "Expanding the Boundaries of Sport and Media Research." *Journal of Sport Management* 25, no. 3 (2011): 202–216.

Karusch, Matthew. "National Identity in the Sports Pages: Football and Mass Media in 1920s Buenos Aires." *Americas* 60, no. 1 (July 2003): 11–32.

Kittleson, Roger. *The Country of Football: Soccer and the Making of Modern Brazil*. Berkeley: University of California Press, 2014.

Klubock, Thomas Miller. *Contested Communities: Class, Gender, and Politics in Chile's El Teniente Copper Mine, 1904–1951*. Durham, NC: Duke University Press, 1998.

Knight, Jennifer L., and Traci A. Giuliano. "She's a 'Looker,' He's a Laker: The Consequences of Gender-Stereotypical Portrayals of Male and Female Athletes by the Print Media." *Sex Roles* 45, nos. 3–4 (August 2001): 217–229.

Knijnik, Jorge. "Visions of Gender Justice: Untested Feasibility on the Football Fields of Brazil." *Journal of Sport and Social Issues* 37, no. 1 (February 2013): 8–30.

Krüger, Arnd, and William J. Murray. *The Nazi Olympics: Sport, Politics and Appeasement in the 1930s*. Urbana: University of Illinois Press, 2003.

LaFevor, David. "Prizefighting and Civilization in the Mexican Public Sphere in the Nineteenth Century." *Radical History Review* 125 (May 2016): 137–158.

Langland, Victoria. *Speaking of Flowers: Student Movements and the Making and Remembering of 1968 in Military Brazil*. Durham, NC: Duke University Press, 2013.

Larraín Mancheño, Fernando. *Fútbol en Chile, 1895–1945*. Santiago, Chile: Molina y Lackington, 1945.

Lauria-Santiago, Aldo, and Leigh Binford, eds. *Landscapes of Struggle: Politics, Society, and Community in El Salvador*. Pittsburgh, PA: University of Pittsburgh Press, 2004.

Ledesma Prietto, Nadia. "Entre la mujer y la madre: Discursos médicos y la construcción de normas de género (Argentina, 1930–1940)." *Trabajos y Comunicaciones* 42 (2015): 1–15.

Leite Lopes, José Sergio. "Da usina de açúcar ao topo do mundo do futebol nacional: Trajetória de um jogador de origem operária." *Cadernas AEL Esportes e Trabalhadores* 16 (2010): 13–40.

Lenharo, Alcir. *A sacralização da política.* São Paulo: Papirus, 1989.

Lenskyj, Helen. *Gender Politics and the Olympic Industry.* Houndmills, UK: Palgrave Macmillan, 2013.

———. *Out of Bounds: Women, Sport and Sexuality.* Toronto, Ontario: Women's Press, 1986.

Lessa, Patricia, and Tais Akemi Dellai Oshita. "La participación de las mujeres en los deportes." *EFDeportes* 11, no. 105 (February 2007). http://www.efdeportes.com/efd105/la-participacion-de-las-mujeres-en-los-deportes.htm.

Livingston, Noyes Burton. "Physical Education in Brazil: Its History, Philosophy and Psychology and Its Present Status as to Administration and Methods." University of Texas, Department of Physical Education, July 7, 1950.

Lobato, Mirta Zaida. "Afectos y sexualidad en el mundo de trabajo entre fines del siglo XIX y la década de 1930." In *Moralidades y comportamientos sexuales: Argentina, 1880–2011,* edited by Dora Barrancos, Donna Guy, and Adriana Valobra, 155–174. Buenos Aires: Biblios, 2014.

López, Oresta. "Women Teachers of Post-Revolutionary Mexico: Feminisation and Everyday Resistance." *Paedagocia Historia* 49, no. 1 (2013): 59–69.

López-Portillo, Esther. *Nosotras también tiramos al gol: Un libro para verdaderos apasionados del fútbol, escrito con la picardia y la gracia de mujeres triunfadores.* Mexico City: Aguilar, 2010.

Lorenzo, María Fernanda, Ana Lía Rey, and Cecilia Tossounian. "Images of Virtuous Women: Morality, Gender, and Power in Argentina between the World Wars." *Gender and History* 17, no. 3 (November 2005): 567–592.

Lucumí Balanta, Yanet. "Aportes de la mujer en la transformación de los estereotipos socio-culturales del deporte colombiano." *Revista UDCA Actualidad & Divulgación Científica* 15 (Supl. Olímpico, 2012): 27–35.

Macías-González, Victor, and Anne Rubenstein, eds. *Masculinity and Sexuality in Modern Mexico.* Albuquerque: University of New Mexico Press, 2012.

Magazine, Roger. *Golden and Blue Like My Heart: Masculinity, Youth, and Power among Soccer Fans in Mexico City.* Tucson: University of Arizona Press, 2007.

Manzano, Valeria. *The Age of Youth in Argentina: Culture, Politics, and Sexuality from Perón to Videla.* Chapel Hill: University of North Carolina Press, 2014.

Maraniss, David. *Rome 1960: The Olympics That Changed the World*. New York: Simon and Schuster, 2008.

Marinho, Inezil Penna. *Contribuição para a história da educação física no Brasil*. Rio de Janeiro: Imprenta Nacional, 1943.

Márquez C., Ramón. "Introducción." In *Crónicas del fútbol mexicano: Por amor de la camiseta, volumen 2 (1933–1950)*, edited by Carlos Calderón Cardoso. Mexico City: Editorial Clio, 1998.

Martinez, François. "¡Que nuestros indios se conviertan en pequeños suecos! La introducción de la gymnasia en las escuelas bolivianas." *Andines* 28, no. 3 (1999): 361–386.

Martínez, Josafat. *Historia del fútbol chileno*. Santiago, Chile: Nacional, 1961.

Martínez Moctezuma, Lucía. "Desencuentros en el desarrollo de la escuela rural mexicana en las primeras decadas del siglo XX: El caso de los institutos de mejoramiento en el estado de Morelos." *Revista Brasileira de História da Educação* 16, no. 2 (2016): 285–310.

———, ed. *Formando el cuerpo del ciudadano. Aportes para una historia de la educación física en Latinoamérica*. Cuernavaca, Mexico: Universidad Autónoma del Estado de Morelos, 2016.

Matos, Maria Izilda, and Andrea Borelli. "Espaço feminino no mercado produtivo." In *Novas histórias das mulheres do Brasil*, edited by Carla Bassanezi Pinsky and Joana Maria Pedro. São Paulo: Editora Contexto, 2012.

McCaa, Robert. "The Peopling of Mexico from Origins to Revolution." In *The Population History of North America*, edited by Richard Staeckel and Michael Haines, 241–304. Cambridge, UK: Cambridge University Press, 2000.

Melo, Victor Andrade de. "Mulheres em movimento: A presença feminina nos primórdios do esporte na cidade do Rio de Janeiro (até 1910)." *Revista Brasileira de História* 27, no. 54 (n.d.): 127–152.

———. *Os sports e as cidades brasileiras: Transição dos séculos XIX e XX*. Rio de Janeiro: Apicuri, 2010.

Mendonça, Anna Amélia de Queiróz Carneiro de. *Alma* (Rio de Janeiro: Empreza Brasil, 1924).

Mignolo, Walter D. *The Idea of Latin America*. Malden, MA: Blackwell, 2005.

Molina Jiménez, Iván. "Educación y sociedad en Costa Rica: De 1821 al presente (una historia no autorizada)." *Diálogos* 8, no. 2 (August 2007–February 2008).

Mora Carvajal, Virginia. "Moda, belleza y publicidad en Costa Rica (1920–1930)." *Boletín AFEHC* 45 (June 2010). http://afehc-historia-centroamericana .org/index.php?action=fi_aff&id=2445.

Moreira, Ramon Missias. "A mulher no futebol brasileiro: Uma ampla visão." *EFDeportes* 13, no. 120 (May 2008). http://www.efdeportes.com/efd120/a-mulher-no-futebol-brasileiro.htm.

Moura, Eriberto José Lessa de. "As relações entre lazer, futebol e gênero." MA thesis, Universidade Estadual de Campinhas, December 2003.

Mourão, Ludmila, and Marcia Morel. "As narrativas sobre o futebol feminino." *Revista Brasileira de Ciências do Esporte* 26, no. 2 (January 2005).

Mueller, Juliane. "La práctica del fútbol entre mujeres bolivianas en Sevilla. Redes sociales, trayectorias migratorias y relaciones de género." *Íconos* 41 (September 2011): 153–169.

Mujeres y hombres en México. Mexico City: Instituto Nacional de Estadística, Geografía e Informática, 2007.

Murad, Mauricio. "Futebol e violência no Brasil." In *Futebol: Síntese da vida brasileira,* edited by Mauricio Murad. Rio de Janeiro: UERJ, 1996.

Murcia Peña, Napoleón, and Luis Guillermo Jaramillo Echeverry. "Fútbol femenino: Estigma de discriminación cultural de las mujeres que practican fútbol en la ciudad de Manizales." *EFDeportes* 6, no. 32 (2001). http://www.efdeportes.com/efd32/futbolf.htm.

Nadel, Joshua. *Fútbol! Why Soccer Matters in Latin America.* Gainesville: University Press of Florida, 2014.

Nari, Marcela. *Políticas de maternidad y maternalismo político.* Buenos Aires: Biblos, 2004.

Naul, Roland, and Ken Hardman, eds. *Sport and Physical Education in Germany.* New York: Routledge, 2002.

Negreiros, Plínio José Labriola de Campos. "Futebol nos anos 1930 e 1940: Construindo a identidade nacional." *História Questões & Debates* 39, no. 2 (2003). http://dx.doi.org/10.5380/his.v39i0.2727.

Núñez Noriega, Guillermo. *Sexo entre varones. Poder y resistencia en el campo sexual.* Mexico City: PUEG-UNAM, 1999.

Olcott, Jocelyn. *Revolutionary Women in Postrevolutionary Mexico.* Durham, NC: Duke University Press, 2005.

Olcott, Jocelyn, Mary Kay Vaughan, and Gabriela Cano, eds. *Sex in Revolution: Gender, Power, and Politics in Modern Mexico.* Durham, NC: Duke University Press, 2006.

Oliveira, Rosa Maria. "Fronteiras invisíveis: Gêneros, questões identitárias e relações entre movimento homossexual e estado no Brasil." *Revista Bagoas* 4 (2009): 160–172.

Oriard, Michael. *King Football: Sport and Spectacle in the Golden Age of Radio and Newsreels, Movies and Magazines, the Weekly and the Daily Press.* Chapel Hill: University of North Carolina Press, 2001.

Owen, Hilary. "Discardable Discourses in Patricia Galvão's *Parque Industrial.*" In *Brazilian Feminisms,* edited by Solange Ribeiro de Oliveira and Judith Still, 68–84. Nottingham, UK: University of Nottingham Monographs in the Humanities, 1999.

Palmer, Steven, and Gladys Rojas Chaves. "Educating Señorita: Teacher Training, Social Mobility, and the Birth of Costa Rican Feminism, 1885–1925." *Hispanic American Historical Review* 78, no. 1 (February 1988): 45–82.

Pandolfo, Gaetano. "Las pioneras del fútbol fueron ticas." Semanario Universidad, May 5, 2009. https://semanariouniversidad.com/deportes/las-pioneras-del-ftbol-fueron-ticas/.

Pensado, Jaime. *Rebel Mexico: Student Unrest and Authoritarian Political Culture during the Long Sixties*. Stanford, CA: Stanford University Press, 2013.

Pérez de Peñamil, Santiago Prado. *El fútbol y los clubes españoles de la Habana, 1911–1937: Asociacionismo y espacios de sociabilidad*. Havana: Fundación Fernando Ortíz, 2013.

Perlaza Concha, Flavio. "Fundamentos básicos para la selección de talentos en el fútbol femenino ecuatoriano." *EFDeportes* 19, no. 199 (December 2014). http://www.efdeportes.com/efd199/seleccion-de-talentos-en-el-futbol-femenino.htm.

Pinsky, Carla Bassanezi, and Joana Maria Pedro, eds. *Nova história das mulheres no Brasil*. São Paulo: Editora Contexto, 2012.

Pontón, Jenny. "Mujeres futbolistas en Ecuador: ¿Afición o profesión?" In *El jugador número 12: Fútbol y sociedad*, edited by Fernando Carrión M., 131–153. Quito, Ecuador: FLACSO, 2006.

Priore, Mary del. *Corpo a corpo com a mulher: Pequena história das transformações do corpo feminino no Brasil*. São Paulo: Editora SENAC, 2000.

Ramacciotti, Karina, and Adriana Valobra. "'Peor que putas': Tríbadas, satisfas y homosexuals en el discurso moral hegemónico del campo medico, 1936–1945." In *Moralidades y comportamientos sexuales: Argentina, 1880–2011*, edited by Dora Barrancos, Donna Guy, and Adriana Valobra, 195–216. Buenos Aires: Biblios, 2014.

Ramírez Hernández, Georgina. "Educar al cuerpo en el Porfiriato: Una mirada a través las revistas pedagógicas." Paper given to XI Congreso Nacional de Investigación Educativa. http://www.comie.org.mx/congreso/memoriaelectronica/v11/ponencias.htm.

Reggiani, Andrés Horacio. "Cultura física, performance atlética e higiene de la nación. El surgimiento de la medicina deportiva en Argentina (1930–1940)." *Historia Crítica* 61 (July–September 2016): 65–84.

Richey, Jeffrey William. "Playing at Nation: Soccer Institutions, Racial Ideology, and National Integration in Argentina, 1912–1931." PhD diss., University of North Carolina at Chapel Hill, 2013.

Rigo, Luiz Carlos, Flávia Garcia Guidotti, Larissa Zanetti Theil, and Marcela Amaral. "Notas acerca do futebol feminino pelotense em 1950: Um estudo genealógico." *Revista Brasileira de Ciências do Esporte* 29, no. 3 (May 2008): 173–188.

Rodríguez, María Graciela. "The Place of Women in Argentinian Football." *International Journal of the History of Sport* 22, no. 2 (March 2005): 231–245.

Rodríguez S., Eugenia. "Cronología: Participación socio-política femenina en Costa Rica (1890–1952)." *Diálogos* 5, nos. 1–2 (2005): 695–722. https://revistas.ucr.ac.cr/index.php/dialogos/article/view/6254/5956.

———. "Visibilizando las facetas ocultas del movimiento de mujeres, el feminismo y las luchas por la ciudadanía femenina en Costa Rica (1890–1953)." *Diálogos* 5, nos. 1–2 (2005): 36–61. https://revistas.ucr.ac.cr/index.php/dialogos/article/view/6230/5933.

Rosemblatt, Karin Alejandra. *Gendered Compromises: Political Cultures and the State in Chile, 1920–1950.* Chapel Hill: University of North Carolina Press, 2000.

Rubenstein, Anne. *Bad Language, Naked Ladies, and Other Threats to the Nation: A Political History of Comic Books in Mexico.* Durham, NC: Duke University Press, 1998.

———. "The War on 'Las Pelonas': Modern Women and Their Enemies, Mexico City, 1924." In *Sex in Revolution: Gender, Politics, and Power in Modern Mexico*, edited by Jocelyn Olcott, Mary Kay Vaughan, and Gabriela Cano, 57–80. Durham, NC: Duke University Press, 2006.

Rubio, Katia, Helena Altmann, Ludmila Mourão, and Silvana Vilodre Goellner. "Women and Sport in Brazil." In *Women and Sport in Latin America*, edited by Rosa López D'Amica, Tansin Benn, and Gertrud Pfister, 69–78. Abingdon, UK: Routledge, 2016.

Salamone, Frank. *The Native American Identity in Sports: Creating and Preserving a Culture.* Lanham, MD: Scarecrow Press, 2013.

Salas M., Demetrios. *Educación física biológica.* Santiago, Chile: Editorial Nascimento, 1930.

Salas Madrigal, Agustín. *Historia del deporte en Costa Rica.* San José, Costa Rica: 1951.

Sánchez-León, Abelardo. "The History of Peruvian Women's Volleyball." In *Sport in Latin America and the Caribbean*, edited by Joseph L. Arbena and David G. LaFrance, 207–217. Wilmington, DE: Scholarly Resources, 2002.

Santillán Esqueda, Martha, and Fausta Gantús. "Transgresiones femeninas: Fútbol. Una mirada desde la caricatura de la prensa, México 1970–1971." *Tzintzun* 52 (July–December 2010): 141–174.

Santos, Martha. *Cleansing Honor with Blood: Masculinity, Violence, and Power in the Backlands of Northeast Brazil, 1845–1889.* Stanford, CA: Stanford University Press, 2012.

Saraví Rivière, Jorge. *Historia de la educación física argentina.* Buenos Aires: Libros de Zorzal, 2012.

Sarlo, Beatriz. *La máquina cultural. Maestras, traductores y vanguardistas.* Buenos Aires: Ariel, 1998.

Scharagrodsky, Pablo Ariel. "Dime cómo te mueves y te diré cuál es tu 'sexo': Discurso médico, educación física y diferencia sexual a finales del siglo XIX y principios del siglo XX." In *Moralidades y comportamientos sexuales: Argentina, 1880–2011,* edited by Dora Barrancos, Donna Guy, and Adriana María Valobra, 73–94. Buenos Aires: Biblos, 2014.

———. "El padre de la educación física argentina: Fabricando una política corporal generizada (1900–1940)." *Perspectiva* 22 (July–December 2004): 83–119.

———. "Los arquitectos corporales en la educación física y los deportes. Entre fichas, saberes y oficios (Argentina primera mitad del siglo XX)." *Trabajos y Comunicaciones* 4 (2015): 1–18.

Schpun, Mônica Raisa. *Beleza em jogo: Cultura física e comportamento em São Paulo nos anos 20.* São Paulo: Editora Senac/Boitempo Editorial, 1999.

Schultz, Jaime. *Qualifying Times: Points of Change in U.S. Women's Sports.* Champaign: University of Illinois Press, 2014.

Sepúlveda Vásquez, Carola. "Esencias en fuga: Dime, mi bien, ¿quién me llorará, si me dan alas y echo a volar? Juana Gremler: Mujer, educadora, directora . . . no rectora. Santiago de Chile (1894–1912)." PhD diss., Universidad de Chile, 2007.

Sol Serrano, Macarena Ponce de León, y Francisca Rengifo. *Historia de la educación en Chile (1810–2010).* Santiago de Chile: Taurus, 2012.

Serret, Estela. "El feminismo mexicano de cara al siglo XXI." *Cotidiano* 16 (March–April 2000). http://www.redalyc.org/articulo.oa.

Sharratt, Sara. "The Suffragist Movement in Costa Rica, 1889–1949: Centennial of Democracy?" In *The Costa Rican Women's Movement: A Reader,* edited by Ilse Abshagen, 61–83. Pittsburgh, PA: University of Pittsburgh Press.

Sheinin, David, ed. *Sport Culture in Latin American History.* Pittsburgh, PA: University of Pittsburgh Press, 2015.

Silva, Marcelo Moraes e, and Mariana Purcote Fontoura. "Educação do corpo feminino: Um estudo na *Revista Brasileira de Educação Física* (1944–1950)." *Revista Brasileira da Educação Física* 25, no. 2 (April/June 2011): 263–275.

Silva Baquero, Georgina. *Tratado de educación física.* Quito, Ecuador: Editorial Casa de la Cultura Ecuatoriana, 1962.

Sluis, Ageeth. "Building Bodies: Creating Urban Landscapes of Athletic Aesthetics in Postrevolutionary Mexico City." In *Sports Culture in Latin America*, edited by David Sheinin, 121–138. Pittsburgh, PA: University of Pittsburgh Press, 2015.

Soares, Carmen Lúcia. *As roupas nas práticas corporais e esportivas: A educação do corpo entre o conforto, a elegância e a eficiência (1920–1940)*. São Paulo: Autores Associados, 2017.

———. "Da arte e da ciência de movimentar-se: Primeiros momentos da ginástica no Brasil." In *História do esporte no Brasil*, edited by Mary del Priore and Victor Andrade de Melo, 133–178. São Paulo: UNESP, 2009.

Soihet, Rachel. "A conquista do espaço público." In *Novas histórias das mulheres do Brasil*, edited by Carla Bassanezi Pinsky and Joana Maria Pedro, 218–237. São Paulo: Editora Contexto, 2012.

Souza, Gabriela Conceição de, and Ludmila Mourão. *Mulheres do tatami: O judo feminino no Brasil*. Rio de Janeiro: MAUAD, 2011.

Sugden, John, and Alan Tomlinson. *Watching the Olympics: Politics, Power and Representation*. Abingdon, UK: Routledge, 2012.

Susto, Juan Antonio. *La educación de la mujer panameña en el siglo XIX*. Panama City: Ediciones del Ministerio de Educación, 1966.

Tamburrini, Claudio. "El retorno de las amazonas: El deporte de élite y la igualdad genérica." *EFDeportes* 17 (n.d.). http://www.efdeportes.com /efd17/amaz.htm.

Tinsman, Heidi. *Partners in Conflict: The Politics of Gender, Sexuality, and Labor in the Chilean Agrarian Reform, 1950–1973*. Durham, NC: Duke University Press, 2000.

Tomlinson, Alan, Christopher Young, and Richard Holt, eds. *Sport and the Transformation of Modern Europe: States, Media, and Markets, 1950–2010*. Abingdon, UK: Routledge, 2011.

Torres, Cesar. "The Latin American 'Olympic Explosion' of the 1920s: Causes and Consequences." *International Journal of the History of Sport* 23, no. 7 (November 2006): 1088–1111.

Toscano, Moema, and Mirian Goldenberg. *A revolução das mulheres: Um balanço do feminismo no Brasil*. Rio de Janeiro: Editora Revan, 1992.

Urbina Gaitán, Chester. "El fútbol femenino en Costa Rica (1924–2015)." *EFDeportes* 21, no.221 (October 2016). http://www.efdeportes.com /efd221/el-futbol-femenino-en-costa-rica.htm.

———. "Estado, política y deporte en El Salvador (1885–1921)." *Realidad y Reflexión* 6, no. 17 (May–August 2006): 17–29.

———. "Fútbol, estado e identidad nacional en El Salvador (1897–1943)." *Realidad y Reflexión* 17, no. 6 (May–August 2006): 53–98.

———. "Génesis del fútbol en Guatemala (1902–1921)." *EFDeportes* 14, no. 135 (August 2009). http://www.efdeportes.com/efd135/genesis-del-futbol -en-guatemala-1902-1921.htm.

———. Orígenes de la política deportiva en Costa Rica (1887–1942)." *EFDeportes* 7, no. 34 (April 2001). http://www.efdeportes.com/efd34 /crica.htm.

———. "Origenes del deporte moderno en El Salvador." *Realidad y Reflexión* 17, no. 6 (May–August 2006): 33–49.

Vasconcelos, Iana dos Santos. "Mulher e mercado de trabalho no Brasil: Notas de uma história em andamento." *Examãpaku* 3 no. 2 (2010). http://dx .doi.org/10.18227/1983-9065ex.v3i2.1497.

Vásconez Cuvi, Victoria. *Actividades domésticas y sociales de la mujer*. Quito, Ecuador: Talleres Tipográficos Nacionales, 1925.

Vaughan, Mary Kay. *Cultural Politics in Revolution: Teachers, Peasants, and Schools in Mexico, 1930–1940*. Tucson: University of Arizona Press, 1997.

———. "Nationalizing the Countryside: Schools and Rural Communities in the 1930s." In *The Eagle and the Virgin: Nation and Cultural Revolution in Mexico, 1920–1940*, edited by Mary Kay Vaughan and Stephen Lewis, 157–176. Durham, NC: Duke University Press, 2006.

Vera, Antonino. *El fútbol en Chile*. Santiago, Chile: Editora Nacional Quimantú, 1973.

Votre, Sebastião, and Ludmila Mourão. 2004. "Women's Football in Brazil: Progress and Problems." In *Soccer, Women, Sexual Liberation: Kicking Off a New Era*, edited by Fan Hong and J. A. Mangan, 254–267. London: Frank Cass.

Weinstein, Barbara. *The Color of Modernity: São Paulo and the Making of Race and Nation in Brazil*. Durham, NC: Duke University Press, 2015.

———. *For Social Peace in Brazil: Industrialists and the Remaking of the Working Class in São Paulo, 1920–1964*. Durham, NC: Duke University Press, 1997.

Wilkson, Adriano. "1a maria-chuteira do Brasil fez poesia para conquistar o goleiro da seleção." *Folha*, February 10, 2014. http://esporte.uol.com.br /futebol/ultimas-noticias/2014/10/02/1-maria-chuteira-do-brasil-fez-poesia -para-conquistar-o-goleiro-da-selecao.htm#fotoNav=1.

Williams, Jean. *A Game for Rough Girls? A History of Women's Football in Britain*. London: Routledge, 2003.

Witherspoon, Kevin B. *Before the Eyes of the World: Mexico and the 1968 Olympic Games*. DeKalb: Northern Illinois University Press, 2008.

Wood, David. *Football and Literature in South America*. New York: Routledge 2017.

Woodward, Kath. *Sex, Power, and the Games*. Houndmills, UK: Palgrave Macmillan, 2012.

Zaikos, Nikos. "Ingeborg Mello: 'Two Lives' in Sport." *Nashim* 26 (Spring 2014): 5–34.

Zeledón Cartín, Elías. *Deportivo Femenino de Costa Rica FC: Primer equipo de fútbol femenino en el mundo*. San José, Costa Rica: Ministerio de Cultura, Juventud y Deportes, 1999.

Zolov, Eric. "Showcasing the 'Land of Tomorrow': Mexico and the 1968 Olympics." *Americas* 61, no. 2 (October 2004): 159–188.

INDEX